# biopolis

# biopolis

Patrick Geddes and the City of Life

VOLKER M. WELTER

The MIT Press
Cambridge, Massachusetts
London, England

This book was set in Monotype Bell and Adobe Copperplate Gothic by Graphic Composition, Inc. and was printed and bound in the United States of America.

Library of Congress Cataloging-in-Publication Data
Welter, Volker.
    Biopolis : Patrick Geddes and the city of life / Volker M. Welter.
        p. cm.
    Includes bibliographical references and index.
    ISBN 0-262-23211-1 (hc. : alk. paper)
      1. Geddes, Patrick, Sir, 1854–1932.   2. City planners—Great Britain–Biography.   3. City planning—Great Britain—History.   4. City planning—Philosophy.   I. Title.

HT169.G7 W45 2001
711′.4′092—dc21
[B]                                                                      00-054820

for Elisabeth &
Werner Welter

# Contents

# List of Illustrations

# List of Tables

# Acknowledgments

I would like to express my gratitude to the following individuals and institutions for kindly granting permission to quote from manuscripts and printed material, and to reproduce images from drawings and photographs in their possession.

Archives Nationales/Institut Français d'Architecture (AN/IFA), Paris

Felicity Ashbee, London

Bildarchiv Foto Marburg, Marburg/Art Resource, New York

Sarah Sabita Branford-McGuinness, London

Madame Bonnier Lordonnois, Provins

The British Museum, London

The Carnegie Dunfermline Trust, Dunfermline

Central Saint Martins Museum and Study Collection, London

Hugh W. J. Crawford, Edinburgh

Roger Mears, London

Musée des Beaux-Arts de Lyon, Lyons

Norval Photographers, Dunfermline

Georges Ottino, Geneva

Patrick Geddes Centre, Department of Architecture, Edinburgh University, Edinburgh

Royal Commission on the Ancient and Historic Monuments of Scotland, Edinburgh

Special Collections, University Library, Edinburgh University, Edinburgh

Staatliche Museen zu Berlin, Kunstbibliothek, Berlin

Staats- und Universitätsbibliothek Hamburg, Hamburg

Trustees of the National Library of Scotland, Edinburgh

University Archives, Strathclyde University, Glasgow

Wenzel Hablik Museum, Itzehoe

Support for the cost of illustrations was gratefully received from the Faculty of Social Sciences and the Department of Architecture, both Edinburgh University, Edinburgh. Support for the project was also received from the Getty Grant Program, Los Angeles, for which I wish to express my thanks.

# Foreword

Writing in the early years of the twentieth century, Max Weber famously condemned modern society as an "iron cage," ruled by experts utterly isolated within the constraints of their particular realm of knowledge. With the triumph of the Enlightenment, the unified world views grounded on religion and metaphysics had been replaced by a separatist culture in which fundamental divisions had emerged between the three main streams of human thinking: science, morality, and art. As a result, in Weber's words, "value spheres of the world stand in irreconcilable conflict with each other."[1] The emancipation from religious dogma and superstition had resulted not in a world in which reason had replaced religion as a basis for moral values, but rather in a world unable to answer the great moral questions posed by human purpose, value, identity, suffering.

In the later nineteenth century, with an ascendant Darwinism challenging the narratives of Christianity as baseless, cultural critics turned to literature and art for moral guidance. As Matthew Arnold claimed in 1879:

> There is not a creed which is not shaken, not an accredited dogma which is not shown to be questionable, not a received tradition which does not threaten to dissolve. Our religion has materialised itself in the fact, in the supposed fact; it has attached its emotion to the fact, and now the fact is failing it. But for poetry the idea is everything; the rest is a world of illusion, of divine illusion. Poetry attaches its emotion to the idea: the idea *is* the fact. The strongest part of our religion today is its unconscious poetry.[2]

It was just as possible, of course, to live a life controlled entirely by artistic sensibility as it was to pursue an exclusively rationalist or pragmatic existence, for the crisis of faith produced not only stoic activism but also a meditative passivity. The well-known lines from Tennyson's *In Memoriam* contrast the harsh world of late Victorian commerce with the willful isolation of the poet, who inhabits an entirely different, solipsistic realm:

> He is not here; but far away
>> The noise of life begins again,
>> And ghastly thro' the drizzling rain
> On the bald street breaks the blank day.[3]

But a purely materialistic understanding of culture and history is just as one-sided as an exclusively aesthetic or spiritualistic interpretation. The former offers the means of action without comprehending the goals, the latter the goals without the means.

As botanist, sociologist, educator, artist, and town planner, Patrick Geddes was committed to the reconciliation of science, morality, and aesthetics. The vehicle for his polymathic wanderings between the disciplines was a very personal system of graphic logic, which he dubbed his thinking machines. The chosen site for the intellectual and emotional reconciliation of the disciplines was the city. In constructing modes of thinking and theoretical models based on the forms of urban society, Geddes returned the word "theory" to its religious origins. As Jürgen Habermas has noted: "The *theoros* was the representative sent by Greek cities to public celebrations. Through *theoria*, that is through looking on, he abandoned himself to the sacred events."[4] Three key themes emerge here that are central to an understanding of Geddesian thought: the Greek *polis* as model, the act of seeing as the source of knowledge, and visual pattern-making as the instrument that transforms this knowledge into theory. The further metamorphosis of theoretical precepts into practical action was, for Geddes, stimulated by the model of nature and of the natural sciences. Geddes was closely acquainted with Ernst

Haeckel of Jena University, and an important inspiration was Haeckel's biogenetic law, which stated that ontogeny recapitulates phylogeny. More simply, a developed organism results from and epitomizes the modifications in form and structure undergone by successive generations of ancestors over the course of their historical evolution. For Geddes, such Darwinian insights were equally applicable to the city and to the protozoa. In an essay on the progress of the arts and sciences toward unity, he concluded:

> The first word of the Sociology of Autumn is the beauty of Nature, the glory of Life, both culminating (as our urban culture only more fully teaches us) in their Decadence. Hence there inevitably comes the second word, the pessimist antithesis: yet a third—the vital one—remains. Amid decay lies the best soil of Renascence: in Autumn its secret: that of survival yet initiative, of inheritance yet fresh variation—the seed; who wills may find, may sow, and in another Autumn also reap.[5]

As this extract suggests, Geddes—for all his polymathic brilliance—was not easy to comprehend. His writing style is rarely felicitous, and as a speaker he was difficult to follow in private, impossible on the lecturer's podium. Even more problematically, his thinking machines, for all their genial insights, can hinder rather than promote the great synthesis of the arts and sciences that was his ultimate goal. Lewis Mumford, who admired Geddes enormously while remaining alert to his shortcomings, is particularly interesting on the central Geddesian figure, the Notation of Life.

> In the course of elaborating his fundamental graph, Geddes had in fact exposed the archetypal drama of life: and what was even more important had restored the missing factors of time and change. In the scenario for this drama the actors, the plot and the scenery, the dialogue, the performance, the

setting actively bring into existence an interwoven sequence of events whose meaning and purpose no single part, however clearly presented, can possibly convey.[6]

The static Notation of Life was, by definition, unable to capture this dynamic and dramatic process. As Mumford himself concluded: "Synthesis is not a goal: it is a process of organization, constantly in operation, never finished. Any attempt to produce a single synthesis good for all times, all places, all cultures, all persons is to reject the very nature of organic existence."[7] Yet the fascination of Patrick Geddes lies precisely in the scale of his ambition, his resolve to resist, single-handed, the pull toward fragmentation, and to replace the "iron cage" of specialization by the generous concordances of his visual graphs.

Patiently dismantling the Geddesian thinking machines in his first chapter, Volker M. Welter reveals the workings of the components, both individually and as part of the whole. From this close reading of the individual cogs, he is able to demonstrate how these machines, and in particular the Notation of Life, drive everything that Geddes subsequently thought and did. At the center of the Geddesian universe was the city, and in particular Edinburgh, the seat of political, civil, intellectual, and spiritual authority in Scotland, a city of stunning topography and weighty architecture. The ideal worlds described by the thinking machines derived from Geddes's close observation of the physical and institutional structures of Edinburgh, and the power of the Geddesian vision derived from this firm attachment to the real world.

While the history and geography of a city are standard points of reference for any urban development, the spiritual components—the sense of place, of particularity, and of belonging—are visited less frequently. Yet the Geddesian project was concerned not only with comprehension of all manifestations of social life through observation, but also with the assimilation of the insights thus gained through a process of solitary contemplation. The visitor to the Outlook Tower in Edinburgh, after viewing the panorama of the Forth Valley from the rooftop terrace and studying successive levels devoted, in descending sequence, to Edinburgh, Scotland, Language, Europe, and the World, would reach the inlook tower, a bare-walled cell containing nothing but a single chair. As Geddes explained: "The Tower of Thought and Action needs a corresponding basement and not merely that of Arts and Sciences in general as hitherto but a sub-basement or catacomb proper in which the Life of Feeling is similarly to be recognized."[8] This simple idea, contained within a tiny space, is symptomatic of Geddes's ability to address the true complexity of human life, shunning easy or conventional wisdom, the obvious, and the banal.

In the realm of town planning, the wealth of new reference introduced by Geddes led the distinguished city planner, Patrick Abercrombie, to despair:

> It is perhaps safe to say that the modern practice of town-planning . . . would have been a much simpler thing if it had not been for Geddes. There was a time when it seemed only necessary to shake up into a bottle the German town-extension plan, the Parisian Boulevard and Vista, and the English Garden Village, to produce a mechanical mixture which might be applied . . . to every town in the country; thus it would be "town planned" according to the most up-to-date notions. Pleasing dream! First shattered by Geddes as he emerged from his Outlook Tower in the frozen north, to produce that nightmare of complexity, the Edinburgh Room at the great Town Planning Exhibition of 1910.[9]

In exploring not only its biological, historical, and geographical basis but also its metaphysical ambitions, Volker M. Welter succeeds in locating Geddes's urban theory in the mainstream of European utopian thought in the early twentieth century. He also opens the way for a long-overdue assessment of the strong revival of interest in Geddes's work that informed the debate on urban development and reconstruction after World War

II. Speaking to UNESCO in December 1947, Walter Gropius called for a synthesis of "art, science and religion." "Only then," he said, "will the individual be integrated with his community, carried by a new faith!"[10] Through the admission of Geddes, our understanding of the richness of urban theory in the early twentieth century is significantly enriched, and the oversimplifying critiques of postmodernism repulsed. Where better to start investigating this richness and complexity than with the thinking machines of Patrick Geddes? In a letter written in 1975 to the Edinburgh Professor Percy Johnson-Marshall, Lewis Mumford confided:

> I finally decided in self-defence to do a critical analysis of Geddes's graphic system, to show both his achievements and his weaknesses. . . . But this task has so far proved beyond my powers: even after writing four drafts I doubt if what I am saying would make sense to anyone who was not as familiar with Geddes's thought as I am. So in the end I may have to leave this critique to some younger scholar.[11]

In Volker M. Welter, both Geddes and Mumford have found a younger scholar equal to the task.

IAIN BOYD WHYTE

# biopolis

# Introduction

"Angling for Cities!—That is the sport on which I am engaged," writes Patrick Geddes in a letter in 1907. Only three years earlier he had published *City Development: A Study of Parks, Gardens and Culture-Institutes*, a planning report with which he participated in an invited competition to design Pittencrieff Park in Dunfermline, Scotland. Geddes's first ever "city design" report guaranteed him a prominent place among contemporary architects and members of the emerging profession of town planning. But what could have been a distinguished career in town planning—comparable to that of Thomas Mawson, Geddes's likewise unsuccessful competitor in Dunfermline—did not take off. Geddes continues the letter by cautiously hinting at some obstacles to the appreciation of his efforts by the targeted cities: "while as you see they nibble, and even bite as at Dunfermline, . . . to land one properly is the difficult matter."[1]

Commonly, Patrick Geddes (1854–1932) is hailed as one of the founding fathers of the modern town planning movement, a forerunner of regional planning, the inventor of "conservative surgery," and the creator of the term "conurbation." Geddes complemented his planning proposals—realized and unrealized—with one of the most comprehensive theories of the city put forward in the decades flanking 1900. While many contemporary urbanistic proposals, for example Ebenezer Howard's Rurisville or garden city, Tony Garnier's Cité Industrielle, Otto Wagner's *Großstadt*, and Le Corbusier's Ville Radieuse, are subjects of intense and detailed scholarly analysis, Geddes's contribution to the debate about the city has remained largely unconsidered. This does not mean that he has been forgotten or, as one occasionally hears in his native Scotland, has been ignored, either deliberately or incidentally. Rather the opposite is correct. Since Geddes's death a small but slowly growing number of essays and books have explored his varied initiatives and activities. Many publications dedicated to Geddes, however, adopt a chronological narrative of events, sometimes incorporated into a biographical framework. They are often highly informative, but also mainly descriptive and selective in their focus. Questions that are of particular interest to historians and students working in the fields of architectural, planning, and urban history are left unconsidered. To look briefly at two examples.

As is well known, Geddes derived his notion of the region from contemporary geographical and botanical concepts. Its alleged naturalness seems to have fostered the assumption that the idea of a region is self-explanatory. Questions are seldom asked regarding the advantages Geddes may have thought could be gained from his idea, or the implications of his understanding of the region for every architect's and planner's work.

Likewise, Geddes's renewal work in Edinburgh's Old Town is one of the best-known examples of conservative surgery—the careful reconstruction rather than demolition of old buildings. But despite his preservation activities in some areas along Edinburgh's Royal Mile, Geddes also proposed the demolition of historic houses in the Old Town, like those adjacent to the Outlook Tower or opposite St. Giles Cathedral. Obviously, conservative surgery relied on judgments regarding the value of historic buildings; yet scholars have not examined the rationale behind Geddes's concept, emphasizing instead the ahead-of-its-time character of conservative surgery.

This book takes an architectural historical interest in Geddes. Its particular concern is his theory of the city and its practical application in the form of "city design," Geddes's preferred term for his activities. "Place," "work," and "folk"—Geddes's famous analytical triad—provide the basic structure for the book. According to Geddes, cities should be understood from three viewpoints: the geographical, the historical, and the spiritual, aspects of the city that correspond to place, work, and folk, and are likewise closely interrelated.

Scholarly analysis to date has concentrated on the first two of these three aspects, each of which, significantly, is generally considered independently of the other. Despite the strong emphasis commonly put on Geddes's holism—his restless striving toward a synthesis of diverse subjects and fields of knowledge—a comparably holistic approach is not normally applied to the study of his urban thought and work. Not surprisingly, then, Geddes's third, spiritual aspect of the city has so far been neglected. Manifold references to Greek gods and Muses in Geddes's city design reports for countries as diverse as Scotland, India, and Palestine, or his grand architectural schemes for religious and secular temple buildings, are either ignored or are welcomed as an opportunity to label him as some kind of maverick. Yet these were not mere fantasies of an imaginative and vivid mind. They were deliberate references to the spiritual aspect of the city, which in Geddes's work must be directly related to its geographical and historical aspects.

Two main analytical themes are pursued throughout the book. One is biology; Geddes's transfer of knowledge from the discipline in which he received his academic education to town planning turns out to be far more sophisticated than the more typical crude assumption that a city is an organic entity. The second is the Greek *polis*, real and ideal, especially that of Plato's *Republic*, a hitherto unacknowledged source of influence that Geddes hinted at continuously with both direct and indirect references. Regarding both sources of inspiration, it is important to bear in mind that this study is concerned with the use that Geddes made of them, rather than the philosophical, historical, or scientific correctness of his exploitation.

Some have stated that the real Geddes can best be discovered in his letters; some of his early biographers even claimed that the only way to *really* understand him was to listen to him in person. His published work is usually dismissed as badly written and of little help. Furthermore, because each work deals primarily with a single subject, it allegedly lacks what Geddes's often-announced *opus magnum* would have provided: the synthesis in one book of his philosophy and thoughts for general public and posterity alike. Although this *opus* remained unwritten, the many existing and easily accessible written and pictorial sources other than his letters, namely Geddes's books, essays, typescripts, manuscripts, notes, diagrams, photographs, drawings, and sketches, have proved to be more than helpful to the present study.

To focus on Geddes's fascination with the city might appear to be unduly narrow, given the breadth of his intellectual outlook and the subsequent synthesis of the many insights he claimed to have gained. Notwithstanding (so runs the major thesis of this book), the city provides the unifying focus for nearly all of his theoretical writings and practical activities. For the biologist Geddes—a scientist of life—the city is *the* form that human life in its highest evolutionary development (which he took to be communal and cooperative) could and should take. Consequently, the city, its past, present, and future, runs like Ariadne's thread through the maze of Geddes's life, and accordingly through this book.

Chapter 1 briefly sets out Geddes's intellectual development within the context of early modernism, with emphasis on his call for a "larger modernism," a modernism that does not exclusively rely on rational knowledge but emphasizes the need to complement rationality with its dialectical opposite, myth and religiosity. Chapter 2 analyzes Geddes's "Notation of Life," his most complex and famous "thinking machine." The analysis focuses on the contributions of the diagram to an understanding of city design, especially by reading it against Plato's *Republic*. The remaining six chapters explore the city and city design in relation to geography, history, and spirituality. Chapter 3 deals with Geddes's idea of a region-city, examining the origin of his concept in the biological sciences and the consequences of biological models for his work as a city designer. In chapter 4 the focus rests on Geddes's understanding of the city as *the* constant expression of human life throughout history. His interest in the city in history envisioned a morphology of cities in which all cities are derivations from an *ur*-city—an abstract notion comparable to Platonic ideas and to Johann Wolfgang von Goethe's elusive *Urpflanze*. Geddes's activities regarding historic buildings and cities are examined in chapter 5. Conservative surgery is unveiled as a means of allowing city and citizen to recollect (in the Platonic understanding of memory) and to recapitulate (according to Ernst Haeckel's biological law of recapitulation) the history of a city. Chapter 6 takes a close look at the popular urge among contemporary architects and town planners to implement a metaphysical city center in the form of a temple as a precondition for further urban design and renewal. Chapter 7 assembles a selection of Geddes's temple schemes, most of which present human life as an eternal phenomenon constantly materializing itself in the form of cities. The arguments from the preceding chapters are united in chapter 8 by analyzing the importance and urban form of Geddes's ideas of a temple of the city and of a cultural acropolis—an idea that anticipates Bruno Taut's *Stadtkrone* by nearly thirty years.

The book frequently refers to Geddes's many city design reports, yet the principal focus rests on his theory of the city within the terms of contemporary European debates about architecture, urbanism, and the city. The circumstances and nature of Geddes's patchy career in Great Britain pushed him to seek work abroad, for example in India after 1914. But Geddes, who was fluent in French, had a good knowledge of German, and allegedly also spoke Italian, actively sought the Continental European context from the outset of his professional life. Once outside the confines of the British Isles, Geddes thrived. Back home, his architecture and town planning colleagues perfected a contemporary version of a principally rural way of life in their garden cities and garden suburbs. Geddes, meanwhile, moving around in countries like France, Switzerland, Germany, and Italy, encountered a debate about architecture and the city that combined easily pragmatic approaches to the improvement of cities—witness the heated discussion in the German-speaking countries toward the end of the nineteenth century about the virtues of straight or crooked streets, or the adaptation of the garden city in Europe—with an idealistic, visionary outlook on a future that despite all antiurban rhetoric never abandoned the city as a way of life. Placed in the context of, for example, the life reform community on Monte Verità, François Garas's Temple à la Pensée, Fritz Schumacher's Monument for Nietzsche, and K. P. C. de Bazel's call for an "architect-priest," many of Geddes's seemingly more fantastic and eccentric ideas unveil themselves as part—often even as predecessors—of a wide range of speculative architectural thought, which in its emphasis on idealism was well beyond the pragmatic horizon of most of the contemporary British architectural and town planning scene.

Sometime after the publication of his report for Dunfermline, Geddes had paper printed with the following letterhead:

Patrick Geddes & Colleagues / Landscape Architects, Park and Garden Designers, Museum Planners, etc. / City Plans and Improvements / Parks and Gardens / Garden Villages / Type Museums / Educational Appliances / School Gardens[2]

This is more than a piece of "some elaborate writing paper" printed in "an effort to drum up 'a client or two.'"[3] It is one of the shortest, most concise pieces of writing about the city he ever produced, for, taken literally, it provides a nearly complete list of the essential elements that constitute, according to Geddes, a "true" city.

*Vivendo Discimus*—by living we learn.

Patrick Geddes

# "Angling for Cities!"

"Now, what I want is, Facts. Teach . . . nothing but Facts. Facts alone are wanted in life. . . . Stick to Facts, sir!" are the opening sentences of Charles Dickens's 1854 novel *Hard Times*, which describes the dislocations that accompanied the Industrial Revolution. Measurable, calculable, and definable facts, according to Dickens's protagonist Mr. Gradgrind, are the basis allowing everyone to master the new life as a better life.[1]

In his *Lectures on Architecture and Painting* published that same year, John Ruskin queried the citizens of Edinburgh on architectural details of the Scottish capital. Referring to the standard window form of the city's Georgian houses, constructed with massive stone lintels on square-cut jambs, Ruskin asked his audience: "How many windows precisely of this form do you suppose there are in the New Town of Edinburgh?" While Ruskin did not conduct a count all over the New Town, he provided the information that on Queen Street alone there were six hundred and seventy-eight of these windows, excluding those with moldings. The sheer number of the windows, however, does not amount to architecture, nor does the rational and Cartesian street pattern of the New Town create a city. For Ruskin, neither windows nor New Town are interesting and attractive nor entertaining and pleasing, for they appeal purely to reason but not to the heart.[2]

Knowledge likewise stands at the center of a third example from that year, Robert Pemberton's Happy Colony, a proposed model settlement to be built for British workers in New Zealand (figure 7.2).[3] Maps of the world and the sky, geometrical shapes and forms, and botanical and horticultural gardens occupy the circular colony's central space, which is surrounded by four colleges. The world Pemberton presents to the working men is thus not merely a heap of isolated facts but a meaningful composition; circular groves occupied by statues representing history, mythology, and the Muses are reminders of a unity and order of the world including but larger than rational knowledge.

Patrick Geddes was born in Ballater, Aberdeenshire, Scotland, in 1854, into a century of cities. In that same year Dickens published his novel, Pemberton brought out his model, and Ruskin presented his lectures in printed form. The broad common interest of these publications—knowledge, its constitutive elements, and higher order or synthesis—and their similar focus—the use of this knowledge for the benefit of life and society, most notably in cities—make the three authors appear to have stood sponsor to Patrick Geddes. While Geddes grew up exploring the hills and river valleys of Perthshire, attended Perth Academy, enrolled as an apprentice with a local bank, and finally decided in 1874 to study botany and the natural sciences at Edinburgh University, modern societies began to collect experiences in dealing with large-scale urban problems, both socially and architecturally.

In 1853 Georges-Eugène Haussmann began to remodel Paris by cutting boulevards into the historic urban fabric. Six years later, in 1859, Ildefonso Cerdà presented his grid plan for an extension of Barcelona, while Vienna began to implement Ludwig Förster's design for the Ringstraße. Each of the three schemes approached the city in a particular way. The rebuilding of the French capital destroyed what was old, rejecting the rights of historic Paris in favor of an ongoing, modern existence; Geddes was later to collect lithographs by the French artist Théodore Joseph Hoffbauer depicting the lost city.[4] Barcelona's expansion provided a rational plan for a new city, turning away from the existing city; Geddes obviously did not like it, as only one, bad reproduction of a map of Barcelona, including Cerdà's extension, survived among his papers.[5] Vienna's Ringstraße celebrated the city's wealth and self-confidence by assembling cultural and civic institutions together with the palatial residences of the bourgeoisie on the sites of the demolished defense systems surrounding the historic city core. This development was a matter of convenience, however, rather than an expression of adoration for the traditional Vienna. Geddes collected plans of Vienna before and after the Ringstraße, a project he approved of because of the concentration of public buildings and functions.[6]

Activities like those in Paris, Barcelona, and Vienna, or contemporary ideas like Arturo Soria y Mata's linear city from 1882, contributed, toward the end of the nineteenth century, to a lively debate on town planning and urban design. Geddes was to become a prominent figure in this debate (figure 1.1), but arrived at it from a different route than many architects and social reformers. He was first of all a biologist, although his career in that field did not begin without its problems. When he first realized that he was supposed to analyze dead plant specimens in a laboratory rather than study life in nature, Geddes left Edinburgh University in a dramatic gesture after only one week. He moved instead to London hoping to study zoology under the biologist Thomas Henry Huxley, a prominent defender of Darwin's evolutionary theories; after a preparatory year at the Royal School of Mines, he was admitted in 1875 to Huxley's classes at the same institution. There he was exposed to some of the most interesting questions of contemporary biology, questions that would fundamentally shape his lifelong interests in the city.

## The Scientist of Life

In the aftermath of Darwin's theory of evolution, forms of life and their relation to the environment were of utmost interest to natural scientists. If Darwin's hypothesis of natural selection was correct, both the existence of a species and variations among representatives of that species would be the result of the survival of those members best equipped to live in particular environments. In order to determine this advantage of the fittest, it was necessary to study both the species and its environmental conditions, so as to identify the conditions to which the characteristic qualities of the species

THE TOWN PLANNER.

FIGURE 1.1

Pàtrick Geddes in India,

c. 1915.

best responded. Without knowledge of the environment, it was impossible to explain the variations between populations of the same species under different conditions from an evolutionary standpoint. It was from this relation between organism and environment that the notion of a biological region emerged, serving as a necessary tool for anyone interested in evolution. Huxley, for example, made it the basis of his study of organisms and life in the Thames basin.[7]

Forms of life and their emergence and development in interaction with the environment were to become a major interest of Geddes, determining his life work from his earliest publication to his last book. A study period at Roscoff marine biological station in Brittany, which Huxley organized for Geddes in 1878, allowed him to begin his investigations with a startling discovery. Geddes succeeded in showing that chlorophyll is not only to be found in plants but also in certain basic forms of animal life, which like plants existed through photosynthesis.[8] In 1931, when Geddes published his last book (written with Arthur Thomson), the two-volume *Life: Outlines of General Biology*, questions about the relation between forms of life and the environment were still the main focus of his biological interest.[9] In this light, Geddes's lifelong interest in the city takes on a meaning far beyond the typical late nineteenth-century social consciousness based in finding relief for urban misery through philanthropic endeavors. The city is for Geddes the most distinct form that human life can take; even more, it is the form human life *should* take, especially in its highest development as cooperative and communal life.

After completing his time at Roscoff, Geddes moved on to Paris where he continued his studies at the Sorbonne and other academic institutions. Paris in 1878 was a city full of excitement, promise, and change. A few years after its defeat in the Franco-Prussian War and the end of the Paris Commune, the French capital appeared ready to compensate national humiliation with visions of imperialist territorial acquisitions. These tendencies were reflected in an upsurge of interest in scientific and commercial geography, exemplified by the world's fair of 1878 with its emphasis on foreign countries, overseas trade connections, and scientific discoveries. Geddes was deeply fascinated by both the intellectual attractions of Paris and the international aspirations of the exhibition, but one of the greatest discoveries he made in Paris was the social theory of the French sociologist Frédéric Le Play.[10] Le Play's social philosophy centered on the triad of *lieu*, *travail*, and *famille*, which Geddes adapted in the following decades either as "place," "work," and "folk" or as "environment," "function," and "organism." Le Play's triad enabled Geddes to place the category of work—human labor and activities—at a central position in the relation between the environment and human beings. This in turn allowed him to emphasize that man, although still an example of organic life, nevertheless distinguishes himself from animals and plants through his ability to change the environment consciously with his own labor, according to his needs.

The emphasis on labor as the main characteristic of man in society was common during the nineteenth century. While for Thomas Carlyle labor had a quasi-religious function, John Ruskin and William Morris considered it more as a possible form of art, an approach that inspired Ruskin's essay on the Gothic in *The Stones of Venice* in particular and the arts and crafts movement in general. Marx and Engels recognized labor as a means by which man raised himself above nature. Geddes develops a different view: Man should not attempt to rise above nature but should adapt himself to his environment through work. While animal and plant life interact with the environment passively or instinctively, human life interacts consciously, and the results of human work—material and cultural products—are unique to human life. Furthermore, through work Geddes's other two societal categories, place and folk, can actively be influenced and determined.

After his year in Paris Geddes returned briefly to Scotland in 1879, only to leave again toward the end of the year on an expedition to Mexico. While collecting scientific data and specimens there, he suffered temporary blindness caused by a combination of strenuous work with the microscope and exposure to the strong southern sun. Geddes attempted to cure himself by living temporarily in a darkened room, avoiding all light. His confinement amounted to a crisis whose importance can be gathered from autobiographic verses he wrote in 1925:

> As with winged eyes I had lived my life,
> Gloating o'er all I saw:
> Through nature and art, in beauty rife,
> Observe! was my life's law!
> . . . . .
> From tropic rides and quests and finds
> Prisoned in night-dark-room!
> Long weeks, then months, its boding binds
> Hope between gloom and doom![11]

During this time of insecurity over the chances of ever returning to laboratory work, Geddes conceived a means by which to order his thoughts and ideas. Trying to follow trains of thought, Geddes resorted to the squares of a window. If the individual panes represented the variables of a problem, and each pane was adjacent to at least one other pane (more likely to three or more), relations and dependencies between the variables could easily be symbolized. Out of this tactile thinking device—due to his blindness it was not initially a visual one—Geddes developed what are today known as thinking machines. These are pieces of paper that Geddes folded several times so that when unfolded they were structured by lines forming smaller squares. Similar to the window panes, the squares represented thoughts, ideas, or symbols and their relationships. As such, these diagrams were a means to create and express order in complex systems.

## The Economics of Nature

After his return from Mexico Geddes settled in Edinburgh in 1880, where he continued his career as a biologist. At the same time he pursued his interest in ordering and classifying phenomena, facts, and things. Following his fascination with the relation between life forms and their environments, the classification of life would become Geddes's second main interest, developed early in his career and sustained throughout. Like the relationship of life forms and environments, the classification of life also strongly informs Geddes's late work, including his last published book *Life: Outlines of General Biology*, in which a classifying thinking machine with the title "General Sciences" illustrates the endpapers. For Geddes the connection between biology and classification is close and logical.

The desire for order, according to the sociologist Zygmunt Bauman, is a main characteristic of modernity.[12] The premodern world just existed, failing to ask how it could be created by those living in it, and passed away at the moment man gained insight into this higher order. Modernity begins with man's reflection on the order of the universe, the place of mankind in the world, and the knowledge that this reflection is a conscious one.

Reflection upon the world leads to classification, which is an attempt to give back to the world a structure by establishing categories and ascribing facts and observations to them. According to Bauman, the ideal of classification is to accommodate all observations and facts in a huge filing cabinet. Each fact is to receive a unique place in the structure; ideally there would be no ambivalence, but cross reference helps in cases of doubt. Classification thus relies on fragmentation, the continuous dissection of the world into ever smaller, solvable questions.

The price for this approach to order, however, is the discovery of yet another layer of chaos underneath the order just arrived at. Order is one of the *foci imaginarii* of modernity, writes Bauman; it moves further away the closer the modern mind seems to come to it. There are "no headquarters to co-ordinate the battles—certainly not commanders-in-chief able to chart the whole vastness of the universe to be conquered," he writes.[13] This weakness, however, is also the source of the continuous strength of modernity.

As early as 1881, in his first and major publication on the subject of classification, Geddes declares that "to biology above all is presented the problem of an innumerable multitude of actual phenomena demanding arrangement."[14] A zoologist occupied with grouping animals, for example, has to specialize in his studies in order to learn about details, but simultaneously must generalize in order to locate these details in their larger context. Because biology in particular must balance individual facts with the larger whole, and because the largest whole biology deals with is life, Geddes proposes in this essay to derive from biological sciences a model for the classification of statistics.

His efforts in classification result in a "colossal balance-sheet," a table that allows for generalizations while accommodating "the most trivial details of common life."[15] Geddes claims that his classification is scientific, systematic, universally applicable to human and animal societies alike, and comprehensive, because it incorporates the results of all sciences. He admits that it would be impossible ever to fill all the pigeonholes of the scheme but argues that it is useful anyway because it assembles the results of statistics in a whole. Furthermore, it allows for their application to a multitude of other topics, among them cities:

> Thus, for instance, it is one of the most marked advantages of the tables that it would be easy to monograph on this principle a city or a village, a single household or even an individual, as well as a nation, to compare these facts of personal and domestic economy among each other, and to generalise bodies of these.[16]

There is a second connection between biology and the proposed classification scheme. Geddes's table develops around his usual triad of place, work, and folk (here "territory," "occupations," and "organisms"), following the underlying assumption that a human society can be looked at along the same lines as animal and plant societies. Animals, plants, and humans all exist in habitats limited in space and time, comprised of multiple organisms that "modify surrounding nature, primarily by seizing part of its matter and energy."[17] The consideration of life as a processing of matter and energy is what allows Geddes to apply his classification to individual organisms, cities, and nations alike; for all are merely different forms of life. In the following years he continued to develop his theories in two areas: in the biological context, where he elaborated his ideas in various essays on cell theory, and in regard to human societies, where he focused his essays on economics.[18] Without embarking on a detailed analysis of Geddes's attempt to root human economy in principles of dissipation of natural matter and energy, two points are important to note in relation to his interest in the city.

First, Geddes distinguishes between the production and consumption of "necessaries" and "super-necessaries."[19] Necessaries are products such as fuel, shelter, food, and the like, required to maintain structure and functions of biological or social organisms. Super-necessaries are purely aesthetic products, for example "articles of ordinary city consumption, such as ashlar housefronts with iron railings, furniture and decorations, cookery and dress"[20]—products meant to stimulate the human sense organs. Because higher forms of life rely on a more developed nervous system, Geddes arrives at the surprising conclusion that higher forms of life—the most developed being the human—need more super-necessaries.

Second, necessaries and super-necessaries differ with regard to their consumption. Necessaries like food or clothing, although of existential importance, are transitory, whereas super-necessaries, Geddes argues, are permanent. From his observation that with the development of capitalism the turnover of commodities accelerates, Geddes concludes that short-lived necessaries increase at the expense of permanent goods. This constitutes a waste of matter and energy, which can only be corrected by redirecting production and consumption toward the creation of super-necessaries. The latter, whether newly produced or already accumulated in the past, are what constitute the real wealth of a society and, ultimately, of mankind.

## The Economics of Cities

That the creation of wealth in the form of permanent super-necessaries is the ideal result of human activity was not a new insight, though it was innovative, according to Geddes, to base the analysis of economics on physical laws and principles. His classification of statistics based on the interaction of place, work, and folk, and his analysis of economics as the transformation of energy and matter, Geddes writes, are "simply a return to the conception from which political economy arose and departed, that of the study of household management and law." In a footnote to this remark Geddes elucidates his points of reference, which are the civil polity (*politeia* or *polis*), the household (*oikos*), and the law (*nomos*).[21] This is one of his earliest references to ancient Greek philosophy and thought. In addition to biology, Geddes adopts the Greek idea of economics—the ethically and morally sound management of an estate and household, most notably expressed and achieved in the field of agriculture—as another basis for his study of the economic activities of contemporary societies.[22] Here he follows John Ruskin, who had proposed that political economy is "the generalized aspect of domestic economy."[23] The first volume of Ruskin's Bibliotheca Pastorum, an ideal literary library for Britain's peasants, was a translation into English of Xenophon's *The Economist*, one of the most famous works of ancient economics. In his introduction to the text (translated by two of Ruskin's students at Oxford), Ruskin draws the connection between agricultural life—the main subject of Xenophon's work—and the city. Only in the shadow of the "Metropolis"— "the city in which the chief temple of the nation's God is built"—Ruskin writes, can the good life be lived. Even more, the relation between rural life and the city is indissoluble, because "the temple of the city being changed into a den of thieves," the surrounding "fields of the country" turn into "a labouring ground of slaves."[24]

Geddes would develop this amalgam of ideas taken from biology, natural sciences, classification of knowledge, and Greek philosophy and culture in a sequence of essays and papers written in Edinburgh during the 1880s.[25] These essays do not present a linear intellectual development proceeding from biology toward sociology and cities. Rather, they aim at the clarification of a set of ideas and a testing of their applicability to various subjects, of which the city is one. Geddes concludes that human organisms, their functions, and their environment all require improvements for the benefit of man. Existing cities run counter to this aim:

> What has any modern industrial city, however stupendous its wealth—on paper—to show save a sorry aggregate of ill-constructed houses, mean or showy without, unhealthy within, and containing little of permanent value; for the rest, dirt and darkness, smoke and sewage everywhere, as if its inhabitants had absolutely framed the ideal of a short life and a dismal one, with which they are dull enough to rest contented.[26]

These cities are examples of wasted energy and matter, formed by what Geddes calls the "paleotechnic age." The new city, on the contrary, is a "city of healthy and happy artists" creating permanent wealth in super-necessaries. It is "surrounded by imperishable treasure," the results of the good rural life conducted in the city's shadow as described earlier by Ruskin.[27] This city is the product of the "neotechnic age"; it is created by the development, expansion, refinement, and economical use of industrial products facilitated by more efficient means of transforming matter into energy—for example, electricity.[28]

## The Order of Cities

Chaos came into being when the premodern divine order collapsed; Bauman calls chaos and order the two sides of modernity. They are the successors to an opposing third, nature, that is, nature as given, the universe as it existed before man started to think about it. Nature as reflected upon implies man's awareness of a lack of structure, in short chaos, since nature no longer expresses a divine order. Nature as reflected upon contains all the elements of a possible new order, but one that no longer comes about unaided. Rather, once recognized, the order in nature requires deliberate effort for its realization and maintenance.[29] This new natural order must also be total and comprehensive. Although fragmentation and classification appear to make this impossible, the aim remains a complete *"mappa mundi."*[30] Once formed, this idea of a comprehensive order becomes the basis of intellectual reasoning and scientific research, its realization the quest of the modern state and society. Against the background of a chaotic, disordered and uncultivated nature as given, Bauman describes the modern mind's perception of itself as a gardener, occupied with the deliberate introduction of rational order for the benefit of man.[31]

"Town-planning," Geddes once wrote, "is not mere place-planning, nor even work-planning. If it is to be successful it must be folk-planning. This means that its task is . . . to find the right places for each sort of people; places where they will really flourish."[32] These places, of course, are not really to be found but have to be made. From his earliest designs for a botanical school garden and urban renewal work in Edinburgh to his latest building initiatives in Montpellier in southern France, Geddes pursued the creation of such places. He perceived himself as a gardener ordering the environment for the benefit of life. The difference between creating gardens as places for plant life and cities as places for human life is only a matter of degree. As Geddes said late in life, "My ambition being . . . to write in reality—here with flower and tree, and elsewhere with house and city—it is all the same."[33]

Geddes attempted to derive from the eternal economics of nature the future economics of society and city. His "neotechnic age" aimed at a threefold result: it would "culminate in the Rehabilitation of Beauty, . . . in the ordering of nature, and the creation and conservation of art."[34] The rehabilitation of beauty is the return to the balance and harmony between input and output in nature, accomplished by returning to nature an order that will help to create permanent wealth in the form of super-necessary art and architecture. Thus according to Geddes both artists and architects were the "natural and eternal leaders" of the new order; artists because of their social idealism and often collective pattern of work, and architects because of their "power of resource and practical organisation."[35]

To realize the neotechnic order requires "productive action in country and city."[36] Geddes's dual focus on country and city aims at a unity he later calls the region. The region is not only a reminder of the scientific roots of Geddes's approach to cities in biology and geography, but also a symbol of the comprehensiveness implicit in his aim to order nature. The region was to become the visual expression of the order he detected in nature. Potentially, the region embraces *in nuce* all possible modes of human life between the two opposing poles of rural and urban, if only life and nature can be made to serve the theoretical model underpinning this microcosm. Geddes's claim for comprehensiveness is total: even nature untouched by human intervention and unexploited by capitalist development has to be incorporated into the neotechnic order in the form of nature reserves or botanic and zoological gardens. Once subdued to the regional order, nature still appears natural while ceasing to be so. This was exactly Geddes's intention.

In 1895, to give an example, Geddes refused to oppose the development of the waterfalls of Foyer in Scotland's Inverness district into a water-driven power station for the British Aluminum Company. Instead he supported the building of the station but recommended that it be constructed in a way that would allow the waterfalls to continue to run, at least periodically. Furthermore, he advised that the buildings of the power station "once devised by the engineers for the economic utilisation of the water should be revised in architectural style, by some architect . . . for . . . all that is wanted is picturesque grouping of roofs and pleasant contouring of white-washed walls."[37] Thus in Geddes's conception, engineers in service with architects could transform a spot of natural beauty into a location of neotechnic beauty and thus an expression of permanent wealth.

## The Revolt against Reason

Besides comprehensiveness, exclusiveness often emerges as a second essential characteristic of the modern order. The clear definition of inside and outside, and a growing awareness of the importance of borders against what Bauman calls common sense, beliefs, superstitions, and ignorance, become indispensable to modernity's battle against ambivalence.[38] Geddes's intellectual development took a different course, however. His approach to classification and the ordering of nature did not depend on a narrow and selective set of intellectual categories. Rather, he broadened his interests over time, widening the focus of his activities to include religious ideas, metaphysics, and mysticism. When Geddes comments in the early 1880s that "the influence of other extra-scientific conceptions, theological or metaphysical . . . has . . . to be guarded against,"[39] this seemingly sensible statement in an essay on economic principles is an early indication of a major intellectual conflict that would occupy him for the remainder of his life: the relation between science or reason and "extra-scientific" conceptions such as metaphysics or religious beliefs.

At about the same time, Geddes came into contact with groups like the Fellowship of the New Life. The Fellowship comprised intellectuals and social reformers with an interest in spiritual development as opposed to the mere pursuit of material aims, who assembled in London around the Scotsman Thomas Davidson.[40] Likewise, since the 1870s Geddes had been acquainted with Annie Besant, a future influential figure in the international theosophical movement and foster mother of an adopted son Krishnamurti. In 1899 she would establish the Central Hindu College, later the University in Benares, India. Thus from the outset of his career as a natural scientist Geddes moved in intellectual circles whose ideas would become known toward the end of the century as the "revolt against reason."

The most prominent representative of this bourgeois, idealistic questioning of materialistic-scientific principles was probably the French philosopher Henri Louis Bergson. Bergson criticized a purely mechanistic understanding of the physical world in which, for example, the idea of evolution appeared to divide the eternal phenomenon of life into short sequences of the existence of numerous species, entirely determined by principles of accident. Against the idea of time as an intellectual abstraction Bergson set the idea of *durée*, thus emphasizing a continuum of becoming and deceasing. Against accidental natural selection he placed an *élan vital*, a mysterious force that directs mechanical evolution toward the evolution of meaningful life. And finally, against reason as the human faculty allowing the creation of knowledge, Bergson favored intuition as the appropriate means of philosophical inquiry.

Geddes and Bergson met in Paris at the 1900 Universal Exposition. By then Geddes's intellectual development had taken a path broadly comparable to that of Bergson and other contemporaries. Like them, he emphasized the equal value of both scientific or rational and extrascientific or metaphysical approaches to the understanding of life and the world; like them, he called for a renewed unity between the two approaches, more commonly seen as opposing poles with the rational one dominant. But Geddes differed from many of his contemporaries on one important point; as a natural scientist he never entirely lost a pragmatic, scientific view of the world. Geddes did not hesitate to marvel at the mysteries of life or capture them in the symbolic, imaginative forms of art and literature. Yet he always went a step further and asked how life could be improved, rather than merely understood or venerated.

Ultimately, Geddes rejected Bergson's undefinable *élan vital*, although his own answer to the quest for a teleological life force, the idea of the *genius loci*, was equally vague. Geddes derived the *genius loci* from the concrete material existence of a regional or urban environment. He likewise wished to root the spiritual there, for it is mankind's interaction with the environment that perpetuates the *genius loci*. Thus Geddes's philosophy of life is characterized by a strong element of activism. Yet his apparently rational approach to the material world, which made *genius loci* seem more concrete than *élan vital*, does not indicate a materialist position. In fact it is materialism turned upside down, for Geddes never accepted that the material world was devoid of meaning other than what the human mind ascribes to it. Instead, he was interested in material facts because they could convey the existence of life as a truth preexisting the material world and human reason.

Geddes's fascination with the fin-de-siècle revolt against reason can be gathered from his depiction as "Professor P. Grosvenor" in the novel *The Cruciform Mark*.[41] Grosvenor, professor of psychology at Edinburgh University, is a central figure in a circle of friends and students gathering in a residence hall high above Edinburgh's Old Town. While their daytime is occupied by the pursuit of rational knowledge, evenings are given over to discussions of psychological and spiritual interests, and nights to strange and mystical events.

After 1900 Geddes spent more and more time in London, where in 1903 he was among the founders of the Sociological Society. His years in London proved to be decisive for his intellectual development; there his fascination with religious, metaphysical, and mystical thoughts received further stimulation, fostered by contacts with old and new friends. Among these, Victor Verasis Branford, an accountant and former student at Geddes's summer schools in Edinburgh, was the driving force in the early years of the Sociological Society.[42] Although a financier by profession, Branford took a keen interest in philosophical and religious questions. Lewis Mumford later praised Branford's "early interpretation of the significance of religion as the binding force in all human societies" for anticipating "by two or three decades a change of philosophic orientation that is still going on."[43] Branford's interest in religion was highly influential on Geddes's analysis of societies and cities and the planning of the latter.

Of a comparable influence was David Montague Eder, one of the first British psychoanalysts of the Freudian school.[44] His friendship with Geddes began in the years around 1908 and developed especially after 1919, when Eder vigorously supported Geddes's design for the Hebrew University at Jerusalem. Eder was also closely acquainted with D. H. Lawrence, who, like Geddes, was a visitor to the utopian community of Monte Verità in Ascona, Switzerland. Through friends like Eder and Branford and contacts with people such as Alfred Richard Orage, the editor of the journal *New Age*, Geddes was part of a movement of renewed interest in religiosity and rising fascination with spirituality, mysticism, and Eastern beliefs.[45] These interests were to become dominant in the final decades of Geddes's life, especially during the years from 1914 to 1924 when he lived and worked as a city designer mainly in India.

## Toward a Larger Modernism

Geddes's time in India was overshadowed by the deaths of Alasdair, his eldest son, killed in military service in France, and of Anna, his wife since 1886. Within less than two months in May and June of 1917, Geddes lost not only one of his staunchest supporters and allies since the couple's early days in Edinburgh, but also his chosen successor in the quest to propagate his philosophy of life. These personal losses contributed to, but did not trigger, the increasing orientation of Geddes's philosophy and activities toward metaphysics and spirituality during the late 1910s and 1920s. Neither was the First World War the cause. Beyond the horrors of the battlefields, the war was for Geddes the confirmation and the climax—unnecessary, though not entirely unexpected—of the ongoing struggle between a dying paleotechnic world order and the coming neotechnic one. In keeping with the activist stance of his philosophy of life, Geddes instantly focused on the future that would follow the war. "The War: Its Social Tasks and Problems" was the title of a conference he organized with some friends at King's College, London, in July of 1915. The main thrust of the event, for which Geddes returned temporarily from India, was to discuss how to end both the war and the paleotechnic age by diverting the forces of destruction toward the reconstruction of life, societies, and cities.[46]

The war did not cause Geddes to totally revise his understanding of the human mind or his outlook on the world, as happened to so many of his European contemporaries. Rather, it reemphasized what he had believed and argued since the 1890s: that the rational-scientific principles on which the order of modern societies rested would only be beneficial to mankind if they were complemented by a metaphysical and spiritual orientation.

Geddes's sojourn in India confirmed this assumption. On his arrival, he felt an overwhelming but also familiar fascination with the country's cultures and traditions, especially its religions and their associated temples and holy shrines. As a subscriber to the fin-de-siècle, neoromantic notion that Eastern cultures were superior to modern European ones, being not yet spiritually depleted in favor of a blunt materialism, Geddes looked at India primarily through the eyes of the European *Lebensreform* movement. This appears to have been the most important cause of the ever-increasing weight he placed on spirituality and metaphysics during the final decades of his life.[47] Architecturally, this tendency finds its apotheosis in his scheme for Hebrew University in Jerusalem, a commission he worked on from 1919 to 1929. He responded to the task by conceiving not only a new place of Jewish learning but a temple of life for Palestine, the ancient cradle of Western civilization.

The Hebrew University commission was also the climax of a professional cooperation between Geddes and his son-in-law, the architect and town planner Frank Mears. A lack of sophisticated architectural drawing skills constantly forced Geddes to engage architects, engineers, or draftsmen for the presentation of his thoughts in plans and drawings. Seldom was he able to ensure the support of an architect as skilled as Mears.[48] Mears has occasionally been described as a faithful architectural translator of Geddes's ideas,[49] but Mears's architectural projects for Geddes are interpretations rather than straightforward translations of the older man's thoughts. Plans like those for Hebrew University are the result of a reciprocal working partnership between an unusual thinker and a gifted artist-architect, in which the individual contributions are sometimes hard to identify.

The literary critic Raymond Williams points out that modernity's obsession with the city invokes less the city as a community than an isolated "man walking through" the urban space.[50] This fragmentation of society into individuals who no longer form a collective is the ultimate experience of subjectivity and individual consciousness, though it nevertheless stimulates the return of a "collective consciousness." This renewed knowledge of community differs from the community lost with the rise of the modern city. The reclaimed collective of its citizens is one of myths and archetypes, an example of a "metaphysical or psychological 'community.'" Accordingly, the experience of a sense of belonging to such communities relies, as Williams puts it, on "the most inward channels" supported by "a whole range of techniques of self-isolation."[51] The often-bemoaned loss of the old community and social consciousness is thus turned into a virtue of modern man.

Geddes's growing interest in religion, metaphysics, and mysticism was not purely theoretical but culminated in his vision of building "Temples of the City" complemented by "thinking-cells." If built, these structures would have institutionalized the self-isolation Williams refers to. The long years in India and the short but intensive working spells in Palestine—the Holy Land of his Christian childhood—nourished in Geddes the conviction that the neotechnic city needed nothing more than a new temple in order to bring about the neotechnic age of mankind.

Geddes had begun his career in the 1880s with a quest to classify knowledge for the benefit of life. Late in his life, the same interest in the classification of knowledge led him to call for the building of temples, as spaces for the synthesis of knowledge and facts for the pursuit both of wisdom and a new sense of community. Geddes's attempts to resuscitate forms of knowledge other than the rational were not a pursuit of an alternative to modernity but, as Victor Branford puts it, "a plea for the larger modernism."[52]

We are, in truth, at the opening of one of those phases of human as of simpler evolution, when individuals casually crowded, loosely grouped, begin to enter upon a new phase of existence— more social, more orderly, and in general more beautiful.

Patrick Geddes, "Town Planning and City Design"

# Patrick Geddes's Theory of the City

Victorian Britain was the first modern society to experience on a grand scale the process of industrialization and the establishment of modern capitalism. Progress and change occurred rapidly but continuously and were readily observable in the fabric of its towns and cities. Railway tracks and telegraph wires drew new lines of transport and communication over the land. Railway stations, stock markets, bank buildings, and department stores came to dominate city centers, rivaling the spires of the churches. Existing cities grew into the countryside, where they threatened the realm of the upper classes, the country house. Extended areas of cherished land became coal fields or disappeared beneath the endless rows of working-class houses that formed new industrial cities. As the landscape changed its appearance, the life of the people changed too. The upper classes benefited from newly created wealth, which they spent sometimes on urban amenities, sometimes on their country estates. Change was more dramatic at the other end of the social hierarchy, for those working in the new factories and living in the row houses. Working-class Britons had to come to terms with unemployment, illness, and bad housing. For them, life in an industrialized society was not necessarily a better life; they were often compelled to give up a poor but somewhat secure life in the countryside for a poorer and insecure town life. Furthermore, because the emerging working class was seen as a potential threat to the rich whose wealth they produced, they became the object of ongoing scrutiny.

Another result of the transformation of Victorian society was the centralization of the state. Administrative and political power guaranteed a stable frame of laws and regulations within which the individual entrepreneur could compete either at home or abroad. The state also attempted to guarantee the economic basis of production by improving the health, living, and labor conditions of the working classes. Yet in the predominantly liberal climate of Victorian Britain any interference with the natural course of economics was deeply unpopular, and state initiatives were accordingly confined to easing the worst results of laissez-faire practices. Additional endeavors were left to churches or philanthropic individuals and organizations, which often concentrated on individual problems like alcohol consumption, or on the improvement of housing through model settlements like Cadbury's Bournville (from 1879) or Lever's Port Sunlight (from 1888). The problems of society were often traced back to the moral and ethical conduct of its individual members rather than to economic, political, and social structures. The underlying issues at stake were the relations between different social classes on the one hand and the individual and the larger society on the other. As the problems of an industrialized capitalist society were new, many of those concerned with the condition of society began to look back into human history for guidance, seeking to reintroduce imaginary models of a happier past into the completely new social, economic, and political environment of Victorian Britain.

## Victorian Britain and Historical Models

The Middle Ages took on such a model character for the Victorians, admired as a period of a great society predominantly structured by Christian thought, with the medieval city as its nearly perfect expression. The life of the city's inhabitants was organized around guilds: unions of citizens of the same profession, which guaranteed economic and social security and advantages to their members. Among these, the mason's guild was of particular interest to many nineteenth-century reformers, especially those involved with art and architecture. The mason's guild was responsible, supported by the rest of the city's inhabitants, for the erection of the cathedral, the edifice that dominated the medieval cityscape both architecturally and symbolically. The cathedral became a symbol of the possible heights to which a society could rise, in which the mutual endeavor of all people, despite their different social positions, was guided toward one unifying aim. A range of nineteenth-century undertakings, including the antiquarian Gothic revival in its early decades, John Ruskin's Guild of St. George, William Morris's Red House designed by Philip Webb in 1859, Morris's guildlike company Morris & Co., or the arts and crafts movement in general, were all influenced by aesthetic and economic principles derived from the Middle Ages, though the primary points of reference differed according to individual social, political, and artistic interests.

But the Middle Ages were only one possible model society, especially popular toward the end of the nineteenth century. This popularity was preceded and paralleled by a strong interest in antiquity, especially classical Greece of the fifth and fourth centuries B.C., which first acquired the status of a model society in the second half of the eighteenth century. The questions Enlightenment philosophers asked about human self-knowledge and man's position in nature, along with political upheavals like the American and French revolutions, seriously shook traditional institutions and the morals and ethical values of the older societies. Thus began a process of societal change that lasted through the whole of the nineteenth century. Classical Greece offered an alternative social model characterized by stable conditions and a coherent body of values. As a model society it could be exploited both by those who argued for change and by those who wanted to preserve the status quo.[1] The latter were represented by the enlightened absolutist rulers who embellished towns and country estates with classicist buildings meant both to impress and to teach their people humanist values. On the other hand the artists, architects, and writers who took the grand tour through Greece and Italy often dreamed of democracy, even if they were financed by the absolutist rulers who made use of their newfound knowledge at home.

In Victorian Britain the classical world occupied a major position in politics, philosophy, and education. The inclusion of classical subjects in higher education fostered a traditional knowledge of Greek civilization among the educated classes. For those who were no longer taught Greek or Latin, new translations of classical authors were deployed in an attempt to maintain the validity of these favored texts of the political elite. The interest in antiquity was a contemporary one rather than historical, for as historian Frank M. Turner explains, "writing about Greece was in part a way for the Victorians to write about themselves."[2] The historicist, evolutionary interpretation of national history as stages in a process of growth allowed for the juxtaposition of Victorian Britain with classical Greece, since both cultures were seen as being on the same level of their development and therefore facing comparable political, moral, and aesthetic problems.

Within this larger frame, the middle of the nineteenth century was marked by a particular revival of interest in Plato. According to Turner, the nineteenth-century revival of Plato was much stronger than its Renaissance counterpart.[3] At a time when the influence of Christian churches was on the wane, Plato offered an alternative intellectual paradigm similarly concerned with such issues as transcendence and the eternity of the soul. Furthermore, Plato's widely read dialogue the *Republic* addresses a question—the relation between the state or society and the individual citizen—that was of utmost importance to the Victorians.

Plato's *Republic* is presented as a dialogue between the philosopher Socrates and some of his pupils on the moral question "What is justice?" The question is not a purely academic one, for Socrates wants to find out whether it pays to live a just life. Socrates suggests it is appropriate to begin this examination at the level of a Greek *polis* or city and then focus in on the individual, since if justice can be found in this larger unit it will be easier to identify the equivalent in the smaller one.[4] However, justice is a matter of both the community and the individual in which the latter is the decisive element, for as Plato writes, "We are bound to admit that the elements and traits that belong to a state must also exist in the individuals that compose it. There is nowhere else for them to come from."[5] A good city should therefore possess the four virtues of wisdom, courage, self-restraint, and justice. If the first three can be found within the city, the fourth, justice, will be immediately evident as well.

Accordingly, the perfectly good city is characterized by a division of the inhabitants into three classes. The majority of people belong to the economic class, serving the ruling class which is divided into auxiliaries (the military) and guardians proper. Courage, defined as the ability to adhere to what is correct and lawful under any circumstances, is the virtue associated with the auxiliaries. The guardians are the old and wise men administering in the interests of the *polis*. Their virtue is wisdom, in this case knowledge about the well-being of the city as a whole and its relations to other cities. The virtue of self-restraint is embodied in the rulership of the good part of a city (the guardians proper) over the other parts.[6] Justice—the principle that each man should pursue only one profession, that which suits him most naturally—is the virtue that concerns all inhabitants of the *polis* equally. Each class should likewise be confined to its functions and none should try to perform the functions of another; if the relations between the classes are determined by this restriction, the city will be a just one.[7] Each individual, like the city itself, is composed of three parts—desire or appetite, reason, and spirit—and the relation between these determines whether the individual is just.[8] The connection between city and individual is thus a matter of scale: both the just city and the just individual are ruled by the same principle of the relation between the four constitutive parts, and insights into justice at one level are reciprocally transferable to the other.

## The Notation of Life

One of Geddes's most sophisticated "thinking machines" is the Notation of Life, occasionally also called Chart of Life, a graphic summary of his ideas about human life (figure 2.1). The diagram puts forward a theory of human interaction with the environment, drawing on subjects ranging from contemporary psychology and politics to sociology, arts, and beyond. The Notation of Life is not merely descriptive or analytic but a call for action, as it contains Geddes's methodology for the improvement of the human condition.

Plato's quest for the just life led to the insight that *polis* and citizens are connected in an interdependent relationship, from which alone the good life can emerge. Geddes assumes a comparable relationship between the two principal forms of human life, the individual and the social or cooperative. "Like flower and butterfly," he writes, "city and citizen are bound in an

PLATE V       THE CHARTING OF LIFE.

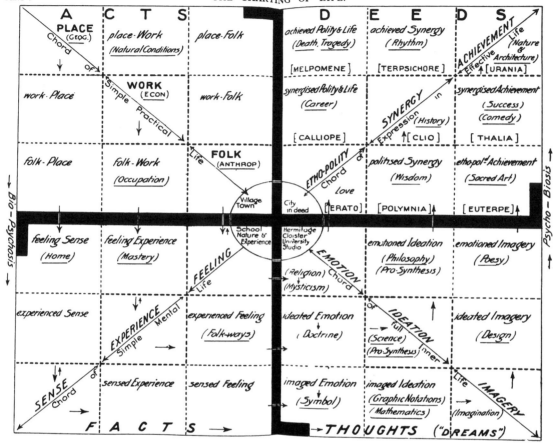

FIGURE 2.1

The Notation of Life, as

published in 1927.

abiding partnership of mutual aid."[9] It is around this mutually beneficial re-lationship that the Notation of Life develops. The central four terms of the diagram, "Town," "School," "Cloister," and "City in deed," represent what one may call the Town-City formula, which comprises the four steps of trans-forming a mere town into a city. Along the outer frame of the diagram the terms "Acts," "Facts," "Thoughts (Dreams)," and "Deeds" constitute accord-ingly the Act-Deed formula, which likewise comprises four steps by which individual human lives are raised to higher levels of conscious existence.[10] Geddes intertwines indissolubly the two formulas in the diagram. Only

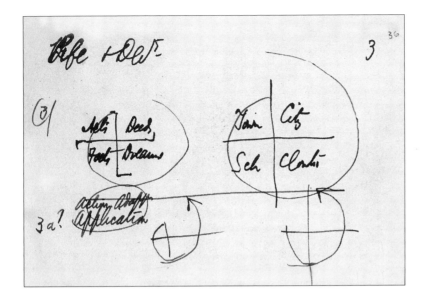

FIGURE 2.2

A sketch by Geddes of
the Act-Deed and Town-
City formulas, not dated.

when taken together as the two parts of a whole do the formulas function properly, guaranteeing the constant evolution of human life—individual and social—toward ever higher forms, an evolution he compares to the upward coiling of a spiral (figure 2.2).

The Notation of Life diagram was published only once during Geddes's lifetime, when Amelia Defries, his first biographer, included it along with a supplementary text by Geddes in her 1927 *The Interpreter Geddes: The Man and His Gospel*.[11] However, several of Geddes's essays and lecture syllabi appear to date the diagram's development to approximately 1904–1905. In those years Geddes read two papers on civics as applied sociology to the newly established Sociological Society in London that make frequent reference to the Town-City formula.[12] According to Defries, Geddes first presented the full diagram to the public in 1914 during a lecture at the Royal Society of Arts in London.[13]

## From Town to City

According to Geddes any human settlement, whether village, town, or city, can be comprehended by applying the triad place-work-folk. A town occupies a certain location, its place, where the inhabitants are involved in all

| PLACE-FOLK | WORK-FOLK | **FOLK** |
|---|---|---|
| ("NATIVES") | ("PRODUCERS") | |
| PLACE-WORK | **WORK** | FOLK-WORK |
| **PLACE** | WORK-PLACE | FOLK-PLACE |

TABLE 2.1
The triad
place-work-folk.

sorts of activities, their work. With their life structured by work and influenced by the conditions of place, the residents would form a folk with a common superstructure of shared beliefs, traditions, and customs. To arrive at a full picture of a town, the interrelations between the main categories, as set out in table 2.1, have to be included in the analysis.[14]

The six subcategories are more than auxiliary means to fill the table. Every aspect of a town and town life can be accounted for with the help of the main and the subcategories. But it is the latter in particular that allow for a dynamic analysis of towns, as for example when Geddes identifies the same group of people as being "Natives" or "Producers," thereby referring to their changing roles within a society. Similarly, place can be looked at from various angles:

> For Place, it is plain, is no mere topographic site. Work, conditioned as it primarily is by natural advantages, is thus really first of all *place-work*. Arises the field or garden, the port, the mine, the workshop, in fact the *work-place*, as we may simply generalise it; while, further, beside this arise the dwellings, the *folk-place*.[15]

The nine categories applied to any town provide a picture of the objective life, the "everyday world of action." A town analyzed as such Geddes names "Town proper."[16]

To this point Geddes's analysis concerns only the daily life composed of objective elements. They are supplemented with, or reflected in, the subjective life made up by the corresponding "thought-world."[17] Each element of the Town has its corresponding element in the thought world, as set out in table 2.2.[18] Geddes introduces "School" as a generic term for the subjective elements of life, comparable to its use in the field of art history.[19]

| FOLK | WORK | PLACE |
|---|---|---|
| **TOWN** | | |
| (a) Individuals | (a) Occupations | (a) Work-Places |
| (b) Institutions | (b) War | (b) War-Places |
| **SCHOOL** | | |
| (b) History | (b) Statistics and History | (b) Geography |
| ("Constitutional") | ("Military") | |
| (a) Biography | (a) Economics | (a) Topography |

TABLE 2.2

The Town proper reflected in the thought world of Schools.

Within the division into the three categories of folk, work, and place, the institutions of the Town proper, for example, are reflected in Schools of history. Likewise, the lives of individual inhabitants become reflected in "Schools of biographies," and occupations of the inhabitants give rise to Schools of economics.

Hence a Town consists of the Town proper—the world of action—and the Schools—the world of thought. A Town proper never exists on its own, for with it a corresponding thought world comes into being. Daily town life and its activities exist as a dialectical process between the two worlds of action and though. A School emerges, it influences the objective elements of which it is the reflection, and thus a new School emerges as the reflection of the changed objective elements. Although the Town proper gives rise to the Schools, Geddes does not wish to express a purely materialistic point of view. The driving force in the dialectic is the subjective life, which influences and changes the objective life:

> Once and again we have noted how from the everyday life of action—the Town proper of our terminology—there arises the corresponding subjective world—the *Schools* of thought, which may express itself sooner or later in schools of education. The types of people, their kinds and styles of work, their whole environment, all become represented in the mind of the community, and these react upon the individuals, their activities, their place itself.[20]

| TOWN | | | | CITY |
|------|------|------|------|------|
| | FOLK | | POLITY | |
| | WORK | | CULTURE | |
| PLACE | | | | ART |
| SURVEY | | | | IMAGERY |
| | KNOWLEDGE | | IDEAS | |
| | | | SOCIAL, ECONOMIC | |
| | MORALS, LAW | | IDEALS, ETHICS | |
| SCHOOL | | | | CLOISTER |

A town or village at this level functions adequately but does not rise to a higher level of societal evolution. The simple process of reflection is not enough to effect the development of a Town into a City. To achieve that something more is necessary.

Throughout the life of a Town, Geddes assumes a continuous production of Schools, some of which would develop into leading centers of thought and engage in "a Synthesis of a new kind." Geddes locates these particular Schools in places he called "Cloisters of contemplation, meditation, imagination."[21] Cloisters are characterized by a deeper insight, speculative and unrestrained thought that goes beyond merely mirroring the objective life of a Town. The activities of the Cloister are again classified in three categories: "ideals," "ideas," and "imagery." The category of ideals, or ethics, is based on the understanding of what is good, while that of ideas, or "synthetics," is based on what is true, and imagery or aesthetics on the beautiful. Accordingly, three different results emerge from the cloister: ideals or ethics lead to "polity," ideas lead to "culture," and imagery leads to "art."[22] The products of the Cloister point toward a City, yet they do not make a City. The "City proper," the fourth step of the Town-City formula, requires the transfer of the ideas emerging from the cloister into practice.

Finally and supremely arises the City proper—its individuality dependent upon the measure and form in which ideals are expressed and harmonised in social life and polity, ideas synthesised in culture, and beauty carried outwards from the study or chamber of the recluse into the world of art.[23]

The City completed, or the "great" or "true city" as Geddes calls it elsewhere,[24] consists of all four components of his analysis—Town, School, Cloister, and City—as shown in table 2.3.[25]

A cross, the four fields inscribed with the words Town, School, Cloister, and City, is sometimes used by Geddes as a simplified graphic version of the Town-City formula. He also transfers this simplified version into the center of the Notation of Life. In the inner top left corner of the Notation of Life are written "town" and "village," the Town proper of Geddes's analysis. In the quadrant below, at the level of Schools, are the words "school," "nature," and "experience." The latter two refer to Geddes's principle that all living beings should be observed in their natural environment, an insight he gained while studying biology under Huxley in London, and which he reiterated with the Town-City formula as a principle also applicable to human beings. The next quadrant to the right contains the words "cloister," "hermitage," "university," and "studio," which are possibilities for human intervention in the development from Town to City. The last quadrant, finally, is inscribed "City in deed," which indicates the transformation of reality according to the ideas and ideals developed in the Cloister.

Strengthening the idealistic orientation of the Town-City formula, Geddes concludes that a City vanishes if its Cloister ceases to exist, or decays. This can happen in two ways. Each Cloister unavoidably declines into a School because of its very success in leading the transformation from Town to City.[26] Decay might also occur while a Cloister still functions, for it can "take place within itself, since imagination and ideal may be evil, and theory false."[27] In either case, Geddes takes the process of decline for granted:

> It must however be kept clearly in view that the city of each day and generation subsides or decays more or less completely into the mere town anew, as the cloister into the schools. The towns and cities of the world are thus classifiable in terms of their past development and present condition.[28]

This final statement emphasizes how strongly Geddes conceives the Town-City formula as a law of the evolution of cities. Contemporary evolutionary biology accepted the degeneration of a species as part of the laws of evolution, even if it meant the end of any further evolution for that species. In a comparable manner Geddes includes the decay of cities in the Town-City formula; the disappearance of a City is a stage in the law of city development rather than a moral statement. Like natural laws, too, which, once understood, allow humans to exploit them for their own good, Geddes's law of the development of cities opens cities up to human intervention.

### From Act to Deed

The Town-City formula describes the transformation of a Town into a City but does not explain how the process is instigated. Furthermore, the role and position of a town's inhabitants are left undefined. The Act-Deed formula, the half of the Notation of Life noted along the diagram's outer frame, provides this information. This formula sets out another course of four steps, those of "acts," "facts," "dreams," and "deeds," which deal with the "mental side" of social life, as Geddes once called it.[29] Each of the four levels consists again of three categories which, Geddes claims, allow the classification of human social behavior.

The first step is that of Acts, classified according to the triad place-work-folk and its interrelations. This triad explains the behavior of the inhabitants in the ordinary Town. The Town inhabitants' objective world (the site of Acts) is complemented by a closely related subjective world. Geddes's interest here is to elaborate with the help of psychological terminology how this mental life of Facts, the second step in the formula, comes into being as a reflection of Acts:

> It is with our senses we come to know our environment, perceiving and observing it. Our feelings are obviously developed from our folk, in earliest infancy by our mothers' love and care. And our experiences are primarily from our activities, of which our work is increasingly the predominant one.[30]

The third step, from Facts to the level of Thoughts or Dreams, is a step from the simple to "deeper psychology":[31]

| ACTS | | | | DEEDS | |
|---|---|---|---|---|---|
| PLACE | | | | | ACHIEVEMENT |
| | | WORK | | SYNERGY | |
| | | | FOLK | ETHNO-POLITY | |
| | | | FEELING | EMOTION | |
| | | EXPERIENCE | | IDEATION | |
| SENSE | | | | | IMAGERY |
| FACTS | | | | THOUGHTS (DREAMS) | |

TABLE 2.4
Geddes's psychological
analysis of social life.

Our primary (*i.e.*, objectively acquired) feelings become transformed
and individualised to us as Emotions, our experience becomes clarified
from ordinary intelligence to rational Ideas, and our sense impressions
not only fade or revive in memory, but rearrange as personal Images.[32]

On the level of Dreams, the inhabitants of a Town develop ideas and plans
concerning their future. From here the inhabitants proceed to the final level
of Deeds, where their ideas, when realized, find expression in a "new type
of community . . . the essential bond being 'not according to the flesh, but
to the spirit.' This new type of group thus needs a type-name; and as fundamentally of ethic bond, yet social purpose, let us call this an Etho-Polity."[33]

Table 2.4 presents the complete Act-Deed formula with all the
main categories on each level, but isolated from the Notation of Life.[34] A
simpler graphical expression of this formula is that of a swastika with the
words Acts, Facts, Dreams, and Deeds in four adjacent fields.[35] While the
Act-Deed formula attempts to explain the social behavior of a group of human beings, the Town-City formula focuses on the environmental results
of this behavior at various levels. Geddes merges these two formulas in the
Notation of Life, where the Act-Deed formula forms the frame while the
Town-City formula occupies the center, thus indicating that the creation of
a City is the goal toward which all human action should be directed. The
formulas are indissolubly connected, as one makes sense only with the
other. "The City Beautiful must be the result of its own life and labour,"
Geddes writes; "it is the expression of the soul and mood of its people."[36]

### From Individual to Communal Psychology

What the Act-Deed formula describes with regard to the collective holds true for individual inhabitants of a Town as well: each has the potential to raise his own life from the level of mere existence to a higher state of being and acting. Geddes elaborated this fundamental idea underlying the Act-Deed formula in a short essay of 1905 with the title "The World Without and the World Within: Sunday Talks with My Children." Here he divides the world into an everyday "out-world" and an "in-world" or "thinking-world." Both worlds together form the habitat of each human being. A garden used as a playground can represent the out-world, made up of facts. The corresponding in-world is composed of the memories of these facts. To think of the garden mainly as a playground is to confine life to these two worlds, but to plan the future of the garden is to step from the in-world of memories into the deeper in-world of plans and designs, which, subsequently transferred to the out-world, leads to acts. Facts, memories, plans, and acts are the four steps of this early version of the Act-Deed formula, Geddes's analysis of the dynamic process of individuals living in, reacting to, and acting upon the environment.

Combining the Act-Deed formula with the Town-City formula amounts to an attempt to derive the behavior of a collective from the psychology of individuals. When Geddes presented both formulas to students at the University of London, he advised them to consult either his essay "The World Without and the World Within" or contemporary psychology manuals for the foundation of his ideas, citing especially the American psychologist William James and his British colleague G. F. Stout.[37] The psychological roots of the Notation of Life, and the close relations it assumes between individual and collective actions and lives, prefigure important aspects of Geddes's work as a city designer.

While the four steps of the Town-City formula once conceived were never altered, Geddes renamed the four steps of the Act-Deed formula, with the early version presented in the 1905 essay later revised in the Notation of Life (see table 2.5). Although the Act-Deed formula describes a circle of life, not all types of life encompass the whole circle. In "The World Without and the World Within" Geddes refers to people who live in the out-world only, or to the "poor Rich" who own a rich out-world but a poor

| LEVEL | TOWN-CITY | ACT-DEED (1905) | ACT-DEED (NOTATION OF LIFE) |
|---|---|---|---|
| 1 OUT-WORLD | Town | Facts | Acts |
| 2 IN-WORLD | School | Memories | Facts |
| 3 IN-WORLD | Cloister | Plans | Dreams |
| 4 OUT-WORLD | City | Acts | Deeds |

TABLE 2.5
Comparison of the Town-City and Act-Deed formulas.

in-world.[38] To these types of life, which are active but confined to the out-world, the term "acts" applies far better than Geddes's initial term "facts." "Acts" indicates a type of life which, although above "reflex activities,"[39] does not enter the in-world of facts (the term that ultimately replaced the word "memory" in Geddes's model).

Memory, Geddes explains in his talks with his children, means to recall in the evening, when going to bed, the garden one has played in during the day. What happens "is another sort of looking. . . . The garden has come in with you; it is in your In-world now."[40] Memory is also the defining characteristic of the Schools in the everyday Town, for "the school is essentially one of memory, the impress of the town-life."[41] Stout's *Manual of Psychology* defines memory as the ideal reproduction of an object or event. The reproduction should happen without recalling inferences connected to the original event or object, and without any interest defined by the moment of the reproduction.[42] Furthermore, as William James emphasizes, memory is necessarily connected with past time. James's interest is less the very obvious fact that memory *refers* to the past than that memory "must be dated in my past. . . . I must think that I directly experienced its occurrence."[43]

Geddes's substitution in the Notation of Life of the word "facts" for "memory" pays tribute to James's individualization of memory. Each human being remembers his or other people's acts as facts in his own past. Geddes reveals himself as a true idealist, because for him there are no facts outside the individual mind. Facts only exist in each individual's in-world, which is, according to Geddes, in "a very true and thorough sense . . . more familiar, more real than the other; for all we know, or can ever know of the Out-world, or of each other, is in our minds."[44] Similarly, the life of a Town, when reflected in the Schools, is individualized as local culture. Schools are "the record and reflex of the life of the hive, the Town: of all its general and particular environment and function, its family type and development." The Town life that Schools reflect is subsequently "expressed in local knowledge, in craft tradition, in kinship and its associated kindness, in habits and customs, and their development up to morals and law."[45]

From the level of facts, the first level of the in-world of individualized memory, human beings can proceed to a further level where plans are conceived to guide future action. In the final version of the Act-Deed formula as incorporated in the Notation of Life, the term "dreams" replaces "plans." For individuals, dreams are the equivalent level to the Cloister in the Town-City formula. The Cloister, as Geddes stresses, initiates "collective action" by the inhabitants of a Town, which is, however, based on the individual endeavors, that is the dreams, of the former.[46]

At this point, the assumed analogy between an individual's psychology and that of the collective inhabitants of a Town constitutes a problem. The assumption that individuals derive their dreams from individualized facts (memories) does not necessarily guarantee collective action by the Town inhabitants on their way toward becoming a City. A brief examination of contemporary psychology helps explain why Geddes could make this assumption.

With regard to memory and the human mind, turn-of-the-century psychology distinguished between sense perceptions, images, and ideas or ideational processes. Sense perception was caused by an object and found expression in an immediate (bodily) reaction to the object.[47] An image was a sketchy mental copy of something already perceived.[48] Images were closely related to ideas or ideational processes, the former being necessary parts of the latter.[49] Stout describes ideational processes as "trains of ideas" that arrange images into new sequences and combinations. He distinguishes two phases of these ideational processes: the reproductive phase or "association of ideas," followed by the productive phase, the "ideal construction" or combination of ideas. According to Stout, ideational processes are mental activities directed toward some practical or theoretical end.[50] It is this that allows human beings to plan into the future, since the "ideational consciousness can cross a bridge before coming to it."[51] Stout explains that the ideational consciousness can anticipate the endpoint of its intended activity and then move forward, backward, and sideways in order to overcome obstacles until the goal is realized. This model describes exactly the difference between the types of consciousness in the two levels of the in-world that Geddes defines in his essay "The World Without and the World Within." Simply to remember the garden means to remain on the level of perceptual consciousness, but to plan the garden's future is a forward-acting mental activity characteristic of the ideational consciousness.

Stout also attempts to explain why individual thoughts would result in collective action. He defines the problems as follows:

> The ideal combinations which arise in the individual mind can only become permanent parts of the ideal structure representing the real world if they are entertained by other minds also, and so become current in the society to which the individual belongs.[52]

To make individual ideas the dominant ones for all members of a society requires communication, for which Stout identifies language as an appropriate means. Without communication, Stout asserts, the very fact that man has the ability to indulge in ideational thought simply makes no sense.

> Such thinking is essentially a social function. Other animals co-operate in work and play, but only men co-operate in thinking. Where many men are united in striving to realise a common end, each single mind is, so to speak, part of a great collective mind. The ideas occurring to each are communicated to all.[53]

Despite Stout's firm assertion, to attribute a social function to the communication of ideational thought processes and their results leaves the problem of the relation between the individual and a social collective essentially unsolved, for even if men cooperate in thinking, this does not explain why they should act in unison accordingly. Language also suffers the disadvantage that it only allows for intragenerational exchange of ideational thought. Accordingly, Stout claims the whole material environment of humankind as a supplementary means of communication used to transfer ideational thought between generations of human beings, an idea—as will be shown in chapter 5—that very likely influenced Geddes's appreciation of historic architecture and cities. Stout notes that "tools, weapons, utensils, buildings, gardens and cultivated fields, are all products of human intelligence. They are material arrangements embodying in outward and visible form trains of ideas which have passed through human minds."[54] This statement accurately describes the step of arrival at the level of a City from the level of Dreams, as Geddes expresses graphically in the Notation of Life.

Why did Geddes employ such a complex, psychologically based model to explain the creation of the city? As early as 1886, in his essay "On the Conditions of Progress of the Capitalist and the Labourer," he rejected a Marxist notion of class in favor of an idea of cooperation influenced by the thought of Peter Kropotkin.[55] But with his rejection of the idea of class, Geddes robbed himself of the opportunity to explain the shaping of a City—understood as a synonym for a human society—as rooted in the diverging and competing interests of various classes, an idea which, for example, strongly informs Max Weber's famous essay "The City" of 1921.[56] Rather than following a line of inquiry similar to Weber's, Geddes focused on the individual's interaction with the environment, arguing that the consonance between an individual's action and that of a larger social group would cut across social classes, even going beyond them.

Yet Geddes was never able to overcome the inherent weakness of this approach to cities, which requires that the parallel movement of individual and collective action be a necessary and not just an incidental one. Not surprisingly, even Geddes introduced a division of the city's inhabitants into smaller social groups, which act as intermediaries between the individual and the whole citizenry. These groups do not compete with each other, but cooperate in order to realize a City according to Geddes's model of human interaction with the environment. Geddes divides the body of citizens into four social types and relates these types to the four steps or levels making up a City. Thus, the type "people" corresponds to the stage of Town, "chiefs" to that of Schools, "intellectuals" to the Cloister, and "emotionals" to the City; these groups are discussed in more detail below in chapter 4.

A second peculiarity of Geddes's thought stems from his view of the underlying springs of human action. In his model, the basic division of all forms of human life is that between an out-world and an in-world. Each of these exists in two versions. The two sequences that constitute the Notation of Life begin in the out-world, run into the in-world, then proceed to a second level in the in-world before emerging in the out-world again. Char-

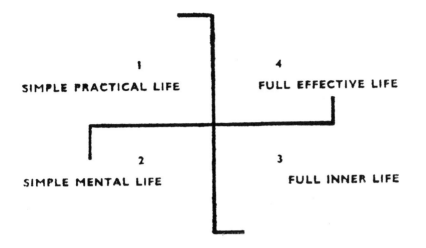

SIMPLE PRACTICAL LIFE 1

FULL EFFECTIVE LIFE 4

SIMPLE MENTAL LIFE 2

FULL INNER LIFE 3

FIGURE 2.3

The Notation of Life as the union of vita activa and vita contemplativa, as published in 1949.

acteristic of these stages is that life becomes more conscious about its possibilities and future in the course of them. The first level of the out-world is that of simple, unreflective activities; the second is that of conscious deeds. A similar division rules the in-world, which consists on the first level of simple sense perceptions, on the second level of ideational activities directed toward the future. Thus, cutting across the division into in-world and out-world is another division into passive and active ways of life. The lower half of the diagram symbolizes the in-world of both an individual and a town; the upper half represents their out-worlds. The left half is the passive way of life; the right half the active (figure 2.3). Accordingly, human life is a process of oscillation: "To be at home in the Out-world and in the In-world, and to be active as well as passive in each by turns; that is what we have seen you can aim at in your education."[57]

Ultimately, this model of life derives from Geddes's research into the metabolism of single-cell organisms. He believed that he could explain their life as a process consisting of a more active (catabolistic) and a more passive (anabolistic) stage, a point to which chapter 7 returns in greater detail. Yet the application of this active-passive dichotomy to human life, and to social life especially, creates a difficulty. The phases in simple organisms follow each other rather mechanically; they are instigated and controlled by external factors like nutrition, temperature, and light. The link between the active and passive sides of human and social life, on the contrary, Geddes locates in the consciousness of the in-world. There human beings, individually and as a group, can leave the passive in favor of the active in-world, thus connecting the two phases of life. But why they should make this step—the decisive precondition to achieving the levels of Deeds and the City—Geddes is reluctant to explain.

> How our simple life-feelings evolve to emotion, become complexed and fixed as sentiment; how they crystallise as ideal, and kindle as passion, is the central mystery of life in its evolution: it is the secret of mystic and saint, of lover and poet also. Yet it is much to see that such evolution does take place.[58]

To understand human life as a mystical glorification of a mechanical process taken from simple organic life is not an alternative explanation but no explanation at all. Together with social classes, Geddes also dismisses notions of human activity as driven by individual and class-determined needs of all kinds—material needs such as shelter and food, and immaterial needs such as the desire for prestige derived from wealth and power—all of which might result in adaptation of the environment in order to satisfy these needs. To leave the step from the passive to the active in-world not only unexplained but mystified undermines the value of the Notation of Life as a coherent theory. Yet this was no problem for Geddes. Even if the central aspect of human life is beyond human understanding, it is not beyond experience, and can therefore be exploited for future development.[59] For Geddes, the diagram provides a theoretical structure coherent and logical enough to base on it his activities in town planning and architecture.

### Geddes's Theory of the City: A Platonic Reading

Geddes, like Plato, connects the *polis* or City with the individual. Plato argues from the individual to the *polis*, although he presents the argument the other way round. A *polis* is for Plato a living individual on a larger scale. Similarly Geddes: "Like the living being it is, a city reacts upon its environment."[60] He also argues from the human being to the city: "For if each human individuality be unique, how much more must that of every city?"[61] While

Plato ascribes an immortal soul to each individual, Geddes ascribes a soul to the city and its community, which in turn is composed of the souls of its inhabitants. Both Plato's and Geddes's souls are likewise subject to a process of rebirth. Plato's concept of rebirth is not a simple repetition of the past; rebirth means to him the return of the soul in different historic manifestations with a knowledge of transhistoric eternal ideas or forms.[62] Geddes writes in an analysis of Chelsea's past:

> Our record of local history and achievement is . . . a perpetual renewal of certain recognisable elements. . . . It is of the very essence of our growing sociological re-interpretation of the past to see its essential life as continuous into the present, and even beyond, and so to maintain the perennation of culture, the immortality of the social soul.[63]

Plato's republic is administered by the guardians or philosophers, living their lives only for the city. Plato insists that they apply their knowledge of the "divine order" (the forms) to "the habits of men both in their private and public lives."[64] This is an obligation, as Plato stresses in the simile of the cave: the enlightened philosophers must return to the men living in the cave; they are not allowed to remain in the upper world where they have seen the divine. The guardians' task is to serve the community by bringing to it knowledge of the divine.[65] The Cloister and the intellectuals of Geddes's City occupy a position comparable to the philosophers' place and function in the *Republic*. Without transferring the ideas of a City from the Cloister to the Town, the City would never come into existence. The philosophers of Geddes's City are a select group within a community; considering universities as Cloisters, Geddes describes their function as the "inspiring intercourse 'of picked adolescents and picked senescents.'" The results of Geddes's Cloister are again Platonic, for the ideals lead to eupolity, a synonym of the "good"; ideas realize the "true" in culture; and imagery expresses the "beautiful" in art.[66]

The connection between *polis* and individual is valid for both the good and the bad *polis* or city. Plato's imperfect societies of timarchy, oligarchy, democracy, and tyranny are each accompanied by a type individual whose character corresponds to the characteristics of the society. For Plato it is beyond doubt that every society, even if organized on the principles laid

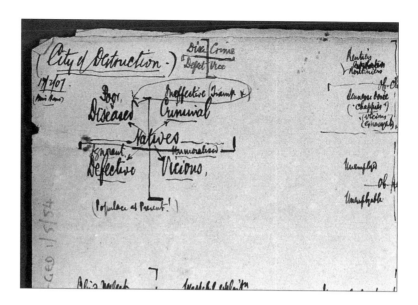

FIGURE 2.4

Notes by Geddes,

1907, on the City of

Destruction.

out in the *Republic*, will one day decline; the decay originates among the auxiliaries and philosophers.[67] Similarly Geddes takes the decline of a City for
granted, and he also locates the initial cause within the leading part of the
City, in his case the Cloister. Accordingly, to the upward evolutionary movement of the Town-City and Act-Deed formulas he conceives a downward-
directed equivalent leading to the "City of Destruction," a name Geddes may
have borrowed from John Bunyan's *Pilgrim's Progress* (1678) (figure 2.4).
The four downward stages of this city he defines as "disease," "defect," "vice,"
"crime," and its inhabitants are characterized as "poor, diseased," "ignorant,
defective," "vicious," and "ineffective, criminal," respectively.[68]

As outlined earlier, Geddes identified two causes for the un-
avoidable decay of a Cloister and subsequently a City. The first cause—the
regression of a successful Cloister to a School due to mummification—
would present the Town-City formula, and the Notation of Life, as a value-
free law for the development of Cities and societies. The second
cause—the decay of a Cloister due to a wrong or evil idea—points toward
a morally rather than scientifically inspired analysis of a City's decay. The
formula of the City of Destruction underlines this moral basis by linking
poverty and disease unavoidably with criminality and ineffective life. Fur-

thermore, both negative results are only understandable via the bypass through the mind—the in-world—of the degenerate individual, the criminal for example. In Geddes's model, criminality is not so much a direct response to economic and social conditions as it is the result of vicious thoughts. If the in-world is more real than the out-world, then criminality is primarily a question of individual character, and society is relieved, at least to a certain extent, from any responsibility for this kind of social behavior. Geddes's attempt to explain contemporary social realities by resorting to individual psychology, putting aside notions of class or economics, leads only to moralizing judgments.

More generally, Geddes like Plato is interested in defining an all-embracing concept of the good life. Plato's concerns are "What is the best life?" and "What is the best order or organization of human society?"[69] Everything has to serve the aim of creating a good *polis:* the position of the individual citizen within the social hierarchy, the pursuit of a citizen's profession within the division of labor of the *polis,* and the education of children, which requires, among other things, a beautiful and healthy environment.[70] Similarly, art is subdued to the larger aim as its function is restricted to guiding children and adults alike to morally right judgments with regard to the *polis.* All these criteria touch upon fields close to the activities Geddes was engaged in: for example, education, art, and architecture as teaching tools, and the improvement of the (built) environment.

Plato's pursuit of the good life centers on philosophical categories like justice, whereas Geddes's concept of the "good life," for which he coined the term civics, is derived from an analysis of life itself. Consequently, civics claims responsibility for all aspects of human life, as Ebe Minerva White, a lecturer in civics with the London County Council and a follower of Geddes, explained:

> The word "Civics," in its derivation, linked with *citizen* and *civilisation,* designates a subject which is yet in the making. . . . "Civics" deals with all that appertains to the life and surroundings of any citizen, and includes far more than the spheres of legislation and administration.[71]

Civics is Geddes's contribution to the contemporary late nineteenth- and early twentieth-century debate about citizenship.[72] Where this debate had been mainly focused on theoretical notions of democracy and voting rights, Geddes put his own distinctive stamp on it. His civics calls for an immediate engagement of citizens in the affairs of their society, leading to an improved environment, for example in the form of garden cities.[73] Beyond this, because civics derives from Geddes's analysis of life, it contributes to the improvement and evolution of life. Civics is Geddes's solution of what he considered to be the most pressing question of his time:

> The central search of our age . . . is for a theory of Life in its Evolution, and this in all its aspects and products; and such a theory must deal, not only with the organic life therefore, but also with the psychic life; similarly with ethical life no less than with social. . . . Furthermore, it must correlate the individual life with the social, and this in no mere abstract, ethical way, but as the citizen with his city.[74]

The need Geddes defines here is nothing else than civics as encrypted in the Notation of Life. Human "life in its evolution" can take only one form, that of a City, the most distinctive, concrete, materialistic creation of human beings. Significantly, Geddes chose for his one major book on cities the title *Cities in Evolution*, which has an ambiguous meaning. It can be read to mean cities in *their* evolution, thus referring to the evolution of cities as such, but it can equally mean cities in *human* evolution, thus referring to the function cities have in the larger evolutionary process of life. Whenever Geddes writes about civics, he writes about towns and cities. In his two essays "Civics: As Applied Sociology" and "Civics: As Concrete and Applied Sociology," he presents the application of sociology—a metascience of life—to cities as a result of necessity rather than choice.[75] Similarly, a 1910 lecture series published as *Civics: The Conditions of Town Planning and City Design* mainly deals, according to the syllabus, with how cities were built at different times and why.[76]

Civics, the analysis of the evolution of human life as a spiral running perpetually through the four stages from Act to Deed, from Town to City, provides Geddes with a philosophical approach to cities. Civics focuses on cities, their function in evolution, and their internal structures and institutions, but leaves the question of practical application unconsidered. For such practical application, whether to new or to existing cities, Geddes employs the terms "city design" and "city development."[77] Both the *polis* and Plato's *Republic* provide him with a working conception:

> Yet now the modern town-planner, for whom Greek citizenship is not a mere learned reminiscence or a moral wonder, but a working conception once more, is in these days actually designing, for the bettering cities of the opening future.[78]

This working conception functions in two ways. First, the *polis* is an example of the good life in a City, and can therefore be considered an application of civics. The good life is achieved because the ideas about it are rooted in "natural origins" on the levels of Act and Town, and refined through artistic and intellectual reflection "into philosophic form[s]" on the level of Dreams and Cloisters. The visible expression of the good life in a City is therefore to be expected, because the creation of the *polis*—City on the final level of the Town-City formula—is the "corresponding evolution" of both "clarified thought and perfected art."[79]

Geddes's interests differ from the contemporary view of Greek citizenship as primarily an abstract politico-philosophical concept. Instead, and this is the second aspect of the *polis* as a working conception, Geddes focuses on the physical structure and urban fabric of the *polis*. Of particular interest are the "natural origins" that gave rise to Greek ethics first of all, and the Cloisters where thoughts are clarified into ideas for a City. When Geddes insists that "Hellas may be more fully recovered, modern life more truly Hellenized,"[80] he does not suggest an aesthetic appreciation of Greek culture, town planning, and architecture, for example in neoclassical buildings. He proposes rather a new, contemporary version of the *polis* as the embodiment of an ideal form, and in particular a return to the "natural origins" and a provision of the "organs for that fuller life" for which the term City stands.[81]

City design is the necessary precondition to activities in town planning. But whereas town planning is primarily concerned with the material aspects of a town, city design also takes care of the psychological side of a City as community.[82] Geddes writes:

Acropolis and Temple, Forum and Cathedral, thus fully reappear, and these not only in their rationale and significance in the past, but in their renewal in the future. To ask—what examples of all these in London today? In Paris, etc.? is obviously to establish a scale of criticism and valuation of cities far beyond the current economic and statistical ones. Furthermore, we may even proceed to apply the same methods towards the ideal cities and their renewal in modern thought.[83]

City design works on three levels. First, it deals with geographical considerations, the natural origins of the *polis* of old, or, at a more general level, with the place. Second are historical considerations, both the attempt to stimulate City building by showing that there were always Cities in history (among which the *polis* was the earliest successful example) and the recognition that Cities are real, historic places whose existing historic structures require attention. Finally, there is the issue of Cities as communities, which is the focus of the spiritual aspect of city design as it attempts to unify citizens into a community, or a folk, by emphasizing the soul of a City.

The evolution of Towns into Cities requires the implementation of Cloisters and structures embodying ideas for a City into the urban fabric, comparable to the Acropolis in Athens or the cathedral in the medieval *Stadt*. Geddes's religious references in his historic examples and the choice of the term Cloister are not accidental but deliberate, as Sybella Branford (née Gurney), the wife of Geddes's friend Victor Branford, explains: "Up to the time of the Renaissance religion was not only in its essence but in its outward form the unifying reality which made a group of individuals into a city . . . and as the tradition dwindled so did the city perish."[84] This spiritual aspect of city design marks the most significant difference between Geddes's approach to cities and contemporary town planning. The term "spiritual" refers to the essence or soul of the city. In Platonic theory the soul not only gives life to matter but is also the carrier of knowledge about ideas and forms.[85] The soul of a City has comparable functions, and the Cloister is its visible expression: as an institution, a Cloister produces ideas for a City. As a built structure, the Cloister symbolizes the ideas it brought to the City, similar to religious buildings whose "outward form," according to Sybella Branford, once symbolized the "unifying reality" of religion. Yet the idea of the City as a symbol of life at the center of a secular religion also recalls once again ancient Greek culture with its religious veneration of the *polis.*

No other historical city proved to be as important for Geddes as the Greek *polis,* to which he refers time and again, both directly and indirectly. Hence his working conception of the *polis* can be used as a methodological tool to analyze his ideas about cities and city design. This working conception allows us to identify aspects of Geddes's life work as belonging to his City idea, when such a connection is not otherwise immediately obvious. The historic pageants he organized, or his Olympus project—a garden for the Greek Muses and a temple for the Greek gods—become necessary elements of city design rather than mere expressions of an otherwise eccentric mind. To paraphrase historian Turner's remark quoted above, it is important to bear in mind that Geddes's references to *polis* and *Republic* are essentially references to his own idea of the City.

Thus begins to appear the essential point. . . . It is to suggest that our town and country divisions . . . are . . . now for the most part totally inadequate for modern purposes.

Patrick Geddes, *City Surveys for Town Planning*

# The City and Geography

Around the turn of the twentieth century, the experience of life in great cities with several hundred thousand or even millions of inhabitants was still a relatively young phenomenon. Great Britain was the first country to undergo a massive shift of population from the countryside into the cities. By the middle of the nineteenth century London's population was already over two million, but during the second half of the century the whole quality of urban growth changed. Not only did some towns grow extensively as a result of the industrial revolution, but the relation between rural and urban population reversed. By 1901, 80 percent of the British population lived in urbanized areas, in one of 74 cities with more than 50,000 inhabitants.[1]

## Town and Country

This rapid urban growth was interpreted from two main points of view. First, the city came to be viewed as a problem, as more people than ever encountered the perils of city life related to housing, health, labor conditions, unemployment, and the like. Second, the countryside was perceived to be in a state of crisis due to the physical growth of cities at the expense of agricultural land, forest, or previously unexploited natural areas. Town and country were perceived as opposites.

The town-country conflict developed into a standard framework for the analysis of urban growth and its related problems. While the city became synonymous with the bad in modern, industrialized life, the country was seen as its victim, and a myth evolved of a better past rooted firmly in rural tradition. Within the parameters of this conflict the city was seen as the active and the country and its economy as the suffering, passive part. The country lost out because the pull of the city was too strong. London, for example, was described as "a tumour, an elephantiasis sucking into its gorged system half the life and the blood and the bone of the rural districts."[2] A possible explanation for this view is that even those people concerned with urban conditions still came from a background in the country.[3]

Despite the city's identification as the cause of the town-country conflict, some attempts to solve the conflict took both sides into account, as a new balance between city and country was sought. Two such solutions were offered in the 1890s by Ebenezer Howard and Peter Kropotkin; both appear to call for a return to the land, but on closer examination represent distinctive approaches that can in fact be taken as opposites.

Ebenezer Howard accepts that cities are attractive to people, and his concept of the social city, or garden city as it is usually called today, starts from this basic premise.[4] Howard envisions a complex of smaller cities surrounding congested places like London; each of these complexes (including the old center) is to be encircled by a country belt and connected by tramway and high-speed train systems. The economic basis of this social city is publicly owned land whose value rises with the city's growth. Rents paid to the public trust finance the public institutions. Howard speculates that after the foundation of several garden cities, each with 32,000 inhabitants, the central older city will become unattractive and subsequently rebuilt at a lower density for a maximum population of 58,000 inhabitants.

Howard claims that the social city is a marriage of town and country, as it distributes the inhabitants of an existing big city over a large area.

Yet both the old cities and the familiar countryside have here disappeared. Although the individual garden cities are separated by green belts, the countryside is no longer made up of dispersed villages dedicated only to agriculture. Each garden city is allocated 6,000 acres of land in Howard's plan, but the city in the literal meaning of the word is confined to 1,000 of these. The remaining 5,000 acres are dedicated to various purposes including agriculture and forestry, but also brick production, asylums for the handicapped, and homes for convalescents and children. What Howard calls country is really an extended city's green fringe accommodating urban institutions. By locating these institutions outside the urban core, he imposes the town permanently on the country, visualized in a network of roads and traffic lines connecting the institutions and their users. Howard's solution for the town-country conflict brings the town to the country and makes the countryside fully available to the needs of the city.

For the Russian-born anarchist Peter Kropotkin it is neither the city nor the smaller town or village but rather the economic situation of industrialized countries that serves as the starting point for the discussion. Kropotkin analyzes the emerging international division of production between older industrialized countries, for example Great Britain, and their more recently developed colonies. The latter provided the raw material for the industry in the mother country, which exported the end products back to the colonies and elsewhere. But Great Britain also received the largest part of its food from the colonies. British agriculture was in decline because home-grown products were too expensive, and it was cheaper to import foodstuffs than to invest in modern technology that would raise productivity. This lack of investment, according to Kropotkin, caused the crisis of the countryside and the subsequent migration into the cities.

Kropotkin suggests a return to a self-sufficient combination of agricultural and industrial work such as prevailed before the industrial revolution.[5] In the Middle Ages, smaller units of human settlements supported individuals who worked in small workshops and farmed as well. Goods were produced mostly for the local market and there was no centralization on a large scale. Long-distance trade was confined to commodities that could not be produced locally. Although Kropotkin wishes to reintroduce this socioeconomic structure, his ideas are no simple return to the past. He suggests both agricultural and industrial production that makes use of the latest technology available but takes place in decentralized units—either in "the factory amidst the fields"[6] or in industrial villages. His vision is directed against both the capitalist dream and the Marxist ideal of a continuous concentration of industry and capital in ever larger units.

The essential element in Kropotkin's socioeconomic and political thinking is the socialization of the means of production and consumption. However, he does not develop any planning or architectural model of future society, favoring instead the village and the medieval town as perfect expressions of the ability of human beings to cooperate.[7] While he mentions Howard's garden city in the second edition of *Fields, Factories and Workshops Tomorrow,* nothing indicates that this is his favorite settlement model. Kropotkin does not develop a program to establish industrial villages on a large scale before a revolution, nor does he insist on the dissolution of big cities like London. Rather, he believes that new, small electric power aggregates will make his decentralized self-determined mode of production possible even in existing big industrial cities. For Kropotkin technology as the most important means of change does not lead to a specific urban form, but rather allows steps toward a nonalienated form of labor. Achieving this goal through a revolutionary change of society is more important to him than solving the town-country conflict. Yet his proposal to combine industrial labor with agriculture—derived from a historical model of a rural economy based in smaller towns and villages—dovetails with the wider societal expectation that a return to the land would create an ideal form of life.

Howard's garden city and Kropotkin's industrial village are similar in their utilization of contemporary technology, but they do not arrive at the same urban form, except for a general preference for smaller settlements. Howard would distribute the various aspects of city life among smaller settlements in rural areas, followed by a subsequent abolition of the large city centers. For largely economic reasons Kropotkin prefers the idea of smaller rural settlements—preferably industrial villages—without thinking of them as a substitute for larger cities. A third, distinctively urban solution for the town-country conflict was envisioned by the French anarchogeographer Elisée Reclus, as published in 1895 in a brief essay titled "The Evolution of Cities." Though an outline more than a fully developed proposal, this essay's uniqueness, and its importance for interpreting Geddes, demand a more detailed analysis.[8]

Reclus begins his reflections with the popular image of the city as an octopus spreading its tentacles over the countryside. But his conclusion runs contrary to the equally popular condemnation of a city's growth, which he instead embraces whole-heartedly. Urban expansion is a positive "sign of healthy and regular evolution" of mankind, since "where the cities increase, humanity is progressing; where they diminish, civilisation itself is in danger."[9] In the final pages of his essay Reclus outlines the form of his ideal city, for which a necessary precondition is that mankind bury all quarrels in order to free its energy for the peaceful development of civilization through city building.[10] Reclus draws on contemporary ideas from the anarcho-socialist and urban reform traditions, foreshadowing ideas that figure prominently three years later in Howard's *To-morrow*. In Reclus's essay one finds the desire to combine the best of town and country, not as a means to limit urban growth but to allow for the opposite, namely the "indefinite extension of . . . towns." Any difference between town and country can be overcome through the permanent expansion of the town, until "throughout the length and breadth of the land the provinces will be scattered with houses which, in spite of the distance, really belong to the town."[11]

Existing cities, especially their historic centers, will be transformed into spaces dedicated to the communal life of the expanding city of Reclus's plan:

> What was once the most densely inhabited part of the city is precisely the part which is now becoming deserted, because it is becoming common property, or at least a common centre of intermittent life. Too useful to the mass of the citizens to be monopolised by private families, the heart of the city is the patrimony of all. . . . The community claims . . . the use of open spaces of the city for public meetings and open-air celebrations. Every town should have its agora, where all who are animated by a common passion can meet together.[12]

Reclus's ideal city is thus characterized by communal ownership focused on the historic urban center with its cultural and educational institutions. From this cultural center the city continuously expands into the countryside. Smaller cultural nodes support the main center by serving smaller groups of citizens. The resulting city, which I call in the following the ever-

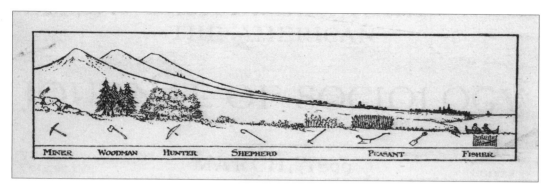

MINER   WOODMAN   HUNTER   SHEPHERD   PEASANT   FISHER

FIGURE 3.1

The valley section, as
published in 1909.

expanding city, is structured hierarchically, so that what was once countryside is now covered by a network of human settlements and individual
houses of different sizes and types. Town and country merge because the
city does not simply return to its rural roots but transforms and elevates
the countryside to its own, more highly evolved level of social and cultural life.

## The Valley Section

Patrick Geddes's best-known contribution to resolving the town-country
conflict is the simple diagram of the "valley section," first published in
1909. Considered against the background of the town-country conflict, the
diagram does not oppose the two antagonists but rather unites them in the
idea of the valley region. The valley section is a longitudinal section that
follows a river from its source in the mountains to its broad entrance to the
sea (figure 3.1). It combines physical conditions—represented in the drawing by plants—with so-called natural or basic occupations—represented
by tools—and includes various types of settlement that refer to the social
organizations arising from the natural occupations best adapted to their
environments. Silhouettes of a city, towns, villages, and individual houses
represent these social organizations. As Geddes explains his model:

> Beneath vast hunting desolations lie the pastoral hillsides, below these
> again scattered arable crofts and sparsely dotted hamlets lead us to the
> small upland village of the main glen: from this again one descends to

the large and prosperous village of the foothills and its railway terminus, where lowland and highland meet. East or west, each mountain valley has its analogous terminal and initial village, upon its fertile fan-shaped slope, and with its corresponding minor market; while, central to the broad agricultural strath with its slow meandering river, stands the prosperous market town, the road and railway junction upon which all the various glen-villages converge. A day's march further down, and at the convergence of several such valleys, stands the larger country-town. . . . Finally, at the mouth of its estuary, rises the smoke of a great manufacturing city, a central world-market in its way. Such a river system is, as geographer after geographer has pointed out, the essential unit for the student of cities and civilisations.[13]

Settlement occurs in the valley region from coast to mountaintop. The city is located at the coast, followed by the country town in the hinterland as the focal point of various valleys. Each of these valleys features a market town on its agricultural plain; in the foothills above are large villages ("initial villages") at the upper terminus of rail lines, each village standing at the beginning of a system of glens, or mountain valleys. Farther up are smaller upland villages in the larger glens. Higher still are hamlets, consisting only of several houses. Even higher up, only isolated crofts (poor farmhouses) are to be found. Thus the region Geddes circumscribes with the valley section encompasses several valleys and an agricultural plain stretching from the bottom of the mountains to the coast (figure 3.2).[14] The valley region is characterized by a strong connection of three major elements—physical environment, occupations, and settlement types—as each influences the other.

Conceptually, the valley region is based on the idea of a plant association, derived from the botanical survey work of the biologist Charles Flahault, a friend of Geddes, in Montpellier, France. In his survey work, published between 1896 and 1900, Flahault mapped the distribution of species of trees. Different trees are best adapted to the given situation in different environments and dominate the plant population there. Flahault labels them "'social' species," because they indicate "the presence of particular associations of subordinate species."[15] Identifying the social species allows one to draw conclusions about environmental conditions and the subordinate species, and accordingly to identify the economic possibilities inherent to the region.

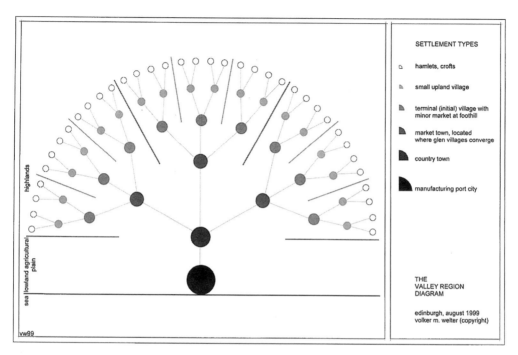

SETTLEMENT TYPES

▫ hamlets, crofts

◗ small upland village

◖ terminal (initial) village with
minor market at foothill

◗ market town, located
where glen villages converge

◗ country town

◗ manufacturing port city

THE
VALLEY REGION
DIAGRAM

edinburgh, august 1999
volker m. welter (copyright)

highlands

sea  lowland agricultural plain

vw99

Geddes draws on the concept of plant association for the study of
human beings and their societies.[16] While Flahault's concern is the regional
distribution of plant species, Geddes focuses on the natural occupations of the
valley region "inhabited by . . . hunter, shepherd, agriculturalist, and fisher,
each at his proper level."[17] These basic or natural occupations—Geddes uses
both terms indiscriminately—represent, analogously to Flahault's "social"
species, the best adaptation of human beings to distinct environments such
as mountains, forests, or agricultural plains. The environment's physical conditions determine human occupation much as they influence plant life. Studying a valley region, Geddes argues, will help us to understand "how far nature
can be shown to have determined man" and "how far the given type of man
has reacted, or may yet react, upon his environment." Geddes's choice of
words—nature determines and man reacts—expresses the primary role of
nature in the process of "mutual adaptation . . . of region and race."[18]

The variety of occupations in Geddes's valley region is equivalent
to the mixture of species in Flahault's plant association. Just as the character
of a plant association is determined by its dominating species, so the valley

region is dominated at various levels by its different occupations. Just as Flahault's social species includes a cluster of subordinated species living, so to speak, under the shadows of the trees, so from each of the natural occupations "distinct types of social organisations" arise, with related political and religious ideas,[19] symbolized in the valley section by the range of human settlements from hamlet to city. Thus the valley section separates the entirety of human beings into smaller units comparable to the separation of species in a plant association.

Flahault's plant associations are hierarchical but cooperative and mutually beneficial. The cooperative nature of Flahault's model may have inspired Geddes to transfer the plant association from the botanical sphere to that of human societies. Doing so allows him to get away from the popular social Darwinist notion of society as a permanent struggle for existence, instead foregrounding cooperation as more important for the evolution of all forms of life. Kropotkin adds an intermediate step as the best-known advocate of such cooperation, though he focuses on cooperation within a single species, just where Darwin located the fiercest struggle for existence. In opposition to Darwin, Kropotkin attempts to prove that animals survive only through mutual aid and cooperation, and he believes the same to be true for humans. Kropotkin cites medieval Europe as the best example of cooperative human society, with the medieval city structured around guilds as its highest expression. Both the medieval city and the guilds are "Mutual Aid Institutions," in Kropotkin's terms.[20]

Geddes's concept of natural occupations aims at strengthening the argument for the superiority of human cooperation by putting it in biological terms. Once man is classified into natural occupations, cooperation among these occupations is more easily within reach. Each natural occupation exploits a specific area of the region; together they create a regionwide cooperative association of human beings. While each species in Flahault's plant association survives due to its adaptation to particular conditions in the environment, all species together create a balanced association taking maximum advantage of the region. The same principle ruled Kropotkin's medieval city, where each citizen pursued his profession as a member of a guild and all guilds contributed to the mutually beneficial institution of the city.

The valley section is not merely rooted in contemporary natural sciences; it contains a strong historic element as well. Geddes writes that "by descending from source to sea we follow the development of civilisation from its simple origins to its complex resultant; nor can any element of this be omitted."[21] The historical development Geddes projects into the valley region is the Enlightenment theory of social evolution that describes the development of mankind through four stages: hunting, pastoral, agricultural, and commercial.[22] One of the main proponents of this theory was the Glasgow philosopher John Millar, of whose 1771 *Observation Concerning the Distinction of Ranks in Society* Geddes owned a first-edition copy. Millar emphasizes that to understand human evolution, one must first analyze the relations among a given environment's conditions: the "species of labour" that arise to exploit this environment, the communities of human beings, and their development of the arts and social life. The reciprocal relations among these four elements define the degree of civilization reached.[23] Thus in Millar's work are already assembled all the ingredients that Geddes later unites in the valley section, though in slightly different form. The natural occupation of the hunter stands in Geddes's model for Millar's hunting stage, the shepherd for the pastoral stage, and the peasant for the agricultural stage. Miner, woodman, and fisher can be allocated to all three. Significantly, Millar's commercial stage—the city in the valley section—is not represented by a natural occupation.

The projection of the four stages of mankind's evolution into the space of a valley is of course a symbolic representation. Even if man's early ancestors hunted in the mountains, mankind's history did not originate there but rather in the fertile plains and coastal areas where Geddes locates the city. By including a reference to mankind's evolution in the valley section, Geddes points out the ongoing importance for the contemporary city of man's roots in rural life. The valley section's hierarchy from hamlet to city describes both a historical and a contemporary spatial relationship between town and country; or as Geddes used to say, "It takes the whole region to make the city. As the river carries down contributions from its whole course, so each complex community, as we descend, is modified by its predecessors. The converse is no doubt true also, but commonly in less degree."[24]

All the smaller settlements located in the mountains and the upper plains, representing social organizations of natural occupations, make for the city at the lower end of the valley region. The one settlement not related to a single natural occupation is the city itself, because as a social organiza-

FIGURE 3.3

The valley in the town:

the valley section and its

manifestation in the

town, before 1925.

tion it is derived from the smaller settlements. All the professions and types of labor in contemporary cities are differentiations of natural occupations. Thus, according to Geddes, the miner is the forerunner of the ironworker and goldsmith. House-, furniture-, and shipbuilders derive from the woodman. The crofter, whose life is a struggle with poor soil in the uplands, creates financial and insurance institutions because his survival depends on the economic and carefully planned use of available resources. The lawyer stems from the peasants in the lower, richer areas of the plain, who need records of land and harvest results for taxation purposes.[25] Modern types of labor like clerical and industrial work, increasingly numerous and characteristic of contemporary cities, are simply neglected in Geddes's model in favor of those contemporary professions whose alleged roots in natural occupations are easily grasped. This concept of natural occupations has therefore rightly been judged as not particularly helpful in explaining social reality, and as missing any concept of class.[26]

A city is more than just an element of a region, however; it acquires a larger symbolic meaning as a microcosm of the macrocosm that is the valley. Accordingly, the whole valley section is mirrored in a section through any city street, and its urban workshops and commercial premises can be taken as modern-day representations of the natural occupations (figure 3.3). Like Flahault's plant association, the city is "a system of life-adaptations," as Geddes writes in a review of Park, Burgess, and McKenzie's 1925 study *The City*, the manifesto of the Chicago School of urban sociology.[27] Geddes shifts the focus of the inquiry. While other sociologists and social reformers concerned themselves with class conflicts, ownership of the means of production, or, like the Chicago School in the 1910s, with urban territory disputed between social or ethnic groups, Geddes identifies misadaptation to the natural environment as the underlying cause of urban problems. For Geddes, conflicts arise not between classes but between occupational groups and the environment. As the aim is to adjust the whole city to the environment, cooperation among citizens becomes not only a viable option but a necessity.

### Edinburgh and Its Region: A Northern Athens and Its *Polis*

Edinburgh and its hinterland offer nearly all the elements Geddes combined into his model of the valley section, and presumably stimulated Geddes's model. The Pentland Hills to the southwest are the mountains. The region of Lothian comprises both pastoral hillsides and agricultural plains with interspersed settlements and villages. Edinburgh itself is the city, despite its location a short distance from the coast, and Leith, the harbor of Edinburgh, is the fishing village. A few elements of the full valley section are missing or exist only in minor form, such as a river binding the region together, or mining areas (which are only to be found in Midlothian). Allowing for these disadvantages, Geddes concludes that Edinburgh and its region, "if not quite an ideal microcosm of geography, [are] yet an exceptionally complete approximation to this."[28]

The region of Edinburgh corresponds to a botanical region defined in a survey by the biologist Robert Smith. Smith was Geddes's assistant at the University of Dundee, and was sent by him to work with Flahault during the winter of 1896–1897 at the University of Montpellier.[29] On his return to Edinburgh Smith began a botanical survey of Scotland, the first two parts of which deal with the Edinburgh and North Perthshire districts.[30] Smith divides the botanical region of Edinburgh into three parts: first, the "Region of Cultivation," or the plains and lower slopes of the Pentland Hills, subdivided into a lower zone of wheat cultivation and a second where oats were the most suitable crop; second, the hills, with mostly uncultivated pasture and moorland, differentiated into areas of heather association, grass association or hill pasture, a mixture of both, and an alpine-like region; and third, a minor littoral zone along the shore.

Not only botanical and geographical characteristics but also historical connotations raise Edinburgh to the status of a model region for Geddes:

FIGURE 3.4

Comparison of the
urban-geographical
structures of Athens
and Edinburgh, as
published in 1911.

Indeed, to understand a city of this type we must go further afield than
ever. Hence the comparison, side by side, of Edinburgh and Athens—
each plainly a hill-fort associated at once with a sea-port, and with an
agricultural plain. This combination of an Acropolis with its Piraeus
and its Attica, is common throughout Mediterranean Europe, though
less frequent in the north. . . . Thus we see the traditional comparison of
Edinburgh with Athens has really little to do with our eighteenth and
nineteenth-century imitations of Greek temples or Greek sophistries,
but lies far deeper, in geographical and historical origins.[31]

Both Edinburgh and Athens are built around a center on high ground—political and spiritual in the case of the former, spiritual in the case of the latter—
with a town below to accommodate the inhabitants and a harbor at some
distance (figure 3.4). Geddes initially based his comparison of the two capitals
on this observation, but the location of both cities in similar geographical areas allowed him to carry the comparison further. Geddes's analysis of the Notation of Life showed that a city emerges as an expression of man's reflection

on the environment and its inherent possibilities. A city is, so to speak, a superstructure erected on the basis of place, work, and folk. It is a cultural reflection of the given environment, comparable to the section through a city street that mirrors the valley section. Looking back through the history of human civilizations, the first cultural equivalent Geddes could identify was the Greek *polis* and its younger sibling, the Roman *civitas*. The link to the valley section is the geographical area occupied by a *polis* or a *civitas*, and the relation between town and country in each. Geddes explains that "the old meaning of *civitas* has to be remembered, since this included both the town (or *municipium*—what we know as the municipal group and area) and the *pagus* or countryside." He continues: "A right concept of country and town, with its schools and its cloisters—in our day not a monastery but a university, art centre, socialized religious centres, too—develops as a city indeed."[32]

Greek and Roman city-states encompassed an urban core and a network of variously sized settlements within a larger territory. Theories about the origin of the *polis* in Geddes's time, for example that of historian William Warde Fowler, stress that the city-state emerges from this hinterland. In this view, a territory is first settled by several families bound by kinship ties. Once settlement takes place, village communities of several families are formed.[33] The moment some of these villages establish a union beyond blood bonds, for reasons like self-defense or common worship of a deity, the *polis* is born. This process of unification then incorporates more and more villages "until some natural boundary is reached, such as the sea and the mountain barriers which enclose Attica or Latium."[34] According to Fowler, in a *polis* like Attica the city, in this case Athens, has a well-defined function as the one point that defines the *polis* politically, intellectually, and religiously, even if its citizens live in the countryside.[35] City and country in the *polis* are by definition a single, coherent whole.[36]

Accounts of the origin of the city-states likes Fowler's were influenced by the contemporary attempt to organize modern nation-states on principles of race, language, or ethnicity—criteria that cannot be easily applied to the ancient city-states.[37] Yet Fowler's explanation of the origin of the *polis* reads like a tailor-made proof of the similarities between the valley section and the *polis*. In each case cities derive from villages in the countryside, and the territories of *polis* and valley region are defined by natural barriers. The city Geddes describes in the valley section is a whole consisting of town and country, as in the *polis* of old: in what follows, I will refer to this concept as the region-city. Its basis in the analogy of the plant association allows Geddes to claim that the region-city is a natural concept, while at the same time it is confirmed historically by its derivation from the ancient *polis*. For Geddes the *polis* represents the most successful model of human settlement because it originated in natural regions and never outgrew, according to Fowler, its constituting "natural boundaries." Thus, as Geddes states, the city-state was "conducive . . . to regional as well as civic culture," two goals the region-city aims to revive.[38]

The idea of a region-city has consequences for Geddes's perception of contemporary cities. Instead of focusing on city or town in opposition to the country, he emphasizes the continuities between them. In his civic surveys, for example, he follows the descent from hamlets to city as found in the valley region model: "For our regional and civic surveys elucidate the evolution of the town and city, as at best a rural concentration towards regional development at its highest as with cloister and cathedral of old, and with University at its coming best."[39] Geddes's analysis of the division of labor in modern cities as derived from natural occupations now makes sense, because it explains the city as the continuation of the country. Everything that happens in a city is rooted in the country. Accordingly, his use of the term city refers to both a larger region, or region-city, and an urban center within that region as the site of the highest concentration of what is principally a rural way of life.

The origin of the city in its larger region is no safeguard against its tendency toward autonomy from the area around it. Geddes accepts the contemporary perception of the metropolitan city as big and rootless, potentially subjugating a region—or even a nation—to its character and needs.[40] But he does not arrive, as do so many of his contemporaries, at an antiurban position. For Geddes, even a metropolis like London continues to display its origin in villages, because it is "still essentially rather the biggest of village-groups than in any deep sense the greatest of cities."[41] This observation suggests a way to redeem the metropolitan city, which can become a great city again not by denying its rural and regional roots but by emphasizing and building on them.

Geddes's valley section and valley region are not so much analytical tools as models expressing what a city should be: a logical extension of the surrounding region, distinguished by a higher degree of differentiation of rural verities. Geddes's preference for "visual thinking," for example the representation of the region-city as a valley section, never fostered a clear expression of this concept. Furthermore, he obviously assumed that sparsely dotted references to the *polis* were understood at a time when knowledge of antiquity was still common among the educated. His catalogue of the Cities and Town Planning Exhibition, as shown in Edinburgh in 1911, states briefly under the heading "Ancient and Historic Cities" that "of these Great Cities everyone has some general knowledge." For those who did not know, or did not know enough, Geddes continued, "beyond this the visitor must depend on his own study or on the oral guidance."[42]

### The Region-City: A Step toward Conurbations and the World City

The valley section as the visualization of a region-city emphasizes a physical unit larger than that described by the existing administrative boundaries of most cities. This raises the issue of how the concept of the region-city affected town and regional planning activities. That cities relied on zones of influence in their nearer and wider environs was not a novel idea. When John Ruskin in his 1873 *Fors Clavigera* lamented the fact that Loch Katrine had become a reservoir for Glasgow, he drew attention to the way cities had already begun to draw on the regions around them to satisfy their material needs.[43] Such observations, along with the conditions of life in big cities and the increasing need to balance diverging economic interests of potential land users, all contributed to the emergence of town planning, and subsequently regional planning, in the decades around 1900. Britain's Housing and Town Planning Act of 1909 marked the end of the preliminary period with the recognition of town and regional planning as a statutory duty in Great Britain. In this context, Geddes is commonly credited with the introduction of the idea of a region into the developing concept of planning. Yet descriptions of the content and character of Geddes's contribution remain vague, hardly going beyond references to the origin of his concept of the region in biological and geographical models, or the observation that he felt that town and region were somehow related and must be considered in parallel.[44] This vagueness on the part of historians of planning can be traced back to Geddes's own references to Edinburgh and its region, if set in the context of his work in that city and its environs.

Geddes never planned the area between the Pentland Hills and Leith—Edinburgh's region—which was the area of Smith's botanical survey and was illustrated in the *Civic Survey of Edinburgh* in 1911. Rather, he worked almost exclusively in Edinburgh's Old Town along the Royal Mile between the Castle and Holyrood Palace. Beyond the Old Town, but still within Edinburgh, he was involved in the planning of a small terrace of cottages at Roseburn Cliff above the Water of Leith.[45] He also claimed to have been responsible for the creation of working men's housing close to a factory near Edinburgh.[46] To what extent the wider region was included in a "vacant land survey," which unveiled 450 unused acres in the city's environs, is today unknown.[47] Geddes also makes various comments about the Midlothian coalfields around Newtongrange southeast of Edinburgh as a suitable area for future industrial development and "industrial garden villages." Farther from Edinburgh, Geddes and Frank Mears designed a garden suburb for the Burgh of Leven on the eastern coast of Fife,[48] and Geddes occasionally mentions the garden city of Rosyth north of the Firth of Forth as an outstanding example of town planning.[49] Finally, it is known that he supported the reconstruction of a shipping canal between the Firth of Forth and the Firth of Clyde.[50]

All this, however, does not amount to a regional scheme as defined by the planning historians Wannop and Cherry. Analyzing the pioneering years of regional planning from 1920 to 1948, the authors identify as key elements of regional plans statements about traffic, zoning, town extensions and new towns, the relation between town and country, and the preservation of areas of outstanding beauty. Regional plans are distinguished from mere urban plans when they tackle areas larger than a borough or district.[51] Considering that Geddes worked in Edinburgh from the late 1880s onward, at a time when concepts of coordinated town and regional planning schemes existed only in earliest form, it is not surprising that he did not propose a comprehensive regional scheme. Yet his renewal scheme for Edinburgh's Old Town is far more comprehensive than a simple slum rebuilding initiative; surely he could have outlined a more comprehensive scheme for the region of Edinburgh had he felt the need to do so. Similarly, when he worked for the Zionist Commission on various projects in Palestine between 1919 and 1925, Geddes talked about the region of Palestine yet his work again concentrated on schemes for urban settings such as Jerusalem, Haifa, Tel

Aviv, and a few smaller settlements.[52] Thus he propagated the ideas of the region and the region-city while pursuing urban renewal work in the centers and town extensions like garden suburbs at the fringe of existing cities, apparently without feeling that there was a contradiction.

Geddes's understanding of a city's function within a region allowed him to confine his planning and renewal work to the urban centers in geographical areas he conceived as region-cities in the making. This was an attempt to regain for these centers a function similar to that of the urban core of an ancient city-state as defined by Fowler.[53] Athens was the center of the *polis* because it was where all important institutions like temples and the agora were assembled. Geddes envisioned a similar function for a city at the center of a region-city. A town like Edinburgh had to be transformed again into a City in Geddes's sense, bound into a region by accommodating the highest regional concentration of civic, cultural, and spiritual institutions and facilities. Once its influence had radiated into the region, city and region would become again an integrated whole, restoring a historic but now-lost unity by overcoming the modern separation of town and country. This marks a shift from the then-current "quantitative and material" distinction between town and country toward the traditional "qualitative and spiritual" distinction.[54] Unlike the biological or geographical regions from which it is derived conceptually, the region-city is ultimately defined by its center, whose spiritual and cultural power determines the character and size of the region. Thus Geddes concentrates on elevating villages and towns to the level of cities, in order to guarantee that a network of spiritual and cultural centers would bind the larger region together.

Regionalism in literature, biology, geography, planning, or any other field faces two main theoretical problems: the definition of the region and, based on this, the question of boundaries.[55] The first question Geddes sufficiently solved for his purpose by resorting to the plant association as a model for the regional organization of human societies. The distinctive cultural production of a region is another way to identify it. But the question of boundaries remains. Natural regions in biology do not necessarily have clear boundaries, but this is not so much of a problem for biologists concerned with plant or animal distributions. Habitats can be mapped, and the regions of various species can yield zones of transition or even overlap without creating a problem for the theoretical concept as a whole. But using regions to distinguish among human societies and cultures puts the question of boundaries at the forefront, especially if regionalism attempts to reorganize existing administrative units. In such cases the regionalist deals with the distribution of power and zones of influence of various local elites, which find their limits at the boundaries.

Geddes never arrived at a well-defined idea of the boundaries of region-cities.[56] He declares at one point that the boundaries of modern nations are "essentially concepts of war, and of that passive, latent, potential war" which is "connected with expansion."[57] Boundaries and war are ultimately caused by the dominant position of the hunter and his descendants amongst the natural occupations. To constrain them requires that society be given a structure composed of region-cities, which, in turn, means basing societies on natural and geographical regions. Existing boundaries of cities, districts, and the like have to be overcome, since "municipal boundaries exist for the sake of cities, and not cities for municipal boundaries."[58] Societies based on natural regions place the development of regional life above the expansion of man-made entities like states. Boundaries then lose their importance, and as they do so the importance of the urban center correspondingly rises. Again, his emphasis on the urban core allows Geddes to insist on immediate urban renewal in existing cities as a step toward the development of region-cities. Beyond the vague idea of a "natural" or "geographical" region, Geddes could safely ignore the definition of boundaries, as the future would render them superfluous.

Thus he never clearly defined the region of Edinburgh. In his writings Edinburgh's region varies between Smith's botanical region and the whole of Scotland. On one occasion Geddes divides Scotland from Aberdeen to the southern border into five distinct regions, yet Edinburgh's is not among them.[59] Despite this lack of a clear geographical definition, for Geddes it is beyond doubt that the city must branch out. With regard to the legal and political implications of the proposed industrial area in the Midlothian coalfields—within the region but outside the administrative boundaries of Edinburgh—Geddes declares that Edinburgh, with its large legal community, should be able "to enlarge at once its area and its powers to an extent worthy alike of the opening social future, and of the continued place of Scotland as one of the Great Powers—of Culture."[60] To lay claim to the hinterland is neither an expression of Edinburgh's imperialism nor an end in itself, insofar as the expansion will not end at the coalfields. Rather, it is part of a broader pattern in the emergence of a new city type Geddes observes in various parts of the United Kingdom. Looking toward Edinburgh from Glasgow on the other side of Scotland, he writes:

> I may describe Glasgow as a vast city, which I venture to name Clyde-Forth, because it extends from the opening of the Firth of Clyde to the Forth at Edinburgh. . . . We have, therefore, to prepare for a great and living city, and that in a large and effective way, a city which would be second to none.[61]

Mergers like that developing between Glasgow and Edinburgh transform the "geographic tradition of town and country in which we were brought up."[62] This transformation had already begun in the emergence of "city-groups," which Geddes identifies as essential elements of a thriving civilization.[63] Such conurbations, as he came to name them, also developed elsewhere in Great Britain, for example as "Greater London," or between Liverpool and Manchester in the form of "Lancaston."[64] Conurbations are extended geographical areas characterized by a network of settlements ranging from villages to towns, cities, and region-cities. Each of the settlements could be a city in its own right (in the terms of Geddes's Town-City formula) while together they form another city on a larger scale. The position of the region-city within the hierarchical structure is thus that of a *primus inter pares*. Conurbations composed of region-cities are rooted in geographical truths—a precondition for their planned, directed growth.[65] Geddes is highly critical of the uncontrolled development of conurbations, but nothing in his writings suggests that he disapproved of them as a city type.[66]

Recall that Ebenezer Howard and Peter Kropotkin represent two different attempts to overcome the town-country conflict. Howard approached the problem from an urban point of view and arrived at a compromise. Kropotkin, who started from the rural viewpoint, never developed a clear idea of what to do with existing cities. Only Elisée Reclus took a firm stand in favor of the urban point of view, since even remote houses and settlements are bound to existing cities. Geddes's conurbation is very likely influenced by Reclus's notion of the ever-expanding city, given Geddes's aim to integrate existing cities into region-cities and conurbations rather than dissolve them into smaller units.[67] Both the conurbation and the ever-expanding city emerge from the country and return to it—in Geddes's case mediated through the region-city—as the highest expression of the possibilities inherent in the country.

It is remarkable how seldom Geddes criticizes the city as sucking everything and everybody out of the country. In fact he finds the opposite to be true, because every "town arises and renews itself from country; and this not only in blood and in temperament but in tendencies, aptitudes, activities, in qualities and defects; in short in character, individual and social."[68] Both Reclus's and Geddes's projected future cities are structured hierarchically. While the conurbation is polycentric, the region-city follows Reclus's scheme in having a clear urban focus that radiates out to the hinterland. Geddes, like Reclus, proposes to concentrate cultural, educational, and spiritual institutions and buildings in that center. Both the conurbation and the region-city allow him to easily incorporate other urban types such as garden cities. Describing the conurbation between Glasgow and Edinburgh as a "future Garden City, stretching from sea to sea,"[69] Geddes establishes a hierarchy in which the conurbation is superior.

Reclus considers peace a precondition of the ever-expanding city. Geddes reverses this order and hopes to achieve world peace through the constructive activity of city building. Uniting all cities in a world confederation would help to bring about international peace and cooperation, aims that nation-states have never achieved. Geddes claims that he originally conceived the idea of a Congrès International des Villes in 1912—roughly the time when the idea of conurbations began to appear in his writings—in collaboration with the Belgian internationalist and bibliographer Paul Otlet,[70] who visited Edinburgh in that year. Although suggestions of a world league of cities are rare in Geddes's publications, the idea is important as it places him within the growing cultural internationalism of his time, which was a reflection of both the increasing economic internationalism of capitalism and the political internationalism of Marxist and socialist movements. Cultural internationalism was characterized by the belief that growing tensions among the capitalist nations in Europe and North America could be checked by cooperative cultural and scientific activities across national borders. Otlet, who since 1895 had pursued the collection of an international bibliography, would expand his activities to the founding of a world museum and world library to be accommodated in the Mundaneum, a world center for knowledge.[71]

For Geddes, a world city is a "Super-Metropolis," the culmination of European and world civilization.[72] With this phrase he refers to a project by the Norwegian architect and sculptor Hendrik Christian Andersen, who in 1912–1913 designed a world city in collaboration with the French architect Ernest M. Hébrard. With this project they sought to establish a single city as the visual center of international knowledge, as a step toward the common good of humanity and world peace.[73] Geddes included the lavishly printed volume of Andersen and Hébrard's scheme in his Cities and Town Planning Exhibition, but he differs from their scheme insofar as he envisions not one world city but a world league of cities, composed of region-cities and conurbations.[74] What began with the valley region and valley section at the local level thus led him finally to the level of the whole world. Despite the vagueness of his statements about a world leagues of cities, his works clearly raise the question of the relation between the region and the world, between the regional and the universal.

## Regional and Universal

Geddes views Edinburgh as a biologist, seeking a solution for the general question by studying a single cell through a microscope. When referring to that city, he emphasizes that it allows one to gain both specialized and generalized knowledge. The specialist focuses on the local and regional aspect of a single city like Edinburgh and its hinterland, while the generalist keeps the "culture of the world, the common heritage of civilisation" always in view.[75] Both aspects are closely connected and can only be understood with and through each other. Edinburgh is a nearly ideal microcosm because it allows for the study of the universal macrocosm. Consequently, Geddes usually prefers to refer to Edinburgh as a model or type.

He is convinced that the valley section, based on the region of Edinburgh, represents a universal model. It can be enlarged or reduced "to any scale, and to any proportions" in Great Britain, Ireland, Scandinavia, Europe, the Siberian plain, North America including Canada, or South America: "Broadly speaking, this way the world is built."[76] Yet, seemingly contrary to this statement, Geddes declares elsewhere that the valley section is not a well-defined natural unit: "There is no such exact thing in nature as our diagrammatic valley, containing all the types and in their right place." But, he continues, "as an ideal unit it is valuable just in proportion as it enables one actual valley with its quantum of regional life to be compared with another, and conformity to the ideal standard or departure from it, observed and defined."[77]

This statement is not a self-criticism but describes the very function of the valley region as an "ideal unit" against which reality and history can be compared. History provides the evidence that the ideal type was realized repeatedly throughout history, most notably in the Greek *polis* and the medieval *Stadt*. The model compared with reality shows how to improve present cities through city design, in order to achieve the ideal once more. Yet the ideal character of the valley region does not lend itself easily to attempts to use it as a planning unit. Rather Geddes describes an idea, outlining important structural elements within the valley section: a mixture of settlement types, a division of labor derived from the natural occupations in order to maximize adaptation to the environment, and a recognizable center, or city, binding together the region into a region-city.

Viewing the valley region as an ideal unit allows for comparison with Plato's notion of ideas or forms. Lewis Mumford confirms the connection in writing on Plato's *Republic*: "As the basis for his ideal city, whether Plato knew it or not, he had an 'ideal' section of land in his mind—what the geographer calls the 'valley section'."[78] Similarly, Geddes's contemporaries required a Platonic idea before embarking on building a city: his Notation of Life showed that the step from the third level—Cloister and Dream—to the fourth level—City and Deed—is the decisive step in the progression of city development. Furthermore, Geddes's declaration that the in-world is more real than the out-world can be taken as a reference to Plato's forms. Reality in Plato's metaphysics is confined to the eternal forms, whereas the sensible world and material phenomena are mere copies, more or less perfect imitations. The form Geddes offers is that of the valley section or region-city, which is detailed enough to allow concrete analysis of regions all over the world, yet abstract enough to allow the classification of these regions as realizations of a universal ideal unit. Thus city design works simultaneously on both the regional and the universal levels.[79]

## The Outlook Tower

Plato's dialogue *Meno* presents the story of an uneducated slave boy who solves a geometrical problem through careful questioning by Socrates.[80] The slave boy is able to provide the solution because he recollects forgotten knowledge of ideas or forms that his soul acquired when it was in touch with the eternal realm while separated from the body. Geddes criticizes citizens for not being able to teach each other about civics. They are unable not because they do not know, but because they have "forgotten most of the history of their own city."[81] Accordingly, he conceives two means, the outlook tower and the regional and historical survey, to enable citizens to recollect the forgotten ideas of the valley region and the region-city.

In 1892 Geddes purchased a six-story building at the upper end of Edinburgh's Royal Mile. Since the mid-1850s the building, whose lower four stories date from the seventeenth century, had been used by a Maria Short as a public observatory. To this end, the building had received two new floors topped by a battlemented roof platform with an octagonal domed cap house where Short installed a camera obscura as a tourist attraction. Geddes began to develop the tower as a unique public institution, at once a tool for the city designer and a civic museum, giving it the name the Outlook Tower. Later he referred to the Edinburgh Outlook Tower as a prototype for similar structures he proposed to erect in other cities, as discussed in chapter 5, though none of these was ever built.

The redeveloped tower is structured to focus visitors on Edinburgh and its region (figure 3.5). The top floor of the tower provides synoptic views of Edinburgh through a camera obscura, and of the immediate hinterland from the open gallery. The stories below contain exhibits about ever-larger spatial units, ranging from Edinburgh through Scotland, the English-speaking world, Europe, and the world. Thus after viewing the city and the region directly and through the camera obscura, a visitor climbs down the tower while the image of city and region merges from floor to floor in ever-widening geographical and cultural zones. The whole world is presented at ground level, with the real Edinburgh just on the other side of the exit—Edinburgh not only as the reality behind the image produced by the camera obscura, but also as a symbol of the world and of life. Geddes writes,

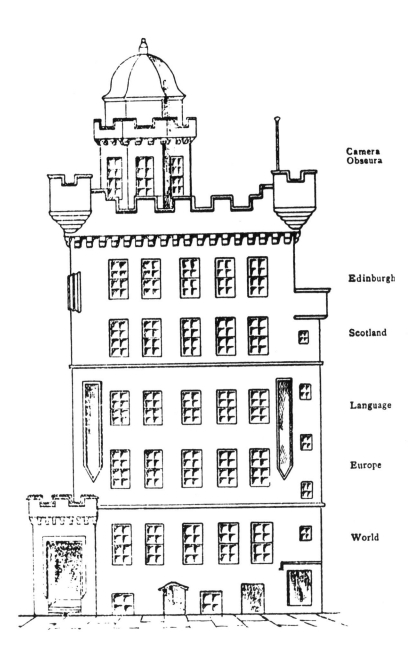

Camera
Obscura

Edinburgh

Scotland

Language

Europe

World

FIGURE 3.5

Diagram of the Outlook
Tower in Edinburgh, as
published in 1915.

Here around us ... is an amphitheatre of social evolution.... In this great amphitheatre we must study man's struggle for life, at first in direct contact with nature, as hunter and fisher, shepherd and peasant, woodman and miner; and thence trace the complex development, yet enduring influence, of these elemental occupations into our modern industrial division of labour.[82]

The type of the outlook tower represents a merger of Geddes's regional idea with an understanding of a universal civilization mediated by categories like city, state, nation, empire, and language, in short with "the whole gradated social framework."[83] The valley section is his symbol of the successful union of regionalism and humanism,[84] offering an ideal, the region-city, against which contemporary towns and cities can be compared in order to establish their history, their current shortcomings, and their needs of improvement. The latter are not achievable without knowledge of the former.[85]

Despite all references to natural and historical roots, the region-city as a concept is ultimately based solely on Geddes's own definition of the future city's desirable form. Here his major contribution to the emerging disciplines of town and regional planning does not differ from many of his contemporaries' ideas.[86] The novelty of his contribution is less the idea of a region as such, but rather that the region-city and the larger conurbation are metastructures accommodating divergent ideas of the city along with new concepts of planning in an even larger, ultimately universal frame of interaction between man and his environment.

History is not ended with our historian's "periods"; the world is ever beginning anew, each community with it, each town and quarter. . . . How then shall we continue the past tradition into the opening future; that is the problem, the essence of our Utopia.

Patrick Geddes, *Chelsea, Past and Possible*

# The City in History

Montesquieu, as historian Moses I. Finley points out, did not consider the city to be an object worthy of particular attention.[1] But by a generation later, the third book of Adam Smith's *Wealth of Nations* began with the famous remark about the reciprocal relation of town and country between which the trade is conducted that characterizes a civilized society.[2] While Smith described the relation as mutually beneficial, he nevertheless held the view that man finally finds fulfillment only in the countryside; human beings are rural beings. Yet the city was for Smith a place of virtue where man enjoys the profits of industry by developing, refining, and ennobling his culture. Voltaire, to name another Enlightenment philosopher, held a similar, even stronger view of the city as a civilizing agent in contemporary society, which was distinguished from all earlier forms of urban life through the existence of industry and pleasure.[3] The novelty of the industrial city and its economic power made it a greater object of interest and study by the early nineteenth century. As Raymond Williams observes, although city life was the life of a minority of people until the end of the nineteenth century, the disproportionate influence of the city on the life of societies was recognized much earlier.[4] By the beginning of the twentieth century the city had become reality for a large part of Great Britain's population. Thus cities as a significant part of modern life could no longer be avoided as objects of study.

The historian Carl E. Schorske puts the city as an object of study above an interest in society at large, although the study of the former nearly always leads to the analysis of the latter.[5] It would be misleading to assume from this that intellectuals in the eighteenth and nineteenth century were thinking primarily about the city. Most of them did not arrive at their studies of society by setting out to understand the city, but exactly the other way round. The attempt to understand contemporary society led to the study of cities as a condensed expression of the new, increasingly urban way of life.[6]

### The City in Nineteenth-Century Thought

The work of Karl Marx and Friedrich Engels illustrates the minor importance of the city for early economic and social studies. Engels published his book *Die Lage der arbeitenden Klasse in England* in 1845. Although the third chapter deals extensively with living conditions of the working class in cities, particularly Manchester, for which a map and typical block and street plans are included, the book is not a study of a city per se.[7] Instead, Engels delivers an analysis of a moment in the development of modern British capitalism, and the cities he refers to are simply a partial expression of the conditions it generated. Marx and Engels are interested in cities only when they are important to understanding society at large. Thus in *Die deutsche Ideologie* they refer to the emergence of the city as distinguished from the country in relation to the ongoing division of labor, with agricultural occupations on one side and industrial and commercial activities on the other.[8] Later, insisting on the abolition of the contrast between town and country, Engels expresses the logical result of the Marxist analysis of capitalist societies rather than an "anti-megalopolitan stance."[9]

Max Weber's preoccupation with the city has a similar place within the body of his work. Weber's posthumously published essay "The City" was never intended to be a separate study of the city, but was part of a larger project dealing with a "Sociology of Domination." (In the book *Economy and Society,* likewise published posthumously, the essay appears with the title "Non-legitimate Domination (Typology of Cities)" as part of a chapter titled "Sociology of Domination.")[10] Weber begins by defining the city as essentially an economic market. This definition signals a different interest in cities than the one advanced by Marx and Engels, for Weber tries to establish an ideal type of a city. Still, the city is not his main interest, because for Weber an ideal type is a theoretical construct meant to aid comprehension of a diverse reality. He quickly moves away from considering cities as economic associations—to which he never returns in the essay—by adding a political-administrative dimension: the city as fortress or garrison.[11] The fortress city is both market and garrison, and its prince or ruler guarantees both the market peace and the military jurisdiction. Weber accordingly identifies the relation between the fortress and the market, and the shifting power from one to the other, as the most important issue.[12] As Weber explains it, the economic and political distinctions between fortress and market gave birth to the ideal type of the medieval, independent city in northern Europe. Depending on the ruler's demands, the citizens often united against him in an act of oath-bound confederation that marked the beginning of independent cities.[13]

Weber compares various forms of European independent medieval cities to the ancient Greek *polis* and to Middle Eastern and Asian cities. The *polis* is based on a deliberate act of fraternalism, expressed symbolically through the existence of a city-god but also in a common *prytaneium,* a space to celebrate the act of *synoikia* (living together).[14] Comparably, the medieval European city heralds its cult-based fraternization in the city church, the city saint, and the symbolic common feast of the Lord's supper.[15] Asian cities were different; Indian cities, for example, contain a fortress, a marketplace, and a palace for the king or royal administration. Their division into the city of the notable men and the economic city reminds Weber of the contrast between *pnyx* and *agora* in Greek cities, or *campus Martius* and *forum* in the Roman city.[16] Accordingly, he concludes that the built expression of the distinction between political fortress and economic market indicates, in all three types of cities, the potential for the emergence of an independent city. But it does not emerge actually in India, where the religious caste system prevents the fraternization of the population.[17]

Weber's real agenda, in fact, is the study of the religious background of cities. In India, salvation and reincarnation depend on living in accordance with the rules of the caste system. This (in Weber's view) irrational aspect of the Indian religion prevents the emergence of cities comparable to those in Europe. The lack of "magical or religious barriers,"[18] or, to put it in a different way, the existence of a religion supporting the ever-growing rationality of capitalism and its predecessors, allows for the necessary fraternization of inhabitants in European towns. Weber identifies various degrees of rationality in different religions as the driving forces behind the emergence of modern economic life. Regarding cities, however, his writings reveal a conviction that city form is shaped by the needs of the strongest of the competing social groups.

An alternative nineteenth-century view emphasizes cities' permanent, eternal existence rather than their emergence from specific economic, material, and historic circumstances. Accordingly, the typical becomes more important than specific historical differences. Here the inhabitants of a city are seen as the collective force that builds it, rather than as members of different interest groups creating an urban environment by interacting with each other. Biological and organic metaphors suit this view of cities and their development very well.

Frederic Harrison, a leading British positivist and acquaintance of Patrick Geddes, is an early representative of this approach. His book *The Meaning of History*, despite its general title, is an attempt to establish the city as an autonomous historical subject. Considering the effects of the French Revolution, Harrison asks which power actually determines man's destiny. "It is the Past. It is the accumulated wills and works of all mankind around us and before us. It is civilization." According to Harrison, in addition to reading books there are two other ways of learning about the past, which he equates with being civilized. One is to study the history of great men—the classic positivist answer. The other is to study not only statues and pictures in museums but also historic buildings in cities. In combination these historical facts unveil the purpose of history: "The history of the human race is the history of a growth. . . . History is a living whole."[19]

Harrison's living whole of history is not only stronger than man, it also exists as a separate force independent of him. It is perceivable through material vestiges like buildings, however. The city as physical embodiment of history thus acquires for Harrison a position far more autonomous than, for example, in Weber's thinking:

> The life that men live in the *City* gives the type and measure of their civilization.... Hence, inasmuch as a city is a highly organized and concentrated type of the general life of an epoch or people, if we compare the various types of the city, we are able to measure the strength and weakness of different kinds of civilization.[20]

Comparative analysis is crucial to Harrison's thinking here. It allows him to order the cities of various civilizations along a single line and thus to judge the value of each civilization through its cities, making possible the construction of an evolutionary order. It also leads him to judge the modern city as being "in a far lower stage of organic life" than some of its predecessors.[21] His evolutionary ordering of cities combined with a holistic understanding of history results in the equation of the city with the living whole. History is civilization, which in turn is embodied in the city.

Although Harrison acknowledges that people build cities, the autonomy his cities acquire relegates man to a secondary status. City building is no longer primarily the expression of the satisfaction of man's needs, but is rather a contribution to the independent life of the city as an organism. Man provides the physical body for the living whole of history, which exists outside his sphere of influence yet determines his life. This view of history as a transcendent force robs Harrison of any chance to understand the development and appearance of modern cities through an analysis of the activities of their inhabitants:

> The Modern City is ever changing, loose in its organization, casual in its form. It grows up, or extends suddenly, no man knows how, in a single generation—in America in a single decade. Its denizens come and go, pass on, changing every few years and even months. Few families have lived in the same city for three generations.... The result is, that a Modern City is an amorphous amœba-like aggregate of buildings, wholly without defined limits, form, permanence, organization, or beauty.[22]

FIGURE 4.1

Arbor Saeculorum—the

tree of the centuries,

1895.

He cannot make sense either of the changing physical appearance of cities or the movements and behavior of the inhabitants.

### Geddes's View of History: The Arbor Saeculorum

Like that of his acquaintance Harrison, Geddes's analysis of the city intertwines his subject with an evolutionary view of human history. The Arbor

Saeculorum, the "Tree of the Centuries," summarizes Geddes's schematic view of all known history (figure 4.1). Originally the Arbor Saeculorum was conceived for a stained glass window, which Geddes incorporated into the Outlook Tower in Edinburgh in 1892. The sketch of the window presents the common nineteenth-century understanding of mankind's history as a succession of highly developed cultures.[23] It begins with Egypt at the bottom, proceeds to Israel, Greece, Rome, the European Middle Ages, the Renaissance, the French Revolution, and finally the contemporary period of industrialism and capitalism. At the center of the illustration stands the Arbor Saeculorum itself, whose branches, each consisting of groups of four leaves, symbolize the periods of past cultures. On the margins at either side, two scrolls display symbols relating to each of the periods. Rome, for example, is represented by a chain for slaves and the standard of the SPQR (*senatus populusque romanorum*), by the fasces for law and justice, and by the chi rho sign of the emerging religion of Christianity. The helmet of chivalry and the charter of the free cities, shown opposite the papal tiara and the barrel (a sign for intemperance in prosperous cities), together stand for the Middle Ages. The Renaissance is signaled by the blazons of noblemen and the hat of the Puritan movement at left, while on the right side Greek letters symbolize intellectual achievement and the Bible evokes the Reformation. Above these, the period of the French Revolution is characterized by the liberty hat rising above the *fleur-de-lis* of the absolutist regime, while the scroll at left shows the sword for conflict and the cogwheel of modern industry. Finally, the purse of the rich and the empty hands of the poor on the left scroll summarize Geddes's criticism of contemporary capitalism, while he puts on the right scroll the red and black flags of socialism and anarchism. Between the two scrolls the tree ends in a bud at its top, which is the future of human history. To the right a butterfly symbolizes the Psyche of thought, and its counterpart to the left is the Phoenix of action. The stem of the tree is wrapped in a spiral of smoke rising from a fire burning at its bottom, which indicates human ignorance of past ages and generations.

The Arbor Saeculorum illustrates Geddes's concept of history as a continuous process of growth. The horizontal structure of each period is accompanied by a vertical division of successive cultures and societies, symbolized by the two scrolls on either side of the tree. The right scroll stands for what Geddes calls the "spiritual powers" and the left for the "temporal powers." Societies or periods of human history are not necessarily related by historical causation, but because all cultures share the same structural division. Geddes borrows the distinction between temporal and spiritual powers from the French sociologist Auguste Comte.[24] Comte divides the temporal powers further into "people" and "chiefs," and the spiritual powers into "intellectuals" and "emotionals"; all four groups together constitute what Geddes calls the four social types. The temporal powers are in charge of a society's material order, while the spiritual powers are responsible for the immaterial order.[25] Geddes further associates the temporal powers with politics, business, and industry, while the spiritual powers relate to religion, science, and academic research.[26] The historic societies embedded in the Arbor Saeculorum can be understood as a dialectical interplay among Geddes's four social types. At the level of the city, Geddes compares the behavior of the four social types to that of actors on a stage, and bases on this assumption his well-known dictum that "a city is more than a place in space, it is a drama in time."[27]

The fourfold division of human beings according to their functions within a society recalls the similar fourfold structure of the Notation of Life. The four leaves of each section of the Arbor Saeculorum symbolize, at once, the four social groups of a society, the four steps of the Town-City formula, and the four stages of the Act-Deed formula as discussed in chapter 2. This correspondence shows that the Town-City formula is not merely an abstract process achievable when a community's individual members live according to the Act-Deed formula. The various elements of the formula—town, school, cloister, city—refer to existing groups within a town's population, and to their role in the functioning and well-being of the whole community. In a little sketch Geddes combines the concept of the four social types with the Town-City formula by writing: "People in Town" and "Chiefs in School."[28] Accordingly, the cloister can be ascribed to the intellectuals and the city to the emotionals.

Geddes's application of the four social types to historic periods and societies is rather loose. In the Middle Ages, for example, he identifies as "people" two distinctive groups of the population: peasants in the country and burghers in towns. The chiefs are the barons or nobility. The regular clergy in abbey and monastery are intellectuals, and the secular clergy in the cathedral church represent emotionals.[29] The distinction between people and chiefs roughly reflects the difference between the ruled and the rulers. The difference between intellectuals and emotionals is that the former are in charge of a community's intellectual life and the latter of its "emotional uplift."[30] Translated into the language of the Notation of Life, this means that the former are responsible for developing an idea of the city, and the latter for bringing this idea into a town, thereby raising it to the level of a city.

The description of the four social types in the modern period, called the "Age of Industrialisation," is equally vague. A general division groups society into the four categories of business (people), politics (chiefs), education (intellectuals), and religion (emotionals).[31] Yet as soon as Geddes embarks on a more detailed analysis, things become difficult. The complex social conditions of modern society require that the category of chiefs accommodate without further differentiation inventors like Arkwright, Watt, and Stephenson; entrepreneurs like Carnegie and Rockefeller; imperialists like Cecil Rhodes; political leaders like Chamberlain; entrepreneurs like Krupp and Emil Rathenau of the Allgemeine Electricitäts-Gesellschaft (AEG) in Berlin; and financial chiefs like Speyers and Morgan.[32] Scientists and academics are intellectuals in the modern abbeys that are universities and colleges. The corresponding emotionals are journalists, musicians, artists, novelists, and playwrights.[33]

The four social types cannot be seriously considered as well-defined sociological categories, but they serve Geddes as a "working model of social life in each of its characteristic historic phases."[34] This model is not so much an analytical as a moral one, ascribing to the four social types eternal functions needed for the success of a society. Individual members of each type have to realize their role within the larger social whole, and their fulfillment of particular tasks is their contribution to the common good. The specific task for Geddes is "to remind the ordinary citizen of the fourfold aspect and responsibilities of his own life . . . and so make him aware of his high calling."[35] Each society wishing to reach an advanced stage of evolution has to organize itself according to the four social types, and these groups, in turn, must correctly fulfill their functions to ensure its highest development. A city is only achievable if the four groups work together harmoniously: "The world-history of City Development shows that this has only adequately taken place when the fertile union has occurred of a deeply civilized and well-skilled people ideally minded too—with an active individual leader—usually therefore their ruling Prince."[36]

The four social types are tangible in the urban reality through the buildings that accommodate social groups and their activities. Human history, symbolically expressed in the Arbor Saeculorum, is made real in towns and cities:

> This tree of history, the observant traveler will find in every city he visits, every village, often hamlet even. Upon the changing town-plan, with its corresponding monuments, edifices, survivals of all kinds, he reconstructs the main aspect of its branching, and this often in the strangest completeness of detail.[37]

To find the Arbor Saeculorum in the urban fabric requires a "direct reading of history from towns and cities and regions with the help of their plans and pictures."[38] The most important of all sources available are a city's buildings. In a medieval city, for example, the castle refers to the chiefs, the town-houses to the people, and the abbeys and cathedral to the intellectuals and emotionals respectively. "Thus it is," Geddes concludes, "that town-house and castle, cloister and cathedral are all needed to understand and express the main life of the cities in the mediæval time."[39] In a similar manner other periods of the Arbor Saeculorum can be traced in the urban fabric, as will be shown below.

## Organicism and Morphology

Yet the city is more for Geddes than a historic textbook or a storeroom of records, for he ascribes to it an active role in human evolution and history. According to him, human life has two types of connections with the past. One is an organic connection with earlier family members and, therefore, past generations of mankind. The other is the human heritage, both the material heritage and the immaterial heritage of traditions and other conventions of a community's social life.[40] Geddes identifies the city as the

> specialized organ of social transmission. It is the vehicle of acquired inheritance. It accumulates and embodies the cultural heritage of a re-

gion, and combines it . . . with the cultural heritage of larger units, national, racial, religious, human. It stamps the resultant product upon each passing generation of its citizens. . . . The city receives the experiences of each passing generation and hands the record on to the next. . . . It is the instrument primarily of the regional memory, but serves also as the memory of larger groups.[41]

Without cities there would be no human evolution and consequently no history. Only through the city are human beings able to transfer their cultural-historical achievements to the future, because "in the scheme of nature it is the essential function of cities to transmit the culture heritage of mankind."[42] Geddes does not dismiss artifacts like books or museum exhibits as means to transfer human knowledge from one generation to another, but he prefers the immediate reading of history from buildings and cities.

For Geddes, then, the city is neither an accidental human product nor the result of a conscious decision to create it, but something essential to human life. He identifies the city as "the organ of human evolution and also, alas, of degeneration," asking: "Does it not seem that the city, in its being and becoming, is, as it were, the very incarnation of the evolutionary process?" The moment man creates his own city as a cultural artifact, he leaves the simple animal world for good. His own evolution and history begin, structured by the concept of the four social types. As Geddes puts it in a rhetorical question: "May not the city be the long-sought missing link between animal and human evolution?"[43]

Geddes arrives at a theory of cities, and consequently of human history, in which man is not the only conscious acting subject determining his life: man shares this position with the city. Geddes's assignment of a place in the natural order to cities, and his use of the city-organ analogy, indicate that he considers cities to be independent of man. Geddes intensifies this stance by arguing that "civic life and city development represent the supreme striving of nature to balance the freedom of the individual and the continuity of the species."[44] But the continuity of the species is nothing less than the continuity of life, of which an individual's life is only a temporary expression. Individual man perishes, while the city as a form of life continues.

Reading history from the city means for Geddes accepting the continuity of life in the form a city bears. There is little room for interpretation, for the reader of history from the city is merely a passive receptor of the knowledge a city's soul provides. "The spirit of the city selects and blends memories of the past with experiences of the present and hopes for the future." Civic life results not from human activities and original ideas but from the activities of a *genius loci*, which Geddes occasionally also refers to as the "regional *élan vital*."[45]

Why does Geddes adopt the simplistic concept of the four social types as a structural model for cities, at a time of increasing insight into the complex social reality of cities? Resorting to biological metaphors allows him to avoid both a purely materialistic and a religious, seemingly irrational world view. Organic metaphors conveniently appeal to modern scientific interests at the same time as they imply that the state of society and cities is natural, and therefore immutable. Hence these metaphors emerge, as György Lukács points out, in the growing antiscientific climate of the late nineteenth century.[46] This climate was not characterized by a general rejection of science, but by a critique of the directions taken by individual sciences. Unable to explain complex social phenomena or the manifest problems in society, scientists seemed to hide behind specialized studies. What was needed was a new unifying world view. Biology, as the science of life, appealed strongly to both scientists and intellectuals, no longer as a rational, empirical discipline but as an irrational, even mystical metaphor for life itself.

The art historian and philosopher Caroline van Eck distinguishes two main concepts of organicism as applied to art. One deals with the general relations between art and living nature, while the other centers around the idea of "organic unity" where the part-whole relationship of living organisms is applied to works of art.[47] The idea of organic unity may be applied to cities in two ways. Cities can be understood as organisms composed of physical elements like roads, buildings, and open spaces, to name only a few. If these parts are coordinated efficiently by the various planning disciplines—which should have the same relation among themselves as their subject matters—the city will function properly as an organism.[48] Organic unity is also useful if the city is viewed as a social whole, composed of various classes or individuals united by a common interest—keeping the organism of the city alive and preventing fragmentation by different interests. Harrison's use of the organic metaphor, discussed above, is a beginning at this application of organic metaphors to cities considered as social wholes. But while Harrison applies the metaphor in a negative and simplistic way, Geddes embarks on a more systematic and positive application.

In doing so, he implicitly refers to the idea of morphology advanced by Johann Wolfgang von Goethe. Morphology as a separate field of biology goes back to Goethe's 1790 essay "An Attempt at the Explanation of the Metamorphosis of Plants," in which he seeks to understand the development of a single plant from one leaf, the primordial leaf, into an entity composed of different organs. He assumes an "inner identity" among all the parts of the plant, even if the outer appearance is different.[49] Goethe next moves from the relation between the parts of a single plant to the question of a probable relation between all existing plants. The variety in the world of plants can only be explained as the result of reactions to specific environments. But this variety does not mean that plants are not comparable; rather the opposite, as there are similarities between even very distant varieties of plants.

Goethe develops the idea of an *Urpflanze* (primordial plant) as the common origin of all plants.[50] Though he could never identify this ancestor, the idea as such has been very influential. Even if viewed only as a transcendental concept, as Goethe himself was later to do, the possibility of connecting species through a common ancestor contributed to the development of an evolutionary view in biology. The *Urpflanze* expresses an underlying unity of all plants comparable to the inner identity of all the organs of a single plant expressed in its form (*Gestalt*), a unity which means life itself, because the parts cannot exist independently of each other.[51] According to Goethe, morphology is the science of form, dealing with the shaping and reshaping of the whole organism in both its outer appearance and its inner structure.[52] Rather than establishing it as another specialization within biology, however, Goethe uses morphology to attempt a reunification of all biology's branches into a convincing whole.

Geddes was well aware of Goethe's research into morphology. In his entry on morphology for the ninth edition of the *Encyclopaedia Britannica*, Geddes credits Goethe with having recognized more clearly than anybody else "the fundamental idea of all morphology—the unity which underlies the multifarious varieties of organic form." The question of whether the *Urpflanze* was "a mere ideal archetype" or "a concrete ancestral form," he continues, was only answerable with the arrival of Darwin's theory of evolution.[53] In Goethe's time the theological dogma of the origin of species due to divine intervention prevented scientists from achieving anything in the study of species beyond their classification, resulting in the theory of types and the constancy of species. As Geddes explains, the idea of an *Urpflanze*, or the "unity of organic composition" as the French biologist Etienne Geoffroy Saint-Hilaire calls it, anticipated an idea of a natural relationship between species that mere classification did not allow for. Still, the type theory and the concept of the *Urpflanze* were insufficient insofar as they left unanswered the question of whether type and *Urpflanze* followed a creative plan or were "purely Platonic and archetypal ideas." An answer was provided by Darwin's theory of evolution, since the *Urpflanze*, types, and other theoretical constructs "at once became intelligible as schematic representations of ancestral organisms, which, in various and varying environments, have undergone differentiation into the vast multitude of existing forms." Accordingly, "all the enigmas of structure became resolved."[54]

By analogy with Goethe's idea of the metamorphosis of plants, the motif of the tree in the Arbor Saeculorum means that all historical periods and cities have a common ground, and that there is a sense of inner identity among all of them. Yet the biological legacy in Geddes's thinking goes deeper. As a methodological approach, morphology helps explain his use of the simplistic idea of the four social types to account for the complex social reality of cities. If a city is like an organism, then the four social groups are the parts of the whole, essential to its functioning. By tracing them as organs in historic and contemporary cities, Geddes can establish a relation among all cities. Since this relation is a structural one, it can best be explained through morphology, which compares organisms, their structure, and their parts or organs.

Morphology makes use of two principal modes of correspondence: homology and analogy. Analogy stresses the same function of different organs in various organisms, which is understood to be the result of adaptation to similar environmental conditions rather than origin in a common ancestor. Homology is concerned with the similarity of organs due to their common evolutionary origin, though their actual appearance and function might vary to the point of complete dissimilarity.[55] The structural similarity Geddes assumes between the social types of people, chiefs, intellectuals, and emo-tionals in all cities can be understood as a homology of organs. The four groups constitute the inner structure of all cities, despite their varying man-ifestations and appearances in cities of different historical periods or cultures. This structural unity enables him to compare city with city morphologically, and thus to establish a "Science of Cities."[56] Table 4.1 gives an overview of the homology Geddes thought could be established between the social types of different historical cities. Within five historical periods he identified "Types of Individuals" (the historical realizations of the social types). To each of these individual types he assigned a "Type of Institution" (representing the indi-vidual type as a collective), such as castle, palace, capital, bureaucracy, and finance in the category of chiefs. Furthermore, he ascribed to them a "Place of Activity or Means of Action" within a city, for example workshop, shop, slum, barracks, and doss house to the social type of people.[57]

But Geddes does not confine the four social types to the cities of those cultures and historic periods he includes in the Arbor Saeculorum. While Max Weber expends considerable effort on understanding the differ-ences between Indian cities and medieval European or ancient Greek cities, Geddes easily identifies the Indian castes of Sudras (laborers), Vaishyas (merchants), Brahmins (priests), and Kshatryas (warriors) as yet another expression of the four social types.[58] Elsewhere, in connection with the divi-sion of labor in society, he emphasizes even more strongly the sameness of the four social types across all periods and cultures. He declares that "in all times, and in all countries . . . the infinite division of labour which charac-terizes our time is nothing more than a development of that of the savage; nothing generically new has ever been introduced, for what seems new is but a differentiation of the old."[59]

The emphasis Geddes puts on the development from an *ur*-type (the savage in this passage) into a large variety of historical examples is also valid for the evolution of cities and of the four social types. They are a case of general homology, of a particular relation "in which a part or series of parts stands to the fundamental or general type, involving a knowledge of the type on which the group in question is constituted."[60] The parts are the individual social types and the series of parts is the city. All derive together from fundamental or general types—the common ancestors of social types and city—which evolve into various forms during the course of history. The

| | PEOPLE | CHIEFS | INTELLECTUALS | EMOTIONALS |
|---|---|---|---|---|
| **MEDIEVAL CITY** | | | | |
| TYPE OF INDIVIDUAL | burgher | baron | monk | priest |
| TYPE OF INSTITUTION | town hall | castle | abbey | cathedral |
| PLACE OF ACTIVITY | workshop | strategic point | retirement | city center |
| **RENAISSANCE CITY** | | | | |
| TYPE OF INDIVIDUAL | roundhead | cavalier | scholar | Bible reader |
| TYPE OF INSTITUTION | camp | palace | college | puritan meeting |
| PLACE OF ACTIVITY | shop | estate | art and song | psalm-singing |
| **INDUSTRIAL CITY** | | | | |
| TYPE OF INDIVIDUAL | laborer | master | barrister | public speaker |
| TYPE OF INSTITUTION | labor | capital | parliament | oratory |
| PLACE OF ACTIVITY | slum | machine | ballot box | pub, including club |
| **EXPANSIONIST CITY** | | | | |
| TYPE OF INDIVIDUAL | guard | clerk | historian | bard |
| TYPE OF INSTITUTION | army | bureaucracy | state instruction | nationalism |
| PLACE OF ACTIVITY | barracks | market | sports and games | flag, music |
| **FINANCIAL CITY** | | | | |
| TYPE OF INDIVIDUAL | borrower | investor | economist | philanthropist |
| TYPE OF INSTITUTION | public taxpayers | finance | advertisement | investment |
| PLACE OF ACTIVITY | doss house | stock exchange, bank | arithmetic | shop window, hoarding |

TABLE 4.1

The homologous four social types in different historical cities.

contemporary variety of forms of social types and cities is nothing else than the result of metamorphoses.[61]

Such an emphasis on morphology, especially homology, raises the question of an *ur*-city from which all cities—European, Indian, and others—are descended. Geddes does not identify a specific historical city as the potential common ancestor, but his valley region model, with its region-city, provides an idea of a city comparable to the *Urpflanze* as a Platonic or archetypal form. The Greek *polis* is the first materialization of this idea of a city, to which the four social types are now added as another constant feature. When Geddes uses terms like Mammonopolis, Strategopolis, Biopolis, Geopolis, and Regionopolis, he is not inventing "nomenclature at its wildest"[62] but drawing on his idea of the region-city. Regardless of their exact meaning, these terms, taken literally and read morphologically, name later derivations of the *polis*, that earliest incarnation of the region-city.

## The Cities and Town Planning Exhibition

Geddes's Cities and Town Planning Exhibition, which went on display for the first time in Chelsea, London, in 1911, is one result of the idea of a morphology of cities. The exhibition partially evolved out of the vast collection of maps, views, plans, architectural drawings, photographs, and other visual images of Edinburgh that he had amassed in the Outlook Tower since 1892. In 1910, Geddes presented his survey of Edinburgh at an exhibition on town planning at the Royal Academy in London which coincided with the Royal Institute of British Architects' First International Conference on Town Planning, likewise in London (10–15 October 1910).[63] The Royal Academy exhibition was dedicated to the historical and contemporary development of towns and town planning, with examples from the United States, Scandinavia, Italy, the Low Countries, the German-speaking countries, and Great Britain. When the 1910 exhibition closed its gates by the end of October, Geddes felt that a dispersal of the displayed material would be a loss of a great educational resource. Among fellow conference participants and town planning colleagues he gathered support for keeping the exhibits together, and in due course a committee was established under the chairmanship of Raymond Unwin. Geddes was made the director of the Cities and Town

Planning Exhibition, which was subsequently shown in London in February 1911. The same year, the exhibition was also displayed in Edinburgh, Dublin, and Belfast (see table 5.1).

In this exhibition Geddes confirms the basic role of the ancient cities, summarizing with this term Egyptian, Mesopotamian, and Indian cities plus Jerusalem, Athens, and Rome. These last three correspond to the first three circles of leaves of his Arbor Saeculorum. The exhibition was meant to remind its viewers of "how the respective heritages of Jerusalem, Athens, and Rome underlies [sic] all subsequent civilization, up to that of to-day, and necessarily also that of to-morrow."[64] Although Geddes mentions the three outstanding buildings of these cities, respectively the Temple, the Acropolis, and the Pantheon, he does not explicitly apply to them the four social types.

The treatment is different for medieval cities. These, and especially continental cities like Bruges in Belgium or Rothenburg and Nuremberg in Germany, are outstanding examples of the division of a city into four social types, as Geddes's friend Victor Branford enthuses:

> The castle and town hall of the temporal power, the cloister and cathedral of the spiritual power, reached, in the mediæval city, an architectural perfection and a social co-adjustment which give to that historic period a particular significance for sociology.[65]

Geddes and Branford appreciate medieval cities because they offer the best societal expression of a well-balanced relation between temporal and spiritual powers. Their enthusiasm is more than the usual nineteenth-century fascination with medieval cities found in Morris, Ruskin, or Camillo Sitte, among others. Just as the *polis* contributes to Geddes's concept of city design the idea of a region and the identity of town and country, so the medieval city shows the importance for city development of the four social types and the balance between them.

The exhibition's consideration of the Renaissance city is brief. The Reformation, with the subsequent seizing of the wealth of abbeys and cloisters by noble classes old and new, brought an upswing for culture and art. Mansion houses and palaces with magnificent gardens supersede the medieval castles as dwellings of the chiefs in the city. Against this improvement of a city's space, the developing technology of war results in their enclosure by sophisticated fortifications. Geddes blames this change for the overcrowding of so many cities, more usually considered a result of the Middle Ages. The fortress dominates the newly enclosed city, which is subsequently reduced to a mere appendix. The Renaissance city therefore destroys the balance between the four social types along with the relation between major and minor cities, thus affecting settlements in the entire region. War as a dominant force of the Renaissance alters both the appearance of individual cities and the hierarchy among cities, as some become centers of military power. This is the beginning of the long development toward "metropolitan greatness" later embodied in cities like Paris, Berlin, London, or Vienna, which are comparable only to imperial Rome.[66] The final stage of evolution, as set out in the exhibition, is the industrial city that emerges after the period of militarized cities comes to an end in the eighteenth century. This final stage is the contemporary paleotechnic city, which Geddes hopes to redevelop toward a future neotechnic city.[67]

Note that the chronological order of cities in Geddes's exhibition is the same as the sequence of historic periods in the Arbor Saeculorum. This order also provides the structure for the ideal route through the exhibition (figure 4.2). The exhibition begins with engravings of cities and regions together with town and county maps, which are "picturesquely but confusedly grouped under [the] course of sun and planets."[68] (Geddes repeated the confusingly arranged entrance hall when the exhibition was on display in Ghent in 1913, with the stated intention of making a visitor feel "the profusion and confusion of the subject.")[69] From this hall, the visitor ideally proceeds through the geographic origin of cities to sections on the *polis*, medieval cities, the Renaissance, and so on, until the route reaches the garden city, the beginning of the future. Apart from this final section, the exhibition, significantly, does not contain detailed suggestions for the future development of cities. In this it echoes once again the Arbor Saeculorum, where the future has not yet found a concrete form but is indicated only by the final bud. Yet even if the Arbor Saeculorum does not disclose details of the future, it can be inferred that the structural elements of the coming period will be the same as those of the past. The same applies to the Cities and Town Planning Exhibition. Its function is not to

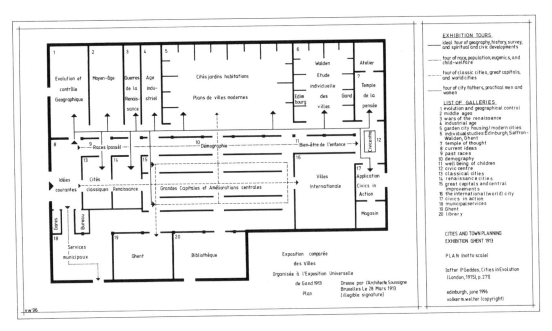

Inside the plan image:

EXHIBITION TOURS
ideal tour of geography, history, survey, and spiritual and civic developments
tour of race, population, eugenics, and child-welfare
tour of classic cities, great capitals, and world cities
tour of city fathers, practical men and women

LIST OF GALLERIES
1 evolution and geographical control
2 middle ages
3 wars of the renaissance
4 industrial age
5 garden city housing/modern cities
6 individual studies Edinburgh, Saffron-Walden, Ghent
7 temple of thought
8 past races
9 current ideas
10 demography
11 well being of children
12 civic centre
13 classical cities
14 renaissance cities
15 great capitals and central improvements
16 the international (world) city
17 civics in action
18 municipal services
19 Ghent
20 library

CITIES AND TOWN PLANNING
EXHIBITION GHENT 1913

PLAN (not to scale)

[after P Geddes, Cities in Evolution
(London, 1915), p. 271]

edinburgh, june 1996
volker m. welter (copyright)

FIGURE 4.2

Plan of the Cities and Town Planning Exhibition in Ghent, 1913, indicating the ideal and three alternative routes through the show.

predict the detailed development of cities but to teach about the elements required for city building.

In the *Meno* Plato offers an account of Socrates's interrogation of a slave boy, as discussed in chapter 3. The experiment begins by putting the boy deliberately into a state of confusion, which is the necessary precondition for questioning that leads to the recollection of forgotten knowledge. Socrates explains that the slave is keen to recollect, as he wishes to leave the confused state of ignorance in favor of the truth.[70] Similarly the visitor to Geddes's exhibition is meant to discover the idea of a city hidden in the confusing entrance hall. Toward this end Geddes—as instigator and interpreter of the exhibition—intends to stimulate a process in his visitors similar to the one Socrates achieved in the boy's mind. His ideal exhibition route offers a way out of the confusion of the entrance hall by emphasizing the historical continuity of the essential elements of city building. Having completed this ideal route, a visitor should be able to produce answers to the problems of cities by applying the elements of city development—most notably the regional origin and the social types as a structural continuum—to his own city.

## Some Problems, Regional and Historical

Geddes's morphological approach to the city in history illuminates another difficulty in his thinking. Although he defines the four social types as the basis of his analysis of existing cities, he dedicates astonishingly little thought to the interaction between these social forces. In his *Encyclopaedia Britannica* entry on morphology he explains that the "morphological aspect of an organism is merely statical." Still, he adds that "though the demonstration of the structural unity of the organic world is in itself a great result, yet the desire of a deeper explanation of form as determined by function and environment is thereby rendered all the more pressing." The morphologist has a "physiological ideal" which is the understanding of life, that is, the vital functions of an organism.[71] Geddes expresses a similar ideal with regard to cities:

> Beyond geographic conditions, beyond occupational beginnings and their economic developments, and beneath all the historic metamorphoses, we have to seek a more vital interpretation of city and citizens alike—in fact a theory of life in its evolution.[72]

It is the interaction of the four social types with the environment that determines the life of an individual city as an organism. Occasionally Geddes mentions a life cycle of individual cities, beginning with the *polis* as the *ur*-city. This cycle comprises the six stages of *polis*, metropolis, megalopolis, parasitopolis, pathopolis, and finally necropolis—all of them deviations of the ideal form.[73] As Geddes left no written elaboration of this cycle, however, no analysis of these six stages can be attempted.[74]

Also important for the life of a city is its relation with the environment, which refers back to the city's geographical aspect, including the derivation of its social composition from the natural occupations of the region. How might this analysis of social reality interface with the four social types as the historically constant social division in each city? Geddes provides the following answer:

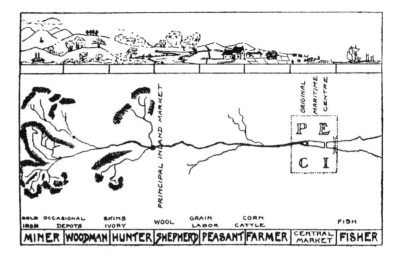

THE ASSOCIATION OF THE VALLEY·PLAN WITH THE VALLEY SECTION

RURAL·OCCUPATION·&·MARKET·TOWN·

FIGURE 4.3

People, chiefs, intellec-
tuals, and emotionals in
the region, as published
in 1917.

With the geographical survey we can easily associate the historical one. The history chart stands vertical to each region, is as it were a representation of the stratum of dust overlying the post-tertiary; the most concrete illustration being in ruined cities like Troy or Lachish.[75]

The region as circumscribed by the valley section is an ahistorical concept. As explained in chapter 3, Geddes refers to the modifying influence on each "complex community" of its predecessors higher up the valley region. But then he adds that "the converse is no doubt true also," indicating that he does not intend this to be an evolutionary, historical order of city development, with the village upriver as the oldest and the city downriver as the youngest settlement.[76] Further, he consistently presents the natural occupations as existing in parallel; it follows from this that the related types of settlements like hamlet, village, and so on exist in parallel as well.[77] All the various types of settlement in a region, representing the original natural occupations and their historical derivations, interact at once. If their adaptation to the environment is perfect, the natural occupations and the associated settlement types will be in balance; no single one will dominate but each will benefit from the others, and all together will form a region-city.

But a city is not only a natural geographical event; it is also a cultural product, different according to place and time. The historical aspect of cities refers to this cultural facet of their existence. The natural occupations represent the social divisions of life seen from a natural point of view. Superimposed onto this, the four social types approach life and society from a historical point of view (figure 4.3). Only the geographical and the historical aspects of human life taken together can explain the dual world of human life.

Thus Geddes reads a city as a historical chart of the evolution of human life, in addition to his reading of it as an expression of the natural occupations. Both readings together form the background against which individual cities can be investigated, which is the subject matter of the next chapter.

Our old city had no lack of historic memories, though these were too little taught us. . . . What has this modern county town, with its active agricultural interests and markets, its special industries, . . . and its large through railway traffic, to do with ancient history?

Patrick Geddes, "City Deterioration and the Need of City Survey"

## History in the City

The nineteenth century experienced what urban historian M. Christine Boyer has called a "memory crisis."[1] The increasing speed of change and innovation diminished the significance of the past, which no longer appeared to be a coherent continuum but rather a mere source of scientific facts and scholarly knowledge. With the perception the presentation also changed, for the "teller of tales" was replaced with the "narrator of history."[2] The substitution of history for tales shed myth and imagination, but the enlightened pursuit of the past did not necessarily improve understanding of the accumulated knowledge of history. In urban terms, the past surrounded the inhabitants of towns and cities, but they could no longer make sense of it.

The founding of the Society of Antiquaries of London (1717) and the Society of Antiquaries of Scotland (1780), at the beginning and toward the end of the eighteenth century respectively, marks the small beginnings of an institutionalized concern for the past in Great Britain.[3] By the mid-nineteenth century an increasing number of local or regional historical

societies were established. Most of them had a combined interest in archae-
ological, historical, architectural, and occasionally natural historical subjects.[4] On the local level, these societies strengthened the sense of place
by emphasizing the importance of smaller towns and cities against the
growing industrial cities and the capital, London. Methodologically, local history societies were often characterized by an undiscriminating,
all-embracing approach to the past.[5] Potentially, every historic object or fact
could arouse their attention simply as a survival that might shed light on
some aspect of the past.

During the nineteenth century, historians and authors like Walter
Scott raised public awareness of the importance of history by combining
in their writings historical facts with fictional liberties. Regardless of the
sometimes liberal use of invented geographical and historical data, deliberately created historic narratives like Scott's did foster a real and lasting interest in history and historical geography. Local historical societies pursued
a similar aim, but from a more scientific point of view. By providing metic-
ulously unearthed and researched facts, they put local artifacts and events
into a historical order and geography. Beyond this, their efforts contributed
to a growing awareness of the importance of historic buildings and other
man-made structures.

## Reading History from the City

The wave of restoration that spread through British towns and cities during
the nineteenth century was a practical expression of the value placed on the
historic environment. A tremendous effort went into the restoration of
churches, castles, and other buildings, although the executed work often
amounted to an alteration of the original buildings in an attempt to recreate
a past style.[6] Restoration became a topic of public debate in 1877 when
William Morris, following earlier criticism of restoration practice by John
Ruskin, founded the Society for the Protection of Ancient Buildings
(SPAB).[7] Morris rejected restoration as it falsified the appearance and the
structure of many buildings, but he did not reject a more general concern for
historic buildings and history. Since for Morris architecture embodied the
efforts of bygone historic periods, one could experience through it the development of man's ideas as well as the continuity of his history. Architec-

ture guaranteed perpetual education about past generations. What Morris looked and hoped for was a style in architecture that was of its time but referred to all earlier history.[8] The very time-boundedness of architecture, of styles, and of the means of production all led him to the conclusion that restoration is impossible and that buildings should therefore not be altered. They belong to both forefathers and coming generations, while the present generation has merely a preservative role: "We are only trustees for those that come after us,"[9] he asserted.

Patrick Geddes widened the frame of reference for this interest in historic architecture. In addition to individual objects and buildings, he advocated including the whole city within the potential scope of preservation activities, for which he coined the term "conservative surgery." Ideally, conservative surgery was to be preceded by a survey of a town and accompanied by a display of the Cities and Town Planning Exhibition.

In Geddes's scheme, the survey is a stocktaking exercise of all possible aspects of a town, as outlined in figure 5.1.[10] It results in a collection of visual images, written sources, statistical tables, diagrams, lists of historic buildings, three-dimensional models, maps, and the like. The first four sections of the survey deal with the geographical and economic conditions of a town as well as with its population. Each aspect is to be considered from both historical and contemporary points of view. The fifth section, "Town Conditions," tackles what Geddes calls the historical survey, whose task is to trace the history of a town as far back as possible, then carry this forward to its present conditions, in order to provide an up-to-date picture of its current physical appearance along with its strengths and its weaknesses. The final section of the survey, "Town Planning; Suggestions and Designs," provides a wider national and international outlook by introducing planning initiatives from British and foreign cities. Only at this last stage does the survey approach particular planning and architectural solutions for the city it is dealing with.

The survey as an endeavor preparatory to town planning envisions the engagement of citizens with their city's history and its contemporary conditions. It is meant to be an open-ended initiative involving each new generation of citizens, who have to familiarize themselves with the existing survey and add new information to it. Within this large-scale, ideally community-wide exercise, Geddes concentrated on the historical survey.

SITUATION, TOPOGRAPHY AND NATURAL ADVANTAGES :—
- (a) Geology, Climate, Water Supply, etc.
- (b) Soils, with Vegetation, Animal Life, etc.
- (c) River or Sea Fisheries.
- (d) Access to Nature (Sea Coast, etc., etc.).

MEANS OF COMMUNICATION, LAND AND WATER :—
- (a) Natural and Historic.
- (b) Present State.
- (c) Anticipated Developments.

INDUSTRIES, MANUFACTURES AND COMMERCE :—
- (a) Native Industries.
- (b) Manufactures.
- (c) Commerce, etc.
- (d) Anticipated Developments.

POPULATION :—
- (a) Movement.
- (b) Occupations.
- (c) Health.
- (d) Density.
- (e) Distribution of Well-Being (Family Conditions, etc.)
- (f) Education and Culture Agencies.
- (g) Anticipated Requirements.

TOWN CONDITIONS :—
- (a) HISTORICAL : Phase by Phase, from Origins onwards. Material Survivals and Associations, etc.
- (b) RECENT : Particularly since 1832 Survey, thus indicating areas, lines of growth and expansion, and local changes under modern conditions, e.g., of streets, open spaces, amenity, etc.
- (c) Local Government Areas, (Municipal, Parochial, etc.)
- (d) PRESENT : Existing Town Plans, in general and detail.
  Streets and Boulevards.
  Open Spaces, Parks, etc.
  Internal Communications, etc.
  Water, Drainage, Lighting, Electricity, etc.
  Housing and Sanitation (of localities in detail).
  Existing activities towards Civic Betterment, both Municipal and Private.

TOWN-PLANNING ; SUGGESTIONS AND DESIGNS :—
- (A) Examples from other Towns and Cities, British and Foreign.
- (B) Contributions and Suggestions towards Town-Planning Scheme, as regards :—
  - (a) Areas.
  - (b) Possibilities of Town Expansion (Suburbs, etc.)
  - (c) Possibilities of City Improvement and Development.
  - (d) Suggested Treatments of these in detail (alternatives when possible).

FIGURE 5.1

Table showing the topics

and themes of a survey,

1911.

This emphasis is mainly for conceptual reasons—as will be shown below—but is probably also a consequence of practical considerations relating to the sheer scale of a general survey.

The possible extent of a town survey is demonstrated by the Survey of London. This enterprise began in the last years of the nineteenth century under the guidance of Charles Robert Ashbee, who initiated it in reaction to the demolition of the Old Palace of Bromley-by-Bow, a Jacobean country house in London.[11] The Survey of London's main purpose was to compile a register of historic buildings, which was to be published together with drawings of buildings, photographs and old views, reprints of historic documents, and a list of occupants and owners; its first volume was published in 1900. The main series of the publication dealt with individual parishes, although in 1896 a series of monographs on single buildings had been launched. The parish of Chelsea was, after Bromley-by-Bow, the second focus of the Survey; a glance at the two volumes published on Chelsea reveals the amount of material a systematic inquiry into a locality's history can provide.[12]

Patrick Geddes was very well aware of the survey of Chelsea and its extent. He was a member of the London Survey Committee that Ashbee had formed in the 1890s, and the architect Walter Hindes Godfrey, editor of the volumes on Chelsea, listed Geddes among the active members of the survey of Chelsea.[13] In fact, the predominantly scholarly character of Ashbee's initiative, which accepted traditional assumptions about which buildings were historic monuments—churches and manor houses, for example—as well as an exclusive focus on architectural history differ markedly from the type of survey Geddes advocates.

The historical survey Geddes proposes as part of a general survey aims not at documenting what has survived, but at unveiling a city's historic social structure as constituted by the four social types of the Arbor Saeculorum. Nor is the historical survey intended simply to record or preserve surviving historic buildings, but to put the historic city at the disposal of the contemporary one. An active city, for Geddes, should "display traces of all the past phases of evolution."[14] Paraphrasing Schelling's famous dictum of architecture as frozen music, Geddes states: "Architecture, it has been said, is crystallized history."[15] The active, contemporary city—a city in deed on the fourth level of the Notation of Life—decrystallizes history and brings it to life again. Once this is accomplished the city regains its soul or spirit, for the city "which has kept alive its ancient culture by using it for modern needs *is* the spiritual treasure-house."[16] Such a city accommodates history as living history, and its citizens can make use of historic vestiges for two purposes: to make them their own, which means to live *in* the city, and to keep them for the sake of the city, which means to live *for* the city.[17]

To further this aim, the historical survey must be primarily narrative rather than scholarly or scientific. A process of selection by interpretation is required, followed by the recombination of the selected elements into a vision, which gives rise to the city in deed. Selection does not mean choosing from neutrally collected facts; rather the inquiry itself is guided by a priori choices made against the background of the four social types. The survey assembles "images and impressions . . . which at its close build themselves into a vision of the city, in all the manifoldness of its being and becoming. In proportion to the fullness and opulence of this vision does the citizen take possession of his social inheritance."[18] Conceptually, this approach to a city's heritage as the transmitter of social inheritance refers to contemporary psychology, which, as elucidated in chapter 2, included the built environment among the nonlingual means of transferring knowledge and thoughts from one generation to the next.

### The *Genius Loci*

Methodologically, the transmitter function of the urban fabric relies on a direct encounter with a city's architecture, a requirement Geddes probably best illustrates in *Our Social Inheritance*, a book he coauthored with his friend Victor Branford. In the second part of the book the authors offer, under the heading "A City Survey for Disoriented Citizens," a series of educative walks through Westminster: from Piccadilly Circus to St. James's Park, for example, or from Leicester Square to Green Park.[19] These walks reveal a borough soaked with history and crammed with buildings in which even minor decorative elements are full of meaning. Lewis Mumford credits these walks with a lasting effect on all his later thinking.[20]

The fifth walk covers the area between Westminster Abbey and the Houses of Parliament, the "sacred centre" of Westminster, London, England, and the British Empire.[21] The walk begins with an outlook from the clock tower of the House of Commons, but for the detailed reading of the history a standpoint closer to the ground is preferred. The appropriate point is Victoria Street, and the first two buildings Geddes interprets are the then National Liberal Club and Westminster Hospital (figure 5.2). Built in 1823, the hospital is, according to Geddes, a "Temple of Suffering" because as a modern hospital it accommodated the people, the victims of the industrial revolution. The National Liberal Club, which during the First World War occupied the former Westminster Palace Hotel (1859), Geddes associates with the chiefs, the second temporal power. Opposite the Club, the "Church House" or Gothic House (1854) embodies the spiritual powers' reaction

FIG. 5.—PRECINCTS OF THE ABBEY: APPROACH FROM VICTORIA STREET.

**A.** National Liberal Club. **B.** Corner of Westminster Hospital. **C.** Church House and Dean's Yard. **D.** Westminster School Column. **E.** The Abbey, West Front. **F.** St. Margaret's Tower. **G.** Corner of Middlesex Guildhall. **H.** Clock Tower. **I.** Office Buildings.

FIGURE 5.2

The precincts of
Westminster Abbey, as
published in 1919.

against the industrial revolution. The Gothic revival style of the building expresses "a pathway to romance, through the pointed arch of medieval mysticism."[22] Behind the National Liberal Club Geddes identifies the Old Wesleyan Central Building (1905–1911), built by Henry V. Lanchester and Edwin Alfred Rickards, as another building related to the spiritual power. The partial occupancy of this building by a bank Geddes declares to be a reminder of the possible aberrations that can befall even a spiritual power like the reformed churches.

In front of Westminster School a column commemorates the fallen of the Crimean and Indian wars. For Geddes, the column is also a reminder of the Renaissance: whereas the reformed churches are symbols of the spiritual powers, which purify the people, the column leads Geddes's thoughts back to the chiefs, a temporal power. As a war memorial it expresses the ideals of a social type devoted, beside political aims, to the ideals of learning. A second symbol of learning, focused on teaching a coming generation of chiefs by intellectuals, is the College Hall of Westminster School, formerly the refectory of Westminster Abbey.

The only remaining witnesses to the Middle Ages are Westminster Abbey and St. Margaret's Church. The church in particular is of great value to Geddes because it dates from the final period of the Middle Ages, the time of the great independent cities. Ideally, this civic phase—which perfectly illustrates a society's division into four social types—would be best embodied in a medieval cathedral, a town hall, a belfry, and a university, but none of them existed in this area of Westminster. However, Geddes reads the rebuilt Middlesex Guildhall (1906–1913) and the new Catholic Westminster Cathedral (1895–1903) as symbols of this civic tradition.

Vestiges of the time before the Middle Ages are very rare, and Geddes is left to seek guidance in much younger buildings and statues. The classical decoration of the National Liberal Club's building recalls Vitruvius, and a male statue in Parliament Square wearing a toga becomes a symbol for Virgil and Cicero. Westminster Hall recalls the "Temple of Justicia," although it lost this direct association with the move of the Law Court to Fleet Street. Remnants of Celtic times are even rarer, but Geddes still finds them. He turns a statue of Queen Boadicea into a symbol of Celtic Britain, and presents the Thames Embankment as the modern equivalent of prehistoric man's earthworks. Even Stonehenge-like ancient standing stones exist in Westminster, at least for Geddes, who recognizes them in the stone posts of an iron fence around the northern side of the Abbey.

Geddes's reading of Westminster's architecture reveals less man's work as embodied in buildings (for which Morris argued) than an interpretation of architecture as a representation of the four social types. The historical survey aims at comprehensiveness. Its goal is to identify in the urban fabric the complete Arbor Saeculorum through all its main periods. The perpetual recurrence of the social types is the *genius loci*, which Geddes believes to be embedded in historic structures and which he hopes a historical survey can unlock. London, as a town of the people, accommodates within its boundaries three centers for the other social types, although no social type is exclusive to any one of them. The City, London's financial district, represents the chiefs. Chelsea and Westminster share the role of being places for intellectuals and emotionals. It is the sacred traditions, expressed in the churches and holy structures like the standing stones, that form the *genius loci* of Westminster. Although the reading of Westminster's architecture is intended as an active step toward discerning the complete *genius loci*, ultimately, Geddes argues, the spirit of a place will unveil itself. When entering Westminster Abbey, for example, he recommends that the visitor "wait in reverence for the genius of the place to work its miracle in its own way."[23]

Geddes's idea of a *genius loci* has consequences for the city designer's work. Most notably, it is impossible to successfully plan against the spirit of a place. Each design that does not take the *genius loci* into account fails, as, according to Geddes, John Nash's plan for Regent Street failed.[24] Nash's proposal to build a "sumptuous boulevard" from Calton House to Regent's Park in the north worked against the spirit of the place by ignoring the continuous history of fairs and trade in the area that became Lower Regent Street. This traditional use began in the Middle Ages when citizens of Westminster founded a hospital dedicated to St. James. The Benedictine abbot gave some land, the later St. James's Park, and the king established an annual fair whose profit financed the hospital. King Henry VIII (1509–1547) enclosed the land as his hunting ground, replacing the hospital with a hunting lodge and later with St. James's Palace. Charles II (1660–1685) finally forbade the fair, but the spirit of the place reappeared in the form of shops and stores both in Restoration London and again in contemporary times. Nash's design, explains Geddes, achieved only "that which the *genius loci* dictated. Lower Regent Street, if you think of it symbolically, is a ceremonious broadway linking into unity the redefined luxury of Pall Mall and the commoner gaieties of Piccadilly Circus."[25] Arcades, which Nash suggested in order to improve the quality of the space, were considered detrimental to the needs of the shops in the ground floors and accordingly were enclosed by shop windows.

A city designer is not so much realizing his own ideas as expressing what is already present in the form of the spirit of the place: "There are deeds and events which cling to a place, and remain an 'unseen hand' in the ordering of its destiny."[26] City design begins by discerning the *genius loci*: "For its definite principle is that we must not too simply begin ... with fundamentals as of communications ... but above all things, seek to enter into the spirit of our city, its historic essence and continuous life."[27]

Once the city's *genius loci* is grasped, the resulting design "will thus express, stimulate and develop its highest possibility, and so deal all the more effectively with its material and fundamental needs."[28] But before the city designer becomes actively engaged in developing a plan, his role is merely a passive one: the survey of the city is a means to study, analyze, observe, and then wait for the *genius loci* to unveil itself. The design or plan, although actively prepared by a city designer, is fundamentally a disclosure: "My re-planning has not been 'designed' in the sense of patterns or inventions, but rather has become disclosed, like a solution of a chess-problem, by the close study of the board and all the pieces on it. There is no other way."[29]

### Conservative Surgery

The city designer is like the romantic artist, through whose intercession independently existing ideas find artistic expression in reality. Considered as the embodiment of a *genius loci*, an existing urban environment requires respect. Consequently, Geddes develops the concept of "conservative surgery" as an appropriate approach to work in an existing city.

Conservative surgery means amending and improving an urban quarter by minimizing the destruction of existing buildings, let alone the demolition of whole areas, for the sake of new houses and structures. Geddes's involvement in repairing and refurbishing old houses began in the Old Town of Edinburgh in 1884 with the foundation of the Edinburgh Social Union, and his subsequent move into James Court at the center of the historic town in 1886. He later recommended the use of conservative surgery while advising the municipality of Dublin between 1913 and 1914 on the improvement of housing conditions there. Some of the best examples of conservative surgery are to be found in his Indian town planning reports.

In India Geddes applied conservative surgery as an alternative to the standard methods of British municipal engineers or other members of the colonial administration. Their approach to improvement mostly involved the design of a new city quarter with a grid of streets replacing the old plan. Consequences like the expulsion of the former inhabitants, who

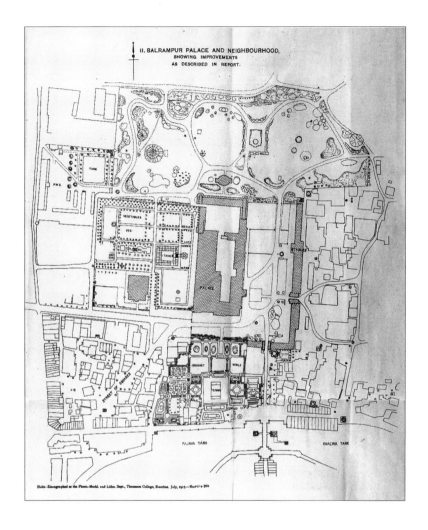

II. BALRAMPUR PALACE AND NEIGHBOURHOOD,
SHOWING IMPROVEMENTS
AS DESCRIBED IN REPORT.

FIGURE 5.3

Balrampur, Street of
Squares (at lower left),
an example of conserva-
tive surgery applied to a
city quarter, 1917.

often could not afford a dwelling in the new quarter, were normally ignored.[30] Geddes worked along different lines. In the Balrampur report, for
example, he suggests widening a narrow street running diagonally through
a neighborhood into a sequence of small squares (figure 5.3). This achieves
the intended improved access to the palace behind the neighborhood while
retaining as many of the existing houses as possible.[31] Trees lining the new
squares mark the improvement and define the borders of the new open
spaces. In the same town Geddes replanned the Tehri Bazar, a quarter south

of the palace beyond a large open water tank, again by applying conservative surgery.[32] The principles are always the same: The worst houses are taken away, and the resulting gain in open space is used to create small squares, often dominated by a temple, a tree, or other features. Trees mark the new spaces and thwart, or at least hinder, future encroachment by new building.[33]

Conservative surgery is concerned with maintaining historic urban quarters. Geddes argues that his approach is less expensive than the standard solution. In the Lahore report he points out that his ideas cost about 35,000 rupees, compared to the 65,000 rupees to be spent on the official plans. In addition his alternative saves 6¼ acres from being used to build roads upon.[34] The second advantage of conservative surgery is the prevention of social upheaval: slums do not simply migrate to those parts of a city where the targeted quarter's former inhabitants next settle, but are improved in situ. The third advantage is that conservative surgery takes the *genius loci* into account. For Lahore Geddes argues: "The existing roads and lanes are the past product of practical life, its movement and experience; and observation and common sense alike show them to be in the right directions, and therefore needing only improvements."[35]

Streets, lanes, houses, temples, in short the whole fabric of an existing city are explained as expressions of the *genius loci*. For Indian towns this *genius loci* comprises ties of antiquity, family, faith, caste, and occupation, along with the tradition of collective action among the inhabitants of a distinct urban quarter.[36] This history and form of life await renewal by the city designer, whose most pressing task is "first of all to put Heart into the community, the City. Say to revive this since plainly [it is] sleeping there; thus renewing the sense of Citizenship."[37] In Baroda, Geddes worked in *poles*, which are traditional municipal units. He stresses in his report the need to "re-cultivate" the city's *poles* "until old advantages of collectivity substantially return."[38] Geddes uses similar language in the Balrampur report, claiming that when the Tehri Bazar and other quarters are "reopen[ed] to one another, the old village life . . . will be seen to be only awaiting renewal."[39] In his Lucknow report Geddes envisions the "recovery and renewal of old-world village life, which is the vital secret of the working quarter, both for east and for west alike."[40] Explained in the symbolic language of the Notation of Life, his many references to renewing and reawakening old, traditional forms of life mean climbing onto a higher coil of the spiral of life embodied in the Arbor Saeculorum.[41]

Because of the respect conservative surgery expresses for a local culture, it provides a substantive alternative to the standard urban development policy of British colonial power. Yet while Geddes criticized the practicalities of this policy, he did not go so far as to question the imperialist framework within which it was conducted. Rather, he offered a realization of the same long-term goal: the urban redevelopment of native Indian cities, initiated and helped by the British colonial power. His solution would be cheaper and simpler than what a municipal engineer could achieve, because of the reduced number of new buildings and lesser social upheaval. Within the imperialist context, conservative surgery was not a radical political alternative but adopted the same patronizing attitude—in this case toward a whole culture rather than a particular social class—characteristic of many middle-class Victorian and Edwardian philanthropic endeavors to improve the urban environment.

Conservative surgery preserves the built heritage by adapting it to "the requirement of the present."[42] According to Geddes, historic buildings must be used in order both to keep them alive and to guarantee the city's functioning as the organ for transmitting the cultural and social heritage. For individual historic buildings, he suggests a pragmatic approach: what it is possible to keep should be kept; what obstructs needed change has to go. But each old building, independent of age, style, or period, has a potential historic value that makes it worthy of consideration. Though a building's value may not be obvious if it lacks beautiful architecture, it may still be an important historic witness as part of a larger ensemble, or as a typical representation of a specific building type.[43]

Geddes's interest is not in keeping romantic ruins for the amusement of tourists or as inspiration for artists. Instead of finding a contradiction between preserving an old, dilapidated house and raising the living conditions of its inhabitants to a modern hygienic level—which might require a choice between keeping the old or erecting a new building—Geddes seeks to achieve both at the same time:

Let us by all means cleanse, then mend, then adapt frankly to our own modern uses; and though in this process a shock may be given to the merely romantic spirit, a better and truer artistic result is reached, at any rate when with time and use the new elements again harmonise into the old.[44]

This position differs from Morris's ideas on the protection of ancient buildings. Both men see architecture as an expression of its time and civilization, and declare a return to or imitation of the past neither desirable nor possible.[45] But whereas Morris pleads for a moratorium on work on ancient buildings, Geddes suggests the opposite. He is not afraid of adding to or substantially changing buildings as long as they can be incorporated into the collection of historic architecture he seeks to create. His intention is to transform a city into an "Open-Air Museum of the Centuries—a series of surviving buildings which would have something characteristic, if not of each generation or even century, at least of each great period of culture, each great phase of social and civic life, each type and stage of national and European culture."[46]

Geddes feels that historic vestiges can even be replaced without harming their ability to carry history onward. He cites the example of a gravestone in a church in Grahamston close to Edinburgh that commemorated one Knight Graham. The stone has been "trampled dim by unthinking feet" several times since it was first placed. But it has also been continuously renewed, and therefore still reminds visitors of the knight.[47] Geddes does not object to such replacements, suggesting that he is primarily interested in the story such historical vestiges can tell, regardless of their state of authenticity.

**The Rebuilding of Crosby Hall**

In this spirit Geddes took on the project of Crosby Hall, the only remnant of a London mansion built in 1466 by Sir John Crosby. In about 1908 a bank's plan to develop the site in Bishopsgate threatened the existence of the building. According to the account of events provided by the Earl of Sandwich, who worked with Geddes on the project to save the hall, the bank decided to take the building down carefully so that it could be moved for use elsewhere.[48] Geddes was suitably interested in the structure for the story it told as "the hall of Sir Thomas More, where he wrote the 'Utopia.'"[49] Geddes

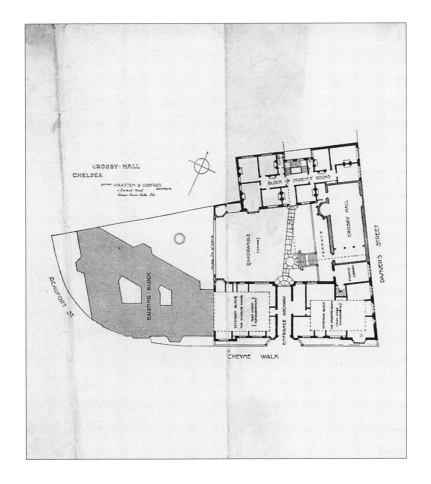

FIGURE **5.4**

Scheme for university

halls of residence at

Cheyne Walk, Chelsea,

1908.

and Sandwich could not offer money but could provide a new use for the
building. In 1903–1904 Geddes had erected a block of flats at the corner of
Beaufort Street and Cheyne Walk in Chelsea. In 1907 this block was con-
verted to an independent university hall of residence and renamed More
Hall, since it occupied space on the site of the garden of the former Beaufort
House, which Sir Thomas More had purchased in 1520 (figure 5.4).[50] The *ge-*
*nius loci* of this site was more than appropriate to establishing a university
hall of residence, for it was in this garden that Thomas More and Desiderius
Erasmus of Rotterdam had debated their ideas about education and the pursuit of knowledge.[51] Beyond this coincidence, Geddes felt his recent

initiative in reviving the *genius loci* to be the latest in a sequence of steps passing the spirit of the place from one generation to the next:

> Again this site . . . had been the favourite haunt of dreamer and Utopist ever since More's day. Here Sir Hans Sloane had practically founded that greatest of all realised Utopias of knowledge, the British Museum; here Carlyle's impassioned dreams had borne their fruit; here Turner, Rossetti, and Whistler had each revolutionised the art of his generation.[52]

To relocate Crosby Hall to Thomas More's former garden would make for a more than welcome addition to More Hall. The architect Walter Hindes Godfrey, an active member of the London Survey committee and editor of the survey's two volumes dealing with Chelsea, guided the reerection of the Hall in 1909–1910 (figure 5.5).[53] Only selected original features of the hall survived the relocation, which, according to Godfrey, required important alterations to both its structure and finishing. Other elements of the rebuilt hall, like a window and a door, were entirely new additions.[54] Geddes's contribution of Crosby Hall to the *genius loci* of Chelsea also required substantial change to its new urban setting, in particular the demolition of four houses dating from the late seventeenth and early eighteenth centuries, pulled down solely to make space for Crosby Hall.[55] Godfrey points out that some features of the demolished buildings were incorporated into the basement underneath the two stories of the rebuilt Crosby Hall. Obviously, the importance of the hall was judged to be greater than that of the ordinary townhouses—further proof that Geddes's attitude toward old buildings is respectful but determined by a pragmatism backed up by a strong conceptual idea.

Geddes grasped the rebuilding of Crosby Hall as an opportunity to contribute to Chelsea's role as the place of the intellectuals within London. He envisioned Chelsea as "the community in its cultural aspect" with his university hall, teaching facilities, and an outlook tower modeled on Edinburgh's, to be named More Tower.[56] Years earlier, in 1895, financial restraints had prevented Geddes from helping to secure Thomas Carlyle's house for the benefit of the community of Chelsea and of London.[57] With his work on More Hall and Crosby Hall, Geddes returned to Chelsea in an attempt to reawaken its *genius*

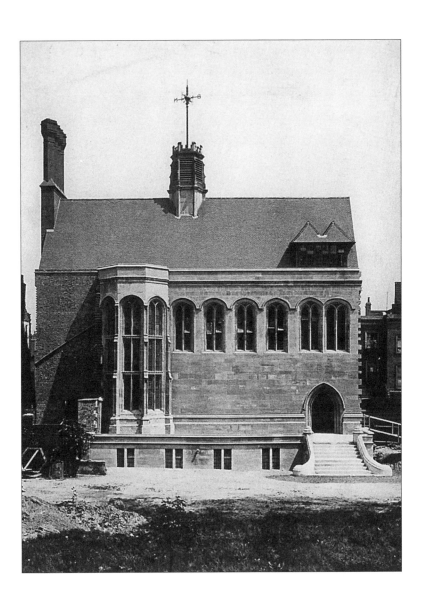

FIGURE 5.5

View of Crosby Hall from the garden after completion of the rebuilding, after 1908.

*loci* by establishing an assemblage of buildings and institutions offering places of learning, culture, and art. This move must be placed in the context of other architects' work in Chelsea, most notably that of Charles Robert Ashbee and Charles Rennie Mackintosh, both friends of Geddes. Since 1893 Ashbee had been involved in designing and building studio houses and artists' flats in Cheyne Walk. In 1912 he designed the London Fraternity House for American and Colonial Students, a large university residence complex centered around a skyscraper-style tower at Cheyne Walk.[58] Mackintosh likewise designed several artists' studios in Chelsea in the late 1910s. Both architects' projects, even if not direct responses to Geddes's initiatives, nevertheless contributed perfectly to his ideas of Chelsea as a center for intellectuals and emotionals.[59]

Crosby Hall is a prime example of Geddes's aim of saving old structures by using them. Crosby Hall was to be used as a dining hall, thus creating together with More Hall a setting comparable to the historic college architecture of Oxford and Cambridge.[60] That the new function required relocating a building was not a problem for Geddes, because of the close affinity between Crosby Hall's old owner and the *genius loci* of More Hall's site. Elsewhere Geddes writes that "for a complete historic environment one should have opportunity of actually living and studying—if possible even dramatizing—in the very dwellings of the historic past, as far as these are obtainable; that is from the middle ages onwards."[61] Crosby Hall exactly achieved this. The students lived and studied in More Hall, and dined and assembled in adjacent Crosby Hall. Additionally, in 1911 Crosby Hall accommodated the Cities and Town Planning Exhibition, affording an opportunity for both students and the public to learn and study the city both conceptual and local. In 1913 the *Masque of Ancient and Modern Learning* was prepared in Crosby Hall, although the performance of this series of *tableaux vivants* by several hundred amateur actors—conceived and directed by Geddes—took place at the Great Hall of the Imperial Institute.[62]

**Exhibitions for Learning**

Geddes's Cities and Town Planning Exhibition was introduced in chapter 4 in the context of his interest in a morphology of cities. It is equally noteworthy for what it shows of the relation between the local and the universal in city history—and for the importance of this for the city designer. Significantly enough, Geddes presented the full exhibition for the first time at Crosby Hall in 1911. As set out earlier, Geddes's exhibition combined his Edinburgh survey as displayed in the Outlook Tower and exhibits of the RIBA town planning exhibition of October 1910. In addition, the exhibition at Crosby Hall incorporated a survey of Chelsea itself, although this new section was rather small, judging from the space it shared on the ground floor with the Edinburgh survey as well as sections on cathedral cities, university cities, and industrial cities (figure 5.6). A visual presentation of the development of the city, from its origins in the region through to the contemporary garden city movement as harbinger of the incipient neotechnic age, was mainly composed with materials from the 1910 exhibition. This general history of the city was by far the largest section of the exhibition: at Crosby Hall it occupied the basement and the top floor. Plans of the exhibition in other venues show that the general history of the city is always the largest section, to which varying local surveys are attached as small appendices (figure 5.7; see also figure 4.2). These smaller local surveys required the presence of the large general section, as it provided information on the general development of cities, on the typology of cities, and on the typical problems of cities and their solutions—in short, all the background information necessary to understand the local city in a larger context and in relation to its own history. The spatial arrangement of the exhibition at various venues emphasizes this function, as the local surveys are always located toward the end of the path through the exhibition.

The bipolarity of the Cities and Town Planning Exhibition translates the idea of a morphological study of cities into a methodological tool for city design. Two aspects of the exhibition's subject are combined in this tool: the evolution of cities in general and the growth of a single city in particular. Table 5.1 shows the various locations and venues the exhibition visited from 1911. Wherever possible, Geddes added a local survey to the exhibition; the show also accompanied him to a great number of places where he was commissioned to report on the city's development. The Cities and Town Planning Exhibition was an essential planning tool for Geddes, but only in its combination of the general morphology of cities with a local historical survey. The exhibition temporarily brought the world of cities to a single city, so to speak.

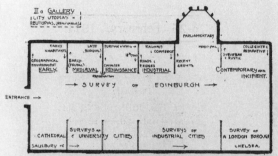

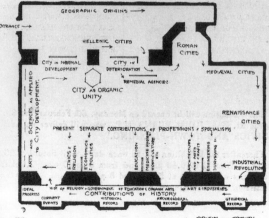

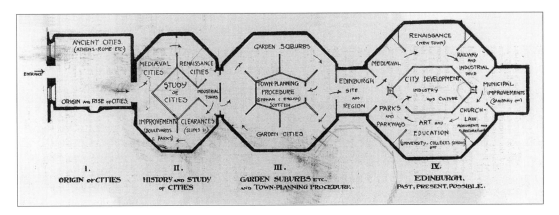

FIGURE 5.7

Cities and Town Plan-

ning Exhibition, plan of

the show in Edinburgh,

1911.

The dual structure of the Cities and Town Planning Exhibition is similar to the organization of an outlook tower as Geddes conceived it. Conceptually, both are built around the relation between the universal and the local, although the sequence between these poles is different: in the outlook tower, the local is related to the world, while in the exhibition the world of cities is related to the local.

With the outlook tower Geddes intends to make available to a community the information obtained by reading and decoding its built heritage. The outlook tower functions as the permanent storage of a city's memory within the urban fabric. Future surveys will be less demanding because they can build on the work already done, concentrating instead on adding more recent data. Geddes prescribes similar foresight to inhabitants of individual buildings by assigning to them the duty to record any fact that might be of future importance. For his student residence halls in Edinburgh's Old Town, for example, he instructs that "a Liber Albus [white book] should be instituted for each house to include photographs of the residents for the year, and to accumulate also all that interests the house and its old residents."[63]

An outlook tower is more than a local history museum, however; it is, as Geddes calls it, an "Index Museum to the world."[64] The local information accumulated through a survey and stored in an outlook tower relates to the world in two ways. First, the lower floors of the tower contain exhibits relevant to the themes of each of the upper floors, thus inviting

| DATES | VENUE | CITY DESIGN REPORTS |
| --- | --- | --- |
| 10–22 OCTOBER 1910 | London, Royal Academy, during Inernational Town Planning Exhibition and Conference (partial materials) | No, but Geddes contributed the Edinburgh survey to the exhibition |
| 6–25 FEBRUARY 1911 | Chelsea, Crosby Hall (first full exhibition) | Yes, exhibition was part of efforts to establish More's garden and Crosby Hall as intellectual center of London |
| 13 MARCH– 1 APRIL 1911 | Edinburgh, Royal Scottish Academy | No, but exhibition was essential to Geddes's renewal work in Edinburgh's Old Town |
| 24 MAY–7 JUNE 1911 | Dublin, Simmondscourt Hall of Royal Dublin Society | No |
| 24 JULY–2 AUGUST 1911 | Belfast, Ulster Halls, during Health Exhibition and Congress of Sanitary Institute | No |
| 27 JULY–1 AUGUST 1913 | Ghent, Belgium, during Exposition Internationale and International Congress of Town Planning and Organisation of City Life; *Grand Prix* awarded | No |
| 1914 | Dublin, Linen Hall | No, but exhibition was shown in preparation of a town planning competition |
| 23 OCTOBER 1914 | exhibition destroyed in war; friends of Geddes later assemble a new exhibition | |
| 18 JANUARY–? 1915 | Madras, Senate Hall of Madras University | Yes |
| OCTOBER–NOVEMBER 1915 | Calcutta, Town Hall | Yes |

TABLE 5.1

Venues for the Cities and Town Planning Exhibition and accompanying city design reports.

| DATES | VENUE | CITY DESIGN REPORTS |
|---|---|---|
| DECEMBER 1915– JANUARY 1916 | Nagpur, Craddock Market | Yes |
| 25 JANUARY– 18 MARCH 1916 | Lucknow, Kaiserbagh | Yes |
| 11 JUNE–? 1916 | Paris, selection of exhibition shown at Exposition de la Ville Reconstituée | No, but exhibition was shown in preparation for the reconstruction of Belgium |
| 1918 | Bombay, Royal Institute of Science | No, permanent display as teaching tool in connection with Geddes's chair in sociology and civics |
| 24 SEPTEMBER– 11 OCTOBER 1920 | Jerusalem, Boys' School | Yes |

comparisons between upper and lower stories, between the local and the universal. Second, each artifact or exhibit derived from the local survey refers not only to its own source or locality but to all similar things elsewhere. An index museum presents universal classes of things and facts by displaying locally generated or found exhibits of these classes. In his report for the city of Indore, Geddes elucidates the museological concept by writing that the "Type Museum" should relate large regional collections to a "small but equally chosen set of Type-collections, thus lucidly summarising the essentials of our knowledge . . . throughout the great world."[65]

Because of their dual function as local memory storage for a city and as a city's link to the larger world, outlook towers feature prominently in Geddes's various city design reports. Usually they are accompanied by additional museum buildings adjacent to the tower. Regardless of the proposed size of an outlook tower and museum complex—for New York City Frank Mears and Geddes designed a skyscraper for this purpose (figure 5.8)—the exhibits not only illuminate characteristics of the local city but also exemplify similar characteristics in other cities. They are a collection of *types* of things and information.

**Recapitulation and Recollection**

Trained as a biologist with an emphasis on botany, and with a keen interest in evolution and morphology, Geddes habitually considers his subject matters as a collection of classifiable types. Each single plant represents not only itself but also its species and the evolution of that species; knowledge about a specific plant is at the same time a reference to the species. Geddes applies this same mode of thinking to other areas, for example to the products he saw during the International Exhibition of Industry, Science and Art in Edinburgh in 1886. He describes the exhibition as "a central museum of industry" which illustrates both the current level of production and the achieved social progress. Problematic for him is that the exhibition emphasizes wealth and quantitative success, whereas it should be "a true museum . . . of real material and social progress in the immediate past, and a school . . . of these in the immediate future." Geddes suggests organizing future industrial exhibitions according to types of labor and products, so that citizens could gain the maximum educational benefit from them. Just as individual plants can offer insight into the evolution of a species, so individual industrial, artistic, and scientifically developed products can offer insight into the "general civilisation of [their] place and time."[66]

The conceptual structures behind an outlook tower and the Cities and Town Planning Exhibition are two more applications of the same idea. By analogy, the universal phenomenon of cities or a group of exhibits in an outlook tower can be considered as representing a species; to exhibit one is to exhibit the other. This correlation not only provides a useful analogy for understanding the concepts of Geddes's museological ideas; it also suggests the ultimate reason why he places such a strong emphasis on the importance of history and historic buildings for city design. Other contemporary town planners and architects, although not denying the importance of history for their own work, do not go as far as Geddes is prepared to. Raymond Unwin, for example, appreciates Geddes's method of the historical survey but warns that "it may not always be practicable to carry the survey to the extent suggested by him."[67]

While Geddes taught at Edinburgh University during the early 1880s, he was in contact with the German biologist Ernst Haeckel. John Arthur Thomson, one of Geddes's students and later his friend, even traveled to Jena University in 1882 to continue his studies under Haeckel.[68] Haeckel was among the leading German biologists supporting and developing Darwin's theory of evolution. In 1866 he published his *General Morphology of Organisms,* in which he introduced the terms "phylogeny" and "ontogeny" into the biological vocabulary. Phylogeny refers to the evolution of a species, ontogeny to the development of an individual member of that species. Haeckel formulated a causal connection between the two, which he later called the "biogenetic basic law":

> Ontogeny is the short and fast recapitulation of phylogeny, caused by the physiological functions of heredity (reproduction) and adaptation (nutrition).[69]

This law, translated to the field of city design, dictates that in order to understand the development of a city (ontogeny), a comparison with the evolution of cities (phylogeny) is required. By analogy with Haeckel's law, a city can only produce a new stage of growth by repeating the evolution of cities as such. This is made possible, for example, through the use of the Cities and Town Planning Exhibition, which offers the evolution of cities at exactly the moment when a specific city is preparing to enter a new phase of its life by commissioning a new plan or town planning report.

But the new phase of a city's life has to be realized by its citizens. Again, the application of Haeckel's biogenetic basic law is helpful. Each citizen is obliged to repeat in his own life the evolution of the larger community, or city, before he can contribute actively to the new phase of the city's life. He can fulfill this obligation conveniently by studying the exhibits in the outlook tower and the museums complex, by participating in the historical and general survey, or by visiting the Cities and Town Planning Exhibition. Citizens, especially adolescents, Geddes writes, have a "birthright in the social and Civic inheritance."[70] To be born in a city does not automatically bestow citizenship, however; to become a citizen requires one to recapitulate the history of one's city, whether of birth or of residence.

In his city design report for the town of Dunfermline, Geddes explicitly confirms the application of Haeckel's law to his own approach to town planning. In connection with an open-air museum of historic "primitive settlements" in Scotland, Geddes writes: "Again, since rapidly to recapitulate the main phases of the past is nature's way of passing beyond these, even of acquiring the impetus for passing in turn the present phase, it may well also be ours."[71] The idea of recapitulation of a town's history has consequences for the work of every town planner, architect, and city designer. Reading history directly from the city's urban fabric is the best way to learn about and make use of the inheritance it embodies. Geddes's survey of Westminster showed that, with some imagination, remnants of every historical period can be traced, which is important for the ontogenetic recapitulation. But London or Edinburgh are existing cities where history is available for recapitulation in the form of historic buildings. What if a city designer plans for an entirely new city not attached to an existing one? Here also, recapitulation is the basis for action. In his entry on morphology for the *Encyclopaedia Britannica*, Geddes rhetorically compares the morphological idea of the *Urpflanze* with a Platonic idea. By the same token, Haeckel's recapitulation and Platonic recollection can also be brought together. In Plato's *Meno*, Socrates's slave boy is made to believe that in his responses to his master's questions he has discovered something completely new, although his answers are in fact the recollection of something age-old or eternal. In the essay on *Industrial Exhibitions* in which Geddes first develops the concept of an index museum, he also makes the deeply conservative statement that nothing truly new can ever be found, as everything believed to be new is only a development of something that already exists.[72] The same applies to city design. As soon as a city designer embarks on his task, he finds himself within a historical framework where there is no other basis for his work than that provided by history and historic cities. "Hence," writes Geddes, each page of history is a palimpsest. Hence our modern town, even when yesterday but prairie, was no mere vacant site, but was at once enriched and encumbered by the surviving traditions of the past; so that even its new buildings are for the most part but vacant shells of past art.[73]

Thus Geddes's fascination with local and regional history went well beyond the contemporary interest in history as a theme for artistic expression. He wanted to make it possible for citizens to learn about their city's history for two distinct reasons. The city considered as an organism has to recapitulate in its own life the history of its "species," in order to advance to another stage of growth. Similarly, its citizens must recollect the earlier stages of their city's life if they want to participate in creating the next stage. Without looking back, forward-looking city design is impossible.

This constant view into the past is reminiscent of what Friedrich Nietzsche calls antiquarian history. Its representative—the antiquarian historian—looks back in time thankfully as his roots lie in that past, and cares for everything old in order to conserve these things for the benefit of coming generations. Furthermore, writes Nietzsche, "the history of his town becomes the history of himself."

> And so, with his "we," he surveys the marvellous individual life of the past and identifies himself with the spirit of the house, the family and the city. He greets the soul of his people from afar as his own, across the dim and troubled centuries: his gifts and his virtues lie in such power of feeling and divination ... his instinctive correctness in reading the scribbled past, and understanding at once its palimpsests—nay, its polypsests.[74]

The identification between the "I," the soul of an individual, and the "we," the soul of a collective, happens according to Nietzsche because the individual's soul transmigrates into things old and makes them its habitat.

Geddes's obsession with historic buildings and their meaning tends toward a similar effect. Yet to root the city in history, and vice versa, does not guarantee momentary or even lasting identification between the contemporary I and the historical we, between the citizen and the city. The historical survey on Geddes's terms requires a deliberate participation by citizens, whose task it is to read the historic buildings. To achieve a lasting identification between the I and the we, it is necessary to bring the city's spirit to the real center—physically and mentally—of the contemporary city. This is what Geddes refers to as the spiritual aspect of cities, which is the topic of the next two chapters.

City Designs, each a New Jerusalem . . . depend for their
character not upon mere breadth of road, but rather upon its
direction, and not upon the mere magnitude and material
purpose of edifices, but upon their ideals.

Patrick Geddes, *Women, the Census, and the Possibilities of the
Future*

# The Metaphysical Imperative in Urban Design around 1900

One characteristic of fin-de-siècle Western cultures was their deep concern with religiosity and spirituality, which forms a remarkable contrast to the rationality dominating the economic and scientific progress of late nineteenth-century societies. Nietzsche's programmatic insight of the death of God did not result in the demise of religion. Rather, while traditional beliefs like Catholicism and Protestantism faced a steady crisis of legitimacy, other forms of religion and pseudo-religion, such as theosophy, anthroposophy, Buddhism, spiritualism, monism, and Tolstoyan Christianity, continued to find supporters and followers, especially within the Europe-wide phenomenon of the life reform movement.[1] Even notions of a people, nation, race, culture, myth, and art became foci of quasi-religious worship and hopes of redemption.

In their study of culture around 1900 in the German-speaking countries, Richard Hamann and Jost Hermand argue that toward the end of the last century idealism emerged as the dominating category in the intellectual debate.[2] In the preceding decades naturalism, which considered man as a question of matter and milieu, and impressionism, for which human beings were an assembly of subjective and personal impressions, had been the points of reference for inquiries into the state of society, art, and culture. In opposition to these ways of thinking, idealism aimed at firmly embedding human beings and society in a structure of moral and ethical values.

The increasing idealism of the time was a reaction against the contemporary capitalist society, with its materialist, positivist, and relativist tendencies. The idealistic approach provided a priori concepts for both the perception of present reality and future developments. According to Hamann and Hermand, idealism determined, for example, the general debate about values in society but likewise a renewed interest in Plato. In science, the appreciation of synthesizing approaches instead of specialized studies expressed a similar idealistic stance. The authors detect other examples of an idealist influence in the rise of educational theories applied to school education and university reforms, or in attempts by historians to describe recurring or eternal phenomena instead of singular historical events. The aim was always to provide holistic concepts of the world, life, art, science, or any other subject matter, to define universally valid ethical and moral guidelines for subjective actions and thoughts.[3] But the concepts thus offered were as diversified as the societies against which they were directed. Hamann and Hermand summarize the attempts to provide new metaphysical concepts for every aspect of human life thus: "With a real 'idealistic' boldness, private ideas about values became presented as ideals that ought to be realized."[4]

## Building the Ideal Community

The idea of community was one point around which proposals for an improved social order crystallized. Across all differences in political conviction, nationality, and belief, the idea of community caught the imagination as a countermodel against contemporary states or cities. Community and society were the opposing poles between which the criticism of contemporary societies moved during the last decades of the nineteenth century, a confrontation that goes back to the German sociologist Ferdinand Tönnies, whose well-known book *Community and Society* was published in 1887.[5]

Tönnies deals with social relations between human beings and their changes during history. He distinguishes two basic types of human associations, which he calls community (*Gemeinschaft*) and society (*Gesellschaft*). The two are contrasted by the different factors that motivate their existence. Causes extraneous to the human association drive the creation of a society, whose members come together in order to achieve mutually agreed ends. A community emerges from within, from the shared awareness of an association as a social entity existing beyond, though not totally independent of, both its members and their endeavors to ensure the community's future.[6] Both types of association are based on shared values, but in a community the values exist independently of the community's members, whereas in a society the relevant values are invented and agreed on by individuals.[7]

Tönnies aimed to provide a theory of social change throughout human history from community toward society, without strictly juxtaposing the two types of associations. Other authors, however, soon used the two terms to classify contemporary reality or to describe a typology of settlements.[8] Tönnies's own writings fostered the latter application in particular, for he located community in historic villages and smaller towns, while the modern city was an example of society. For Tönnies the reference to the past indicated merely the starting point of a historical development, but for others it could serve to indicate both an idealized time that had once existed and a model for a better future. Tönnies's emphasis on values or ideas as an a priori condition for the existence of a community particularly appealed to the contemporary urge to provide society with new metaphysical ideas in order to give a new central basis for its renewal.

Among the a priori concepts around which turn-of-the-century communitarian visions evolved were religious and sectarian beliefs, economic theories suggesting solutions to the town-country conflict, and philanthropic endeavors to bridge the class conflict. Similar ideas were spawned by the wish to return to nature, to a simpler way of life, or to the lost physical features of the life of earlier generations, like villages or small towns. On a more abstract, sociological level, the recovery of the family and the redefinition of town inhabitants as burghers comparable to those of medieval towns, or as citizens as in a Greek *polis*, were possible foci of communitarian thought. Common to many of these were ideas of the equality, real or assumed, of the community members, and a unity centered around a shared idea of life. Among the newly founded communities were such diverse examples as Charles Robert Ashbee's arts and crafts workshop the Guild of Handicraft, in the village of Chipping Campden, England, or the Neue Gemeinschaft, a group of artists, anarchists, and literati seeking a simpler life in a suburb of Berlin.[9] One of the more famous communities was Monte Verità in Ascona, Switzerland. Since the last third of the nineteenth century a colorful mixture of anarchists, vegetarians, spiritualists, theosophists, and followers of other reform ideas settled there and in nearby Locarno, attracted by the allegedly unique spiritual atmosphere of the site.[10]

Turn-of-the-century art and architecture reflect the growing interest in metaphysical and in communitarian ideas, a reflection that culminates in the German-speaking countries in the search for a *Stilkunst*. Earlier in the nineteenth century, historicist art and architecture were already concerned with the question of style. But the question then was "What historical style, for which building task and type?"[11] The notion of style changes toward the end of the century, when style develops into a synonym for an attitude to life. Peter Behrens explains the different meaning in his pamphlet *Feste des Lebens und der Kunst,* where he defines style as "the symbol of the entire condition of a time, of its whole attitude to life."[12]

The British arts and crafts movement is among the first of a series of movements in European art and architecture insisting on the artist's comprehensive responsibility for all aspects of the human environment and life. Already in 1881 William Morris defines the task of architecture, the union of the arts, as the shaping of the whole face of the earth according to the needs of mankind, the only exception being very isolated areas of the deserts. This task is an imperative, for if mankind doesn't engage in it, Morris concludes, the coming generations will inherit an earth of considerably less worth than the one the contemporary generation inherited.[13] The artistic results of this holistic claim should improve the quality of life and thus generate a new attitude toward it. Similarly, Art Nouveau in the French-speaking countries, Secession in Austria-Hungary, Jugendstil and later the Bauhaus in Germany are comparable, despite differences in artistic means, in their comprehensive claim to provide a style for life.

Different areas of life are gradually enclosed in ever-widening circles of artistic interventions. Hermann Muthesius paraphrases this tendency with the formula "from sofa cushion to town planning."[14] What began in two-dimensional art forms like drawing or painting found its continuation in the designs of basic commodities, interiors of rooms, plans for houses, suburbs, and colonies, and led finally to schemes for whole cities. "We must build a city, a whole city," the Austrian architect Joseph Maria Olbrich proclaims in 1898 on the occasion of the opening of the first Secession exhibition at Vienna. He continues:

> Anything less would be pointless. . . . We shall create a world. . . . From the overall design down to the last detail, all governed by the same spirit, the streets and the gardens and the palaces and the cottages and the tables and the armchairs and the lamps and the spoons, all expressions of the same sensibility, and in the middle, like a temple in a sacred grove, a house of labor, both artists' studio and craftsmen's workshop, where the artist will always have the reassuring and ordering crafts, and the craftsman the liberating and purifying arts about him, until the two finally merge, as it were, into a single person.[15]

Architectural schemes for communities and ideal cities are often mergers of the sociological concept of community with the assumption that a comprehensively designed environment would bring about change in a society. According to art historian Helen Rosenau, ideal cities emphasize personal happiness but always under the umbrella of a community that is responsible for itself and the well-being of the individual. Schemes for ideal cities and communities fuse a social consciousness, religiously or secularly inspired, with a design concept characterized by "artistic unity."[16]

Groups attempting to create ideal communities rarely managed to build their own physical environment. Economic restraints forced many to make use of existing buildings; others were prevented from any building work by their short existence. Occasionally, communities existed without an ideal plan as a unifying feature. In Monte Verità the mixture of different groups, often hostile to each other, made it impossible to conceive and implement a coherent plan for the whole area. This does not mean that the question of the physical environment and the architecture of the housing was neglected. In the case of Monte Verità the hut—a symbol of a simple life close to nature—became the preferred ideal dwelling for members of the larger community, regardless of their personal affiliations.[17]

For other community ideas, however, it was extremely important to match the social vision with an architectural one. Architectural designs could help gather support, idealistic and financial, for the realization of the schemes. Images of James Silk Buckingham's city Victoria (1849) or Robert Owen's Villages of Unity and Mutual Co-operation (1817) are visual promises of the immediate betterment of life for the members of the group. Still, reality was different. Owen's village of New Lanark in Scotland does not resemble the ideal scheme, and Buckingham's Victoria remained a mere dream. The Mathildenhöhe in Darmstadt is one of the rare examples where the idea for an ideal community became reality (figure 6.1). Joseph Maria Olbrich was invited by the grand duke of Hesse in Germany, Ernst Ludwig, to design this artists' colony in 1899, only a year after he declared the building of a new city to be his ultimate aim. The intention of the grand duke in sponsoring the colony was to renew the arts and to give a fresh impulse to local trade and commerce. Between 1899 and 1901 Olbrich designed houses for six artists; a seventh member of the group, Peter Behrens, was responsible for his own house.

The center of the colony is the Ernst Ludwig House, likewise designed by Olbrich, which accommodates artists' studios and exhibition spaces (figure 6.2).[18] There the arts and crafts became physically united. This building is a realization of the "house of labor," the center of the coherently designed city Olbrich described at the opening of the Secession exhibition in 1898. Besides being the artists' colony's functional center, the Ernst Ludwig House plays a second important role as the community's metaphysical center. The unification of the arts and crafts is not a mere rational, economic demand but aims to redeem contemporary life from the deadening consequences of industrial and mechanical production. Hence Olbrich's comparison in his Secession speech of the "house of labor" with a temple in a scared grove. The Ernst Ludwig House is a temple of creation for the Mathildenhöhe, a place where a new attitude to life can be conceived.

While architectural unity offers advantages for an ideal community or city scheme, absolutely necessary is a metaphysical center, which is also often though not necessarily the geographical center of the scheme. In New Lanark, the New Institution for the Formation of Character (1809–1813) provides such a center. In Darmstadt, the Ernst Ludwig House is the temple of the Mathildenhöhe. Ebenezer Howard insists in his garden city concept on a central park as a symbol for a closer contact with nature; the public build-

FIGURE 6.1

Site plan of the artists'
colony at Mathilden-
höhe, Darmstadt,
1899–1901, by Joseph
Maria Olbrich.

ings in this park additionally embody ideas of cooperation and mutual aid. A
building or a group of buildings as a metaphysical center allows one to define an ideal community visually, even if the overall settlement lacks aesthetic unity. The center as a place for group activities of any kind makes the
participating individual experience himself as a member of this group.

Thus the social consciousness which, as Rosenau emphasizes, un-
derpins ideal city schemes can materialize itself in either (or both) of two

ways: with a perfect architecturally and artistically unified environment or with a metaphysical city center, a building or ensemble of buildings that expresses the ideas behind the city or community. Depending on its creator, the metaphysical center could become the most important, defining element of an ideal city, guaranteeing the community's perfect character above and beyond any environmental improvement. The metaphysical center can safeguard the character of the ideal city by the very fact that it addresses something other (usually the souls of city and inhabitants) than mere material considerations. This potential power of a metaphysical center has consequences for ideal city schemes but also for the approaches of architects and social reformers to existing cities.

Ideal community schemes tend to abandon existing cities in favor of locations closer to nature, in the countryside or at least at the fringe of existing cities. But the emphasis many of these schemes place on the metaphysical center also opens a way to redirect their underlying reform ideas into existing cities. The sheer size of many existing cities was a serious obstacle to remodeling them along ideal lines comparable to the Mathildenhöhe. Initiatives like the City Beautiful movement, which originated in Chicago in the 1890s, or the Greater Berlin competition from 1910 often strove for the large-scale rebuilding of existing cities. Nevertheless, successful implementations of such schemes were rare. The creation of new cities or of large town extensions like that of Barcelona by Cerdà were the exception. More often, ideal plans for new and old cities remained unrealized or were implemented only partially, usually for political and economic reasons. Despite several decades of planning efforts and urban design schemes, existing cities continued to present neither a real nor an ideal order. As late as 1920 the British arts and crafts architect William Richard Lethaby still insists: "A civilized life cannot be lived in undisciplined towns."[19] But if the urban environment cannot be civilized, which means totally rebuilt in an architecturally unified, disciplined manner, the implementation of a metaphysical center can at least provide an idea of what the city should be. Before we examine typical attempts by architects to reorder existing cities by implementing a metaphysical center—for which the terms temple and temple-like are here employed—the urge around 1900 among architects to design and erect religious and secular temples has to be looked at.

**Temple Ideas around 1900**

W. R. Lethaby's book *Architecture, Mysticism and Myth* was one of the first attempts in that era to examine the ability of architecture to express philosophical, psychological, and other ideas.[20] Reacting against the prevalent historicism of the nineteenth century, which equated architecture with questions of style or aesthetics, Lethaby is interested in exploring "the purposes behind structure and form which may be called the esoteric principles of architecture."[21] Such esoteric principles are the dividing line between mere buildings and architecture proper: buildings are simply expression of form, while architecture concerns the thought behind the form. "Architecture, then," Lethaby continues, "interpenetrates building, not for satisfaction of the simple needs of the body, but the complex ones of the intellect."[22] Next to the needs of men, and the necessities arising from structure and material, nature determines the form of architecture, where "nature" refers to "the known and imagined facts of the universe." Declaring all artistic form to be imitation of nature, respectively the universe, Lethaby names the connection between nature and architecture as the theme of his book.[23] One type of building in particular, the temple, catches his interest; he writes that "we shall find that the intention of the temple (speaking of the temple *idea*, as we understand it) was to set up a local reduplication of the temple not made with hands, the World Temple itself—a sort of model to scale."[24]

The temple as a built expression of man's understanding of the universe is for Lethaby not simply a historical phenomenon. Although he analyzes historical buildings and myths, his concern is with future art and architecture. Architecture, if it wants to exercise influence, needs a new symbolism that is immediately comprehensible to everybody.[25] Though still based on ideas of nature, man, order, and beauty, this symbolism would no longer spread mystery and terror, as in historic temples, but aim at aiding and training life.[26]

The appeal to beauty as a means of improving life recalls Lethaby's roots in the arts and crafts movement. But the insistence on the need for a new symbolism emphasizes a distinctive idealistic-metaphysical aspect in his thinking. The enthusiastic reception of Lethaby's book shows that it responded to a widespread concern among artists and architects. Part of its success stems from its provision of a theoretical-historical analysis, to the effect that mankind has always needed to express its understanding of the macrocosm in the microcosm of a temple. More importantly, Lethaby's book allows for the conclusion that a new symbolism and eventually a new temple building can bring about a reform of life and society by providing new ideals for both—a reversal of the naturalistic relation between the material basis of a society and its subsequent expression in a temple or church.

One finds numerous examples of secular temples and cult buildings in nineteenth-century architecture. The art historian Antje von Graevenitz dates the emergence of this phenomenon to the second half of the eighteenth century, when temple ideas become popular as a "mystical pendant to the Enlightenment."[27] In the aftermath of the French Revolution, everywhere in France temple-like buildings and structures, for example holy mountains (occasionally placed in churches), trees of freedom, and parks of virtues, celebrated this most ambitious attempt to create a new ideal society.[28] In 1900 the German art historian Cornelius Gurlitt compiled a list of the most important temple projects of the nineteenth century, a list that included Karl Friedrich Schinkel's Altes Museum (1823–1830) in Berlin, the national monument Walhalla (1830–1842) in southern Germany and the Befreiungshalle (1842–1863) in Kelheim, both by Leo von Klenze, Richard Wagner's Festspielhaus (1872–1875) in Bayreuth, designed in cooperation with Otto Brueckwald, Otto Wagner's plans for an academy of art (Artibus project, 1880), and finally Olbrich's House for the Secession in Vienna (1898).[29]

But there is an important difference between the earlier and the later temple ideas. Many projects of the eighteenth century and the early nineteenth century are artistic reactions to changes in society or to important discoveries in science. Architects dedicated buildings to the new ideologies and ideas influencing life and society. These projects are cultural and architectural responses to foregoing social and scientific changes. The later projects, on the other hand, show the same reversal of the relationship between the material basis of a society and its ideal or metaphysical expression as already observed in Lethaby: change, it is thought, can be brought about by purely cultural means. The Bayreuth Festspielhaus and Otto Wagner's and Olbrich's projects are not so much artistic responses to earlier change but artistic anticipation of an ideal future condition.

The enduring criticism of the state of society, architecture, and art in the decades flanking 1900 led to a surge in the number and variety of temple projects intended as vehicles to bring about a renewal of architecture and society. Architects, who mainly conceived these schemes, acquired the role of instigators of social and artistic change. They perceived their own position in society as similar to that of a priest of old, as the Dutch architect K. P. C. de Bazel explains in his essay "Bouwkunst" from 1898. The task of the architect-priest, de Bazel writes, is "to present the divine order, to form a relation between earth and heaven, between the material nature of man and his spiritual being." To achieve this, it is necessary to erect "a temple, in which the lost son can find again his spiritual father, a house to consummate the marriage between the soul and its heavenly bridegroom."[30]

Against this background, the wave of temple projects that began in the late nineteenth century and lasted well into the second decade of the twentieth becomes understandable. These temple designs no longer embody a current ideal of society but a wide spectrum of potential ideals, presenting individual beliefs held by single architects or small groups of adepts of various convictions, and the almost desperate search for any faith. Common to all of them is a dream of a different and better life, although the way to achieve this depends entirely on the individual architect's or artist's preference. Despite this variety in form and content, it is possible to distinguish broad themes among the temple designs.

Among the many schemes, of which table 6.1 gives a selective overview, one finds, for example, a Monument for Nietzsche (1900), based on an archaic circular temple (figure 6.3), and a Temple of the Holy Grail (1900), both designed by the German architect Fritz Schumacher.[31] Whereas the first project expresses the widespread interest of Schumacher's generation in Nietzsche's philosophy and cultural criticism, the latter is important for its reference to the search for the Holy Grail, particularly popular in the aftermath of Richard Wagner's opera *Parsifal* (1882). Schumacher later also applies the monumental architectural style of the sketches to other buildings, among them the crematorium in Dresden-Tolkewitz from 1908–1911 (figure 6.4). The crematorium—a temple of death—is the counterpart to the Monument for Nietzsche—a temple of life. Both together celebrate the cycle of life and the immortality of all matter. To resolve the dichotomy of life and death with interchangeable temple projects is a constant feature of many similar designs by other architects. The various temples designed from 1892 onward by the German artist Fidus (Hugo Höppner) illustrate another popular theme. Even if the actual purposes of the projects (such as Temples of the Earth, of Theosophy, of Nudism, of Great Unity, of Dance, of Fire, and of Music) are left ill defined, they all propagate an archaic veneration of Mother Earth and Nature.[32] From there it is only a small step, at least for Fidus, to becoming a staunch supporter of a blood and soil ideology that later nurtured German National Socialism.

Cult buildings are also an important theme for Viennese architects around 1900. They particularly elaborated temples of the arts, of which one of the earliest representatives is the exhibition building for the Secession in Vienna by Joseph Maria Olbrich (figure 6.5). This design—a cube crowned by a dome—provides also a general model for other temple

FIGURE 6.3

Temple of life: Monu-

ment for Nietzsche,

1898–1900, by Fritz

Schumacher.

| | |
|---|---|
| 1875 | Richard Wagner: Festspielhaus, Bayreuth |
| 1886 | Hermann Obrist: vision of an ideal city with temples in the mountains |
| 1890–1893 | Herbert P. Horne: Chapel of Ascension, London, built |
| 1891 | Charles Harrison Townsend: Bishopsgate Institute, London, built |
| 1895, 1901 | Fidus: Temple of the Earth |
| 1895 | Hermann Obrist: monuments on mountaintops |
| 1896 | William Richard Lethaby: sacred way for central London |
| 1896 | Charles Harrison Townsend: Whitechapel Gallery, London, first design |
| 1896–1901 | Charles Harrison Townsend: Horniman Museum, London, built |
| 1898 | Joseph Maria Olbrich: House for the Secession, Vienna, built |
| 1898 | Fritz Schumacher: *Studien* including Monument for Nietzsche and Temple of the Holy Grail |
| 1899–1901 | Charles Harrison Townsend: Whitechapel Gallery, London, built |
| 1900 | Joseph Maria Olbrich: Ernst Ludwig House, Darmstadt, built |
| 1902 | Alois Bastl: Palace for Societies of Occult Sciences |
| 1902 | Wenzel Hablik: temple on mountaintops |
| 1902 | Fidus: Temple of Music |
| 1903 | Wenzel Hablik: Crystal Palace |
| 1907 | François Garas: Temple à la Vie, Temple à la Mort, Temple à la Pensée |
| 1907–1908 | Hendrik Petrus Berlage: Beethovenhuis, Bloemendaal |
| 1908–1911 | Fritz Schumacher: crematorium, Dresden-Tolkewitz |
| 1910 | Charles Harrison Townsend: extension to the Horniman Museum, London, built |
| 1911 | Rudolf Steiner: Johannesbau, Munich-Schwabing |
| 1913 | Edwin Landseer Lutyens: Theosophy Society headquarters, London |

TABLE 6.1
Secular and quasi-religious temple projects, 1880s to 1920s.

| | |
|---|---|
| 1913–1914 | Rudolf Steiner: Goetheanum I, Dornach, built |
| 1914 | Wenzel Hablik: *Sketch for a Display Temple as a Monument of a City* |
| 1914 | Hermann Obrist: model of a mountain church |
| 1914 | Bruno Taut: glass house at Werkbund exhibition, Cologne, built |
| 1915 | Hendrik Petrus Berlage: Pantheon of Humanity |
| 1916 | Henry Wilson: annual Arts and Crafts Exhibition, conceived as a temple of the city, London, built |
| 1917 | Charles Robert Ashbee: arts and crafts center for a city |
| 1919 | Lyonel Feininger: cathedral on first Bauhaus manifesto |
| 1919 | Hans and Wassili Luckhardt: Monument an die Freude |
| 1919 | Hans Poelzig: Große Schaupielhaus Salzburg |
| 1919 | Hans Scharoun: Volkshaus |
| 1919 | Bruno Taut: *Die Stadtkrone, Alpine Architektur* |
| 1919–1920 | Bruno Taut: Folkwang Schule, project for Hagen |
| 1920 | Competition for Hygiene Museum, Dresden |
| 1921 | Frederick van Eeden: City of Light with a temple at the center |
| 1923 | Rudolf Steiner: Goetheanum II, Dornach, built |

FIGURE 6.4

Temple of death: crema-
torium in Dresden-
Tolkewitz, 1908, by
Fritz Schumacher.

FIGURE 6.5

Temple of the arts:
exhibition building for
the Vienna Secession,
1898, by Joseph Maria
Olbrich.

FIGURE 6.6

Temple of death: project
for a cemetery church,
1901, by Otto Schönthal.

projects dedicated either to traditional religion or to a vague notion of religiosity. Otto Wagner's church of St. Leopold, Steinhof, Vienna (1903–1907),
is inspired by Olbrich's model, as are projects by some of Wagner's pupils,
for example Otto Schönthal's project for a cemetery church (1901; figure
6.6). Alois Bastl, a lesser-known student of Wagner, transfers the motif into
a Palace for Societies of Occult Sciences (1902; figure 6.7), thereby making
a connection between the Viennese projects and their more spiritually ori-
ented counterparts like those by Fidus.[33]

Representative of a different strand of temple ideas is a tripartite
scheme by the French architect François Garas.[34] It represents an example
of what can be called temples of synthesis, for it unites several ideas into a
small group of buildings. (Geddes stressed this aspect when he mentioned
Garas's temple ideas in *Cities in Evolution*.)[35] Garas's scheme consists of a
Temple à la Vie, a Temple à la Mort, and a Temple à la Pensée.[36] The author's
intention is to overcome the finite nature of human life, confined to the cycle
from birth to death, and arrive on a level of eternal thought.[37] This aim embraces both the traditional Christian concept of a transcendental, eternal life
after death and a more secular philosophical understanding of an eternal
idea. Garas claims that he conceived the Temple à la Pensée intuitively while
listening in isolation to the complete oeuvre of Beethoven; therefore he dedicates this temple to the composer. Nonetheless, as Garas explains, the temple is not a transformation of Beethoven's music into architecture but a
parallel concept of the eternal idea only triggered by the music.[38] Accordingly, Garas's temple should instigate similar experiences in other people.

FIGURE 6.7

Project for a Palace for
Societies of Occult Sci-
ences, Paris, 1902, by
Alois Bastl.

Whereas the Temple à la Vie and Temple à la Mort are only described vaguely, Garras published a detailed description of the Temple à la
Pensée and also produced a model (figure 6.8).[39] The model shows a central
domed temple surrounded by smaller domes and an adjacent tower located
on a mountaintop; the complex actually grows out of the rock. The basic
composition reminds one of traditional churches consisting of a nave with
an adjacent tower. The upward-shooting tower is Garas's visualization of a
sudden thought. The approach to the temple symbolizes the evolution of
this thought. A visitor to the temple, climbing the steps leading to the entrance, passes several faceless sphinx statues and faces threatening sculptures supporting the entrance arch. This composition expresses the anxiety
and doubts overwhelming the visitor who confronts infinity. The shape of
the dome is an anthropomorphic form modeled on a human skull and stands,
according to Garas, for the acceptance of doubts and fears in calm meditation. The sphinx figures on the supporting buttresses symbolize the quiet
contemplation of the riddles of the world and the universe.

The interior, in particular, emphasizes the character of the building
as a temple of synthesis. It is dominated by eight columns, each with sculp-
tural decoration depicting typical situations of human life such as war, pastoral life, industry, religion, philosophy, science, birth, and death. The
columns are also reminders of the first eight symphonies by Beethoven; the
column for the ninth symphony is at the same time a monument to the

FIGURE 6.8

Temple of thought:
model of the Temple à la
Pensée, before 1907, by
François Garas.

composer himself. The capital of each column repeats the theme in an allegoric figure. Above the capitals, Garas suggests mosaics depicting geographic zones of the earth, mixed with images of the four seasons and the cycle of the birth and death of cities (a decorative scheme that certainly found Geddes's approval). The small chapels between the columns Garas intends to decorate with murals picturing the stages of the evolution of mankind. Even higher, a series of figures in mosaic symbolize music giving birth to human dreams. The climax is an ancient Buddha whose facial expression of eternal calmness embraces all philosophies and religions. A little Swiss chalet below the temple on the rock corresponds to the final section of Garas's booklet, with the title "Ma petite maison."[40] In this section Garas attempts to reconcile the grand idea of the temple with the individual life, which should consider itself lucky to be allowed to take part in building the temple.

Despite its more than doubtful architectural and symbolic merits, Garas's scheme is typical of many temple ideas in its combination of characteristic architectural and intellectual features. Among them are an initiation route as the approach to the temple, with subsequent redemption on entering the sanctuary; the combination of references to different religions and philosophies, occasionally including modern natural sciences, in both the built form and the decoration scheme; and the perception of the temple, despite its often monumental seize, as an introverted space, a cave an adept must enter in his quest for truth, knowledge, or his inner self. The cavelike space is often accompanied by a tower symbolizing overview, elevation, and separation, but also closeness to the truth.[41] Garas's scheme is also typical in choosing the seclusion of a mountaintop as the location of his temple, underlining intentions comparable to the motif of the tower. The solitary location, away from civilization and mankind, reflects the architect's perception of his separation from society, implying both disgust with contemporary society and the exclusiveness of his ideas compared to mainstream thought. Like Nietzsche's Zarathustra, who went into the mountains to meditate and find the truth, architects designed temples on mountain peaks, where those who wished might find a new ideal for their life.

The isolation of the temple in the mountains also refers to the romantic notion of the sublime encapsulated in nature. To the romantic mind, nature itself was best able to create extreme scenes and locations where a spectator in search of the sublime could gain insights into his own mind and experience the close connections between the individual soul and a universal spirit.[42] This notion changes during the course of the nineteenth century. Especially toward the end of the century, nature as such is no longer considered capable of stimulating experiences of the sublime; promising natural locations require architectural refinement in order to unlock their sublime potential. Already nineteenth-century romantic paintings often include man-made objects like factories, bridges, or churches in the presentation of dramatic natural scenes, usually in order to dramatize the effects of the natural location. Paintings like Karl Friedrich Schinkel's images of Gothic cathedrals hidden in the woods, and the watercolor *The Rock and Castle of Seclusion* by the English painter Richard Dadd from 1861 (figure 6.9), indicate the shift from pure nature to the inclusion of man-made architecture. A comparison of Dadd's picture with Caspar David Friedrich's 1808 *A Cross in the Mountains* is revealing. The Christian symbol of the crucified Jesus is for Friedrich the perfect symbol of the highest man can attain. The cross as such is not enough, however, for Friedrich locates it in a challenging natural scene. Although the man-made object seems to dominate the mountain, the actual revelation and redemption come from the experience of the sublime location; the cross is simply a symbolic pointer toward the truth rather than a depiction of a real object. Dadd, on the contrary, places an awesome building on top of a mountain at the center of his watercolor. This indicates not so much a loss of Christian faith as the diminished belief in the sublime power of nature. Whatever redemption the inhabitants of the town at the foot of the rock may seek in the extreme natural location high above them, they will find it only with the help of the building towering even higher.

The combination of buildings with ideal natural scenes is not a confrontation of nature and man-made artifact, but a creation of a third thing, an "artificial-natural double being,"[43] with an inherent, mutually beneficial relation working in both directions. The temple on the mountain peak makes this two-way relation explicit. Man is able to erect great buildings on nearly inaccessible sites, but the temple once built also participates in the sublime qualities already inherent in the mountains. The way the rock of the mountain and the stone of Garas's temple merge into one another expresses this relation. Yet it also emphasizes an identity between the natural rock and the stone of the man-made building; both are only different states of the same matter. This identity is almost certainly influenced by Ernst Haeckel's

FIGURE 6.9

*The Rock and Castle of*

*Seclusion,* 1861, by

Richard Dadd.

monism, a philosophy popular around 1900. Monism assumes that there exists a single law or idea unifying all matter, thoughts, and beliefs. Truth, according to Haeckel, can be found nearly everywhere, but wherever one finds it, it lives in a temple: "The Goddess of truth dwells in the temple of nature, in the green woods, on the blue sea, on the snowy mountain summit."[44]

After ten years Zarathustra realizes that meditation and the accumulation of knowledge are one thing, but to make use of the wisdom for the benefit of the people living in the plains is another. Accordingly, Nietzsche makes him leave his seclusion in favor of teaching among the people in the city. Many contemporary temple schemes took a similar path.[45] If these were to attempt to instigate reform by cultural and architectural means, a sublime isolation away from the city—the focus of the problems—could not satisfy. Furthermore, if the insight gained through the experience of the macrocosm of nature could be encapsulated in the microcosm of a temple, as Lethaby claimed, then the exclusive location of temple buildings on sublime natural sites was unnecessary. With a temple, architects, artists, and social reformers could bring the idea of nature, the universe, and any other idea into the heart of an ideal community or an existing city.

## Temples of Art and Culture

From the outset, schemes for new temple buildings, even those in secluded natural environments, were designed with the city in mind.[46] The architect Hermann Obrist, one of the founders of the Jugendstil in Munich, claimed that his fantastic architectural designs derived from a series of visions he experienced during the 1880s. Significantly, the earliest of these is an image of an ideal city somewhere in a mountain range.[47] Obrist never attempted to design a city similar to the one described in the notes of his visions. Instead, he developed his fantastic structures into a variety of grave and tomb designs, but also models for a chapel (before 1914) and a *Bergkirche* (1914), thus returning to the idea of a temple in a secluded location.

While Obrist was still attracted to a traditional Christian symbolism and building types, the German painter and etcher Wenzel Hablik devised his own new ideas for temples.[48] Hablik also transferred temple schemes from extreme natural locations into the city, thereby transforming them from isolated cult buildings to urban temples of art and culture. As with Obrist,

FIGURE 6.10

Crystal castle behind
clouds, 1906–1907, by
Wenzel Hablik.

visions were Hablik's starting point. In 1902 he recorded in his notebook a
dream during which he saw "castles towering above clouds: . . . castles where
others see mountains or rocks."[49] This dream evolved over the following years
into a variety of temple-like buildings in crystalline shapes mostly located on
mountains or other extreme natural locations (figure 6.10). As for many contemporary artists, the crystal is for Hablik a symbol of a unifying basic principle inherent in the inorganic but also the organic world.[50] A 1914 drawing
titled *Sketch for a Display Temple as a Monument of a City* shows a raised central building with a crystal-shaped dome. The interior consists of a range of
galleries leading to the top of the dome (figure 6.11), an arrangement that recalls the series of six staggered hexagons in Guarino Guarini's dome of the
chapel of the Holy Shroud (SS. Sindone, 1668–1682) in Turin Cathedral. Each

6 **THE METAPHYSICAL IMPERATIVE IN URBAN DESIGN AROUND 1900**

FIGURE 6.11

Temple of the city: interior of a display temple conceived as a monument of a city, 7 July 1914, by Wenzel Hablik.

level offers exhibition space for a different class of artworks: prints and paintings on the first level, sculptures on the second, craft objects on the third. The fourth level is reserved for a library and reading areas. The display temple is a place within a city where insights can be gained into the higher ideals Hablik found in nature, especially inorganic nature, and embodied in his etchings and paintings.[51] The exceptionally clear aesthetic and philosophical relation between Hablik's secluded temples from around 1900 and the display temple in a city makes this particular temple, although only designed in 1914, one of the best examples of what we may call urban temples of art and culture. Chronologically, however, comparable schemes— similar in intention, although very different in form—were already being proposed and built in Great Britain in the 1890s.

The English architect Charles Harrison Townsend is today best known for three buildings in London.[52] From 1892 to 1894 Townsend worked on the Bishopsgate Institute, a lending and reference library and a hall for meetings, concerts, and picture exhibitions for the parish of St. Botolph in Bishopsgate.[53] From 1895 to 1901 he built the Whitechapel Art Gallery in the East End, while from 1896 to 1901 he was responsible for the erection of the Horniman Museum in Forest Hill. All three buildings were for cultural institutions that provided a wide range of urban educational and cultural facilities.

Townsend was a member of the arts and crafts movement and joined the Art Workers' Guild in 1888.[54] The commissions for the three cultural institutions presented him with an opportunity to achieve buildings that expressed both the arts and crafts ideals and the character of these institutions as foci of learning and education directed toward the renewal of life in cities. In the facades of all three designs, towers announce that there is an important public building, and Romanesque arches emphasize the entrances with an inviting gesture. These are also typical features of church buildings, however, and it is enlightening to observe how Townsend's facades more and more take on the impression of sacral buildings or temples.

The Whitechapel Art Gallery goes back to an initiative of the Church of England vicar of St. Jude's in Whitechapel, Samuel Augustus Barnett. Barnett's aim was to overcome the division of society into social classes by facilitating the contacts between them. In 1884 he established with Toynbee Hall a university settlement in the parish, which accommodated

FIGURE 6.12

Temple of art and culture: first design for the Whitechapel Art Gallery, London, 1896, by Charles Harrison Townsend.

young graduates from Oxford University. It was hoped that contact and mutual initiatives between these graduates and the slum inhabitants would positively influence the latter's life. For this end Barnett and his students, among them C. R. Ashbee, organized social and educational events like lecture series, evening classes, and art exhibitions. For the latter Barnett commissioned Townsend in 1895 to design an art gallery. Townsend's first design was dated 1896, but financial difficulties required him to submit a second, smaller version in 1899. The gallery was finally opened in 1901.55

 The first design for the Whitechapel Art Gallery shows a building on a wide, elongated site (figure 6.12). A tower at either side frames the facade; the small entrance arch is inviting but not dominating. The upper part of the facade is structured by a row of Romanesque arched windows, adorned by a mosaic by Walter Crane, and covered by a huge pitched roof. The elements of the design are the same as Townsend had used in the earlier design for the Bishopsgate Institute, but the architect gave the art gallery a distinctly sacral impression. The facade could well have been that of an unconventional church, with a nave under the pitched roof flanked by two towers. This impression is not only an invention of the architect, but is rooted in Barnett's understanding of the function of art within his Christian social reform work. Barnett writes that "the Gospel of the higher life . . . now reaches men through the thousand influences of literature, art, society, which have been touched by the spirit of Christ."[56] The design finally built, for a narrower site, improves on the architectural quality of the earlier design—the entrance arch shifts to the left, thereby breaking the symmetry, which Townsend only regains in the upper half of the building—but is characterized by a loss of the sacral aura.

The Horniman Museum design develops further the theme of a sacrally inspired building as a place for arts and educational initiatives (figure 6.13). The Horniman Museum and Gardens goes back to the initiative of F. J. Horniman, MP (1835–1906), a tea merchant who built up a private anthropological collection. In 1890 Horniman decided in a typical philanthropic endeavor to share his collection with the public and opened his house to visitors. This proved very successful, and in 1896 Horniman asked Townsend to submit a design for a museum in Forest Hill in south London, on the site of his private house. Horniman's house was demolished in 1898, and after the opening of the museum in 1901 Horniman presented the new building and the collection to the London County Council. In 1910 Townsend was working at the Horniman Museum again, this time extending the building with a lecture hall and a library.[57]

For the design of the main museum building Townsend employs again the features of tower and arch, but in a new manner. A single tower is placed beside the building and connected with it through the entrance formed by a Romanesque arch. Two battered pylons each ending in a cupola frame the main facade of the museum. They are reminiscent of the towers of the Whitechapel Art Gallery, but here crowned by an arched tympanum. The main feature of the wall is a mosaic by Robert Anning Bell that depicts various arts and virtues offering presents to the god of humanity. If the overall impression of the building plays again on the form of a church—a nave with a tower on a little hill among detached houses—the mosaic removes any doubt about the character of the building: it is a temple of the arts. The entrance approach, designed as a way of initiation, underlines this idea.[58] A visitor walks straight toward the mosaic, which announces what sacred place he is about to enter. But before he can worship the god of hu-

FIGURE 6.13

Temple of art and
culture: Horniman
Museum, London,
1896–1901, by Charles
Harrison Townsend.

manity, he has to turn right, then pass underneath the arch and through the dark entrance hall with the tower above. The similarity to the motif of the cave and tower is obvious.

Unlike Townsend, Charles Robert Ashbee elaborated a theoretical position on cultural institutions within cities. Ashbee's interest in cities and their improvement through arts and crafts workshops began in Barnett's Toynbee Hall. Ashbee not only lived there from 1886 to 1889 but

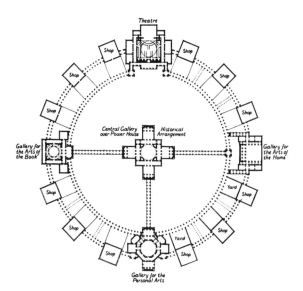

FIGURE 6.14

Temple of arts and crafts: plan for an art institute, before 1917, by Charles Robert Ashbee.

established his Guild of Handicraft in connection with the university settlement in 1888. In 1902 Ashbee moved the Guild out of London to the small village of Chipping Campden, where it existed for another six years until it finally collapsed in 1908.

In 1917 Ashbee published *Where the Great City Stands: A Study in the New Civics*, his major book on cities and their renewal. The book is a return, from a theoretical point of view, to the experience of living and working in the East End of London thirty years earlier. What began there on a small scale Ashbee now presents as a general palliative for contemporary cities. The final chapters of the book deal with Ashbee's idea of a "Crafts Museum" or "Art Institute" in combination with a "Creative Guild" (figure 6.14).[59] Ashbee's concern is to insert groups of artists and craftsmen into the "empty shells" of existing cities, because "unless in every city there are men inventing, dreaming, finding the city its soul," every attempt to reform cities and life in them will be in vain.[60]

The art institute is a place of production. The guild members are to come from various crafts, and their main task is to produce craftwork in order to set an example of what can be done without the help of modern machinery and related modes of production. The art institute is organized into four groups of workshops focusing on private homes, development of individual personalities, books, and printing.[61] Each of the groups has its own gallery in which to exhibit its products. In addition, a central gallery accommodates permanent and loan collections given to the city. Ashbee characterizes the institute as a "little University of the Arts in every city," and its objective is "to 'democratize' the arts, to make them wanted in the city."[62]

The emphasis on the relation between the city and the art institute marks the difference between Ashbee's earlier East End experience and the later plan. While the Guild of Handicraft was essentially a private initiative that wanted to set an example, Ashbee now suggests that the art institute should be regarded as the central function of a city. The city should endow the institute in order to guarantee its financial independence and proper functioning. In return, the art institute will serve the city, because "through the Arts, coordinated and applied to the needs of the City," the current machine culture can be checked with the help of the humanities.[63] The diagrammatic plan underlines the central function and position of the art institute within a city. Ashbee envisages a cruciform plan for the central gallery, which houses a power station in the basement, administration and meeting rooms above, and exhibition rooms on the upper floor. Covered walkways lead to the three smaller galleries and the theater, which are connected by a circular arrangement of single-story workshops. Ashbee stresses that the cruciform plan of the central gallery is not necessary; it could instead have been seven-sided. The latter would not make the plan less formal: Ashbee insists on a centralized arrangement for the whole complex, because the institute "must radiate outwards from the power center."[64] Ashbee presents his return to the city as the final stage of the evolution of the arts and crafts movement. Thirty years ago, he writes in 1916, the original task was "to free the artist craftsman, . . . make him independent of the trade and the factory." The second stage was characterized by a desire for a "greater regard for tradition." This meant emphasizing the workshop as a larger unit maintaining artistic and crafts traditions and passing them on to the individual members. Now the third stage is to incorporate the accumulated skills and traditions of the workshop into an even larger unit, which is "the point where we touch the wider issue of the city."[65] By touching the city at selective points with the temple of the art institute, Ashbee attempts to reform the city into an ideal community.

### Temples of the City

A final development is marked by proposals that consider the city itself as the new ideal to be celebrated in the metaphysical center. Significantly, W. R. Lethaby, whose analysis of the temple as the embodiment of the macrocosm contributed so much to the emergence of a metaphysical imperative in the approach to cities, presents also an early scheme along these lines.

In 1896 Lethaby proposed to resuscitate London by imposing a new metaphysical order, because "before it can be thought of as a whole—a city—there must be some sort of more or less actual, or sentimental, order and unity given to it."[66] Lethaby wanted to build an avenue from Waterloo Bridge to the British Museum, which "would alone almost give an organic system to London" (figure 6.15). The new street divides the hypotenuse of an imaginary triangle with a church—St. Paul's Cathedral and Westminster Abbey—at either end of its base line, and the British Museum and Library— a temple of knowledge appropriately designed with a Greek portico and a domed central reading room—at the apex. Lethaby describes the new avenue as a "Sacred Way" that would be decorated with fountains, trees, statues to the "Fortune of the City" and to the city fathers.[67] An omphalos placed at the crossing of the sacred way with the Strand underlines the temple-like character of the triangle and the avenue: the corresponding macrocosm embodied in the scheme is the British Empire, with London at its center.

Lethaby makes this proposal in a paper read during a lecture series coinciding with the fifth exhibition of the Arts and Crafts Exhibition Society in London in 1896. The theme of the lecture series is "Art and Life, and the Building and Decoration of Cities."[68] Lethaby's lecture culminates in his call for the sacred way, which he intends to be the beginning but also the climax of the new London. The importance of the scheme and its radical nature (at least for Lethaby) are particularly obvious when compared with his ideas for the rest of London and cities in general. Their improvement, Lethaby suggests, should "begin on the humblest plane by sweeping streets better, washing and white-washing the houses, and taking care that such railings and lamp-posts as are required are good lamp-posts and railings, the work of the best artists attainable."[69] Their extreme modesty makes these proposals a hopelessly inadequate contribution to the solution of the contempo-

FIGURE 6.15

Sacred way dedicated
to the City of London,
sketch, c. 1896, by
William Richard
Lethaby.

rary, pressing task of improving vast areas of substandard housing and
working conditions in cities like London. But this modesty—characteristic
also of many other papers read during the lecture series—underlines by
contrast the crucial importance Lethaby places on the new metaphysical
city center as a means of city improvement.

The climax—but also the conceptual end—of endeavors to reform
cities by implementing new metaphysical centers is the 1916 exhibition of

FIGURE 6.16

The arts (serving the
city): mural by Maurice
Greiffenhagen, on dis-
play in the "Municipal
Hall" at the 1916 exhibi-
tion in London of the
Arts and Crafts Exhibi-
tion Society.

the Arts and Crafts Exhibition Society.[70] That year the event was held for
the first time at Burlington House, the building of the Royal Academy in
London. On this occasion the architect Henry Wilson, the president of the
society from 1915 to 1922, took it upon himself to design the exhibition
along conceptual lines.[71] The underlying theme was the city.

The main part of the exhibition was a series of thematic rooms all
relating to the issue of the city. Two rooms, grouped under the title of "Domus," displayed decorative schemes for private homes, thus declaring a totally designed environment or "House Beautiful" to be a necessary element
of an ideal city.[72] A "University Room" emphasized the need to bridge the
gap between town and gown, with murals presenting colorful picturesque
university processions contrasting others depicting the dull life of modern
town-dwellers. But the heart of the exhibition comprised three other rooms.
The first was a "Municipal Hall," with a mural titled *The Arts* by Maurice
Greiffenhagen as the main exhibit (figure 6.16). In the center of the painting a female figure, the City, sits underneath a baldachin and is approached
from either side by the different arts. The City is placed on a plinth flanked
by two putti, the one holding a Greek temple and the other a model of the
Hagia Sophia, with a Gothic church spire in the background. In the second,
"Ecclesiastic" room were a series of altars in apsidal chapels, dedicated to

FIGURE 6.17

Temple of life and death:
the "Hall of Heroes,"
by Henry Wilson, at the
1916 exhibition in
London of the Arts
and Crafts Exhibition
Society.

various religions that were important elements of a fully developed civic life. The culmination of the show was a "Central Hall of Heroes" (figure 6.17) with the motto "Usui civium decori urbis."[73] The key exhibit was a painting of the *Mother and Child* by Reginald Hallward. The room was dedicated to the victims of the First World War; accordingly the other exhibits illustrated human suffering and solidarity. Most notable among them was a model of a *campo santo*, a building based on the Hagia Sophia, which stood in the center of the hall.

Through its symbolism, the exhibition acquires a meaning that transcends its display of the latest products of the arts and crafts movement. The "Domus" rooms present the city as a coherently designed environment, comparable to Olbrich's demand from the late 1890s. The "University Room" underlines the city as a place of learning and education, similar to initiatives like Barnett's university settlement. The "Municipal Room" is a temple of a city, comparable to Lethaby's London scheme. Although the mural shows the arts and crafts contributing to the city, the attributes of the city—the Greek temple, the Hagia Sophia, and the Gothic spire—reveal her as an object of religious origin and quasi-religious veneration. The same idea is again presented in the "Ecclesiastic" room, which, with its churchlike character, is also a temple of contemplation. The "Hall of Heroes," apart from being a response to the ongoing war, is a temple of life. The two key exhibits—the painting of the mother and child and the model of the *campo santo*—cannot make sense of the death of the soldiers. But taking these symbols of life and death together, the hall becomes a place for the veneration of the cycle of life, comparable to the interchangeable temples dedicated to life and death by Schumacher.

The overall symbolism of the exhibition indicates something else. Every theme dealt with, every exhibit presented, is turned into an object with quasi-religious overtones. To elevate the city, whose miserable state was the origin of reform initiatives, into the very *idea* guiding possible interventions is a circular argument that leads the idealistic approach toward cities into a conceptual cul-de-sac. Under the dome of a temple of the city, everything and nothing can be assembled. What began in opposition to traditional religious thought, whose perfected city of the New Jerusalem is deferred to the afterlife, finally became a quasi-religion itself. As in ancient Greece, the city is suddenly perceived as an object of worship. In 1924 another temple scheme, a "Hall of Vision," very similar to the 1916 exhibition, was presented during a "Conference on Some Living Religions within the Empire" in London. That project, prepared by Victor Branford, is the culmination of all the temple ideas of Patrick Geddes, which the following chapter analyzes in detail.

Life individual, associated, collective; Love, through all passions, simplest to highest; Death too, in all its mysteries, its fears, its hopes; . . . Religious emotions and aspirations, ideas and doctrines, . . . they find expression in new imagery, in fresh symbolism; and thus at length in Temples, to house and synthesise them, each and all.

Patrick Geddes, "The Temple Cities"

# The City and Spirituality

Like many of his contemporaries, some of them discussed in the preceding chapter, Geddes recognized the need for a metaphysical city center. But whereas Ashbee, for example, elaborated on one particular idea, the art institute as the core of urban renewal, Geddes conceived many temple schemes, including buildings designed in collaboration with architects, reinterpretations of historic structures, and symbolic forms and spaces to be erected temporarily in exhibitions or incorporated permanently into the urban fabric of existing or new cities. The number and variety of such schemes was part of Geddes's methodological approach to city design:

Let us then go on with our comprehensive designing of the Culture-Institutes of the Future. Such designs have their educative value—& thus they tend to reach execution some day. The social & political reformer has always to state and re-state his ideas, long before he forms that resolute minority, which by and by—by restating these ideas more widely still—persuades a sufficient majority to [adopt] them.[1]

The repetitive content of many of Geddes's temple ideas allows one to order them roughly into two groups. One comprises temple schemes evolving around the theme of knowledge and its synthesis, the other temples dedicated to the phenomenon of life itself. The two groups follow each other chronologically. In the years up to 1900 Geddes was primarily concerned with temples of knowledge. While he never abandoned this idea, he concentrated increasingly in later years on temples of life. This marks a significant shift in his intellectual development, expressing a step away from the primarily scientific analysis of life toward a quasi-religious veneration of the phenomenon of life in its material and metaphysical totality.

## The Temple of Geography

Two-dimensional representations of the earth's surface have a long tradition in cartography. Three-dimensional representations became especially popular after the invention of the panorama by Robert Barker in Edinburgh in 1788. This device spread rapidly through Europe and was complemented in 1822 by the first diorama, invented by Louis Jacques Mandé Daguerre.[2] From a much earlier date globes had shown the known geography of the earth; but panorama and diorama marked a significant change in the method of representation. Both devices depicted reality, for example a cityscape, a natural scene, or a historical event, in such a way that a visitor gained the impression of participating in it. Artists painting a panorama often made use of natural components like pieces of wood or stones arranged in the foreground of the image, so as to enhance the realistic effect by creating a smoother transition between the visitor and the painting. The aim of the panorama was not so much to "deceive observers into believing that they were in the presence of the authentic,"[3] but to present a recreated, man-made nature. The panorama was another "natural-artificial double being" comparable to the temples on mountaintops encountered in the last chapter, where nature and artifacts became one.[4]

In 1851 the map publisher James Wyld opened a panorama of the earth in London, originally conceived for the Great Exhibition of that year

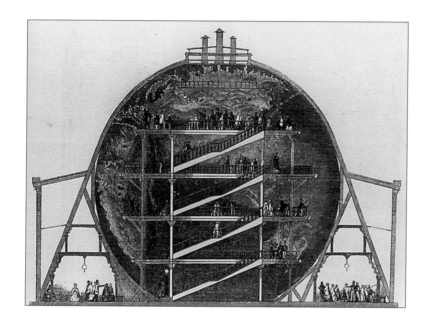

FIGURE 7.1

Temple of geography:

the monster globe, 1851,

by James Wyld.

but built at Leicester Square. This panorama consisted of a globe, 60 feet in diameter, with a relief representation of the earth's surface on its inner side (figure 7.1). Four platforms allowed visitors to view the earth from various levels. Maps, astronomic and other exhibits turned the "Monster Globe" into a center for geography. While Wyld's globe, despite its scientific accuracy, can easily be seen as a tourist attraction, this is not possible in the case of Robert Pemberton's Happy Colony from 1854, a scheme for an ideal settlement in New Zealand. The center of the proposed colony consists of four colleges surrounding a park with a small farm, representations of the Muses, and models of geometrical forms (figure 7.2).[5] Two terrestrial and two celestial maps put the universe and the earth at the feet of the colonists for educational purposes. Wyld's globe and Pemberton's maps are incentives to consider universe and earth as open to human inquiry and, in the latter case, to intervention.

Geddes's friend, the anarchist geographer Elisée Reclus, pursued similar intentions with his Great Globe from 1895.[6] Reclus intended to exhibit the globe during the Universal Exposition in Paris in 1900. The French architect Louis Bonnier conceived a design for an egg-shaped construction

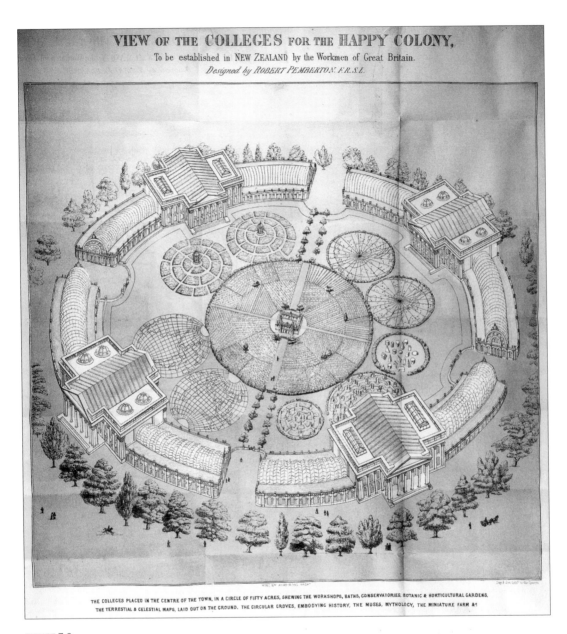

FIGURE 7.2

Terrestrial and celestial maps in the center of Robert Pemberton's Happy Colony, from 1854.

accommodating the globe, documentation center, library, and a collection of dioramas (figure 7.3).[7] As a scientist, Reclus's main concern was the inaccuracy of two-dimensional maps representing three-dimensional sections of the earth. This he wished to overcome with the globe on a large scale, accompanied by models on an even larger scale for individual sections of the earth. A second aim was to make the earth and scientific information about its surface available to those scientists who did not have opportunities to personally explore unknown territories. The third aim was to provide for the public "a model of the Earth, under the shape of a globe, . . . where every man will find himself at home, and even will learn to know his own country better than before." The globe was a device to root man and the masses again in a world steadily becoming larger due to increasing scientific knowledge, but whose lucidity did not grow in parallel. For this, it would be necessary to synthesize specialized knowledge into an idea of the Earth. "Now Globes must be temples themselves," Reclus insists, referring to size, workmanship, and scientific representations, but in particular to the globe's quasi-religious function, which was to arouse respect for the achievements of science and a feeling of awe for humanity, the inhabitants of the earth.[8]

Thus Reclus presents his globe as an instrument of knowledge and as a kind of temple. Geddes picks up on exactly these two notions. Responding to a lecture by Reclus in 1898, Geddes stresses the scientific value of the project and the action it demands.[9] In an obituary after Reclus's death in 1905, Geddes underlines the temple character of the globe. Recalling Lethaby's temple definition, Geddes describes the globe as the "microcosm of the macrocosm itself," as "the image, and shrine, and temple of the Earth-Mother," and finally as expressing "the unity of the world" which was "the basis and symbol of the brotherhood of man."[10] Geddes's and Reclus's idealism is firmly rooted in an enlightened pursuit of knowledge. They wish the temple to be a temple of the brotherhood of man, but it is first of all a temple of knowledge.

As such, Geddes incorporates Reclus's globe into his own scheme for a temple of geography. With the support of the Edinburgh map publisher and cartographer John George Bartholomew, Geddes in 1902 presented a project for a National Institute of Geography to be established in Edinburgh.[11] The project comprises three elements. There is Reclus's globe on a reduced scale, surrounded by maps, reliefs, and other geographical

FIGURE 7.3

Temple of geography:

the Great Globe by

Elisée Reclus, building

designed 1897–1898

by Louis Bonnier.

illustrations and instruments. Complementing the representation of the earth is an image of the universe in the form of a celestial globe designed by the French architect Paul Louis Albert Galeron, intended to be a center of astronomical education and research. (Galeron had already built a celestial globe for the Universal Exposition in Paris in 1900 [figure 7.4], where Geddes met the architect.) An outlook tower is the third element of the institute.

Geddes developed the design for the institute building together with Galeron, who produced a first sketch in 1901 (figure 7.5). The drawing shows an outlook tower with receding stories ending in a protruding platform with a turret on top. The turret is obviously derived from the existing Outlook Tower in Edinburgh and would probably have accommodated an-

FIGURE 7.4

View of the 1900 Universal Exposition in Paris, showing Paul Louis Albert Galeron's celestial globe.

other camera obscura. Two identical halls with stepped roofs connected by an entrance hall with an Egyptian gateway accommodate the globes of Reclus and Galeron. Around the globes, smaller cubicles offer space for reliefs and other exhibits. The final published design (figure 7.6) follows closely the organization of the 1901 plan, although the neo-Egyptian entrance has disappeared. The two stepped roofs are replaced by two domes, underneath which semicircular windows allow visitors glimpses of the globes. Both halls are enlarged at the outer ends by semicircular rooms offering exhibition space and a lecture hall in the form of an amphitheater. This addition results in a significant change in the footprint of the building. Once the two half-circles are added, the plan of the National Institute of Geography becomes a direct reference to a sixteenth-century astronomical laboratory by the Danish astronomer Tycho Brahe (1546–1601), of which Geddes obviously wishes his institute to be a direct descendant.

In 1576 Tycho Brahe was awarded the island of Hveen near Copenhagen by Frederick II of Denmark.[12] The king also provided Brahe with funding that allowed him to erect in the following years what was to

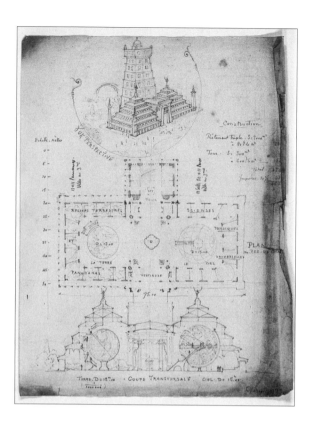

FIGURE 7.5

Temple of geography:

first design from 1901

by Paul Louis Albert

Galeron for Geddes's

National Institute of

Geography.

become a forerunner of modern observatories. From 1576 onward Brahe built on Hveen the unique castle of Uraniborg, combining private and student accommodation with laboratories and study rooms housing astronomical and other scientific equipment. The ground plan of Uraniborg (figure 7.7) shows a quadrangular building divided crosswise by two corridors, and enlarged by semicircular rooms on two opposing sides of the square. One of these rooms accommodates a kitchen, the other Brahe's library and a globe. Uraniborg became famous soon after its completion. It is one of the very few places, other than cities, included by Georg Braun and Frans Hogenberg in their five-volume opus *Civitatis orbis terrarum*, published from 1586 onward.[13] Brahe and Uraniborg again attracted attention when a biography of the scientist by John Louis Emil Dreyer was published in Edinburgh in 1890.[14] It is very likely that Geddes read the book. The fact that he acquired

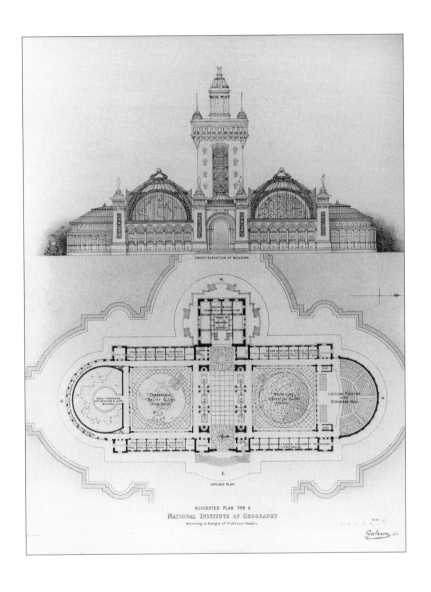

FIGURE 7.6

Temple of geography: National Institute of Geography, drawing, before 1902, by Paul Louis Albert Galeron after design sketches by Patrick Geddes.

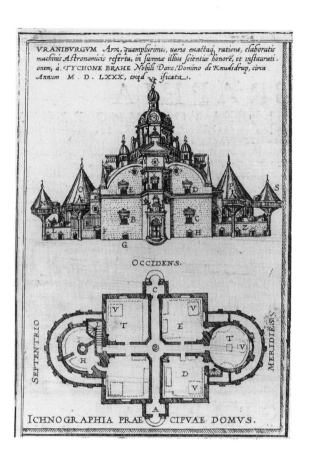

VRANIBVRGVM Arx, quamplurimis, uaria exactaq, ratione, elaboratis
machinis Astronomicis refertis, in summæ illius scientiæ honore, et instaurati-
onem, à, TYCHONE BRAHE Nobili Dano, Domino de Knudsdrup, circa
Annum M . D . LXXX, excæd ificata .

OCCIDENS.

SEPTENTRIO

MERIDIES

ICHNOGRAPHIA PRAE CIPVAE DOMVS.

FIGURE 7.7

Ground plan and view of
the main facade of Tycho
Brahe's Uraniborg on the
island of Hveen, Den-
mark, begun 1576.

at some point in his life an impression of the engraving of Uraniborg from
Braun and Hogenberg's *Civitatis orbis terrarum*, of which figure 7.7 is a detail,
further emphasizes his fascination with Brahe's creation.

Both Uraniborg and Geddes's geographical institute were considered by their creators to be the most advanced scientific institutes of their
time. Uraniborg emphasizes the Renaissance fascination with scientific inquiry as an aid to the rational organization of the world. The building's position at the center of a formally designed quadrangular garden, which in
turn is the heart of the small island of Hveen, underlines this intention. Similarly, Geddes intends his geographical institute, as a center of rational cog-
nition, to become the focus of an ordered environment. The aim is to provide
information and study facilities for scientists, practical information about

foreign countries for manufacturers and politicians, and educational services to laymen. The insights gained should subsequently be applied to the city, the region-city, and finally the world. Beyond this, Geddes aims at a "cosmic presentment of Universal Geography."[15] The geographical institute is to offer a new cosmography, harmonizing philosophically with Reclus's globe but leaving the latter behind by including the universe. The institute is "a Temple of Geography, devoted to the Universe in general and the Earth in particular."[16]

Reclus does not suggest a particular connection between his globe and a city. Restraints of space and costs, he speculates, would prevent the erection of such globes in inner-city areas.[17] Geddes, however, conceived the National Institute of Geography for the inner city of Edinburgh. Despite some initial support, the project was not realized, and Geddes never returned to it. But he continued to elaborate temples of geography in the form of geographical institutes, geographical gardens, or outlook towers. Two years after the plan for the Edinburgh institute, Geddes suggested a similar institution in his report for Pittencrieff Park in Dunfermline, Scotland, this time in collaboration with architect George Shaw Aitken.

The Nature Palace, as Geddes calls the temple of geography in Dunfermline, continues the concept developed for its Edinburgh predecessor, but the content is broadened by the inclusion of biology and anthropology in addition to astronomy, geology, and geography (figure 7.8). The building is designed on a traditional Latin cross plan of a church—this was intended to be a two-story-high perambulation area covered by a steel and glass roof—with an additional rectangular space for a library and a lecture theater at the northern end. Four quadrangular towers with domes, each two stories high, stand in the angles of the cross. An outlook tower is provided by Geddes elsewhere in Pittencrieff Park.[18]

A visitor would ideally enter the Nature Palace from the north and proceed first to the basement, where an installation of about a hundred panoramas of three different sizes represents various continents, countries, and geographical zones. After this imaginary travel, during which a visitor would make the world his own, the upper two stories offer opportunities for more specialized studies. In the four towers, index museums are dedicated to anthropology, geology, biology, and astronomy, the last including a small copy of Galeron's celestial globe. A reduced version of Reclus's

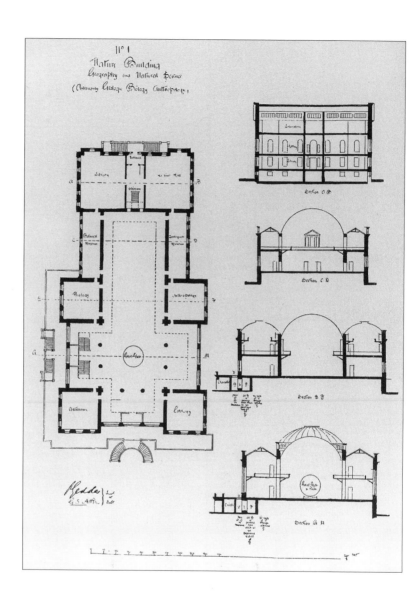

FIGURE 7.8

Temple of geography:
plan, 1904, for the
Nature Palace in
Pittencrieff Park,
Dunfermline, by Patrick
Geddes and George
Shaw Aitken.

globe of the earth stands at the center of the Latin cross as the main feature of the hall.

The intention of the project is to present a unified cosmography based on the synthesis of individual scientific subjects. Geddes emphasizes the cosmographic aspect of the Nature Palace with a reference to biblical cosmology. He suggests four fountains in the outer ends of the cross (although they are omitted in the plan), dedicated to the main human types represented by "ethnological sculptures."[19] Besides the racial symbolism, these fountains are a reference to the Garden of Eden in Genesis, where four rivers originated from one spring. Thus Dunfermline's Nature Palace is turned into an image of the Garden of Eden both lost and regained, the latter, through the synthesis of science into a new cosmography as the guiding principle of human activities, aiming at the renewal of life.

## Biological Views of the City: Eugenic and Metabolic

Darwin's theory of evolution, which secured man a place within the sequence of organic life, cast a new light on discussions of the improvement of human life. Did natural selection, as the mechanism of evolution, apply to man in a similar way as it applied to other forms of organic life? Most felt that civilization and its benefits, regardless of their unequal distribution, tended to overrule natural selection.[20] But that still left the question of how the characteristics of organic life, in particular of human beings, were transmitted to the next generation. Speaking in biological terms, two schools of thought—neo-Lamarckism and neo-Darwinism—confronted each other during the decades preceding the turn of the century. Neo-Lamarckists believed that characteristics acquired in one generation by adaptation to the environment could be inherited by the following generations. Neo-Darwinists assumed that characteristics of organic life were fixed and inherited as such by subsequent generations. This was not a new idea when Darwin put forward his theory of evolution, but suffered from a lack of knowledge about the exact working of the hereditary process. This changed at the beginning of the 1890s, when the German biologist August Weismann announced his germ-plasm theory, a direct attack on the belief in the inheritability of acquired characteristics.[21] Despite this setback, neo-Lamarckism was still influential in the early twentieth century.

The debate between the two schools of thought was not confined to biologists, but was also of interest to social theoreticians and reformers. Their most pressing issue was the steady growth of towns and cities with bad living conditions. Slum restoration and charitable, philanthropic, and educational efforts had so far not led to a lasting improvement of urban conditions of life, especially for the working class. Current views of the theory of evolution described not only the evolution of organic life toward higher stages but also the possibility of a species declining and finally disappearing. This idea was reflected in the thinking of social reformers, for whom towns and urban life became possible expressions of a degeneration of human beings or the human race.[22] For example, already in 1866 John Edward Morgan published a booklet titled *The Danger of Deterioration of Race from the Too Rapid Increase of Great Cities.*[23] The same idea was still prevalent toward the end of the century, most notably in the famous book *Degeneration* by the doctor and man of letters Max Nordau. Nordau subsumes "residence in large towns" among the "noxious influences" of modern life and society, comparable to tobacco, alcohol, and drugs.[24]

Within this context the eugenics movement emerged. It was based on the assumption that an increasing knowledge of heredity would allow human beings to control their reproduction by artificial selection, thus leading mankind to a higher stage in the evolution of organic life. The term "eugenic" was coined by Francis Galton in 1886 as a name for "the science of improving stock, which is by no means confined to questions of judicious mating, but which, especially in the case of man, takes cognizance of all influences that tend in however remote a degree to give to the more suitable races or strains of blood a better chance of prevailing speedily over the less suitable than they otherwise would have had."[25] Eugenics offered a new, supposedly scientific approach to dealing with all kinds of social problems through the control of marriages, birth control, sterilization, and the education of women toward a more responsible selection of their husbands. By 1890 the idea of eugenics was well established both in scientific circles and among the educated public, but it became especially popular in Great Britain in the years after the turn of the century, when military conscription for the Boer War highlighted the allegedly bad stock of the population in the larger British towns.[26]

The idea that organic characteristics are fixed meant that environmental reforms not only were powerless to effect the future improvement of the human race, but probably did active harm, especially in an urban environment. If cities are considered as a natural habitat, differences regarding health, wealth, and social and moral life become not the results of the prevailing socioeconomic order but expressions of the biological characteristics of the inhabitants. The most radical conclusion from this line of argument is that, in order to improve life in cities, the characteristics of the inhabitants have to be looked at rather than the mere physical improvement of the urban fabric.[27]

Galton describes in a utopian novel the ideal state and city of Kantsaywhere, organized around the ideals of eugenics.[28] His novel, of which only fragments survive, gives a good impression of how little value eugenicists assigned to the environment. The center of Kantsaywhere is the Eugenic College. Its task is to examine the citizens with the aim of "weeding out" any unfit inhabitants who were "undesirable as individuals, and dangerous to the community."[29] Toward the end of the surviving part of the novel Galton briefly mentions the environmental aspect of life in Kantsaywhere, which is roughly along garden city lines.[30] While for Galton the environment supports only the inherited qualities of life, it has the opposite function for Geddes. For him the qualities of organic life are determined through its interaction with the environment, and from this basic assumption Geddes, as a biologist, derives the concept of life he wishes to embody in a temple of life.

In an 1886 paper Geddes summarizes the development of biology as a process of accumulating ever more detailed knowledge about organic life.[31] The two main branches of biology—morphology and physiology—both finally arrive at the level of protoplasm, the ultimate substance of which body cells and all organic life are made. Accordingly, he suggests that all phenomena of organic life have to be interpreted through protoplasmic analysis and declares that life is the "fundamental conception of protoplasm." Analyzing protoplasm unlocks the "fundamental secret, that of constructive and destructive metabolism—anabolism and katabolism."[32]

Metabolism means the intake of nutritious substances by a cell and the excretion of waste products. The early period of a cell's life cycle is the anabolic phase, characterized by growth and nutrition; the latter phase is catabolic, because the waste and excretion products take over. From Herbert Spencer's observation that a body's "mass increases as the cube of the

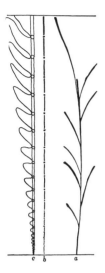

FIGURE 7.9

Genealogical tree,

sketch by Patrick

Geddes, c. 1885.

dimensions" but "the surface only as the square," Geddes concludes that "in the growing cell the nutritive necessities of the increasing mass are ever less adequately supplied by the less rapidly increasing absorbing surface."[33] The ability of a cell to interact with the environment according to its needs controls the succession of the two phases. The changing relation between mass and surface could have three consequences for a cell: either a temporary balance between anabolism and catabolism with no further growth, or death of the cell due to increasing waste products, or, the usual case, a division of the cell.[34]

This dichotomy of anabolism and catabolism is for Geddes the paradigm in biology, one that is responsible for form and functions of cells, tissue, organs, and the appearance of and differences between the male and female sexes.[35] The male sex is catabolistic; accordingly male beings are active, creative, and competitive. The female sex is anabolistic; therefore females are constructive, nourishing, and passive. Which sex develops from an embryo depends on the environmental conditions. A lack of food, light, moisture, and high temperature result in a male being, and the opposite conditions in a female being.[36] This is not only the case in plants and animals, but also in human beings.[37]

The continuity of organic life relies on both metabolic phases. Within single-cell organisms the point of reversal between anabolism and catabolism leads to reproduction by division. In forms of life with distinctive male and female beings, the two sexes have to complement each other in reproducing life. Geddes summarizes this idea in a diagram of a "genealogical tree" (figure 7.9). The stem of the tree stands for the continuity of life in the form of protoplasm, and the leaves symbolize the life cycle of individuals, who become more and more specialized throughout evolution as expressed in the gradually enlarged leaves farther up the stem. At the bottom of the stem, where reproduction means the death of the cell, one finds the single-cell organism. Higher up, the points of contact between the leaves and the stem signify the moments of reproduction due to the unification of male and female.[38] The balance between anabolism and catabolism, between female and male, is "the ideal of all organic life."[39] Elsewhere, Geddes defines as "the quest of life" the "ideal of love . . . which our fathers called romantic, which we now call eugenic."[40]

Like the eugenicists, Geddes looked at society and the city from a biological point of view. He even joined the Eugenics Education Society,[41] which was founded in 1908, and acknowledged in his writings on biology the growing knowledge of the heredity of human biological characteristics. But he never entirely gave up his neo-Lamarckian position and continued to stress the improvement of the environment as the main field of human intervention in all matters urban. Considering Geddes as a biologist, this attachment to neo-Lamarckism makes him appear, with growing age, to be losing touch with developments in biology. Considering him as sociologist and city designer, this loyalty allows for a different reading. Even if acquired characteristics are not inheritable, the environment, especially the built one, is still of utmost importance. As described in chapter 4, Geddes develops the concept of social heritage as the embodiment of man's past cultural development. The social heritage, in turn, is a crucial component of his application of Haeckel's biogenetic basic law to the development of cities and their future progress. In the end, it does not matter to Geddes whether acquired characteristics are not transmittable through genetic mechanisms, because the social heritage provides another means by which human beings can inherit the results of earlier generations' interaction with the environment.

The genealogical tree reminds one strongly of the Arbor Saeculorum (figure 4.1). Both diagrams emphasize Geddes's belief in everlasting evolution. The relatively new discipline of evolution is not classifiable within morphology and physiology, the two main branches of biology, but represents the higher, unifying aim of life. Geddes explains that "evolution considers form and function no longer statically, but in movement."[42] The analysis of the two main branches provides all the facts of life, which can be arranged—as Geddes does in the paper—in a rectangular two-dimensional table. Evolution adds to this table a third dimension "and must be traced through the pile of accumulated concrete facts at right angles."[43]

Like the Arbor Saeculorum, which stands vertically in every city and region, the genealogical tree arises vertically out of the morphological and physiological facts of life. What the Arbor Saeculorum represents for a city as an organism, the genealogical tree represents for the individual citizen. The idea of life is for Geddes the idea of permanent evolution, achievable through the complementary relationship, or love, between male and female sex as the expression of catabolism and anabolism. It is this rather complex construct of ideas that Geddes attempts to symbolize in his temple of life.

### The Temple of the Greek Gods: A Temple of Life

In 1908 Geddes received an invitation to give a lecture to the biology group of the Fabian Society. David Montague Eder, the representative of the group, asked Geddes to talk on eugenics.[44] Geddes's lecture, delivered sometime in December 1908, presented life as a process of individual evolution spanning the period between birth and death.[45] Habitually Geddes divides the life cycle of plants into the seven phases of "Swelling and Budding," "Shooting and Leafing," "Flowering," "Greening," "Fruiting and Seeding," "Drying," and finally "Resting or Dying."[46] His lecture suggests analogous periods for human life, which he separates into the three main phases of youth or rise, maturity, and decline. Each phase is divided again, so that Geddes arrives at seven phases of human life.[47] He visualizes these periods in a half circle accompanied by the question "What is the ideal time of life?" The answer is that there is no single ideal time of life but rather "the optimum development of the optimum quality of life at each stage of life history (ontogeny)."[48]

Geddes assumes that if human beings have ever perfected the male and female life cycles—as ideal illustrations of life in evolution—they must have expressed it artistically or culturally as a historical fact.

> Yet in history and literature there are great and gifted people who have done this. Who are they? The Greeks. They expressed the ideals of humanity as gods! . . . Here we have an indefinite Pantheon which literature has never yet unified.[49]

Thus Geddes resorts again to the ancient Greek culture, "the most marvellous period of human evolution, both civic and individual."[50] As the *polis* influenced Geddes's idea of a region-city and as the Greek gods once ruled the *polis*, so they should also become the ideal for the life in the region. Geddes reinterprets the gods as being "the ideal, or supernorm, of a phase of life. . . . Each goddess, each god, is the essential and characteristic, the logical and necessary, expression of the corresponding life-phase of Woman and of Man." Artistic representations of the gods and buildings associated with them are essential components of Greek and other ancient cities. Accordingly, Geddes insists on the "return of the Olympians" into the contemporary city, "for the Greeks there developed what for us is again dawning in our ideals of eugenics and of education."[51]

In his lecture to the Fabian Society Geddes presents a small sketch of a temple of life which he calls a "sacred grove."[52] The sketch shows two opposing crescents representing the male and female curves of life; the resulting circle symbolizes the complementary relation between the sexes. Geddes allocates to each phase in human life a Greek god or goddess. The crescents and the gods are also the centerpieces of a later, more developed design of the temple (figure 7.10). Again, the male and female curves face each other, this time within an oval structure. Reading the diagram as an architectural plan, each curve comprises four platforms arranged as a series of steps, with the highest at the middle of the curve. On either end of the platforms Geddes places a sculpture of a god or goddess (figure 7.11). The curves of life rise toward Apollo on the one, and toward Pallas on the other side; and both decline toward the exit. The sculptures represent the ideal of human life in its individual phases, and the rising and declining curves symbolize the ideal course of that life. But the representation of life in the temple attempts to include also the less ideal reality of human life.

Contemporary life showed many deviations from the ideal course, either toward what Geddes considered to be the normal human life or even toward a subnormal level. Within the temple of life, the inner steps symbolize the former and the outer steps the latter deviations. The dotted lines of the design indicate ways of bypassing the ideal line of individual evolution. If, as Geddes explains, a woman does not "effectivate her sex," she would thus pass "from girlhood phase of Artemis to the grey hairs of Demeter. Hence again her way divides: at best to sisterhood and vice-motherhood," or, without "psychic compensations and consolation" for the lost sex, she would turn into an "old maid." Similar deviations are identifiable in man's life, as indicated in the diagram.[53]

Geddes traces the social diversity of urban life back to biological principles, although he does not arrive at the same conclusions as the eugenicists. Geddes's concept roots social differences in the variously worked out cooperation between the sexes, considered as the expression of the two metabolic principles of an organism's interaction with the environment. But despite his belief in biological principles, his concept does not offer an explanation of human life, urban or otherwise. What it offers instead is an

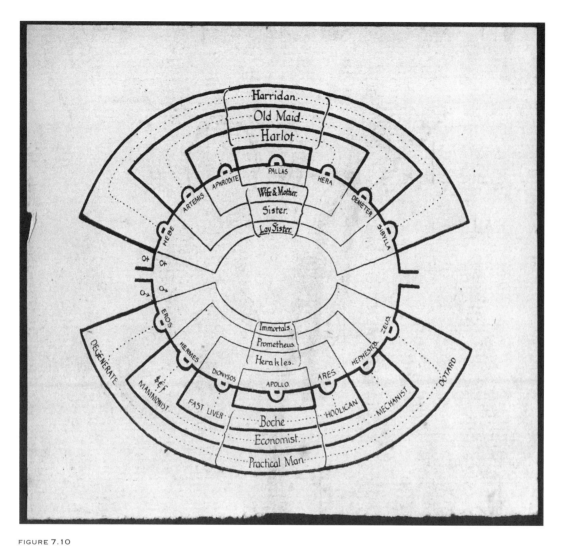

FIGURE 7.10

Temple of life: plan of
the temple of the Greek
gods according to ideas
of Patrick Geddes, as
published in 1921.

FIGURE 7.11

Temple of life: the Greek gods and goddesses representing phases of human life, as published in 1926.

accommodation of all phenomena of a city in a meaningful picture. The guiding interest is the creation of an image of cooperation, which focuses on the relation between the two sexes. This is comparable to the concepts of the natural occupations in the valley region and the four social types in the city, introduced in earlier chapters. In all three cases, Geddes's scientific or historical analysis results in models that explain little of contemporary society but evoke the potential for cooperation between individuals, classes, and occupations for the benefit of both the individual and society.

Historically, the ancient Greek city embodied and perfected the ideal life based on biological principles. Geddes considers medieval cities another perfect example of his theoretical ideas: "In the medieval city there were on the woman's side the homes and the sisterhoods; on the man's side the workshops of crafts and arts, the cloistered study and scriptorium; and for both and all, the Cathedral and the Town-House."[54] In the gender-specific division of work in a medieval city Geddes recognizes the complementary relation between the sexes, reinterpreted in terms of anabolism (the woman working in the home) and catabolism (the man acting out his energy in the guild workshop). He also connects this assumption with the four social types. The housewife and the craftsman represent the people in the town. On the level of the intellectuals in the cloister he establishes the same dichotomy, for women serve their fellow human beings in sisterhoods, whereas men are occupied with studies and writing. Finally, on the level of the city both sexes are united in the cathedral and town-house, and their cooperation results in a new city.

But as the evolution of species embraces the idea of degeneration, so does Geddes's biological analysis of cities. Greek and medieval cities are prototypes of evolution toward the ideal course of life; contemporary cities are the opposite: "Hence the slum, the ghetto; hence our squalor of factory and mine; our garish centres of debasing pleasures. Each is an inverted temple-precinct, and all are the nemesis of our lack of worthier ones."[55] Geddes's temple of life is an attempt to provide a temple worthy of a city (though the description of slums as "inverted temple-precincts" allows one to argue that ultimately he wants to turn the whole city into a temple of life comparable to the medieval city). There each sex lives and works during the various phases of his or her life in the best-suited environment. Applied to the contemporary city, this means creating again an appropriate urban environment that fosters the phases of life each citizen has to pass through.[56] Except for a minor scheme of a temple of the Greek gods in the garden of the Scots College at Montpellier, France, this most ambitious of Geddes's temple projects was never realized.[57]

The curve of life leads finally to death. The genealogical tree emphasizes the continuity of life in the form of protoplasm, as the Arbor Saeculorum embodies the idea of the eternal existence of a city and of history. Like Fritz Schumacher, some of whose temple projects establish a metaphysical relation between life and death, Geddes attempts a sublimation of the individual death into the idea of eternity. He complements his temple of life with a temple of death, based on the same oval shape as the temple of life but with an adjoining structure for a "Crem[atorium]," occupying the space where the exit in the temple of life is located. The oval of the main building becomes a "Col[umbarium]" to keep urns with the ashes of cremated bodies.[58]

## The Garden for the Nine Greek Muses: Life in Action

The final project of Geddes to be discussed in the group of temples of life is one he called the garden for the nine Greek Muses. Geddes develops this type of garden in parallel with the temple of the Greek gods around 1907, and these two reinterpretations of Greek mythology are conceptually linked.

In 1909 Geddes reports in a letter that Frank C. Mears designed "a Parnassolympus of the most extraordinary complexity—to [?] each God nine gardens."[59] Even if Mears's design is now lost, the theoretical concept is important. The gods symbolize again the phases of human life. To understand the function of the nine gardens, one has to resort to the Notation of Life (figure 2.1). The final quarter of the diagram signifies the transfer of ideas from the cloister into the city, and from dreams to deeds. City and deed are the outward-oriented, highest stages of communal and individual life, which express themselves in artistic and cultural activities (the nine squares of this quarter of the diagram). To each of these activities Geddes assigns one of the Greek Muses, the goddesses of poetry, arts, and sciences.[60]

Accordingly, the nine gardens to each god in Mears's design for a Parnassolympus are visualizations of the symbolic role Geddes reserves for the Muses in the final quarter of the Notation of Life.

> For they [the Muses] are demonstrably the (nine) possible modes and
> alternatives of that action of the psychic life upon its environment,
> which is life indeed, the "good life" of the Greek aspiration—transcend-
> ing mere vegetative continuance.[61]

At each phase of human life, the nine Muses symbolize artistic and cultural
activities that Geddes considers the appropriate means to realize the good
life, whose ideals, in turn, are represented by the Greek god or goddess in
his temple of the Greek gods.

For Geddes, the Muses are more than just a convenient symbol for
cultural activities. The Greek poet Hesiod wrote the classic account of the
origin of the Muses in his *Theogony*, a poem Geddes occasionally refers to.
The Muses were born in Pieria at the bottom of Mount Parnassus as the
daughters of Mnemosyne (memory) and Zeus.[62] The Muses teach Hesiod to
sing because they "breathed a sacred voice into my mouth/With which to
celebrate the things to come/And things which were before." The Muses also
sang for "father Zeus/Within Olympus, telling of things that are,/That will
be, and that were."[63] In his *Masque of Learning* Geddes connects the Muses to
the perfection of Greek life: "Hence after their common mother, Mnemosyne
(Memory) the Muses appear, each with her activity or its symbol.
. . . They are here presented as recovered in terms of science, as again becoming manifest through the study of life and mind in evolution."[64]

Geddes's tool of the historical survey documents the past and present of a region and city for the benefit of the future. This future is incipient
because it is already embodied in the past and present. To discover the future requires recapitulating history by reading historic artifacts in the urban structure or in a museum. Hence Geddes's fascination with the Muses:
their mother is Memory; but memory—remembering the history of a
city—is also the first step toward the city's future. The recapitulation of history relies on surviving cultural and artistic artifacts; but these in turn are
products of the Muses, the goddesses of the arts and sciences. And as the
Muses sing about past, present, and future, these artifacts tell about the
same. Each human generation that is inspired by the Muses leaves a layer of
artifacts in a city or region-city, which can tell the next generation about its
predecessors. The city considered as a museum of historical remnants is a
place of the Muses; the word *museum* derives etymologically from Museion,

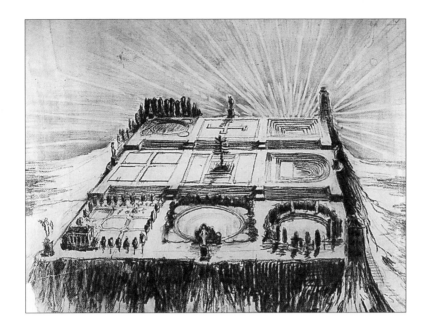

FIGURE 7.12

Garden for the nine
Greek Muses, perspec-
tive, c. 1913–1914, by
Adrian Berrington after
Patrick Geddes.

a hill in Athens facing the Acropolis and sacred to the Muses. A city designer
can renew a city's dedication to the Muses by "designing, for the bettering
cities of the opening future, their veritable 'Museion,' sometimes even with
all its nine Muse-gardens, and their fitting palaces."[65]

Geddes never had an opportunity to build an actual garden for the
Muses, but an undated perspective drawing by Adrian Berrington
(1887–1923), a young architect who collaborated with Geddes on various architectural and exhibition schemes, gives a good idea of such a garden's design (figure 7.12).[66] The garden is located on a mountaintop and divided into
nine smaller gardens, each dedicated to one of the Muses. A sculpture of the
Arbor Saeculorum identifies the central square as the garden of Clio, the
Muse of history. The fourth quadrant of the Notation of Life (figure 2.1) allows us to ascribe the surrounding squares to the remaining Muses. Each
individual garden contains an architectural or landscape feature, among
them sunken horseshoe-shaped and square performance spaces, a stone
circle, and a circular stage. The intention is to provide spaces appropriate to
the artistic activity associated with each of the Muses.[67] The whole garden
is enclosed by an ambulatory with female statues placed at the midpoint of

each side and statues of Apollo, the leader of the choir of the Muses, at two corners. At the other two corners a tower for regional history and a tower of regional science are located.

Whereas this drawing is only a speculative sketch, Geddes's 1922 city design report for Patiala state and city contains a detailed description of a garden for the nine Greek Muses.[68] In Pinjaur, a small town with a royal palace and garden in Patiala state, Geddes reinterprets a classical Indian Mughal garden as both a garden of the Notation of Life and a garden for the nine Muses. The actual seventeenth-century enclosed garden is arranged in terraces.[69] Two channels divide the garden into four quadrangles, each of them in turn subdivided by walkways into four smaller squares.[70] The geometrical plan is the starting point of Geddes's reinterpretation (figure 7.13). He proposes to conserve some of the still existing original planting, but otherwise to renew it. The main quadrangles he ascribes to the four social types. Within each quadrangle he suggests planting gardens whose plants relate to its particular social type. For the people, for example, he plans a domestic orchard and vegetable garden, while a forest as a place of meditation and religious retreat is the appropriate type of garden for the intellectuals.[71] Thus the whole garden expresses for Geddes the "microcosm of the great world," a direct reference to Lethaby's definition of a temple. The central junction of two water channels additionally emphasizes the temple character of the garden; this crossing is a "central and cosmic crossing," similar to the paradise rivers in the Nature Palace at Dunfermline.[72] Finally, Geddes dedicates the garden to the Greek Muses. At the center one finds again a statue of Clio, with statues of the other muses placed on the smaller crossing of the walkways.[73]

## The Temple as the Union between Science and Religion

A chronological ordering of those of Geddes's temple projects and related ideas that can be dated reveals an increasing sense of religiosity in their symbolism (table 7.1). More and more he incorporates cosmographic and mythological ideas. One of his earliest spatial designs is a botanic garden at Grange School in Edinburgh (1883), which primarily visualizes the evolutionary development of plants. A botanic garden at University College, Dundee, only five years later acquires already an additional meaning, expressing the ideas Geddes had recently elaborated about the continuity of

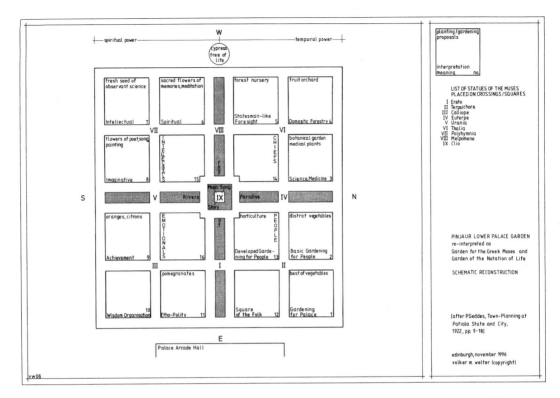

Inside the diagram, the following labels appear:

W

spiritual power — temporal power

cypress tree of life

planting/gardening proposals

interpretation meaning no.

LIST OF STATUES OF THE MUSES
PLACED ON CROSSINGS/SQUARES

I Erato
II Terpsichore
III Calliope
IV Euterpe
V Urania
VI Thalia
VII Polyhymnia
VIII Melpomene
IX Clio

PINJAUR LOWER PALACE GARDEN
re-interpreted as
Garden for the Greek Muses and
Garden of the Notation of Life

SCHEMATIC RECONSTRUCTION

[after P.Geddes, Town-Planning at
Patiala State and City,
1922, pp. 9-18]

edinburgh, november 1996
volker m. welter (copyright)

fresh seed of observant science — Intellectual 7
sacred flowers of memories, meditation — Spiritual 6
VIII
forest nursery / Statesman-like Foresight — Domestic Forestry 5
fruit orchard — Domestic Forestry 4
VII
flowers of poet, song painting — Imaginative 8
INTELLECTUALS 15
F
CHIEFS 14
botanical garden medical plants — Science, Medicine 3
VI
S — V Rivers — IX Music, Song, Story — Paradise IV — N
oranges, citrons — Achievement 9
EMOTIONALS 16
III
horticulture / Developed Gardening for People 13
PEOPLE
district vegetables / Basic Gardening for People 2
II
pomegranates — Wisdom Organisation 10 / Etho-Polity 11
Square of the Folk 12
I
best of vegetables / Gardening for Palace 1

E

Palace Arcade Hall

vw96

anabolic and catabolic forms of life in evolution. The National Institute of Geography (1902) emphasizes this larger interest even more strongly by focusing on the earth and the cosmos as the environment for anabolic and catabolic forms of life.

With Geddes's growing interest in the Greek gods and Muses, the focus of his temple projects changes again in two respects. First, the interpretation of life acquires a different meaning; in the temple of life accommodating the Greek gods, and its counterpart the *campo santo*, the mere scientific analysis of life according to Geddes's theory of metabolism gives way to a presentation of an ideal course of life as a teleological aim. A similar shift can be observed between the temple of geography and the garden of the Muses. The former, although already incorporating religious references to the Garden of Eden, is still primarily a call for action to make use of the earth for mankind's benefit. The latter presents human activities

FIGURE 7.13

Garden for the nine Greek Muses and the four social types, reconstruction drawing based on Geddes's description of the replanning of the palace garden in Pinjaur, 1922.

| 1883 | Botanic garden, Grange House School, Edinburgh (temple of life) |
|---|---|
| 1886 | Beginning of cultural acropolis in Edinburgh (temple of the city) |
| 1888 | Botanic garden, University College, Dundee (temple of life) |
| 1892 | Arbor Saeculorum (symbolic temple of life); Outlook Tower (temple of geography) |
| 1902 | National Institute of Geography, Edinburgh (temple of geography) |
| 1903 | Botanic garden, Horniman Museum, London (temple of life) |
| 1904 | Nature Palace, Dunfermline (temple of geography) |
| 1907 | Temple of the Greek gods (temple of life) |
| 1907 | Garden for the nine Greek Muses (temple of life) |
| [1907] | *Campo santo* (temple of death/temple of life) |
| 1911 | Chapel of the City, Edinburgh (temple of the city) |
| 1918 | Gardens of the phases of life and of evolution, Indore (temples of life and garden of the Muses) |
| 1919 | Great Hall, Hebrew University, Jerusalem (temple of life and synthesis) |
| 1922 | Garden of the Notation of Life and for the nine Greek Muses in Pinjaur, Patiala, India (temple of life) |
| 1922 | Bahá'í Temple, Allahabad, India (temple of life and synthesis) |
| 1924 | Hall of Vision, Conference on Some Living Religions within the Empire, London (temple of life and synthesis) |
| 1925 | Cultural acropolis for the city of Tel Aviv (temple of the city) |

TABLE 7.1

Projects and schemes by Patrick Geddes for temples and temple-like structures.

teleologically; the Muses are a religiously inspired glorification of human cultural and artistic activities and their results.

While Geddes's thoughts about life and human activities grow more and more complex, his means to represent them take the reverse direction: they appear to become ever simpler. The development from the geographical institute—a vast machinery of knowledge—to the statues for the Muses may have been a small step for Geddes; it is, however, a large step for anybody else. The former expects a visitor to immerse himself in knowledge to gain understanding; the latter asks him to believe what Geddes thinks the Muses stand for.

Like many Victorians, Geddes lost his belief in traditional religion sometime during youth or early adulthood. But he never lost the conviction that there is a need, and a space, for religiosity in human life. As an appropriate basis for a contemporary religiosity Geddes identifies biology, the science of life. Geddes as a biologist understands life as the eternal existence of protoplasm, and its anabolic and catabolic interactions with the environment. But the ideas of protoplasm and metabolism as the common denominator of life are not an explanation for life as such. Metabolism is a mechanism, and a "mechanism does not explain anything!"[74] Life is more, but what this more is Geddes has difficulty explaining. He rejects notions of a life force but admits that something similar is necessary, for "the phenomena distinctive of life cannot at present be restated in the language of chemistry and physics."[75]

This conflict is for Geddes more than a dispute between modern biology and traditional religious beliefs. It is a conflict with immediate consequences for the conduct and development of human life, individual and communal, in the city. Although religion appears to have been dethroned by the development of modern science, in historical perspective religion has proven its value for societies and individuals by nurturing the spiritual powers of intellectuals and the cloister and those of emotionals and the cathedral. Even if the gap between biology and religion cannot, at least for the time being, be closed, the contemporary function and importance of religiosity is beyond question. The task is to reconcile both immediately for the benefit of the city. An appropriate space to achieve this is a contemporary temple appealing to man's need for religiosity and directing it toward the understanding of life.

In 1905 the philosopher John Alexander Stewart published a study of the function of myths in Plato's dialogues with the title *The Myths of Plato*, a book Geddes was well familiar with. Stewart argues that Plato engaged myths in order to introduce man into the secret of "Universal Nature" and to the "Value of Life itself," both being beyond the level of thinking in which man worked out his own concept of the world.[76] A myth is successful if the listeners believe what the story said; it is a "deliberate make-believe":

> It is in the spirit of this serious make-believe that . . . we . . . make pilgrimages to places associated with the events of great fiction. . . . The topography of the *Inferno* and that of the Roman Forum are approached in much the same spirit by the interested student in each case.[77]

Geddes's temples are exactly such places of make-believe, putting forward with an ever-increasing religiosity his ideas about life and its improvement. His idea of the temple of life found a fitting climax in a design for a Bahá'í temple in Allahabad, India, from 1922 (unrealized).[78] Contacts between Geddes and the Bahá'í movement, a religious sect that emerged in Persia during the 1860s, can be traced back to a visit of 'Abdu'l-Bahá, the spiritual leader of the movement, to Edinburgh in 1913. Geddes was one of the hosts of the prominent visitor. He renewed this contact in 1920 when he worked in Haifa, which by then had become the spiritual world center of the movement. While it cannot reasonably be claimed that Geddes was a convert to the Bahá'í cause, he was attracted to the movement for its teachings of the unity of all religions, spiritual universalism, universal education, and world peace.

The plan of the Bahá'í temple evolved around a central dome surrounded by nine smaller "cloisters" or "cells of meditation," which are dedicated to major world religions (figure 7.14). A pool with a fountain forms the center of each cloister, while a "pillar of unity" is the central feature of the large dome. Geddes proposed to complement the temple with libraries, a school of comparative religions, and a range of museums.[79] Apart from the number of the cloisters, which refers back to the nine Muses and their function within the city, all the other elements of the design are likewise derived from earlier temple designs by Geddes. The water fountain is a feature of his plan for the Nature Palace in Dunfermline, the educational and museum facilities feature prominently in the National Institute of Geography for

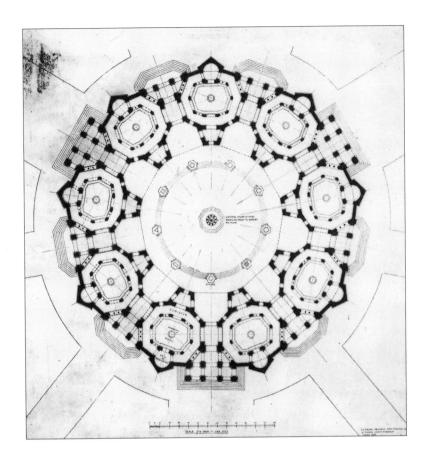

FIGURE 7.14

Ground plan of the
Bahá'í temple, 1922, by
Frank C. Mears and
Patrick Geddes.

Edinburgh, and finally the "pillar of unity," which supports the ribbed vault of the dome, can be read as a tree of life (figure 7.15).

In the context of Geddes's theory of city design, the Bahá'í temple is of particular importance for two reasons. First, in a twenty-four-page explanatory letter to Mears Geddes presents the Bahá'í temple as the climax of a list of comparable schemes. This list comprises Reclus's and Galeron's globes, Geddes's own Edinburgh Outlook Tower, the temples of Garas, but also Rudolf Steiner's Goetheanum in Dornach, Switzerland, and similar buildings or designs. Geddes thus confirms his intention to unite in one temple science, represented by the globes and the Outlook Tower, and religion, represented by the Bahá'í temple and the Goetheanum. Second, toward the end of the letter Geddes specifically declares the design of such temples of life

FIGURE 7.15

Interior view of the
Bahá'í temple, 1922, by
Frank C. Mears and
Patrick Geddes.

as a task for a city designer, despite the fact that "communities are rarely advanced enough as yet to imagine much less to commission" such buildings.[80]

## A Hall of Vision

Two years after the failed scheme for the Bahá'í temple, Geddes at long last succeeded in realizing, although only temporarily, one of his many temple ideas.
In late September of 1924 the School for Oriental Studies and Geddes's circle
of friends in the Sociological Society organized a joint event in London with the
title "Conference on Some Living Religions within the Empire." The aim of the

meeting was to emphasize, in the words of the imperialist turned mystic Francis Younghusband, that the basis of the British Empire should be religion and not political constitutions or economic agreements.[81] The venue was the Upper West Gallery of the Imperial Institute, where Geddes and his friends installed for the duration of the conference a "Hall of Vision." This hall provided the appropriate setting for a series of papers read by them and accommodated at the same time an exhibition of Geddes's ideas about religion and life.[82] The task facing the participants in the event was, in the words of Branford, to address the question of collaboration between science and religion with the aim of arriving at a better order of contemporary civilization.[83] The gap between science and religion is the same as the one Geddes identifies between religion and biology. The speakers at the conference stressed that to close this gap one must resort to Geddes's analysis of the historic function of religion: the provision of cloister and cathedral, of intellectuals and emotionals.

The exhibition underlines the same point. The Hall of Vision assembles drawings and sketches illustrating Geddes's ideas about life, cities, and temples. It is a belated realization of his call for a "house of synthesis for our own times," his description of Reclus's temple of geography from about twenty years earlier.[84] The exhibition starts with a section presenting Geddes's cosmography by showing maps of the world and the heavens and a drawing of a sunburst in a valley section. The idea of life in evolution is captured in a sketch of a many-breasted Life-Mother sitting on a pyramid of substance with ancient Pan and Darwin, Pan's modern reincarnation, at her feet. Ancient Greece is the theme of the next sequence of exhibits. Greek culture is singled out for its ability to weld together man and nature, town and country, and landscape and architecture, pairs that can only be brought together through religious life. A fourth such pair is male and female life, symbolically united by statues of the Greek gods and goddesses of the Olympic Pantheon.

But life fulfillment requires interaction between individual and communal life. The classical means for this end is religion, which, if successful, results in the creation of a "Sacred City" as the expression of the inner visions of the citizens.[85] Usually, the sacred city is dominated by important public buildings or spaces like the Dome of the Rock in Jerusalem, the Piazza del Popolo in Rome, the Acropolis in Athens, or Westminster's group of civic buildings from Big Ben to Westminster Cathedral (figure 7.16). Finally, the exhibition amounts to a religious approach toward civics:

FIGURE 7.16

Hall of Vision at the
Conference on Some
Living Religions within
the Empire, 1924: the
city acropolis in the sa-
cred cities of Jerusalem,
Rome, and Athens and
in Westminster, London.

GREAT CITIES : ATHENS

VIEW FROM
LEPLAY HOUSE

Now the Ideal, when really incarnated in Man, impels him to the building and maintenance of cities made to a pattern revealed on the consecrate Mount of Vision. But that is an affair at once communal and personal. It implies the attunement and unison of all those preceding dramas of the World, of Life and Labour, of Politics and History, of Art and Morals. . . . Here in this concerted play of the high unity, is our sacred Civic Drama. . . . The approach to religion from Civics comes therefore very near to theology.[86]

The unity underlying civics is visualized in a sketch by Philip Mairet with the title "The Classico-Christian Ideal" (figure 7.17). In the foreground is an image of the natural life in the countryside, symbolized by Mary and the child Jesus together with the Trees of Knowledge and of Life, and an ox and donkey. This rural life is not self-fulfilling but gives access to the highest life fulfillment, the life in a city. A road leads from the Tree of Knowledge to a triumphal arch in front of a neoclassical building, a government palace dominating a town. To arrive at a city, however, the path originating at the Tree of Life has to be taken. It winds through a stylized valley section toward the Hagia Sophia, a symbol for religion dominating the city.

The Hall of Vision is a megatemple uniting Geddes's earlier temple projects in two ways. With respect to the Town-City formula, the hall is a cloister of the intellectuals and a cathedral of the emotionals in one. Regarding its contents, the Hall of Vision is the climax of his attempts to provide a new vision for life and cities. The exhibits bring together the idea of the region and geography, stressing the importance of history and natural sciences and the continuous evolution of cities and individual life. The Hall of Vision is a built embodiment of his envisioned synthesis of all branches of knowledge, of the unification of all individual sciences into a vision of life. Geddes anticipates that the future development of sciences will disclose more and more of this coming synthesis and unity, which has traditionally been propagated by religious faiths. Accordingly, the gap between sciences and religion will ultimately be closed by uniting the two into a religious science—or a scientific religion—of life. The Hall of Vision is an anticipation of this merger.

The 1916 Arts and Crafts Exhibition led the metaphysical approach toward cities into a conceptual cul-de-sac by turning the city itself

FIGURE 7.17

Hall of Vision, 1924: "The Classico-Christian Ideal" with the paths toward the big city and the true city, sketch by Philip Mairet.

into an object of veneration. The Hall of Vision indicates a similar development of Geddes's theory of city design. The valley section, the concept of life in evolution, and all other Geddesian ideas are turned into subjects to be venerated in a temple. The London Hall of Vision is merely a temporary solution, but ultimately every city is in need of a comparable hall, a "Hall of Modern Vision fit to stand alongside the Temples of Ancient Faith."[87]

Regardless of the emphasis Geddes put on sciences like biology and geography as the basis of the predicted synthesis, the future that the Hall of Vision depicts is a deliberate composition, consciously created by the exhibitor, and not a logical and necessary consequence of the sciences it allegedly unites. Like the temple schemes of turn-of-the-century architects and artists discussed in chapter 6, which idealized their inventors' ideas, Geddes's temples express nothing more than his own anticipation of an ideal future condition.

Labour in Nature again renews Arcadia. Our town becomes a City indeed, with Acropolis and Temples, Academe and Forum, Stadium and Theatre.

Patrick Geddes, *The Returning Gods*

# From the Temple of the City to the Cultural Acropolis

In the preceding chapter the focus was on Geddes's temples of knowledge and life. A third group of his temple schemes—temples and temple-like structures dedicated to the city—will be discussed in this chapter. Although many of them were conceived at the same time as the previous examples, they are temples of a higher order, as they incorporate elements from the schemes for temples of knowledge and temples of life for the benefit of the city.

## The Temple of the City

Despite Geddes's intention to see a Hall of Vision in every city, an existing city was more likely to be dominated by a traditional religious building, in the case of European cities normally a church or cathedral. We saw in chapter 4 how Geddes appreciates medieval cities as the most perfect expression of a city built by the four social types. Within this structure he identifies the cathedral as the building associated with the emotionals, responsible for transferring the idea of a city from the cloister into the city. Consequently, he reinterprets existing cathedrals as temple structures that express civic virtues and venerate the city itself. The cathedral is for Geddes a temple of the city, a "living and throbbing organ of social life which gathered into itself, and re-expressed as corporate individuality, the finer aspiration of citizen and rustic alike." In its construction, the cathedral allows craftsmen to express their own personalities and ideas but also "those of their city and region."[1] The craftsmen expressing their individuality are a reference to Ruskin's essay *The Stones of Venice*, in which he argues that the achievements of Gothic church architecture were made possible by the individual freedom of the artist.[2] But to consider the cathedral as the expression of a city and region comes closer to Goethe's veneration of Strasbourg cathedral, its expression of truth and beauty derived from the feelings of the soul of the (in this case) German people.[3]

For Geddes, the cathedral is the incorporation of the soul or spirit of a city, because it is "the highest agency of the times towards bringing to bear upon the community the best cultural resources, the synthesis of ideals and of knowledge, . . . the orchestration of all the arts—painting, sculpture, and architecture, music and symbol-drama."[4] It presents in stone the results of those civic activities that the garden of the Muses intends to celebrate. Furthermore, the cathedral normally includes various chapels and altars dedicated to the varying ideals of individual citizens and classes.[5] The cathedral unifies groups of citizens, as all religions are unified in the temple for the Bahá'í faith. Finally, the cathedral is a "veritable popular encyclopaedia," because its decoration depicts astronomic symbolism, the story of the creation and fall of man, and national and civic history.[6] Thus it incorporates temples of knowledge like the Geographical Institute, but also all history as embodied in the Arbor Saeculorum. All these qualities are the product of the Town-City formula's final two stages, the cloister and the city in deed. The cathedral is the city in condensed form. From it ultimately the city will emerge, because the synthesis that is achieved in the cathedral radiates into the existing town and country and thus guarantees that the whole city will become "the cathedral of the People."[7]

Even more condensed symbols of a city than the cathedral are crystallike hexagon and octagon shapes. Among Geddes's papers are many cards and scrap papers on which he scribbled these geometrical forms. Usually, each side of the crystal is dedicated to a different aspect of human life. For example, on one card Geddes notes at one side of the hexagon "Current events/Ethiodrama" together with a symbol for the Arbor Saeculorum, followed on the other sides by the words "autodrama," "technodrama" with a sketch of a valley section, "cosmodrama," "aesthetodrama," and finally "chronodrama." In this case Geddes writes in the bottom right corner "Apply to city +"; this is to be read as "Apply to city cross." On another card a hexagon is identified as a city cross.[8] The hexagon expresses graphically the unity and synthesis of all human activities; it is "the six-sided crystal of life."[9] This symbol of unity is exhibited in the 1924 Hall of Vision (figure 8.1), but already in 1911 a hexagon was displayed at the Cities and Town Planning Exhibition at Chelsea that is identified on the exhibition's layout plan as a symbol of the "city as organic unity" (see figure 5.6). In 1918 a hexagon also figures prominently on the comprehensive plan accompanying Geddes's report for the city of Indore (figure 8.2).[10] Furthermore, Geddes does not confine himself to using the hexagon as a graphic symbol, but attempts on several occasions to insert this form into the urban fabric of cities in the form of either a city cross, a "Chapel of the City," or a public square.

Historically, the cathedral expressed the unity of human activities directed toward the good of the community. A city cross, the traditional structure for official announcements or the center of festive activities, can potentially achieve the same status, as indicated on Geddes's card notes referred to above. It is for Geddes a "peculiarly fitting . . . symbol not only of Citizenship, but of Civic Revivance."

> The many-sided activities of a great city, spiritual and social, educational and hygienic, architectural and industrial—or most simply ideal and material—all these may be fitly symbolised upon the many sides of this characteristic building, as aspects of a real and living unity.[11]

It is this reinterpretation of a historic civic monument which, for example, makes Geddes suggest in his city design report for Dunfermline placing the old city cross on the proposed Carnegie Place above the new city hall.[12]

FIGURE 8.1

Hall of Vision, 1924: the hexagon crystal of life as "The Scholar's Ideal of Life's Six-Fold Drama."

The synthesis embodied in the crystal is also the guiding idea for a "Chapel of the City" that Geddes temporarily installed in one of the octagons in the Royal Scottish Academy during the Cities and Town Planning Exhibition in Edinburgh in 1911. Inside the chapel, six tables form a hexagon. Each table represents a branch of knowledge and human activities: morals, economics, education, hygiene, art, and industry. A central table inside the hexagon symbolizes the sought-for cooperation. Two paintings of old and new Edinburgh complete the chapel as expression of this city's incipient future.[13] Both Geddes's "Chapel of the City" from 1911 and the temple of the city at the Arts and Crafts Exhibition in 1916 are dedicated to the city, but the former's emphasis on knowledge and its application to reality contains a strong call for all citizens to join in creating a city.

A crystal of life, this time an octagon, is also a prominent feature in the master plan Geddes conceived for the city of Tel Aviv in 1925.[14] Geddes structures the extension of Tel Aviv with a grid of north-south and east-west

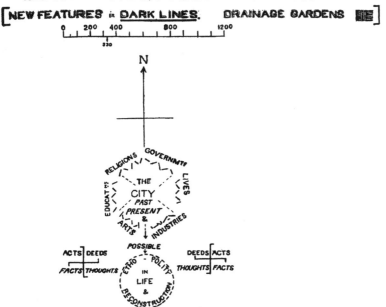

**X**

**INDORE**

**IMPROVEMENTS & EXTENSIONS**

[ NEW FEATURES in DARK LINES. DRAINAGE GARDENS ▦ ]

0    200    400        800        1200

330

N

RELIGIONS    GOVERNMT?
EDUCAT?    THE
CITY
PAST
PRESENT
&
ARTS    INDUSTRIES
LIVES
POSSIBLE
ACTS DEEDS    DEEDS ACTS
FACTS THOUGHTS    THOUGHTS FACTS
ETHO POLITY
IN
LIFE
&
RECONSTRUCTION

FIGURE 8.2

The hexagon as a symbol for the city as organic unity, illustrated on the plan for Indore, 1918, by Patrick Geddes.

streets. At the center of the resulting superblocks he locates open spaces and gardens. While the open spaces are accessible to everybody by means of narrow lanes, they are primarily private gardens for those living in the detached houses of each individual block. The one, large public square Geddes suggests for the extension of Tel Aviv is located exactly on the border between the old and the new town. He gives this square the shape of an octagon, thus emphasizing the need to unite both halves of the city into a larger whole.

The plan for Tel Aviv is a prime example of Geddes's idea of "comprehensive planning" of temple-like structures, which he mentions in his letter to Mears explaining the ideas behind the Bahá'í temple. But the Tel Aviv plan also highlights the gap between Geddes's highly developed structure of thought and his preference for simple symbolic forms. The symbol of the crystal contains all of his complex ideas about the city, but this is obvious only to him and to those already initiated into his thoughts. Nothing suggests how this form should actually transmit an idea form the city designer to the citizens. The final Tel Aviv report gives only the slightest hint regarding the choice of the shape of octagon and the civic importance of the square for the city. Architecturally, Geddes envisions the square as surrounded by four-story buildings, ideally designed by a single architect because "only in this way can this Central City feature be made really and permanently effective."[15] That the expression "Central City feature" refers to more than its location—approximately in the geographical center of Tel Aviv—Geddes does not disclose. Consequently, the form of the octagon was of no great concern to the architect Genia Averbouch, who in 1935 won the competition for today's Dizengoff Square. Her design substitutes a circular space surrounded by streamlined buildings for Geddes's suggested symbol of unity.

Geddes's temples are spaces where a city as a community should gain insights into his vision of life. He complements these communal spaces with "thinking cells," secluded spaces for individual meditation and thought. This dichotomy in the urban fabric between communal and individual spaces dedicated to metaphysical ideas reflects the dual structure of the Notation of Life, which analyzes the city as emerging from the relation between the community and the individual citizen.

In the Outlook Tower in Edinburgh Geddes provides a thinking cell on the top floor adjacent to the camera obscura. To locate the cell above the city is a deliberate choice that recalls the isolated temple schemes on mountain peaks.[16] After the outlook on the region and world, a visitor should enter the small room for "turning over in memory the outlook and its mirrored reflection, and the particular studies of these." It is "the place where one's picture is conceived—not copied—from Nature. It is the room of the Weaving of Dreams."[17] Nothing in the cell is to disturb the inner visions. The Outlook Tower cell contains only a chair. Similarly, a proposed "cell of retirement" that Geddes describes in the Dunfermline report consists of a simple whitewashed room, adjacent to a room of synthesis.[18]

The renunciation of any decoration indicates the degree of temporary isolation in the thinking cell from the contemporary and historic urban environment, especially in comparison with the elaborated decorative schemes Geddes pursues for other buildings and public spaces in a city. The isolation in the cell has to be total; Geddes insists on a space offering time, peace, and quietness within the restless urban life.[19] This recalls Nietzsche's dictum in *The Joyful Wisdom*, under the heading "Architecture for Thinkers," that cities are in need of "quiet, spacious, and widely extended places for reflection" whose architecture and spatial arrangement should "express the sublimity of self-communion and seclusion from the world." Rejecting religious buildings as adequate spaces for a *vita contemplativa*, Nietzsche concludes: "We want to have *ourselves* translated into stone and plant, we want to go for a walk in *ourselves* when we wander in these halls and gardens."[20] To enter Nietzsche's hall of contemplation is to affirm the identity between all matter—stone, plants, and man—an identity evoking an image of eternity similar to the monism of Haeckel. While Nietzsche's Zarathustra instigates many temple schemes in sublime natural locations, Nietzsche's "Architecture for Thinkers" can be seen as a model for introspective temple spaces within cities.

One of the earliest examples of an urban space for a *vita contemplativa* is the Chapel of the Ascension (1890–1893) built by the architect Herbert P. Horne in London. Walter Crane characterizes the building as "intended, not for service, but simply as a quiet place for meditation, for any one weary of the rush and roar of London streets."[21] Traditional churches, according to Geddes, are places where a citizen, after a walk through a city dedicated to reading its history, can conceive and communicate with the *genius loci*. The thinking cell provides another such space within a city. Although not derived from religious buildings itself, its function—the internalization of the macrocosm in the microcosm of the individual—makes it a temple-like structure. The *vita contemplativa* is an important preparation for the *vita activa* of citizens and city designer, aiming at the city in deed; or as Geddes occasionally writes: "The principle thus emerges that Town Planning is the product of Town Thinking, Town Feeling, and is no mere material resultant of geographical situation and occupation, of government or defence."[22]

## Celebrating the City

The elevation of a town to a city requires not only the individual experience of "Town Thinking" and "Town Feeling" in the thinking cell, but also a comparable communal experience. Consequently, Geddes develops into an element of city design the public ritual he experienced on the occasion of the funeral of his acquaintance John Stuart Blackie in Edinburgh in 1895.

Blackie was Professor of Greek at Edinburgh University and a well-known public advocate of Scottish nationalism and home rule. Geddes paid tribute to him in his essay "The Scots Renascence," beginning emphatically with the words: "Blackie was buried yesterday." Geddes describes the funeral procession as a "communion of multitudinous sorrow, that reverent throng amid which the broad Cathedral was but the sounding chancel, the square and street the silent transept and nave." He continues:

> In front went a long procession of Societies headed by kilt and plaid; behind came the mourning kinsmen, with the Advocates, the Senate, the Students, and the Town Council, in their varied robes; then the interminable carriages of personal friends. But the better than all these, the Town itself was out; the working people in their thousands and tens of thousands lined the Way from St. Giles' to the Dean; the very windows and balconies were white with faces.[23]

With the exception of a very few names, mentioned elsewhere in the essay, Geddes merges the inhabitants of Edinburgh into an anonymous mass of citizens. They are divided only into the four social types of intellectuals, chiefs, people, and a small group of municipal dignitaries who conduct "this pageant of Edinburgh" as the emotionals.[24] Edinburgh is mourning the death of one of its intellectuals, yet at the same time celebrating itself by temporarily turning its squares and streets into a cathedral—one of Geddes's symbols of the city. In all of his writing there is hardly a better description of the city as a community and living organism which can be experienced in a public celebration.

What Geddes experienced at Blackie's funeral, more or less accidentally, others elsewhere initiated deliberately. In 1899, for example, Fritz Schumacher wrote a theatrical piece, a dialogue between Faust and Mephisto, that featured *tableaux vivants* involving about two hundred lay actors. A number of artists were in charge of designing the costumes, but Schumacher stresses in a letter to his brother that the whole city was involved in making the performance a success.[25] The year before, Schumacher had begun to work on his temples for cities and sublime locations. The two activities can be considered as related: the temples are built foci providing new ideas for a society or city; the theater play attempts to evoke a sense of community by engaging a large number of citizens as participants in a communal activity. Two years later, in 1901, the Ernst Ludwig House in Darmstadt, the temple of creation of the artist community of Mathildenhöhe, was the focus of a festive ceremony on the occasion of its opening. Conceived by Peter Behrens, the ceremony celebrated a crystal as a sign of the coming redemption through the union of art and life. Beyond this, the event emphasized the sense of a small, close-knit community unified by a common aim.

Geddes was engaged in similar activities, although on a much smaller scale. In 1892 at the upper end of Edinburgh's High Street, the Royal Mile, opposite Castle Esplanade, he had begun to build a speculative development comprising a student hall of residence, artists' studios, and a number of flats. As it was erected on land surrounding the former house of Scottish poet Allan Ramsay, which was incorporated into the new student hall of residence, the complex came to be called Ramsay Garden. The completion of the first part of the project in 1894 was celebrated with an opening ceremony conducted by Blackie. Part of the event was a "ceremonial of the torch," a symbolic presentation of a lighted torch by one of the youngest residents of Ramsay Garden, Geddes's daughter Norah, to the oldest participant in the event, Professor Blackie.[26] He in turn passed the torch on to the youngest member of the student community in the hall of residence, who placed it above the courtyard of Ramsay Garden, thus ending the symbolic circle of life from young to old to young.[27] Geddes lit a torch not only for a single house but also for a city, for example during the final scene of his *Masque of Ancient and Modern Learning*, the pageant through the history of civilization and education that he performed in Edinburgh for the first time in 1912 and later repeated in London.[28]

The *Masque of Learning* is a sequence of *tableaux vivants* portraying man's enlightenment since ancient times through the pursuit of knowledge and education, to be performed by over 300 lay actors. Amelia Defries, Geddes's first biographer, recalls the closing scene of the performance during which the participants pass to each other the lighted "torch of civilisation." The effect is, in the words of Defries, "some realization, of the past—and the pricelessness of modern culture; some perception of our responsibility, to keep alight this divine fire. . . . What indeed is the Divine Adventure if not the quest for Life and Truth?"[29] The torch of civilization symbolizes for Geddes the continuity of life in evolution, presented in the *Masque* in the form of knowledge and its universal transmission from one culture to the other through past, present, and future. Accordingly, the Arbor Saeculorum was a permanent feature in the background of each stage where the *Masque* was performed.[30]

The *Masque of Learning*'s vision of life is specifically related to citizen and city. Its final tableau is an outlook into the future (figure 8.3). At the center of this scene two women—Alma Mater and Edina, eponymous Mater Civitatis for the Scottish capital—are sitting on a small pedestal. They are served from both sides by graduates of various university faculties and by different city institutions, among them the University of Edinburgh and the Outlook Tower. The unison of city and university, of life and learning for it, is the ultimate aim the *Masque* venerated, an aim that every citizen should serve. The *Masque* complements the thinking cell. In the latter the individual citizen internalizes the vision of life and its forms that he might have learned about in the outlook tower, Geddes's temples, and the Cities and Town Planning Exhibition. The *Masque* achieves the same for all citizens as a community. By participating in its performance, citizens reenact and recapitulate the history of human civilization and thereby make it their own. The *Masque* provides a universal outlook on history and life complementing the local history to be read from historic buildings in a city.

The *Masque*, Blackie's funeral, and the festivities around the opening of Ramsay Garden are events evoking a sense of city through communal participation. For Geddes they are not ends in themselves but important means for the renewal of citizenship and the city. Even more, they are a resuscitation of a traditional means of city building, one that has prominent historical precedents in the ancient Greek and the medieval civilization. With respect to his own masques, Geddes points out the importance of legends and myths and their public enactment on the occasion of religious festivals and theatrical performances in the ancient Greek city. The medieval miracle and mystery plays are similar means of sharing traditions between generations of citizens. According to Geddes, it is this "transmission of sacred legend" that "gave birth to the characteristic expressions and the spiritual achievement of the medieval City—its Great Place and Belfry Tower, its Town-House and its Cathedral."[31]

The city at the center of myths and legends refers back to the religious veneration of the Greek *polis*.[32] Religion in the *polis* meant fostering the relation between *polis*, citizen, and city gods rather than redeeming individuals from sin as in Christian religions. The *polis* was dominated by temples, sanctuaries, and other sacred spaces interspersed in its urban and rural areas and concentrated in certain places like the Acropolis in Athens. The life of the citizens and other inhabitants was structured by religious celebrations. Religion as a public and civic matter expressed itself in sacrifices and festivities, often preceded by a procession through the city as a "symbolic reappropriation of the city's space by the community."[33] Part of the religious activities were athletic and dramatic competitions for which the *polis* provided suitable spaces like gymnasia for training, stadia, and theaters. Winning a competition brought honor equally to the athlete and his city, and the drama enacted in the theaters by actors taking on the roles of gods and mythical figures often had an immediate bearing on the politics of the *polis*.

FIGURE 8.3

Celebrating the city: sketch for the closing scene of the *Masque of Ancient and Modern Learning* showing the unison between Alma Mater and Mater Civitatis, 1912.

The statues of the Greek gods in Geddes's various temples of life are intended to visualize within a city his idea of life. To transfer this symbolic representation into reality means to transform a town into a city as the highest expression of life. This requires instigating ordinary citizens to transform themselves and their successors into images of the gods, or at least to attempt to come as close as possible to the ideal course of life. The masque is an intermediate step toward this aim. It brings temporarily to life past embodiments of the gods at various historic periods in different cultures, as the Greek drama brings the gods to the citizens of a *polis*.

Based on the understanding of the Greek drama as serving life and the city, Geddes borrows from the *polis* the amphitheater as an appropriate space in which to perform masques, the descendants of ancient drama. Regarding a proposed amphitheater in the city of Indore, Geddes refers specifically to the role of the theater in the Greek civilization and not to any possible tradition of Indian theater. Geddes describes his proposal as creating a "living theatre, setting forth by turns the main elements of that heritage of legend and myth, of drama and tragedy" that is the basis for the creation of any local culture.[34] Amphitheaters, open-air stages, and performance spaces in theaters and public halls are standard features in Geddes's city design reports. He suggests an amphitheater as early as 1904 in his report for Dunfermline and proposes one again in his last city design report from 1925 for Tel Aviv.[35] Without an amphitheater a city is not complete.

The sense of city Geddes recognizes in the funeral ceremony for Blackie relies not only on the masses of citizens participating, but also on their movement through the urban space. Following this event, Geddes begins to provide appropriate routes through a city for similar expressions of civic spirit. On several occasions in his city design reports he describes a *via sacra*, an idea derived from the sacred ways through a *polis* (for example roads connecting rural sanctuaries and a city) or from procession routes for religious feasts in medieval cities. As early as 1900 for the Universal Exposition at Paris he proposes the transformation of the Rue des Nations with its sequence of national exhibition pavilions into a "'Sacred Way' which would transform Paris into a new Delphi."[36] In the Dunfermline report he elaborates the *via sacra* in more detail. He proposes to make Pittencrieff Park an assembly of cultural and museological institutions comprising the Nature Palace, botanic and zoological gardens, numerous indoor and outdoor exhibition areas presenting the history of labor and of arts and crafts development, a library, public meeting halls, an amphitheater, and similar institutions. As mentioned above, Geddes's intention is to symbolically transform the park into a cathedral. Accordingly, he interprets the individual cultural institutions as having the same function as small chapels in a large cathedral, which is to express "the various ideals to which individuals and classes are devoted."[37]

Geddes's plan for Pittencrieff Park (figure 8.4) combines his understanding of the cathedral as a building of synthesis with the image of a community of citizens moving through the building's space. Like a religious procession that progresses through a church or a city and pauses at different chapels or monuments for worship, walking through Pittencrieff Park becomes a sacred act. Interpreting the cultural institutions in the park as chapels means offering places to venerate past generations, their history, their work, and the spirit that governed their city and their life. Geddes considers the roads and paths through Pittencrieff Park to constitute "the processional routes of future festivals—the *Via Sacra* and *Via Triumphalis* of Labour." He envisions "crafts processions" moving along these routes in order to celebrate the development and achievements of labor and art for the benefit of the city.[38]

While the condensed symbolism of a cathedral and of Pittencrieff Park are to be the focus of communal acts of civic worship, Geddes intends plenty of opportunities for similar emotions on the level of individual citizens. Every street of a city he wishes to become a minor *via sacra*, in which historic buildings, sculptures and memorials, and meaningful embellishments and decorations are all potential "stations of the individual meditative pilgrimage" of citizens on their daily ways through their city. Beyond practical considerations like width or surface, Geddes states that the design and planning of roads should be suggestive and educative, "individually emotional" for citizens and "collectively dramatic" for the community.[39]

Geddes's and Mears's design for the Great Hall of Hebrew University in Jerusalem from 1919, the final project to be looked at in this section, combines the idea of a *via sacra* with a temple of life. In the aftermath of the Balfour Declaration, the Zionist movement commissioned numerous reports by experts on a variety of questions and problems faced by the Zionist resettlement of Palestine. David Eder, the psychoanalyst who in 1908

FIGURE 8.4

Plan for Pittencrieff

Park, Dunfermline,

1904, by Patrick Geddes.

had invited Geddes to present his temple of life to the Fabian Society during a lecture on eugenics, was crucial in convincing Chaim Weizmann to entrust Geddes, in cooperation with Mears, with the master plan and design for the future university. Visually, the main feature of Geddes's plan is the Great Hall, a space for graduations and other large-scale events. Beyond this, Geddes conceived the hall as a temple of life.[40] Connecting the points of the Zionist symbol of the Star of David results in a hexagon, Geddes's symbol for unity in life and the city. Consequently, Mears's interior design shows a hall covered with Stars of David alternating with hexagons (figure 8.5). Additional decorations refer to the valley section and the natural occupations in the valley region.

A series of presentation drawings by Mears clearly shows the intended temple character of the building, which was to be located on Mount Scopus just outside the old city of Jerusalem. One of Mears's perspectives shows a road—a *via sacra*—winding up Mount Scopus like a procession way. Halfway up the hill, the road enters the university precinct through a gate in a wall that encircled the complex (figure 8.6). Another perspective depicts a group of people approaching the Great Hall, guided by a banner that displays the Star of David (figure 8.7). They may be students on their way to a graduation ceremony or—given their folded hands and the knowledge that the Star of David is for Geddes a version of his hexagon symbol—worshipers of life approaching their temple of life.

In a 1914 book Victor Branford proposes a unification of city and university—a merger of town and cloister, in the language of the Notation of Life—with the help of an "Institute of Synthesis." Such an institute would raise "Town Plans . . . into City Design," which is identical with the step from a mere "topographical analysis of Site and Structures" toward a plan structured by "Sacred Ways, [outlook] Towers and Temples." He continues: "The Town Plan is the guide of the city's external and secular existence; the City Design is the dream of its inner and sacred life."[41] The Great Hall in Jerusalem is such an institute of synthesis; it would have raised the Zionist resettlement project to the level of building a city in the region of Palestine. But despite the spiritual feeling evoked by Mears's perspective drawings, the contents and form the spirituality should take among the citizens is left ill defined. Elsewhere Branford hints at the kind of civic ceremony the Great Hall should accommodate: according to him,

the upper of two ambulatories right beneath the dome offers a space for
"outlook upon city and country" and for "processional chant of those
psalms which proclaim an indissoluble unity of the moral and the cosmic
order."[42]

    Geddes's search for a new spiritual and metaphysical center for a
city, which begins with his Outlook Tower and the proposed National Institute of Geography in Edinburgh in the 1890s as a call for the synthesis of
rational knowledge and sciences for the benefit of cities and citizens, ends
two decades later in the chanting of psalms around the Great Hall of Hebrew University conceived as an institute of synthesis. The temple as the cli-

FIGURE 8.6

Distant perspective view
of Hebrew University,
Jerusalem, c. 1919–1920,
by Frank C. Mears and
Benjamin Chaikin for
Patrick Geddes.

max of the city as a form of life—equally rooted in sciences and religion—
becomes the center of ecstatic and joyful celebrations. Such celebrations are
not confined to the temple of life proposed for Jerusalem. Sybella Branford,
married to Victor Branford and likewise a close ally of Geddes, envisions
Richmond, a garden city near London, as a culture city engaged in the pursuit of beauty and celebrating permanent festivities. Its inhabitants were to
be "craftsmen, musicians and artists, thinkers and poets, dramatists and psy-
chologists, sociologists and students," and their daily life was to be filled
with cultural activities comprising everything "from dancing on the green
to writing a poem; from acting a play or taking part in a pageant, to com-
posing an opera."[43]

The paleotechnic town forced its inhabitants into a society of
shared suffering and a passive life; the neotechnic city would unite its citizens in a community of celebrations and active life. Finally, the Muses and
the Greek gods would return to the city. Significantly, however, Geddes's always vivid imagination remains silent on what should actually happen
around the temple or in the city whose metaphysical center the temple is. It
was possible to arouse a feeling of community in the relatively small community of Ramsay Garden, but Geddes's discipline of city design failed to
transpose this idea successfully into the larger city. In retrospect, his many
repetitive temple schemes reveal themselves as an optimistic—but at the
same time desperate—series of attempts to realize at least once, somewhere,
somehow, a built manifestation of an idea of life he had conceived, which was

a utopian idea despite all his efforts to derive it from social, regional, and scientific realities.

## The Cultural Acropolis

In his dialogue *Laws* Plato makes a distinction between towns as mere
"dwelling places" and as "true cities," "polities," while telling the myth of
the golden age of Chronos:

> [Athenian:] *The Cities whereof we just now spake are not* polities, *or
> true cities, but mere* dwelling-*places*, the inhabitants whereof are slaves
> in subjection unto certain ones among themselves; and each one of
> these dwelling-places is called "the government of such and such,"
> after them that be masters therein: but, if it is meet that a city should
> be called after her masters, *the True City will be called after God, who
> verily ruleth over men of understanding.* [Cleinias:] And who is this
> God? [Athenian:] I must ... use Fable for the more convenient
> answering of thy inquiry.... *Chronus*, saith the Tale, *knowing that
> Human Nature could in no wise be left with sole authority in the adminis-*

*tration of all things human . . . took thought of the matter, and set over our*
*cities, to be kings and ruler thereof, not men, but those of a more divine and*
*excellent sort, to wit, Daemons.*[44]

A true city is ruled by God, whose rulership is mediated by daemons. These
divine powers, which stand between gods and human beings in the cosmic
hierarchy, can interfere with human affairs for both good or evil.[45] Accordingly, a city's affairs are guided by a force outside the historical, in the eternal realm of God and ideas.

     The Platonic distinction between dwelling place and true city is
one source for Geddes's dichotomy of town and city. (The italicized parts of
the quoted passage are sentences Geddes considered worth noting when he
read the myth.)[46] In *Cities in Evolution* Geddes recalls Plato's distinction:

> The great city is not that which shows the palace of government at the
> origin and climax of every radiating avenue: the true city—small or
> great, whatever its style of architecture or plan, be this like Rothenburg
> or Florence—is that of a burgher people, governing themselves from
> their own townhall and yet expressing also the spiritual ideals which
> govern their lives, as once in ancient acropolis or again in medieval
> church or cathedral.[47]

Geddes's city is not ruled by God but by the eternal idea of life symbolized
in the temple of the Greek gods (figure 8.8).[48] The mediators between the
ruling idea and the citizens are the intellectuals and emotionals. Because of
their deeper insight into the synthesis of sciences and synergy of the arts,
the intellectuals and emotionals can be compared with Plato's daemons. To
the generic term cloister (the place of the intellectuals) Geddes subsumes
institutions like universities, artists' studios, monasteries, and hermitages
(see figure 2.1), places of retreat like the thinking cells. Historic cloisters
are Plato's Academy and Aristotle's Lyceum, and as contemporary equiva-
lents Geddes identifies, for example, science laboratories and research
institutes.[49]

     Dream and deed—the development of ideas in the cloister and
their subsequent application to reality—"interact with religion and polity,
with thought and action, art and drama; these create Acropolis, Temple,

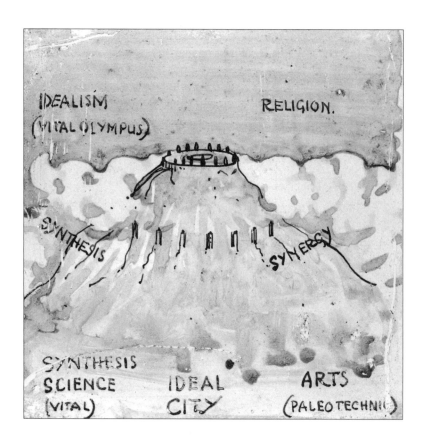

Academe and Theatre."[50] The last four words Geddes uses again as generic terms. Temples, as analyzed in the preceding two chapters, are religious or quasi-religious buildings and spaces implementing a metaphysical idea within a city. Geddes's interest in educational initiatives and institutions like index museums, outlook towers, and universities can be grouped under the term academe. The theater, as already discussed, is for Geddes a place to perform masques and to celebrate the city with communal festive events. Acropolis refers to both an assemblage of temple, academe, and theater, and to its physical location within the urban fabric. This leads back to the quoted passage from Plato's *Laws*.

In *Cities in Evolution* Geddes transforms Plato's hierarchy of gods, daemons, and man into a spatial order. Taking literally Plato's expression of daemons set over a city, Geddes aims at a visual domination of a city by the intellectuals and emotionals. To achieve this goal he habitually reserves the highest available location within an urban topography for buildings and institutions related to these two social types. Pointing to the "sublime situation" of historic examples like the ancient Jewish Temple in Jerusalem, the acropolis of many Greek cities, and the medieval cathedral, he states:

> Every city of the past which has adequately risen to the conception of the Culture-Institutions seen and felt appropriate to the expression of its ideals ... has chosen for these purposes the very noblest site within its area. ... Such location was not merely matter of architecture or esthetics; it carried with it a full yet ever deepening civic sense, an extending and enduring influence throughout the city; and thus in time became its main glory; and this alike for its people and even for humanity beyond— as witness the Temple, and the Acropolis or Cathedral once more.[51]

In Greek cities the sublime location is occupied by the temples and other buildings on the acropolis (figure 8.9). Medieval cities are visually dominated by the cathedral, whose tall tower or spire occasionally compensates for the lack of a sublime location as the cathedral is not always erected on a naturally raised plot of land (figure 8.10).

In order to become a city, a town needs a cloister, wherever possible located on ground raised above the town. To have been built too low (on the same level as the town) is a criticism Geddes utters against the University of Dundee in the 1880s.[52] While Dundee only achieved a negative acropolis, so to speak, Edinburgh's natural topography favored the development of the Old Town's rock as the city's sublime location. There Geddes established the Outlook Tower, his regional laboratory, and nearby he wished to build the National Institute of Geography. In the Old Town of Edinburgh Geddes established his student hall of residence and erected Ramsay Garden (1892–1894), both offering accommodation for academics, students, and artists, Edinburgh's new generation of intellectuals and emotionals. His intention was to transform the whole of the Old Town into the new cultural and educational center of Edinburgh and its region.[53] In Indore in 1918, Geddes proposes to locate a variety of cultural and university institutions, among them a central library, museums, and an open-air

FIGURE 8.9

The altar of Zeus at
Pergamon, reproduction
of a reconstruction: one
of the many images
Geddes collected of
acropolis-style groups of
buildings in Greek cities.

FIGURE 8.10

Furnes (Belgium), "La
Grand' Place," c.
1918–1920: the civic
square as a metaphysical
city center complete
with townhouses, town
hall, and Gothic cathe-
dral: one of the many im-
ages Geddes collected of
medieval city centers.

FIGURE 8.11

The University of Central India as a city crown of Indore; perspective view by Frank C. Mears for Patrick Geddes, c. 1918.

theater, on the "high point of the Ghatio peninsula" (figures 8.11, 8.12). He explains:

> For this is the highest and the most striking site the entire city affords; and a well designed mass of buildings upon this picturesquely wooden shore . . . will here show to the very best advantage. . . . But it is the purpose and use of any such improvement, that is the main thing, its significance in City-Design. . . . For this monumental group is to embody the intellectual centre and crossing-point of the City, and to be its educational focus and centre as well. For the buildings desired are those of Library, Museum, and Theatre, the centres of literature and learning, of the sciences and the arts, and thus appropriately beside the Temples and Ghat of the elder idealisation of life.[54]

Similarly, the land on Mount Scopus that the Zionist movement purchased in 1913 for the future Hebrew University supports Geddes's idea of a sublime location.[55] Situated just outside of Jerusalem's old city, the site guaranteed that Geddes's and Mears's design of the university would have dominated the city below (figure 8.13). To give a final example, in Tel Aviv Geddes planned to concentrate workmen's and women's colleges, museums, a theater, an outlook tower within a water tower, and further cultural and educational institutions on the highest available ground within the otherwise relatively flat and even urban topography.[56]

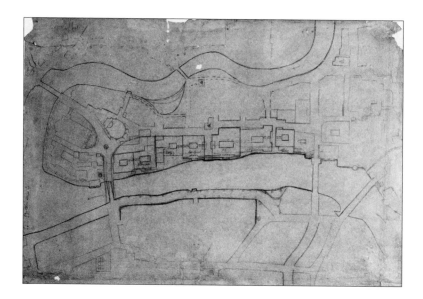

Apart from their sublime locations, most of these proposals for a cultural acropolis, as I would name such groups of buildings, share another characteristic feature. They all attempt to concentrate a variety of cultural institutions in close proximity. This is not a consequence of a shortage of available space in existing cities. Rather, it is an expression of Geddes's interest in reuniting all branches of human knowledge and activities. Cooperation between various disciplines requires first of all a spatial concentration and architectural unity in closely related buildings. In the Dunfermline report from 1904, he explains the cultural acropolis in Pittencrieff Park (figure 8.4) as the result "of designing . . . a unified group of institutions capable of assuring a real and substantial culture development to the city."[57]

According to Geddes, the lack of exactly this spatial and architectural unity is a reason why, for example, in London the Royal Anthropological Institute, the Royal Geographical Society, and the Royal Economic Society did not cooperate in their work, research, and other endeavors,[58] a shortcoming both caused and expressed by the spatial separation of the three societies' headquarters (figure 8.14). Any other consideration than this spatial one—for example institutional traditions hindering cooperation, or

FIGURE 8.13

Hebrew University on

Mount Scopus,

Jerusalem, as a city

crown of Palestine;

model by Avraham Mel-

nikoff for Patrick

Geddes, c. 1919.

the possibility of an informal exchange of research through private contacts—Geddes does not mention. For him, the visual separation on the map
points toward an institutional separation; accordingly, this graphically di-
agnosed problem can be solved by resorting to another graphic, the diagram
of the Notation of Life.

As set out in chapter 2, the Notation of Life is based on the triad of
place, work, and folk on the level of the town, and each of the three aspects
is reflected on the level of the school by subjects like geography, economics,
and anthropology. Accordingly, in order to unite place, work, and folk again
into a city, the respective institutions of the intellectuals and emotionals on
the third and fourth level of the diagram—in the case of London the Royal
Anthropological Institute, the Royal Geographical Society, and the Royal
Economic Society—have to be unified first. The Notation of Life is an elaboration of the thinking machines Geddes conceived during his temporary
blindness while in Mexico in the 1880s. What was then an *aide-mémoire* to
overcome the inability to support thinking by seeing, Geddes develops
later—in the form of the Notation of Life—into a widely applicable tool.
Among other purposes it is a tool to diagnose towns and to plan their

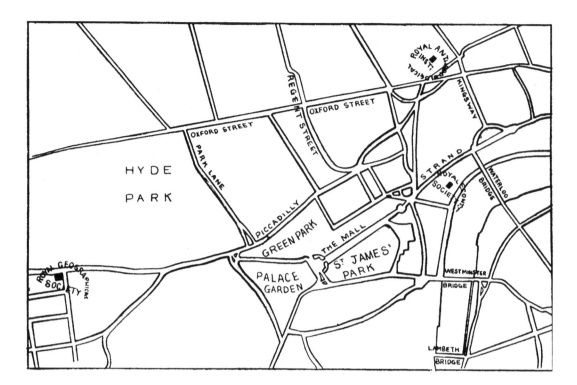

FIGURE 8.14

Geddes's map showing
the physical separation
of the headquarters of
the Royal Geographical
Society, the Royal Eco-
nomic Society, and the
Royal Anthropological
Institute in London, as
published in 1924.

development toward the status of cities. Geddes explains: "Many pages of
further and fuller elaboration are needed for the exposition of the concrete
applicability of this fuller Schema. . . . If the reader be interested in Town-
study and planning, he may use this (even for zoning)."[59]

Geddes's city design plans are concrete visualizations of the Notation of Life, which in turn is an abstract visualization of a complex structure
of thought. As the four quarters of the Notation of Life center on the crossing of the Celtic swastika, where the Town-City formula as the essence of
the whole diagram is noted, the cultural acropolis is the most important
component of Geddes's city design proposals. A new circle of a city's life has
to be designed around this group of buildings from which the new idea of
life, and thus the city, will emerge.

To renew towns as cities, and to establish new cities, requires "not
only new dwellings for the people, but new houses of a new spirit." Geddes
emphasizes that these demands are "two associated and simultaneous tasks,

not separate and distinct ones, as utilitarian and idealist go on believing."[60] But both tasks are not of the same importance, because a true city depends first of all on a new spirit, which subsequently leads to "new dwellings for the people." When Geddes defines the true city in *Cities in Evolution* by paraphrasing Plato, the decisive characteristic is not that the citizens themselves (and no longer a government) constitute the temporal power, but that they in turn are ruled by a spiritual idea. Equally important, however, is that this definition does not include any reference to housing or a city's material and technical infrastructure. Geddes does not ignore these questions, as is shown by the discussion of housing in separate chapters in *Cities in Evolution* and paragraphs on infrastructure problems in his city design reports. But his main concern is a different one.

A city for Geddes is not simply an accumulation of buildings, of space, or of people. It is a "community as an integrate, with material and immaterial structures and functions."[61] Geddes's primary interest is improving on these immaterial structures and functions. Only when this superstructure has been provided with appropriate cultural institutions can one begin to improve the material basis of a city. The material expression of a city has to derive from, but also relate to, the city's metaphysical center, or as Geddes insists, "unless the ideal build the house—and with it the city also—they labour in vain that build it."[62]

A simple and rather naive sketch by Geddes for an extension of the Indian town of Conjeevaram (Kanchipuram) is probably among the best illustrations of the importance of the metaphysical city center (figure 8.15). A square, colored yellow and marked "Temple building," is surrounded by sketchy rectangular forms representing a proposal for a "Village of 200 houses."[63] In its simplicity this sketch can easily be overlooked as an example of city design, but it summarizes in exemplary form Geddes's remark on the need for "new houses" for both people and spirit. The extension of Conjeevaram without the temple would simply be a dwelling place or town. Yet the temple without the surrounding settlement would still be more than merely a religious building, for it is the beginning of a small city. The importance of the temple can be gathered from the whole map of Conjeevaram. This does not show any planning proposal other than the small extension to the north, but every existing temple in the town has been colored in yellow, and many streets surrounding and approaching these temples are highlighted in red.

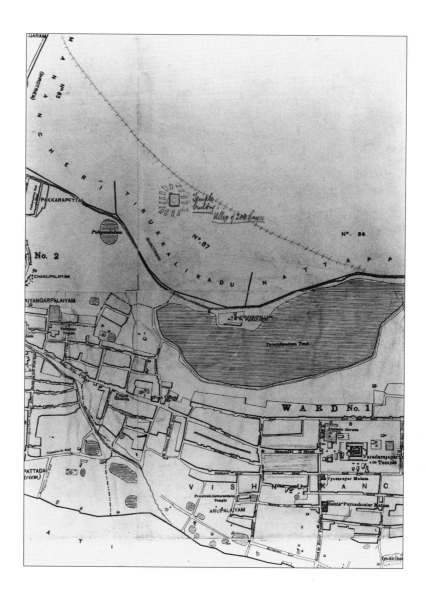

FIGURE 8.15

Map of Conjeevaram,
India, with a proposal by
Geddes for an extension
to the northeast of Ward
No. 2.

Conjeevaram is made up of small cities, or communities, each focusing on a temple as a house of the spirit, with streets and roads relating to the building and of possible use as a *via sacra* when celebrating the city. Geddes adopts this analysis as the basis for proposing the extension at Conjeevaram; on a more general level, it is also to be found in his plan for the city of Tel Aviv.

The extension to the north of the existing Tel Aviv comprises a number of blocks defined by the surrounding streets. Open spaces form the center of most of the blocks, serving as small parks for the inhabitants of the two rows of houses along the borders of each block. This can be understood as Geddes's adaptation of garden city and garden suburb planning principles in an attempt to provide housing with immediate access to open spaces. Yet the underlying idea appears to be a different one. The plan of the extension of Tel Aviv resembles the analysis of the older town of Conjeevaram. In both cases, the city is formed by a number of smaller communities. These focus in Conjeevaram on traditional temples, whereas in Tel Aviv gardens—nature—substitute for the religious buildings. The symbolic octagonal square links the group of new communities with the older part of Tel Aviv. Old and new Tel Aviv together are dominated by the cultural acropolis mentioned earlier. Tel Aviv is also part of the larger region of Palestine; this relation finds its expression in the dominating location of Hebrew University in Palestine's region-city. Thus the structure of the future Palestine as envisioned by Geddes resembles the hierarchical but multifocal models of the region-city and conurbation.

To identify the location and composition of the cultural acropolis is an important key to Geddes's city design proposals. The size, form, and elements of the cultural acropolis are variable, ranging from the large Pittencrieff Park in Dunfermline to a single temple in an urban quarter, or a simple house in country town or village.[64] Regarding the latter, Geddes suggests "the acquirement of some fine old country-house or château for its culture centre."[65] In whatever form, the existence of this city center indicates that the citizens are engaged in transforming their town into a city with a true plan:

> But the true town plan, the only one worth having, is the outcome and flower of the whole civilisation of a community and of an age. While starting from its fundamentals, of port and roads, of market and depot; and from its essentials, too, of family dwellings worthy to be perma-

nent and hereditary homes, it develops onwards to the supreme organs of the city's life—its acropolis and forum, its cloister and cathedral.[66]

For Geddes, the cultural acropolis is two things in one: a means to create a city according to his theory, and a symbolic expression of this achievement. With regard to the cultural acropolis as a means, Geddes is interested in cultural, educational, and spiritual institutions because they allow for the necessary communal interactions and individual self-improvement. This interest partially reaffirms what was often already municipal practice: the sublimation of the economic basis of a successful city in cultural and educational institutions. What is new in Geddes's concept of city design is the degree of importance he ascribes to such institutions and his insistence on the inclusion of contemporary secular temples. With regard to the cultural acropolis as a symbol, Geddes takes a keen interest in the historical and cultural variety of city centers that he believes can be compared to the cultural acropolis. This is a structural interest rather than an attempt to copy architectural forms or styles. However, this interest limits the critical character of Geddes's idea, for in order to make reality and history fit his model he relies on an ahistorical overarching interpretation of these alleged historic precedents. This methodology shows little regard for historical, cultural, political, or any other differences.

## The City Crown

Geddes did not conceive the idea of a cultural acropolis in an intellectual vacuum. A contemporary line of study sought to understand a city through a symbolic building or a group of buildings which, it was thought, captured the essence of the city. Like many of his Beaux-Arts-trained colleagues, Tony Garnier, for example, was engaged in a reconstruction of an ancient city. After winning the Prix de Rome in 1899 he worked on drawings reconstructing the Roman city of Tusculum. At the same time Garnier conceived the Cité Industrielle, which was exhibited for the first time in 1904 and published in its final form in 1917. This blueprint for a future city is influenced by the work on Tusculum, which provides a source for the faint reminiscences of classical architecture in Garnier's design of individual housing. More importantly, his reconstruction of the center of Tusculum appears to be reflected

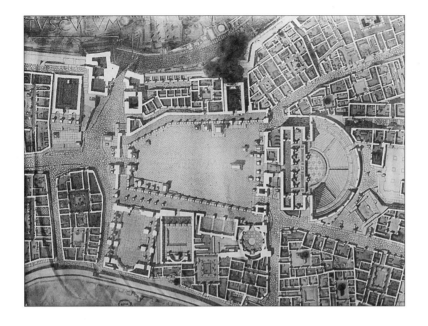

FIGURE 8.16

Plan of the forum at
Tusculum, 1903, by
Tony Garnier.

in the city center of the Cité Industrielle. Garnier's drawings of Tusculum visualize the overriding importance he ascribes to the central area of that city, with its numerous temples, assembly buildings, and other public spaces. These buildings constitute the city; accordingly, in Garnier's plan of Tusculum they are literally carved out of the dense urban fabric (figure 8.16).

For the Cité Industrielle, Garnier provides a similar center—comparable to Tusculum's in its function as the constituting element of the city—in the "Square of the Public" (figure 8.17). The square features a central building complex with assembly and lecture halls and amphitheaters. Next to the diamond-shaped central building he locates a clock tower with a 24-hour clock, and in adjacent buildings he accommodates a theater, a museum, and a library, with a sports arena nearby. Obviously, Garnier feels that the Cité Industrielle requires a clearly identifiable center that defines and refines, through its assembly of cultural and educational facilities, the character of the city as the climax of an industrialized mass society. Finally, he complements the Square of the Public with elaborated visualizations of the industrial complex of the Cité Industrielle, which acknowledge the

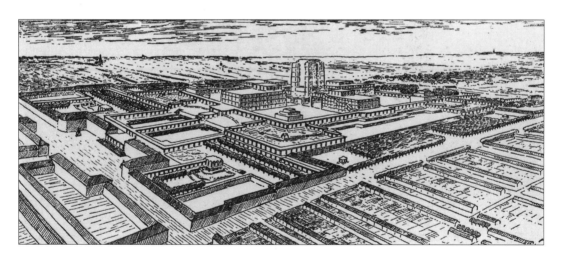

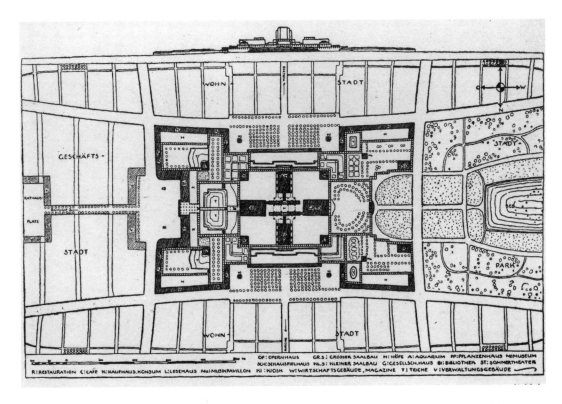

FIGURE 8.19

Plan of the city crown, 1916–1917, by Bruno Taut.

economic basis of the city and aim at balancing it with the city's cultural achievements.

However, the most prominent example of an assembly of cultural and educational buildings at the center of a future city, comparable to Geddes's cultural acropolis, emerged in Germany during the First World War. Between 1916 and 1917 Bruno Taut wrote and drew *Die Stadtkrone* (The city crown).[67] Taut conceives a city of three million inhabitants who live in garden-city-style housing organized around the city crown (figure 8.18). The city crown occupies a rectangular plot of land where Taut envisions a hierarchically structured complex of buildings (figure 8.19). Shopping facilities are located at the outer border; libraries, reading rooms, art museums, natural science exhibitions, and similar institutions are accommodated in the buildings toward the center. The climax of the city crown is formed by an opera house, a small and a large assembly hall, and a theater. The space between these institutions is dedicated to offices and service buildings, which are surmounted by a huge structure, the visual focus of the city crown.

Taut's city crown and Geddes's cultural acropolis show strong similarities, although also significant differences. Both place cultural institutions at the center of the future city, whether this is an entirely new or a transformed historic city. In each concept the city center is related to the surrounding town through a spatial hierarchy; Taut achieves this by varying the building heights, whereas Geddes relies on variations in the natural topography. City crown and cultural acropolis distinguish between the proposed cultural and educational center and traditional foci of cities like the town hall or cathedral, which in both cases are subdued to the new center. Both men also develop very similar historical pedigrees for their proposals that combine—with the same methodological inaccuracies—examples of cityscapes dominated by religious, cultural, and political buildings from ancient or medieval periods, and from distant cultures like the Indian, the Jewish, or the Egyptian. The architectural form and style mark the strongest difference between them; it is obvious that Taut approaches the city crown from an architectural point of view, while Geddes applies a social scientist's approach concerned with social groups and structures and their expression in, and interaction with, the built environment. Nevertheless, Geddes's cultural acropolis can be considered as a predecessor of the city crown.

Usually, Taut's city crown is analyzed within a specific historical and cultural situation in post–World War I Germany that gave rise to expressionism in German architecture. However, the brief discussion here makes clear that Taut's idea is part of a wider phenomenon in the contemporary debate about the city, a phenomenon with roots not only German and stretching back much further than the time of the First World War.[68]

# Epilogue

The attempt to define the elements of a theory of the city informs both Geddes's manifold writings in different intellectual fields and his realized and unrealized city design proposals. His analysis of the forces and events that create and shape the human environment, undertaken in order to understand why and how human life organizes itself spatially and socially in the form of cities, hardly qualifies as a theory according to the definition of the term in the natural sciences. Nevertheless, his education in the natural sciences was helpful in framing—across the many intellectual, professional, and geographical shifts of his life—a body of ideas about the city that is astonishingly consistent. It is so consistent that its transferral into city design makes reading town planning reports by Geddes an unrewardingly predictable endeavor: somewhere in the pages of such a report the reader will inevitably encounter a cultural acropolis, a historical museum, a zoological garden modeled on the valley section, proposals to apply conservative surgery, or any other of the elements that according to Geddes constitute a city. The actual architectural form of these elements may vary; their functions for the city remain the same. The idiosyncratic and ornamental style of his writing may obscure but does not hide the repetitiveness of his assumptions about the city. Once these were conceived, Geddes was more concerned with persistently proving the correctness of his ideas by illustrating their wide applicability, than with exploring their creative exploitation in changing urban and architectural situations in different cities.

The three broad themes around which Geddes constructed his theory—the city and the region, history, and spirituality—are not his inventions but his answers to questions posed by the circumstances of his time. For Geddes these three aspects of a city were not primarily an anticipation of a future utopia but determining characteristics of the existing, contemporary reality. Even if the region had become obscured by the nation-state, or the spiritual aspect of a city was under threat from contemporary secular tendencies, the three themes continued to describe the reality of human life.

This assumption allowed him to refer to the three aspects of the city without always making the references explicit. Likewise, because the three aspects were so obviously real and still influential for the city's appearance, Geddes may not have felt a strong urge or obligation to summarize his theory of the city in the metanarrative of a town planning history-cum-planning manual. *Cities in Evolution*, Geddes's best-known book on the subject, is not his *opus magnum*, for the book assembles earlier published papers without managing to present in a coherent manner the larger metanarrative that informed all of the individual essays.

This lack of an *opus magnum* along the lines of Raymond Unwin's *Town Planning in Practise* or one of the German *Städtebauhandbücher*, for example, appears to have been instrumental, paradoxically, in keeping the interest in Geddes's ideas about the city alive to a degree hardly enjoyed by any other of the early modern town planning theorists, with the exceptions of Camillo Sitte and, possibly, Ebenezer Howard. Geddes's emphasis on the practical application of his ideas about the city rather than on their rigid, theoretical elucidation helped to hide their time-bound character. At the same time it helped to heighten the impression that these ideas are visionary and, despite their simplicity, have far-reaching implications still of value to us today.

While a century later the ideas of contemporaries such as Thomas H. Mawson, Raymond Unwin, and Thomas Adam are mainly of interest to historians of architecture and town planning, Geddes's legacy appears to invite regular rediscovery. Attempts to cast him as an early forerunner of late twentieth-century concerns such as regionalism, environmentalism, or conservation of historic architecture not only tend to obscure the contents of his ideas but to turn them into their very opposite. The change in the meaning of the term "conurbation" is only one example, but a good one. For Geddes a conurbation was the potential pinnacle of mankind's tendency to urbanize large stretches of land; today the term has become a synonym for mankind's allegedly self-destructive tendency to create unsustainable artificial environments. This observation is not an argument against changes in meaning or judgment, but about selective historiography.

The standard historiography of modern architecture and town planning stresses the growing influence of rationality and functionality in the development of modernism, a tendency that reached it climax during the 1950s and 1960s. The postmodern criticism of architectural modernism barely goes beyond the parameters of the modernist historiography. By simply inverting the argument, postmodernist criticism locates modernism's downfall in the overemphasis of rationality and functionality and recommends as the adequate cure the reintroduction of less rational and functional themes into architecture and the debate about the city. Even the most recent attempts at defining a so-called other modernity—a modernity that was not solely determined by rational and functional concepts but acknowledged metaphysics and idealism—still follow the established pattern. Rationalism and functionalism and idealistic and visionary ideas about architecture and urban design continue to be conceived as opposites, whose balance requires establishing the right mixture between them. Yet the history of modernist architecture and town planning cannot be reduced to a decision between two poles, whether understood as opposites or as complementary; for the two are essentially identical (even if apparently contradictory), as Horkheimer and Adorno emphasize in *The Dialectic of Enlightenment* (1947).

The more complex course of the history of modernist architecture and urban planning is highlighted by the continuous references to Geddes's theory of the city during the 1940s, '50s, and '60s, allegedly the high period of a strictly rational and functional modernism. Having been conceived within the context of the emerging modernism, all aspects of Geddes's theory remained central to the debate about the modern city, as the following brief examples show.

One of the foremost exponents of a strictly rational and functional modernism was the Berlin architect Ludwig Hilberseimer. He became known especially for his design of a *Wohlfahrtsstadt* (welfare city) from 1924, an ideal utopian city entirely composed of continuous rows of horizontal slabs. While it is easy to portray Hilberseimer as one of the villains of modern architecture and town planning, a brief glance at his book *The New Regional Pattern: Industries and Gardens, Workshops and Farms* (1949) makes clear that such a judgment is far too simple. There Hilberseimer sets out his idea of regional, modernist societies; among other sources he refers to Geddes, for example when tracing the idea of a region back to ancient Greek and Roman city-states or trying to define a region by applying Geddes's valley section. A few years later Hilberseimer published *The Nature of Cities* (1955), which outlines a vision of a decentralized Chicago, rebuilt as a network of different-sized communities in the region between Lake Michigan and the Fox River. Hilberseimer was not the only one who developed modern concepts of the region with references to Geddes. Projects such as the Tennessee Valley Authority or the work of such planners and urban theorists as Erwin Anton Gutkind and Artur Glikson spring to mind.[1]

Ever since Geddes conceived the historic survey and outlined a general history of the city in his Cities and Town Planning Exhibition, compilations of comprehensive historical pedigrees have been important elements in the debate about modernist architecture and the city. Bruno Taut's overview of the development of historic cities in *Die Stadtkrone* has already been referred to. Similar attempts can be found in the "New Architecture" exhibition of the MARS group in London in 1938, which deliberately put modern architecture in a sequence of historic architectural styles beginning with a Norman castle. Likewise, Lewis Mumford's *The Culture of Cities* (1938) is dedicated to a historical overview of the development and meaning of cities. Similarly, Hilberseimer's *The Nature of Cities* begins with a long and detailed historical survey of the emergence of cities. This interest of modernist architects and theoreticians in the historical pedigree of cities and architecture culminates in Gutkind's multivolume *International History of City Development*, whose publication began in 1964.

Even Geddes's idea of a spiritual focus for the city found an echo among modern architects and planners. Some two decades after his death an idea very similar to the cultural acropolis resurfaced at the eighth CIAM congress at Hoddesdon, Great Britain, in 1951, which was dedicated to "The Core of the City." At the sixth congress, which had taken place in Bridgwater, Great Britain, in 1947, the analytical categories of dwelling, work, transportation, and recreation had been amended when the meeting substituted "cultivation of mind and body" for recreation.[2] Accordingly, the declaration of the 1947 gathering describes the aims of CIAM as "to work for the creation of a physical environment that will satisfy man's emotional and material needs and stimulate his *spiritual* growth."[3]

The exact circumstances of this shift merit further investigation, but a strong direct input of Geddesian theory has been documented.[4] One of the key organizers of CIAM 8 was the British horticulturist, landscape gardener, and town planner Jaqueline Tyrwhitt (1905–1983). After joining the MARS group in 1941, Tyrwhitt developed into an influential figure in the British architecture and planning scene of the 1940s and 1950s. At that time she was deeply impressed by Geddes's thoughts and ideas, which she aimed at nurturing and developing.

CIAM 8 understood the core to be both the physical (though not necessarily geographical) and the ideal center of a city: "The Core is an artefact: a man-made essential element of city planning. It is the expression of the collective mind and spirit of the community which humanises and gives meaning and form to the city itself."[5] The core constitutes a city, for it is "the element that makes a community a community and not merely an aggregate of individuals."[6] This definition was put forward by the MARS group and can be read as directly derived from Geddes's reference to a "community as an integrate." A community can arise from the core because the core stimulates a transformation from passive individuals to active citizens.[7] The core is the interface between the part and the whole; it interprets "the human activities that take place there: *both the relations of individuals to one another, and the relations of individuals with the community*."[8]

In short, CIAM's core of the city stands conceptually in the tradition of Geddes's cultural acropolis and even of Taut's *Stadtkrone*. Tyrwhitt was very likely aware of the Geddesian root. While the conference was called "The Core of the City," the subsequent publication of the proceedings is entitled *The Heart of the City*. This is the same term Geddes's close friend Elisée Reclus had used more than fifty years earlier to describe the communal center of the ever-expanding city, which, as discussed in chapter 3, stimulated Geddes's idea of a region-city with a cultural acropolis at its center.

However, out of CIAM 8 emerged also a poignant though indirect criticism of Geddes's theory of the city. When Sigfried Giedion, in *The Heart of the City*, accepts somewhat reluctantly the existence of a relationship between the social structure of a city and the urban form of its core, he states that this relationship "is not at all so simple and so rational as we once thought," and concludes by emphasizing that it "does not always obey the law of effect and cause."[9]

Throughout his life and work, Geddes aimed at establishing the laws of cause and effect that govern the city. Yet his legacy is not a long-outdated, schematic body of rules setting out how to analyze, plan, and build a city. Rather, it is his attempt to substitute a larger modernism for mankind's two, allegedly separate worlds, the real and the ideal one. The failure of this attempt reminds us that for both a meaningful history of architectural modernism and a useful contemporary criticism or even self-criticism of modern architecture and urban planning, the essential, even if apparently contradictory, identity of mankind's two worlds has to be made the focus of the inquiry.

# Appendix
# Synoptic Overview of Geddes's Life and Time

| LIFE OF PATRICK GEDDES | CONTEMPORARY EVENTS |
|---|---|
| 1854: Geddes born in Ballater, west Aberdeenshire, Scotland; three years later family moves to Mount Tabor, a cottage near Perth | since 1853: Georges-Eugène Haussmann rebuilds Paris<br><br>1854: *The Happy Colony* by Robert Pemberton<br><br>1859: Ildefonso Cerdà's plan for the extension of Barcelona<br><br>1859–1872: Ringstraße, Vienna, after plans by Ludwig Förster |
| 1862–1870: attends Perth Academy<br><br>1871: begins an eighteen-month (unfinished) apprenticeship with the National Bank of Scotland | 1871: the French geographers Elisée and Elie Reclus participate in the Paris Commune<br><br>1872–1875: building of Richard Wagner's Festspielhaus in Bayreuth (first Festspiele, 1876) |
| October 1874: studies in Botany and the Natural Sciences at Edinburgh University, leaves after one week<br><br>Winter 1875: studies of zoology under Thomas H. Huxley at Royal School of Mines, London; subsequently works as demonstrator at University College, London | 1875–1894: *Géographie universelle: La terre et les hommes* by Elisée Reclus, a key publication of regional geography<br><br>1877: William Morris establishes Society for Protection of Ancient Buildings (SPAB)<br><br>1877: Thomas Coghlan Horsfall opens Art Museum and University Settlement at Manchester |
| 1878: works under Professor Henry de Lacaze-Duthiers at marine biological station, Roscoff, Brittany; meets there Charles Flahault, later Professor of Botany at Montpellier University | 1878: Universal Exposition, Paris |

| LIFE OF PATRICK GEDDES | CONTEMPORARY EVENTS |
|---|---|
| 1878–1879: studies biology at the Sorbonne and histology at Ecole de Médicine, Paris (autumn and winter)<br><br>attends lectures by Edmond Demolins where he learns about Frédéric Le Play's social theory | |
| October 1879–April 1880: scientific research work in Mexico; temporary blindness, invention of thinking machines | 1879: George Cadbury begins to build Bourneville as a workers' model settlement; main development starts in 1895 |
| 1880: works as demonstrator in practical botany and vegetable histology at Edinburgh University | |
| 1881: *The Classification of Statistics and Its Results* by Geddes | |
| 1882: Geddes in contact with Fellowship of New Life, introduction to Indian philosophy and religion | 1882: Fellowship of the New Life founded in London by Scottish philosopher Thomas Davidson, with three aims: new educational theory, new relations between sexes, and pursuit of culture |
| 1883: Botanic Garden at Grange House School, Edinburgh, first garden design by Geddes<br><br>Summer 1883: travels to Jena University to visit his friend J. Arthur Thomson and to meet evolutionist Ernst Haeckel | |
| 1884: *An Analysis of the Principles of Economics* by Geddes<br><br>*John Ruskin, Economist* by Geddes<br><br>involved in founding of Edinburgh Social Union, philanthropic organization for relief work in Edinburgh's Old Town | 1884: Fabian Society founded in London as a separation from Fellowship of the New Life |

| LIFE OF PATRICK GEDDES | CONTEMPORARY EVENTS |
| --- | --- |
| 1885: lecture on "Conditions of Progress of the Capitalist and of the Labourer" (published 1886) at Industrial Remuneration Conference in London; other speakers are William Morris and Alfred Russel Wallace | |
| 1886: marries Anna Morton; moves from Princes Street into James Court in Edinburgh's Old Town<br><br>travels with friend and benefactor James Martin White to Athens, Rome, Venice, Constantinople, and Cannes (February to April)<br><br>Peter Kropotkin visits Geddes at his new home<br><br>"Theory of Growth, Reproduction, Sex and Heredity," outlines Geddes's theory of cell metabolism | 1886: International Exhibition of Industry, Science, and Art in Edinburgh; main feature is the "Old Edinburgh Street" designed by Sydney Mitchell<br><br>Peter Kropotkin writes approvingly about Geddes's move into the Old Town of Edinburgh in a letter to Elisée Reclus |
| 1887: birth of Norah Geddes (1887–1967)<br><br>*Every Man His Own Art Critic at the Manchester Exhibition* by Geddes<br><br>opening of Edinburgh's first university hall of residence in the refurbished building No. 2, The Mound | 1887: *Gemeinschaft und Gesellschaft. Abhandlung des Communismus und des Socialismus als empirische Kulturformen* by Ferdinand Tönnies |
| 1888: *Co-operation versus Socialism* by Geddes<br><br>James Martin White Chair of Botany endowed at University College, Dundee; Geddes accepts chair with teaching obligation only during winter term (Geddes resigns from chair in 1919) | 1888: Charles Robert Ashbee establishes Guild of Handicraft in connection with the university settlement Toynbee Hall in the East End of London<br><br>Beginning of Port Sunlight as workers' model settlement of the Lever Company |

| LIFE OF PATRICK GEDDES | CONTEMPORARY EVENTS |
|---|---|
| 1889: *The Evolution of Sex* by Geddes and J. Arthur Thomson | 1889: Universal Exposition, Paris; the tower and the Galerie des Machines by Eiffel are the most famous buildings |
| | *Der Städtebau nach seinen künstlerischen Grundsätzen* by Camillo Sitte |
| 1890: purchases Ramsay Lodge, Edinburgh, former home of Scottish poet Allan Ramsay, and adjacent properties | 1890: Chapel of Ascension, London, built by Herbert P. Horne, conceived as a quiet space within the busy and noisy city |
| 1891: birth of Alasdair Geddes (1891–1917)<br><br>first summer school in Edinburgh, after Geddes had offered summer courses at Granton Marine Station since 1885; last summer school takes place in 1899 | |
| 1892: purchase of Short's Observatory near future Ramsay Garden; building subsequently refurbished as Outlook Tower<br><br>foundation of Old Edinburgh School of Art, John Duncan, director; school ceases to exist in 1900 | 1892: William Richard Lethaby publishes *Architecture, Mysticism and Myth*, a study in the symbolic and cosmic meaning of architecture |
| 1892–1894: building of Ramsay Garden complex, Edinburgh, architects Samuel Henbest Capper and Sydney Mitchell and George Wilson | |
| 1893: renovation of Riddle's Court (acquired in 1889); this project marks a series of similar undertakings in Edinburgh's Old Town after the initial refurbishment of the first university hall of residence in 1887 | 1893: William Warde Fowler's *The City State of the Greeks and Romans* claims the identity between *polis* and natural regions<br><br>Elisée Reclus attends Edinburgh Summer School (again in 1895) |

| LIFE OF PATRICK GEDDES | CONTEMPORARY EVENTS |
|---|---|
| 1894: opening of Ramsay Garden with a performance of a "Ceremony of the Torch" (April) | 1894: British positivist Frederic Harrison republishes *The Meaning of History*, an attempt at a historiography strongly focusing on cities (originally published in 1862) |
| 1895: birth of Arthur Geddes (1895–1968)<br><br>obituary by Geddes for John Stuart Blackie, Professor of Greek at Edinburgh University and Scottish nationalist; describes the funeral procession through Edinburgh as a manifestation of the city as a community | 1895: Elisée Reclus begins to publicize Great Globe for the forthcoming Universal Exposition at Paris in 1900<br><br>"The Evolution of Cities" by Elisée Reclus, proposes idea of ever-expanding cities<br><br>*Degeneration* by Max Nordau |
| 1896: friends of Geddes establish Town and Gown Association to relieve him of the burden of the financial collapse of his renovation and building schemes<br><br>Eastern and Colonial Association established to support financially Geddes's relief work for the benefit of Armenian refugees on Cyprus (autumn) | 1896: Arts and Crafts Exhibition Society organizes lecture series on "Art and Life, and the Building and Decoration of Cities" during their fifth exhibition at London<br><br>*The Cruciform Mark*, a roman à clef by Riccardo Stephens, depicts life in Geddes's university hall of residence in Edinburgh<br><br>*Renouveau d'une cité (On the Social Work of Patrick Geddes at Edinburgh)* by Elie and Elisée Reclus<br><br>First modern Olympic Games propagate classic Greek ideas on art, architecture, physical education, and competition as contemporary ideal |
| 1897: first ideas for Roseburn Cliff, a suburban terrace of cottages in the west of Edinburgh, built only in 1911 by architects McArthy and Watson | 1897: Robert Smith, Geddes's assistant at University College, Dundee, begins botanical survey of Scotland by investigating natural region of Edinburgh<br><br>First World Zionist Congress assembles in Basel |
| 1898: first ideas for university hall of residence in More's garden in Chelsea put forward by Geddes, William Richard Lethaby, and F. W. Troup; built 1902–1904 by Edinburgh architects Dunn and Watson; since 1907 a university hall of residence | 1898: *Tomorrow: A Peaceful Path to Real Reform* by Ebenezer Howard, marks the beginning of the garden city movement |

| LIFE OF PATRICK GEDDES | CONTEMPORARY EVENTS |
|---|---|
| | 1899: Charles Robert Ashbee initiates the Survey of London |
| | Joseph Maria Olbrich begins work on artists' colony at Mathildenhöhe, Darmstadt, Germany |
| | Whitechapel Art Gallery, London, by Charles H. Townsend |
| | *Fields, Factories and Workshops Tomorrow* by Peter Kropotkin |
| | Tony Garnier designs his Cité Industrielle while working on reconstruction of Tusculum at Villa Medici, Rome (published in 1917) |
| 1899–1900: two tours to USA (February to April 1899; September 1899 to April 1900) lecturing and fundraising for forthcoming summer school at Paris and for Reclus's globe; Geddes meets educationalist G. Stanley Hall, philosopher John Dewey, sociologist Charles Zueblin, urban reformer Jane Addams of Hull House, Chicago, and Indian philosopher Swami Vivekananda | 1899–1900: Architect Fritz Schumacher organizes and designs *tableaux vivants* performance of a dialogue between Faust and Mephisto, conceived as a civic event |
| 1900: organizes the International Summer School at the Universal Exposition at Paris, together with the International Association for the Advancement of Science, Arts and Education (IAASAE) | 1900: Universal Exposition, Paris (May to October) |
| | French architect Galeron designs and builds a celestial globe for the Exposition |
| meets in Paris architect Paul Louis Albert Galeron, philosopher Henri Bergson, and Paul Otlet and Henri Lafontaine from the International Office of Bibliography (later Mundaneum), Brussels | from the turn of the century, Monte Verità, Ascona, Switzerland, attracts followers of all sorts of life reform ideas; formerly famous as home of exiled anarchists such as Elisée Reclus and Mikhail Bakunin, the mountain develops into one of the best-known European life reform communities |
| fruitless attempts to save the pavilions of the Rue des Nations as a *via sacra* of international peace and cooperation | |

| LIFE OF PATRICK GEDDES | CONTEMPORARY EVENTS |
|---|---|
| 1901: organizes with the Glasgow branch of the IAASAE a summer school at the International Exhibition at Glasgow<br><br>Galeron visits Glasgow and conceives first design sketch for Geddes's National Institute of Geography | 1901: Horniman Museum opens in London, built by Charles H. Townsend<br><br>Chaim Weizmann proposes at 5th World Zionist Congress the foundation of a Hebrew University |
| 1902: publicizes the National Institute of Geography, to be built in Edinburgh according to a design by Galeron (unbuilt) | 1902: *Mutual Aid: A Factor in Evolution* by Peter Kropotkin |
| 1903: begins to plant Botanic Garden at Horniman Museum in London; garden remains unfinished and is built over when the museum erects an extension in 1910 | 1903: *Die Großstadt und das Geistesleben* by Georg Simmel<br><br>first-ever exhibition on urban design and town planning at Dresden |
| 1903–1904: design for Pittencrieff Park, Dunfermline, competing plan by Thomas W. Mawson (both unbuilt)<br><br>with Victor Verasis Branford, among founding members of Sociological Society in London | 1903–1904: construction begins at Letchworth, the first garden city, by Barry Parker and Raymond Unwin |
|  | 1904: *The Improvement of the Dwellings and Surroundings of the People: The Example of Germany* by Thomas Coghlan Horsfall |
| 1904–1906: lecture series "Civics as Applied Sociology" presents his theory of civics and city design to the Sociological Society | 1904–1906: during the same sessions, Francis Galton presents lectures on eugenics to the Sociological Society |
|  | 1905: *The Myths of Plato* by John Alexander Stewart |

| LIFE OF PATRICK GEDDES | CONTEMPORARY EVENTS |
|---|---|
| | 1906: international architecture competition for Peace Palace at The Hague |
| 1907: opening of Castle Wynd Garden, the first of several open spaces established in Edinburgh's Old Town | 1907: French architect François Garas publishes *Mes temples*, a study describing a tripartite temple scheme |
| idea of a temple of life appears for the first time in Geddes's notes | |
| 1908: saving of Crosby Hall by Geddes and others, subsequently rebuilt in Chelsea by architect Walter Hindes Godfrey | 1908: Chair and Department of Civic Design established at Liverpool University |
| David Montague Eder, Freudian psychoanalyst and later a leading British Zionist, invites Geddes to lecture on eugenics to biology group of Fabian Society | |
| 1909: participates in a town planning tour to Germany organized by the National Housing Reform Council | 1909: Housing and Town Planning Act, first British town planning legislation |
| | *Town Planning in Practise* by Raymond Unwin |
| | urban master plan for Chicago by D. H. Burnham and E. H. Bennett |
| | Founding of Tel Aviv as a suburb of Yafo |
| 1910: displays the survey of Edinburgh at Town Planning Conference in London | 1910: International Town Planning Conference at the Royal Academy in London, organized by the Royal Institute of British Architects |
| introduces term "conurbation" in a paper read at a health congress | Greater Berlin town planning competition |

| LIFE OF PATRICK GEDDES | CONTEMPORARY EVENTS |
|---|---|
| 1911: first display of the Cities and Town Planning Exhibition at Crosby Hall in Chelsea, London; subsequently in Edinburgh, Belfast, and Dublin | 1911: Rudolf Steiner proposes to build Johannesbau in Munich

*Civic Art* by Thomas H. Mawson

*Die Großstadt, eine Studie über diese* by Otto Wagner |
| 1912: performance of *Masque of Ancient and Modern Learning* in Edinburgh to mark the 25th anniversary of the university hall of residence | 1912: Ramsay Traquair and Frank Mears conceive completion of the National Monument on Edinburgh's Calton Hill as a temple of life

Edwin Lutyens begins working on New Delhi master plan |
| 1913: Cities and Town Planning Exhibition displayed at International Congress of Town Planning and the Organisation of City Life, Ghent, Belgium

designs with Frank Mears the Edinburgh Zoological Garden as a three-dimensional valley section, the first of several zoological gardens Geddes proposes | 1913: Hendrik Christian Andersen and Ernest M. Hébrard publish project of a World City as a center of peace and cooperation

1913–1914: Rudolf Steiner builds Goetheanum I in Dornach

*Città Nuova* by Antonio Sant'Elia |
| 1914: Cities and Town Planning Exhibition shown a second time in Dublin; Geddes proposes to build a Catholic cathedral, a *via sacra*, and a garden suburb near Dublin to relieve political tensions (all unbuilt)

travel to India for city design consultancy work

Cities and Town Planning Exhibition sinks in Indian Ocean after an attack by a German warship | 1914: Bruno Taut builds glass house pavilion at Werkbund exhibition in Cologne

Frank Mears works with Edwin Lutyens in London on headquarters for Theosophical Society

friends of Geddes assemble second Cities and Town Planning Exhibition, including material from the Outlook Tower |
| 1915: *Cities in Evolution* by Geddes | 1915: Lewis Mumford contacts the Outlook Tower, Edinburgh |

| LIFE OF PATRICK GEDDES | CONTEMPORARY EVENTS |
| --- | --- |
| 1915 (continued): coorganizes with Gilbert Slater, Principal of Ruskin College, Oxford, summer school "The War: Its Social Tasks and Problems" at King's College, London | |
| 1916–1923: city design work in India; publication of numerous reports, most notably *Town Planning towards City Development: A Report to the Durbar of Indore* (2 vols., Indore, 1918) | 1916: Louis Bourgeois begins model for a Bahá'í Temple; the model is completed in 1920; the temple opens in Wilmette, near Chicago, in 1953 |
| 1916: selection of the Cities and Town Planning Exhibition displayed at Exposition de la Cité Reconstituée in Paris | 1916: annual exhibition of the Arts and Crafts Exhibition Society dedicated to the city, designed by Henry Wilson as a temple of the city |
| 1917: Alasdair Geddes dies in May while on active military service in France<br><br>Anna Geddes dies in India in June | 1917: *Where the Great City Stands: A Study in the New Civics* by Charles Robert Ashbee |
| 1919: visit to Jerusalem for city design report on Jerusalem and planning of Hebrew University, in collaboration with Frank Mears | 1919: *Die Stadtkrone* and *Alpine Architektur* by Bruno Taut<br><br>Frank Mears designs "Scottish National Memorial to Scots who fell in the Great War" to form with Ramsay Garden a city crown for Edinburgh<br><br>Bauhaus founded in Weimar |
| 1920: second visit to Palestine; city design reports for Haifa and other Zionist settlements and projects | 1920: *Die Auflösung der Städte* by Bruno Taut<br><br>first idea for a regional plan for industrial Ruhr area in Germany |

| LIFE OF PATRICK GEDDES | CONTEMPORARY EVENTS |
|---|---|
| 1920–1923: holds Chair of Sociology and Civics at the University of Bombay; Cities and Town Planning Exhibition on permanent display in university | 1922: Lewis Mumford, in *The Story of Utopia*, states the identity between *polis* and Geddes's valley section |
| 1922: design with Frank Mears a Bahá'í temple for Allahabad, India (unbuilt)<br><br>redesigns an Indian palace garden in Patiala as temple for Greek gods and Muses and a symbolic garden of Notation of Life (unbuilt) | 1922: Ville Contemporaine by Le Corbusier |
| 1923: lecture tour to USA; finally meets Lewis Mumford | 1923: Rudolf Steiner builds Goetheanum II in Dornach<br><br>Lewis Mumford and friends establish Regional Planning Association of America |
| 1924: returns from India, travels in Europe<br><br>foundation of Scots College in Montpellier, France<br><br>exhibition of Hall of Vision at Conference on Some Living Religions within the Empire, London | |
| 1925: third visit to Palestine on occasion of the opening of Hebrew University Jerusalem; city design report for Tel Aviv-Yafo | 1925: Plan Voisin for Paris by Le Corbusier and Pierre Jeanneret<br><br>Großsiedlung Berlin-Britz (Hufeisensiedlung) by Bruno Taut (1925–1927) |
| 1927: Amelia Defries publishes *The Interpreter Geddes: The Man and His Gospel*, the first biography of Geddes | 1927: International architecture competition for design of League of Nations building in Geneva |

| LIFE OF PATRICK GEDDES | CONTEMPORARY EVENTS |
| --- | --- |
| 1928: marries Lilian Brown, his second wife | 1928: Congrès Internationaux d'Architecture Moderne (CIAM) assembles for first time at La Sarraz, Switzerland |
| | 1929: Le Corbusier designs Mundaneum for Geddes's friend Paul Otlet |
| 1931: *Life: Outlines of General Biology* by Geddes and J. Arthur Thomson | 1931: *The Science of Life* by Herbert George Wells, George Philip Wells, and Julian Sorel Huxley |
| negotiates together with Frank Mears a design for a Hindu temple, London (unbuilt) | Ville Radieuse by Le Corbusier (published 1935) |
| 1932: accepts knighthood for educational services; dies at Montpellier after return from England | |

# Notes

## Abbreviations

NLS, MS          National Library of Scotland,
Manuscript division

SUA             Strathclyde University Archives

## Foreword

**1.** Max Weber, "Wissenschaft als Beruf" (1919), English translation as "Science as a Vocation," in H. H. Gerth and C. Wright Mills, eds., *From Max Weber* (London: Routledge, 1948), p. 147.

**2.** Matthew Arnold, introduction to *Ward's English Poets* (1880), quoted in David Daiches, *Some Late Victorian Attitudes* (London: Andre Deutsch, 1969), p. 87.

**3.** Alfred Lord Tennyson, *In Memoriam*, VII, in *The Works of Alfred Lord Tennyson* (London: Macmillan, 1894), p. 249.

**4.** Jürgen Habermas, *Knowledge and Human Interests* (London: Heinemann, 1972), p. 301.

**5.** Patrick Geddes, "The Sociology of Autumn," *The Evergreen: A Northern Seasonal* 1 (Autumn 1895), p. 38.

**6.** Lewis Mumford, "The Geddesian Gambit," in *Lewis Mumford and Patrick Geddes: The Correspondence*, ed. Frank G. Novak (London: Routledge, 1995), p. 360.

**7.** Ibid., p. 362.

**8.** Patrick Geddes, letter to Victor Branford, quoted from Philip Boardman, *The Worlds of Patrick Geddes: Biologist, Town Planner, Re-educator, Peace-warrior* (London: Routledge and Kegan Paul, 1978), p. 194.

**9.** Patrick Abercrombie, quoted in Helen Meller, *Patrick Geddes: Social Evolutionist and City Planner* (London: Routledge, 1990), p. 157.

**10.** Walter Gropius, text of speech to UNESCO, December 1947, CIAM 1946–47, 850 865/2, Special Collections, Getty Research Institute, Santa Monica.

**11.** Lewis Mumford, letter to Percy Johnson-Marshall, 1 January 1975, Edinburgh University Library, Special Collections.

## Introduction

**1.** Letter, Patrick Geddes to _____ Large, 16 April 1907 (NLS, MS 10512, f. 20).

**2.** Philip Boardman, *The Worlds of Patrick Geddes: Biologist, Town Planner, Re-educator, Peace-Warrior* (London: Routledge and Kegan Paul, 1978), p. 230.

**3.** Paddy Kitchen, *A Most Unsettling Person: An Introduction to the Ideas and Life of Patrick Geddes* (London: Victor Gollancz, 1975), p. 220.

## 1  "Angling for Cities!"

**1.** Charles Dickens, *Hard Times* (London: Bradbury, 1854; repr. London: Dent, 1964), pp. 1, 2.

**2.** John Ruskin, *Lectures on Architecture and Painting, Delivered at Edinburgh in November, 1853* (London: Smith, Elder and Co., 1854), pp. 6–7, 9. The lectures had been delivered at Royal Physicians Hall in Queen Street.

**3.** Robert Pemberton, *The Happy Colony* (London: Saunders and Otley, 1854).

**4.** See for example SUA, T-GED 22/1/1326.1.

**5.** Reproduction of a map of Barcelona by D. J. Serra from 1890 (SUA, T-GED 22/1/1744).

**6.** Two plans of the Ringstraße are today in the Patrick Geddes collection at Special Collections, Edinburgh University

Library, Edinburgh University. See Patrick Geddes Centre for Planning Studies, ed., *Catalogue of the Cities Exhibition* (University of Edinburgh, 1988), nos. 59, 60.

**7.** Thomas Henry Huxley, *Physiography: An Introduction to the Study of Nature* (1877), quoted in Helen Meller, *Patrick Geddes: Social Evolutionist and City Planner* (London: Routledge, 1990), p. 38.

**8.** Patrick Geddes, "Chlorophylle animale et la physiologie des planaires vertes," *Archives de Zoologie expérimentale et générale* (Paris, 1879).

**9.** Patrick Geddes and Arthur J. Thomson, *Life: Outlines of General Biology*, 2 vols. (London: Williams & Norgate, 1931).

**10.** See Meller, *Patrick Geddes*, pp. 34–37.

**11.** Quoted in Philip Boardman, *The Worlds of Patrick Geddes: Biologist, Town Planner, Re-educator, Peace-Warrior* (London: Routledge and Kegan Paul, 1978), p. 46.

**12.** The following relies strongly on Zygmunt Bauman, *Modernity and Ambivalence* (London: Polity Press, 1991), pp. 4–12.

**13.** Ibid., pp. 11–12.

**14.** Patrick Geddes, "The Classification of Statistics and Its Results," *Proceedings of the Royal Society of Edinburgh* 11 (1881), p. 302.

**15.** Ibid., p. 310.

**16.** Ibid., p. 316.

**17.** Ibid., pp. 303–304.

**18.** Patrick Geddes, "A Re-statement of the Cell Theory, with Application to the Morphology, Classification, and Physiology of Protists, Plants, and Animals. Together with an Hypothesis of Cell-Structure, and an Hypothesis of Contractility," *Proceedings of the Royal Society of Edinburgh* 12 (1883–1884), pp. 266–292; Patrick Geddes, "An Analysis of the Principles of Economics," *Proceedings of the Royal Society of Edinburgh* 12 (1883–1884), pp. 943–980; Patrick Geddes, *John Ruskin: Economist* (Edinburgh: Brown, 1885), reprinted as "John Ruskin, as Economist," *International Monthly* 1 (1900), pp. 280–308; Patrick Geddes, "Theory of Growth, Reproduction, Sex and Heredity," *Proceedings of the Royal Society of Edinburgh* 13 (1885–1886), pp. 911–931. For a discussion of Geddes's economic theories see especially John Patrick Reilly, *The Early Social Thought of Patrick Geddes* (Ann Arbor: University Microfilms, 1975), pp. 81–164, and Meller, *Patrick Geddes*, pp. 58–62.

**19.** Geddes, "Analysis of the Principles of Economics," p. 960.

**20.** Geddes, "John Ruskin, as Economist," p. 298.

**21.** Geddes, "Classification of Statistics," p. 316.

**22.** See Moses I. Finley, *The Ancient Economy* (London: Hogarth Press, 1985; repr. Harmondsworth: Penguin, 1992), pp. 17–22.

**23.** Geddes, "John Ruskin, as Economist," p. 296.

**24.** John Ruskin, introduction to *The Economist of Xenophon*, trans. Alexander D. O. Wedderburn and W. Gershom Collingwood, in *The Complete Works of John Ruskin*, ed. Edward Tyas Cook and Alexander Wedderburn, 39 vols. (London: Allen, 1907), vol. 31, pp. 9, 11.

**25.** See the essays listed in note 18 above; also Patrick Geddes, *Every Man His Own Art Critic at the Manchester Exhibition, 1887* (Manchester: John Heywood, 1887); Patrick Geddes, *Every Man His Own Art Critic* (*Glasgow Exhibition, 1888*) (Edinburgh: William Brown; Glasgow: John Menzies, 1888); Patrick Geddes, *Co-operation versus Socialism* (Manchester: Co-operative Printing Society, 1888).

**26.** Geddes, "John Ruskin, as Economist," p. 304.

**27.** Ibid.

**28.** Ibid., pp. 307–308.

**29.** Bauman, *Modernity and Ambivalence*, pp. 6–7.

**30.** Ibid., p. 8.

**31.** Ibid., pp. 20–30.

**32.** Patrick Geddes, "Report on the Towns in the Madras Presidency" (Madura, 1915), p. 91, quoted in Jaqueline Tyrwhitt, ed., *Patrick Geddes in India* (London: Lund Humphries, 1947), p. 22.

**33.** Patrick Geddes quoted in Amelia Defries, *The Interpreter Geddes: The Man and His Gospel* (London: George Routledge & Sons, 1927), p. 168.

**34.** Geddes, "John Ruskin, as Economist," p. 303.

**35.** Geddes, *Co-operation versus Socialism*, p. 23.

**36.** Geddes, "John Ruskin, as Economist," p. 303.

**37.** Letter, Patrick Geddes to unknown correspondent, 23 February 1895 (NLS, MS 10508 A, f. 98).

**38.** Bauman, *Modernity and Ambivalence*, pp. 23–26.

**39.** Geddes, "Analysis of the Principles of Economics," p. 944.

**40.** See Walter Harry Green Armytage, *Heavens Below: Utopian Experiments in England 1560–1960* (London: Routledge and Kegan Paul, 1961), pp. 327–341.

**41.** Riccardo Stephens, *The Cruciform Mark: The Strange Story of Richard Tregenna Bachelor of Medicine (Univ. Edin.)* (London: Chatto & Windus, 1896).

**42.** Victor Verasis Branford (1864–1930) came into contact with Geddes while studying at Edinburgh University. A close intellectual and personal friendship developed between them, in which Branford, an accountant, became one of Geddes's financial advisors, often saviors. The intellectual agreement between the two was so close that jointly published books do not identify each author's contribution. An analysis of the mutual influences between Branford and Geddes would be an intriguing study, but one beyond the scope of this book. On Branford see Lewis Mumford, *Sketches from Life: The Autobiography of Lewis Mumford, the Early Years* (Boston: Bacon Press, 1982), pp. 252–269.

**43.** Ibid., p. 259.

**44.** David Montague Eder (1865–1936) was a trained physician who had worked in the slums of London's East End but had also practiced in the republic of Colombia. His cousin Israel Zangwill introduced Eder to the Zionist Movement. Eder became a member of the Jewish Territorial Organisation and a prominent figure within the Zionist movement; from 1918 to 1923 he lived in Palestine, working on the establishment of the Hebrew University. Eder became interested in psychoanalysis and founded the Psychoanalytical Association in Great Britain in 1913. See J. B. Hobman, ed., *David Eder: Memoirs of a Modern Pioneer* (London: Victor Gollancz, 1945). Eder and D. H. Lawrence had met in 1914: see Mark Kinkead-

Weekes, *D. H. Lawrence: Triumph to Exile, 1912–1922* (Cambridge: Cambridge University Press, 1996), p. 133.

**45.** For a description of Geddes's circle in London see Philip Mairet, *Autobiographical and Other Papers*, ed. Charles Hubert Sisson (Manchester: Carcanet, 1981).

**46.** See Volker M. Welter, "Arcades for Lucknow: Patrick Geddes, Charles Rennie Mackintosh and the Reconstruction of the City," *Architectural History* 42 (1999), pp. 316–332.

**47.** With the exception of the recently published study by the late Giovanni Ferraro, Geddes's work in India has not been subject to a detailed and critical scholarly investigation. See Giovanni Ferraro, *Rieducazione alla speranza. Patrick Geddes planner in India, 1914–1924* (Milan: Jaca, 1998).

**48.** Frank Mears (1880–1953) had been apprentice to the Edinburgh architect Hippolyte Blanc and had studied part-time at the School of Applied Art. Mears completed his training with the Edinburgh architect Robert Rowand Anderson and qualified as an architect in 1901. He then worked with Robert Weir Schultz in London on the design for a cathedral at Khartoum. In 1906 he returned to Edinburgh to the office of Sidney Mitchell and George Wilson, a practice Geddes had commissioned to design and build various projects in the 1890s. The connection between Mears and Geddes originated in the years around 1908, when Mears collaborated with the young architect Ramsay Traquair, son of the artist Phoebe Traquair who was, in turn, a close acquaintance of Geddes and his circle. A survey of historic Edinburgh and the city's development was Mears and Geddes's first project together. Their relationship progressed from professional to personal when in 1915 Mears married Norah, Geddes's daughter, who was herself trained as a landscape architect. See Graeme Purves, "The Life and Work of Sir Frank Mears: Planning with a Cultural Perspective" (doctoral thesis, Heriot-Watt University, 1987).

**49.** Purves, "Life and Work of Sir Frank Mears," p. 17.

**50.** Raymond Williams, *The Country and the City* (London: Chatto & Windus, 1973; repr. London: Hogarth Press, 1993), p. 243.

**51.** Ibid., p. 246.

**52.** Victor Verasis Branford, *Living Religions: A Plea for the Larger Modernism* (London: Le Play House Press and Williams & Norgate, 1924).

## 2   Patrick Geddes's Theory of the City

**1.** Frank M. Turner, *The Greek Heritage in Victorian Britain* (New Haven: Yale University Press, 1981), p. 2. The following summary of the importance of Greek civilization for Victorian Britain relies strongly on Turner's book.

**2.** Ibid., p. 8.

**3.** See chapter 8, "The Victorian Platonic Revival," in ibid., pp. 369–414.

**4.** Plato, *The Republic*, trans. Desmond Lee, 2d ed. (Harmondsworth: Penguin, 1987), 368e–369.

**5.** Ibid., 435e.

**6.** Ibid., 430b, 428d, 430d–432.

**7.** Ibid., 432b–434d.

**8.** Ibid., 437–441c, 443c–443e.

**9.** Victor Branford and Patrick Geddes, *Our Social Inheritance* (London: Williams & Norgate, 1919), p. 24.

**10.** Probably the best contemporary description of the Notation of Life was provided by Victor Branford in his essay "A More Realistic Approach to the Social Synthesis," *Sociological Review* 22 (1930), pp. 195–218. What I call the Act-Deed formula Branford named "formula of Personality," and for the Town-City formula he used the term "civic formula" (p. 215).

**11.** Amelia Defries, *The Interpreter Geddes: The Man and His Gospel* (London: George Routledge & Sons, 1927), pp. 129–144 and plate V.

**12.** Patrick Geddes, "Civics: As Applied Sociology. Part I," in *Sociological Papers 1904* (London: Macmillan, 1905), pp. 103–

118; Patrick Geddes, "Civics: As Concrete and Applied Sociology. Part II," in *Sociological Papers 1905* (London: Macmillan, 1906), pp. 57–111.

**13.** Defries, *The Interpreter Geddes*, p. 129, footnote 2.

**14.** Geddes, "Civics, Part II," p. 72.

**15.** Ibid., p. 71.

**16.** Ibid., pp. 68, 72. Following Geddes, I will use the word Town (or Town proper) with a capital initial in this discussion to indicate that I am referring to his particular understanding of a Town as opposed to any town. Similarly, in the following pages, School, Cloister, and City (in deed) will refer to specific terms in Geddes's analysis.

**17.** Ibid., p. 68.

**18.** Ibid., p. 69.

**19.** Ibid., p. 74.

**20.** Ibid., p. 72.

**21.** Ibid., pp. 83, 84.

**22.** Ibid., p. 87.

**23.** Ibid., p. 92.

**24.** Patrick Geddes, *Cities in Evolution: An Introduction to the Town Planning Movement and to the Study of Civics* (London: Williams & Norgate, 1915), p. 254.

**25.** Geddes, "Civics, Part II," p. 89.

**26.** Ibid., pp. 80–81.

**27.** Ibid., p. 85.

**28.** Ibid., p. 91.

**29.** Patrick Geddes, "The Mapping of Life," *Sociological Review* 16 (1924), p. 195.

**30.** Ibid., pp. 195–196.

**31.** Ibid., p. 196.

**32.** Patrick Geddes, *Syllabus of a Course of Ten Lectures on Evolution in Life, Mind, Morals and Society* (London: University of London, 1910), p. 9.

**33.** Patrick Geddes, "The Charting of Life," *Sociological Review* 19 (1927), p. 59.

**34.** Ibid.

**35.** Geddes employed the symbol of a swastika because he considered it to be an ancient Celtic symbol of life. Its division into four quadrants and the indication of a circular movement made the swastika an ideal symbol to express the spiral movement of the Notation of Life in a two-dimensional representation. Patrick Geddes, "The World Without and the World Within: Sunday Talks with My Children," undated typescript, p. 10 (SUA, T-GED 12/2/171).

**36.** Patrick Geddes, "The City Beautiful—In Theory and Practise," *Garden Cities & Town Planning Magazine* 3 (1913), p. 199.

**37.** Geddes knew William James (1842–1910) personally, for James had lectured at some sessions of the Edinburgh Summer Meeting, a series of international summer schools organized by Geddes in the years 1887–1899. James was in Edinburgh again in May and June of 1901 and 1902 to deliver the Gifford Lectures on Natural Religions. Geddes and George Frederick Stout (1860–1944) were members of "The Heretics," a Cambridge-based society that aimed "to promote the discussion on problems of religion, philosophy and art." Among the other members were George Bernard Shaw, Bertrand Russell, and Jane Ellen Harrison. (SUA, T-GED 23/13/10.) Geddes might have referred to books like G. F. Stout, *A Manual of Psychology*, 2 vols. (London: University Tutorial Press, 1898–1899), or William James, *Psychology: A Briefer Course* (London: Macmillan and Co., 1892).

**38.** Geddes, "The World Without and the World Within," pp. 2, 7–8.

**39.** Geddes, *Syllabus of a Course on Evolution*, p. 9.

**40.** Geddes, "The World Without and the World Within," p. 4.

**41.** Geddes, "Civics, Part II," p. 80.

**42.** Stout, *Manual of Psychology*, pp. 435–436.

**43.** James, *Psychology*, p. 288.

**44.** Geddes, "The World Without and the World Within," p. 3.

**45.** Geddes, "Civics, Part II," p. 91.

**46.** Geddes, "Mapping of Life," p. 200.

**47.** Stout, *Manual of Psychology*, p. 393.

**48.** James, *Psychology*, p. 302.

**49.** Stout, *Manual of Psychology*, pp. 394–396.

**50.** Ibid., p. 418.

**51.** Ibid., pp. 447–448.

**52.** Ibid., p. 514.

**53.** Ibid., pp. 509–510.

**54.** Ibid., pp. 512–513.

**55.** Patrick Geddes, "On the Conditions of Progress of the Capitalist and the Labourer," in *The Claims of Labour* (Edinburgh: Co-operative Printing Co., 1886).

**56.** Max Weber, "Die Stadt," *Archiv für Sozialwissenschaften und Sozialpolitik* 47 (1921), pp. 621ff.

**57.** Geddes, "The World Without and the World Within," p. 12.

**58.** Geddes, *Syllabus of a Course on Evolution*, pp. 12–13.

**59.** Ibid., p. 13.

**60.** Geddes, *Cities in Evolution*, p. 264.

**61.** Geddes, "Civics, Part II," p. 102.

**62.** Plato, *Phaedo*, in *The Last Days of Socrates*, trans. Hugh Tredennick, 2d ed. rev. Harold Tarrant (Harmondsworth: Penguin, 1993), pp. 81–84.

**63.** Geddes, *Cities in Evolution*, p. 372.

**64.** Plato, *Republic*, 500d.

**65.** Plato, *Republic*, 519c–520b.

**66.** Geddes, "Civics, Part II," pp. 88, 89.

**67.** Plato, *Republic*, books VIII–IX, esp. 545d–546b.

**68.** Patrick Geddes, manuscript notes on the City of Destruction (SUA, T-GED 1/5/54).

**69.** Richard Lewis Nettleship, *Lectures on the Republic of Plato*, ed. G. R. Benson (London: Macmillan, 1898), p. 5.

**70.** Plato, *Republic*, 401c.

**71.** Ebe Minerva White, *The Foundations of Civics* (London: Syndicate Publishing, 1927), p. 7.

**72.** For a summary of this debate see Paul Barry Clarke, *Citizenship* (London: Pluto, 1994).

**73.** See for example Sybella Gurney, "Civic Reconstruction and the Garden City Movement," *Sociological Review* 3 (1910), pp. 35–43, or Sybella Branford [née Gurney], "Citizenship and the Civic Association," *Sociological Review* 13 (1921), pp. 228–234.

**74.** Patrick Geddes, *Country and Town in Development, Deterioration, and Renewal* (n.pl.: n.pub., n.d. [c. 1909–1910]), pp. 17–18.

**75.** See Geddes, "Civics, Part I" and "Civics, Part II."

**76.** Patrick Geddes, *Civics: The Conditions of Town Planning and City Design* (London: Hampton, 1910).

**77.** For example, see Patrick Geddes, *City Development: A Study of Parks, Gardens and Culture-Institutes. A Report to the Carnegie Dunfermline Trust* (Edinburgh: Geddes and Company; Birmingham: Saint George Press, 1904); Patrick Geddes, *Town Planning and City Design—in Sociology and in Citizenship* (London: Sociological Society, 1908).

**78.** Patrick Geddes, *The Masque of Learning and Its Many Meanings: A Pageant of Education through the Ages, Devised and Interpreted by Patrick Geddes. Semi-Jubilee of University Hall, 1912* (Edinburgh: Patrick Geddes and Colleagues, 1912), p. 19.

**79.** Geddes provides the definition: "Greek ethics, their natural origins. Expressions of these, mythic, poetic, artistic. (a) Development of these in temple and statue, in ritual and drama. (b) Elaboration through discussion into philosophic form. (c) Corresponding evolution of the City, in its dual completeness; *i.e.*, as not only a Town of labour and daily life, but an Acropolis of temporal and spiritual idealism, of clarified thought and perfected art." Patrick Geddes, *Syllabus of a Course of Ten Lectures on Evolutionary Ethics, Based on Natural Science and Sociology* (London: Hampton, 1905), p. 3.

**80.** Patrick Geddes, *The Returning Gods* (London: n.p., 1914), p. 2.

**81.** Branford, "Citizenship and the Civic Association," p. 229.

**82.** Geddes made this distinction, for example, in a lecture series, "Cities in Evolution," that he delivered in Madras in 1915. See syllabus "Cities in Evolution (University of Madras)," n.d. (c. 1915) (SUA, T-GED 1/1/4).

**83.** Geddes, *Country and Town*, p. 21.

**84.** Gurney, "Civic Reconstruction," p. 37.

**85.** Plato, *Phaedo*, 75a–77a; Plato, *Meno*, in *Protagoras and Meno*, trans. W. K. C. Guthrie (Harmondsworth: Penguin, 1956), 81c–e.

## 3  The City and Geography

**1.** Figures from H. C. G. Matthew, "The Liberal Age (1851–1914)," in Kenneth O. Morgan, ed., *The Sphere Illustrated History of Britain, 1789–1983* (Oxford: Oxford University Press, 1984; repr. London: Sphere, 1991), p. 60.

**2.** Quoted in Ebenezer Howard, *Garden Cities of To-morrow (Being the Second Edition of "To-morrow: A Peaceful Path to Real Reform")* (London: Swan Sonnenschein, 1902; repr. Builth Wells: Attic, 1985), p. 4.

**3.** See Raymond Williams, *The Country and the City* (London: Chatto & Windus, 1973; repr. London: Hogarth Press, 1993).

**4.** Howard, *Garden Cities*, pp. 6–9.

**5.** Peter Kropotkin, *Fields, Factories and Workshops Tomorrow*, ed. Colin Ward (London: Hutchinson, 1899; repr. London: Freedom Press, 1985).

**6.** Ibid., p. 151.

**7.** Peter Kropotkin, *Mutual Aid: A Factor of Evolution* (London: William Heinemann, 1902; repr. London: Freedom Press, 1987), especially chapters 4 through 6.

**8.** Elisée Reclus, "The Evolution of Cities," *Contemporary Review* 67 (1895), pp. 246–264.

**9.** Ibid., p. 246.

**10.** The following summary is based on ibid., pp. 263–264.

**11.** Ibid., pp. 264, 263.

**12.** Ibid., p. 264.

**13.** Patrick Geddes, "Civics: As Applied Sociology. Part I," in *Sociological Papers 1904* (London: Macmillan, 1905), p. 105.

**14.** Unlike reproductions of the valley section used by Geddes, reproductions of the diagram since c. 1950 usually omit all human settlements other than the large city at the coast.

**15.** Described in Robert Smith, "Botanical Survey of Scotland I. Edinburgh District," *Scottish Geographical Magazine* 16 (1900), p. 387.

**16.** Patrick Geddes, "The Influence of Geographical Conditions on Social Development," *Geographical Journal* 12 (1898), p. 582.

**17.** Ibid., p. 583.

**18.** Ibid., p. 581.

**19.** Ibid., p. 580.

**20.** Kropotkin, *Mutual Aid*, p. 18.

**21.** Geddes, "Civics, Part I," p. 105.

**22.** See Moses I. Finley, "The Ancient City: From Fustel de Coulanges to Max Weber and Beyond," in Finley, *Economy and Society in Ancient Greece*, ed. B. D. Shaw and R. P. Saller (London: Chatto & Windus, 1981), p. 10.

**23.** John Millar, *The Origin of the Distinction of Ranks*, 4th ed. (Edinburgh, 1806; repr. Bristol: Thoemmes, 1990), p. 2. Geddes owned a copy of the first edition of Millar's book, published with a slightly different title: John Millar, *Observation Concerning the Distinction of Ranks in Society* (Dublin: T. Ewing, 1771). (SUA, T-GED 24/292.)

**24.** Geddes, "Civics, Part I," p. 106.

**25.** Patrick Geddes, "The Valley Plan of Civilization (the Third of the Talks from the Outlook Tower)," *Survey Graphic* (June 1925), p. 323.

**26.** Michael Cuthbert, "The Concept of the Outlook Tower in the Work of Patrick Geddes" (master's thesis, University of St. Andrews, 1987), p. 68; Rosalind Williams, "Lewis Mumford as a Historian of Technology in Technics and Civilization," in Thomas P. Hughes and Agatha C. Hughes, eds., *Lewis Mumford:*

*Public Intellectual* (New York: Oxford University Press, 1990), p. 56.

**27.** Patrick Geddes, review of *The City* by Robert E. Park, Ernest W. Burgess, [and Roderick D. McKenzie,] *Sociological Review* 18 (1926), p. 167.

**28.** Patrick Geddes, "Edinburgh and Its Region, Geographic and Historical," *Scottish Geographical Magazine* 18 (1902), p. 306.

**29.** William G. Smith, "A Botanical Survey of Scotland," *Scottish Geographical Magazine* 18 (1902), p. 135.

**30.** Robert Smith, "Botanical Survey of Scotland I"; Robert Smith, "Botanical Survey of Scotland II: North Perthshire District," *Scottish Geographical Magazine* 16 (1900), pp. 441–467, map following p. 504.

**31.** Patrick Geddes, *The Civic Survey of Edinburgh* (Edinburgh: Outlook Tower; Chelsea: Crosby Hall, 1911), p. 542. (Offprint from Royal Institute of British Architects, ed., *Townplanning Conference London, 10–15 October 1910, Transactions* [London: RIBA, 1910], pp. 537–574.)

**32.** Quoted in Amelia Defries, *The Interpreter Geddes: The Man and His Gospel* (London: George Routledge & Sons, 1927), pp. 224–225.

**33.** William Warde Fowler, *The City-State of the Greeks and Romans: A Survey Introductory to the Study of Ancient History* (London: Macmillan, 1893), p. 28.

**34.** Ibid., p. 43.

**35.** Ibid., p. 9.

**36.** Ibid., p. 52.

**37.** See Eric J. Hobsbawm, *Nations and Nationalism since 1780: Programme, Myth, Reality* (Cambridge: Cambridge University Press, 1990), pp. 58–59.

**38.** Geddes, *Civic Survey of Edinburgh*, p. 542.

**39.** Patrick Geddes and Victor Branford, "Rural and Urban Thought: A Contribution to the Theory of Progress and Decay," *Sociological Review* 21 (1929), pp. 14–15.

**40.** Ibid., p. 15.

**41.** Patrick Geddes, "A Suggested Plan for a Civic Museum (or Civic Exhibition) and Its Associated Studies," in *Sociological Papers 1906* (London: Macmillan, 1907), p. 201.

**42.** Patrick Geddes and Frank C. Mears, *Cities and Town Planning Exhibition, Edinburgh, 13th March–1st April 1911, Explanatory Guide Book and Outline Catalogue* (Edinburgh: A. Hutchinson, 1911), p. 20.

**43.** John Ruskin, *Fors Clavigera: Letters to the Workmen and Labourers of Great Britain*, vol. 27 of *The Works of John Ruskin*, ed. Edward Tyas Cook and Alexander Wedderburn (London: Allen, 1907), p. 497.

**44.** See for example Helen Meller, "Patrick Geddes," in Gordon Cherry, ed., *Pioneers in British Planning* (London: Architectural Press, 1981), pp. 46–71, esp. p. 51.

**45.** Patrick Geddes, *Cities in Evolution: An Introduction to the Town Planning Movement and to the Study of Civics* (London: Williams & Norgate, 1915), p. 381.

**46.** Letter, Patrick Geddes to unknown correspondent, 23 February 1895 (NLS, MS, 10508A, f. 98).

**47.** Geddes, *Civic Survey of Edinburgh*, p. 540.

**48.** Geddes, *Cities in Evolution*, p. 390.

**49.** Geddes and Mears, *Cities and Town Planning Exhibition*, p. 37.

**50.** Geddes, *Civic Survey of Edinburgh*, p. 558.

**51.** Urlan Wannop and Gordon E. Cherry, "The Development of Regional Planning in the United Kingdom," *Planning Perspectives* 9 (1994), pp. 33, 35.

**52.** Benjamin Hyman, "British Planners in Palestine, 1918–1936" (doctoral thesis, London School of Economics and Political Science, University of London, 1994); Volker M. Welter, "The Geddes Vision of the Region as City—Palestine as a Polis," in Jeannine Fiedler, ed., *Social Utopias of the Twenties: Bauhaus, Kibbutz and the Dream of the New Man* (Wuppertal: Müller + Busmann, 1995), pp. 72–79.

**53.** Fowler, *City-State*, p. 8.

**54.** Victor Branford and Patrick Geddes, *The Coming Polity: A Study in Reconstruction* (London: Williams & Norgate, 1917), p. 133.

**55.** William John Keith, *Regions of Imagination: The Development of Rural British Fiction* (Toronto: University of Toronto Press, 1988), p. 3.

**56.** See Helen Meller, *Patrick Geddes: Social Evolutionist and City Planner* (London: Routledge, 1990), p. 134.

**57.** Patrick Geddes, "Boundaries and Frontiers: Their Origin and Their Significance," *Westminster Review* 169 (1908), pp. 258, 259.

**58.** Geddes, *Civic Survey of Edinburgh*, p. 564.

**59.** Patrick Geddes, "The Valley in the Town (the Fourth of the Talks from the Outlook Tower)," *Survey Graphic*, July 1925, p. 400.

**60.** Geddes, *Civic Survey of Edinburgh*, p. 564.

**61.** Patrick Geddes, "Opening Address" for a "Discussion on Housing in Scotland," *Proceedings of the Royal Philosophical Society of Glasgow* 44 (1913), p. 246.

**62.** Geddes, *Cities in Evolution*, p. 34.

**63.** Geddes, "Opening Address," p. 247.

**64.** See Patrick Geddes, *City Surveys for Town Planning* (Edinburgh and Chelsea: Geddes and Colleagues, 1911). This is a reprint of a paper Geddes had read at the Birkenhead Health Congress in 1910.

**65.** Geddes, *City Surveys for Town Planning*, p. 10.

**66.** See Phipps Turnbull, "Patrick Geddes and the Planning Unit Today," reprint from *Quarterly Journal of the Royal Incorporation of Architects in Scotland*, n.d. [1947] (SUA, T-GED 1/7/45).

**67.** Reclus referred to Geddes's activities in Edinburgh; see Reclus, "Evolution of Cities," p. 262. In turn, Geddes referred to Reclus's essay in his own writings; see Geddes, "Civics, Part I," p. 106.

**68.** Geddes, *City Surveys for Town Planning*, p. 4.

**69.** Geddes, *Civic Survey of Edinburgh*, p. 558.

**70.** Patrick Geddes, "A World League of Cities," *Sociological Review* 18 (1926), 166.

**71.** In the late 1920s Otlet could assure the collaboration of Le Corbusier, who contributed a design for the Mundaneum centered around a pyramidal structure. See Jean-Louis Cohen, *Le Corbusier and the Mystique of the USSR: Theories and Projects for Moscow, 1928–1936* (Princeton: Princeton University Press, 1987), pp. 111–114.

**72.** Patrick Geddes, *Two Steps in Civics: "Cities and Town Planning Exhibition" and the "International Congress of Cities," Ghent International Exhibition, 1913* (Liverpool: University Press, 1913), p. 11. This is a reprint from the *Town Planning Review*, July 1913, pp. 1–16.

**73.** Hendrik Christian Andersen, *"World Conscience": An International Society for the Creation of a World-Centre to House International Interest and to Unite Peoples and Nations for the Attainment of Peace and Progress upon Broader Humanitarian Lines* (Rome: World Conscience Society, 1913); Hendrik Christian Andersen and Ernest M. Hébrard, *Creation of a World Centre of Communication* (Paris: n.pub., 1913).

**74.** Geddes, *Two Steps in Civics*, p. 11.

**75.** Geddes, "Edinburgh and Its Region," p. 302.

**76.** Geddes, "Valley Plan," p. 289.

**77.** Branford and Geddes, *Coming Polity*, pp. 188–189.

**78.** Lewis Mumford, *The Story of Utopias*, 2d ed. (New York: Viking, 1974), p. 33.

**79.** Geddes, "Edinburgh and Its Region," p. 303.

**80.** Plato, *Meno*, in *Protagoras and Meno*, trans. W. K. C. Guthrie (Harmondsworth: Penguin, 1956), 82b–85e.

**81.** Geddes, *Cities in Evolution*, p. 18.

**82.** Geddes, "Edinburgh and Its Region," p. 306.

**83.** Patrick Geddes, "A Great Geographer: Elisée Reclus," *Scottish Geographical Magazine* 21 (1905), p. 552.

**84.** Branford and Geddes, *Coming Polity*, p. 15.

**85.** Geddes, "Edinburgh and Its Region," p. 304.

**86.** David Massey, "Regional Planning 1909–1939: 'The Experimental Era,'" in Patricia L. Garside and Michael Hebbert, eds., *British Regionalism 1900–2000* (London: Mansell, 1989), p. 72.


4   **The City in History**

**1.**   Moses I. Finley, "The Ancient City: From Fustel de Coulanges to Max Weber and Beyond," in Finley, *Economy and Society in Ancient Greece*, ed. B. D. Shaw and R. P. Saller (London: Chatto & Windus, 1981), p. 7.

**2.**   Adam Smith, *The Wealth of Nations*, quoted in ibid.

**3.**   Carl E. Schorske, "The Idea of the City in European Thought: Voltaire to Spengler," in Oscar Handlin and John Burchard, eds., *The Historian and the City* (Cambridge: MIT Press, 1963), pp. 95–114.

**4.**   Raymond Williams, *The Country and the City* (London: Chatto & Windus, 1973; repr. London: Hogarth Press, 1993), p. 217.

**5.**   Schorske, "Idea of the City," p. 95.

**6.**   Ira Katznelson, "The Centrality of the City in Social Theory," in Irit Rogoff, ed., *The Divided Heritage: Themes and Problems in German Modernism* (Cambridge: Cambridge University Press, 1991), p. 254.

**7.**   Friedrich Engels, *Die Lage der arbeitenden Klasse in England*, in Karl Marx and Friedrich Engels, *Werke*, vol. 2 (Berlin: Dietz, 1969), pp. 277, 281, 287–288.

**8.**   Karl Marx and Friedrich Engels, *Die deutsche Ideologie. Kritik der neuesten deutschen Philosophie in ihren Repräsentanten Feuerbach, B. Bauer, Stirner und des deutschen Sozialismus in seinen verschiedenen Propheten*, in Marx and Engels, *Werke*, vol. 3 (Berlin: Dietz, 1969), p. 22.

**9.**   Schorske, "Idea of the City," p. 107.

**10.**   Max Weber, "Die Stadt," *Archiv für Sozialwissenschaft und Sozialpolitik* 47 (1921), repr. in Max Weber, *Wirtschaft und Gesellschaft. Grundriß der verstehenden Soziologie*, ed. Johannes

Winckelmann (Cologne and Berlin: Kiepenheuer & Witsch, 1964), pp. 923–1033. In the following I refer to Weber, *The City*, trans. and ed. Don Martindale and Gertrud Neuwirth (New York: Free Press, 1958).

**11.** Weber, *The City*, pp. 75–77.

**12.** Ibid., p. 78.

**13.** Ibid., pp. 91–120.

**14.** Ibid., pp. 97–98.

**15.** Ibid., pp. 102–103.

**16.** Ibid., p. 87.

**17.** Ibid., p. 84.

**18.** Ibid., p. 106.

**19.** Frederic Harrison, *The Meaning of History and Other Historical Pieces* (London: Trübner, 1862; repr. London: Macmillan, 1894), pp. 19, 22.

**20.** Ibid., p. 233.

**21.** Ibid., pp. 250–251.

**22.** Ibid., p. 251.

**23.** The following description is based on Patrick Geddes and Gilbert Slater, *Ideas at War* (London: Williams & Norgate, 1917), pp. 23–27.

**24.** See Patrick Geddes, "A Suggested Plan for a Civic Museum (or Civic Exhibition) and Its Associated Studies," in *Sociological Papers 1906* (London: Macmillan, 1907), pp. 215–217.

**25.** Patrick Geddes, "Civics: As Applied Sociology. Part I," in *Sociological Papers 1904* (London: Macmillan, 1905), p. 109.

**26.** Victor Branford and Patrick Geddes, *The Coming Polity: A Study in Reconstruction* (London: Williams & Norgate, 1917), p. 25.

**27.** Geddes, "Civics, Part I," p. 107.

**28.** Manuscript notes, diagrams, and sketches by Patrick Geddes, n.d. (SUA, T-GED 3/7/36).

**29.** Geddes and Slater, *Ideas at War*, pp. 62–63.

**30.** Victor Branford and Patrick Geddes, *The Coming Polity: A Study in Reconstruction*, new and enlarged edition (London: Williams & Norgate, 1919), p. 234.

**31.** Branford and Geddes, *Coming Polity* (1917 ed.), p. 216.

**32.** Geddes and Slater, *Ideas at War*, pp. 129–130.

**33.** Ibid., pp. 64–65.

**34.** Victor Branford, "A More Realistic Approach to the Social Synthesis," *Sociological Review* 22 (1930), p. 212.

**35.** Geddes, "Suggested Plan for a Civic Museum," p. 218.

**36.** Patrick Geddes, *Town-Planning in Patiala State and City: A Report to the H. H. Maharaja of Patiala* (Lucknow: Perry's Printing Press, 1922), p. x.

**37.** Geddes and Slater, *Ideas at War*, p. 28.

**38.** Ibid., p. 32.

**39.** Geddes, "Suggested Plan for a Civic Museum," pp. 217–218.

**40.** Patrick Geddes, "Civics: As Concrete and Applied Sociology. Part II," in *Sociological Papers 1905* (London: Macmillan, 1906), p. 73.

**41.** Branford and Geddes, *Coming Polity* (1917 ed.), p. 154. The expression "acquired inheritance" refers to a nineteenth-century debate in biology in which evolutionists faced the problem of explaining the transmission of any characteristic of animals or plants to the next generation. Geddes might have taken this expression directly from the biologist Lamarck, who had argued that characteristics acquired in response to environmental conditions by a living being during its lifetime are inherited by the offspring. This is called "the inheritance of acquired characteristics."

**42.** Ibid., p. 157.

**43.** Ibid., pp. 155, 153.

**44.** Ibid., p. 153.

**45.** Ibid., pp. 154–155, 156.

**46.** Georg [György] Lukács, *Die Zerstörung der Vernunft* (Berlin: Aufbau, 1955; repr. 1984), pp. 460–463.

**47.** Caroline van Eck, *Organicism in Nineteenth-Century Architecture: An Inquiry into Its Theoretical and Philosophical Background* (Amsterdam: Architectura & Natura Press, 1994), p. 20.

**48.** Giorgio Piccinato, *Städtebau in Deutschland 1871–1914. Genese einer wissenschaftlichen Disziplin*, trans. Michael Peterek (Braunschweig: Vieweg, 1983), pp. 35–36.

**49.** Johann Wolfgang von Goethe, *Versuch die Metamorphose der Pflanzen zu erklären* (Gotha: C. W. Ettinger, 1790); repr. in *Goethes naturwissenschaftliche Schriften. Zur Morphologie*, ed. Rudolf Steiner (Weimar: Böhlau, 1891), vol. 6, p. 60.

**50.** Johann Wolfgang von Goethe, *Versuch über die Metamorphose der Pflanzen* (Stuttgart: Cottasche Buchhandlung, 1831), repr. in ibid., pp. 120–121.

**51.** Johann Wolfgang von Goethe, "Vorarbeiten zu einer Physiologie der Pflanzen," repr. in ibid., p. 296.

**52.** Ibid., p. 293.

**53.** Patrick Geddes, "Morphology," in *Encyclopaedia Britannica*, 9th ed., 24 vols. (Edinburgh: A. & C. Black, 1875–1889), vol. 16, p. 839.

**54.** Ibid., p. 840.

**55.** Ibid., pp. 844–845. A case of homology is the relationship between the wings of a bat and the arms of man: different functions but same evolutionary origin. A case of analogy is the relationship between the wings of a butterfly and the wings of a bird: same function but different origin.

**56.** Patrick Geddes, *Cities in Evolution: An Introduction to the Town Planning Movement and to the Study of Civics* (London: Williams & Norgate, 1915), p. 269.

**57.** Compiled from Victor Branford and Patrick Geddes, *Our Social Inheritance* (London: Williams & Norgate, 1919), p. 36, fig. 1; p. 38, fig. 2.

**58.** Patrick Geddes, *The Masque of Learning and Its Many Meanings: A Pageant of Education through the Ages* (Edinburgh: Patrick Geddes and Colleagues, 1912), p. 12.

**59.** Patrick Geddes, *Industrial Exhibitions and Modern Progress* (Edinburgh: Douglas, 1887), p. 23.

**60.** Geddes, "Morphology," p. 845.

**61.** Patrick Geddes, *Syllabus of a Series of Ten Lectures on the Study of London* (London: P. S. King and Son, 1909), pp. 3, 4.

**62.** Philip Boardman, *The Worlds of Patrick Geddes: Biologist, Town Planner, Re-educator, Peace-Warrior* (London: Routledge and Kegan Paul, 1978), p. 337. Geddes mentioned all these expressions in a draft of a letter to Lewis Mumford: Patrick Geddes to Lewis Mumford, 25 January 1923 (NLS, MS 10515, f. 52).

**63.** Royal Institute of British Architects, ed., *Town Planning Conference, London, 10th to 15th October 1910; Exhibition of Drawings and Models at the Royal Academy from the 10th to the 22nd October* (London: Clowes & Son, 1910). See also Volker M. Welter, "Stages of an Exhibition: The Cities and Town Planning Exhibition of Patrick Geddes," *Planning History* 20 (1998), 25–35; and Volker M. Welter, *Collecting Cities: Images from Patrick Geddes' Cities and Town Planning Exhibition* (Glasgow: Collins Gallery, 1999).

**64.** Patrick Geddes and Frank C. Mears, *Cities and Town Planning Exhibition, Edinburgh, 13th March–1st April 1911, Explanatory Guide Book and Outline Catalogue* (Edinburgh: A. T. Hutchinson, 1911), p. 20.

**65.** Branford, "A More Realistic Approach," p. 213.

**66.** Geddes and Mears, *Cities and Town Planning Exhibition*, p. 30.

**67.** Geddes, *Cities in Evolution*, p. 281; see the discussion in chapter 1 above, under the heading "Toward a Larger Modernism."

**68.** Geddes and Mears, *Cities and Town Planning Exhibition*, p. 11.

**69.** Geddes, *Cities in Evolution*, p. 270. The following account of the structure of the exhibition focuses mainly on the Ghent show from 1913 (see ibid., pp. 270–282). In Ghent Geddes could arrange his exhibition in a more ideal form than within the constraints of Crosby Hall in Chelsea in 1911.

**70.** Plato, *Meno*, in *Protagoras and Meno*, trans. W. K. C. Guthrie (Harmondsworth: Penguin, 1956), 84b–c.

**71.** Geddes, "Morphology," p. 846.

**72.** Geddes, *Syllabus of a Series on the Study of London*, p. 4.

**73.** Patrick Geddes and Victor Branford, "Rural and Urban Thought: A Contribution to the Theory of Progress and Decay," *Sociological Review* 21 (1929), p. 15. Geddes mentioned the six stages also in a letter to Lewis Mumford, 25 January 1923 (NLS, MS 10515, f. 52).

**74.** See Lewis Mumford's *The Culture of Cities* from 1938 for an account of the six stages, whose order and sequence Mumford changes and adapts for his own purposes. Mumford adds a stage earlier than the *polis*, which he called "eopolis." Geddes uses the term "eupolis" in the letter quoted in note 73 above, which might have inspired the word Mumford finally chose for the new stage. Mumford further combines the fourth and the fifth stages of Geddes's scheme, "parasitopolis" and "patholopolis," into a single stage, "tyrannopolis," a term Geddes also uses in the same letter. Lewis Mumford, *The Culture of Cities* (New York: Harcourt, Brace & World, 1938), pp. 283–292.

**75.** Patrick Geddes, unpublished "Paper on Geographic Survey," 1894, p. 3 (SUA, T-GED 1/5/1).

**76.** Geddes, "Civics, Part I," p. 106.

**77.** See for example Patrick Geddes, *A Course of Three Lectures on Inland Towns & Cities: Their Main Origins*, ed. Royal Geographical Society (n.p.: n.pub., n.d.).


## 5  History in the City

**1.** M. Christine Boyer, *The City of Collective Memory: Its Historical Imagery and Architectural Entertainments* (Cambridge: MIT Press, 1996), p. 26.

**2.** Ibid., p. 22.

**3.** Charles Dellheim, *The Face of the Past: The Preservation of the Medieval Inheritance in Victorian England* (Cambridge: Cambridge University Press, 1982), p. 46.

**4.** Ibid., pp. 47–48. Dellheim lists 38 local history societies founded in England alone between 1834 and 1897.

**5.** Ibid., pp. 55–56.

**6.** Ibid., pp. 77–130; Nikolaus Pevsner, "Scrape and Antiscrape," in Jane Fawcett, ed., *The Future of the Past: Attitudes to*

*Conservation, 1174–1974* (London: Thames and Hudson, 1976), pp. 35–54.

**7.** See Edward Palmer Thompson, *William Morris: Romantic to Revolutionary* (London: Merlin Press, 1955), pp. 226–242; Pevsner, "Scrape and Anti-scrape." Geddes was not a member of the SPAB but corresponded with the Society concerning the restoration of a church in Aberdeen during 1885 (letter of the SPAB to the author, 16 January 1995).

**8.** William Morris, "Address at the Second Annual Meeting [of the SPAB], 28 June 1879," in *William Morris: Artist, Writer, Socialist,* ed. May Morris, 2 vols. (Oxford: Basil Blackwell, 1936), vol. 1, p. 123.

**9.** William Morris, "Address at the Twelfth Annual Meeting [of the SPAB], 3 July 1889," in Morris, ed., *William Morris,* vol. 1, p. 148.

**10.** Figure 5.1 is taken from Sociological Society, Cities Committee, *Memorandum on the Need of City Survey Preparatory to Town-Planning* (n.pl.: n.pub., n.d. [1911]), p. 6.

**11.** Francis Henry Wollaston Sheppard, "Sources and Methods Used for the Survey of London," in Harold James Dyos, ed., *The Study of Urban History* (London: Arnold, 1967), p. 131.

**12.** Walter Hindes Godfrey, *The Parish of Chelsea,* in two parts (London: County Council, 1909, 1913).

**13.** Geddes is mentioned as a member of the Survey committee in Godfrey, *Parish of Chelsea,* part I.

**14.** Patrick Geddes, "Civics: As Applied Sociology. Part I," in *Sociological Papers 1904* (London: Macmillan, 1905), p. 108.

**15.** Victor Branford and Patrick Geddes, *Our Social Inheritance* (London: Williams & Norgate, 1919), p. 151.

**16.** Ibid., p. 131.

**17.** Ibid., p. 124.

**18.** Ibid., pp. 138–139.

**19.** Ibid., pp. 129–293.

**20.** Lewis Mumford, *The City in History: Its Origin, Its Transformation, and Its Prospects* (London: Secker & Warburg, 1961), p. 585.

21. The following analysis refers to Branford and Geddes, *Our Social Inheritance*, pp. 262–293.

22. Ibid., p. 269.

23. Ibid., p. 280.

24. This paragraph draws on ibid., pp. 182–187.

25. Ibid., pp. 186–187.

26. Ibid., p. 183.

27. Patrick Geddes, *Cities in Evolution: An Introduction to the Town Planning Movement and to the Study of Civics* (London: Williams & Norgate, 1915), p. vi.

28. Ibid.

29. Patrick Geddes, *Town Planning in Lahore: A Report to the Municipal Council* (Lahore: Commercial Printing Works, 1917), p. 42.

30. See Jaqueline Tyrwhitt, ed., *Geddes in India* (London: Lund Humphries, 1947); Helen Meller, "Geddes and His Indian Reports," in *Patrick Geddes: A Symposium, 1 March 1982* (Dundee: Duncan of Jordanstone College of Art/University of Dundee, [1985]), pp. 1–25; Attilio Petruccioli, "Patrick Geddes in Indore: Some Questions of Method," *Lotus International*, no. 34 (1982), pp. 106–115.

31. Patrick Geddes, *Town Planning in Balrampur: A Report to the Hon'ble the Maharaja Bahadur* (Lucknow: Murray's London Printing Press, 1917), p. 11.

32. Ibid., pp. 41–42.

33. See Tyrwhitt, ed., *Geddes in India*, pp. 40–59, for further examples of conservative surgery in Indian reports.

34. Geddes, *Town Planning in Lahore*, p. 9.

35. Ibid., p. 7.

36. Tyrwhitt, ed., *Geddes in India*, pp. 63–64.

37. Patrick Geddes, *Town-Planning in Patiala State and City: A Report to the H. H. Maharaja of Patiala* (Lucknow: Perry's Printing Press, 1922), p. viii.

38. Patrick Geddes, *A Report on the Development and Expansion of the City of Baroda by Patrick Geddes* (Baroda: Lakshmi Vilas Press, 1916), p. 15.

**39.** Geddes, *Town Planning in Balrampur*, p. 41.

**40.** Patrick Geddes, *Town Planning in Lucknow: A Second Report to the Municipal Council* (Lucknow, 1917), quoted in Tyrwhitt, ed., *Geddes in India*, p. 57.

**41.** Ibid.

**42.** Geddes, *A Report on the Development of Baroda*, p. 7.

**43.** Patrick Geddes, "Civic Education and City Development," *Contemporary Review* 88 (1905), pp. 417, 419.

**44.** Ibid., p. 418.

**45.** Patrick Geddes, *City Development: A Study of Parks, Gardens and Culture-Institutes. A Report to the Carnegie Dunfermline Trust* (Edinburgh: Geddes and Company; Birmingham: Saint George Press, 1904), p. 212.

**46.** Geddes, "Civic Education and City Development," p. 418.

**47.** Patrick Geddes, "The Scots Renascence," *The Evergreen: A Northern Seasonal* 1 (Spring 1895), p. 138.

**48.** See Earl of Sandwich, "The Saving of Crosby Hall," *Sociological Review* 24 (1932), pp. 362–364; Andrew Saint, "Ashbee, Geddes, Lethaby and the Rebuilding of Crosby Hall," *Architectural History* 34 (1991), pp. 206–217.

**49.** Letter by Patrick Geddes to _____ Schrader, 2 June 1908 (NLS, MS 10512, f. 129).

**50.** Harold P. Clunn, *The Face of London: The Record of a Century's Changes and Development* (London: Marshall, 1933), pp. 367–368.

**51.** Anonymous, "Purpose of Crosby Hall" (annotated typescript, n.d.), p. 2 (SUA, T-GED 12/1/344).

**52.** Ibid., pp. 2–3.

**53.** Godfrey, *Parish of Chelsea*, part II, pp. 9–17; Philip Norman, *Crosby Place*, part of the Survey of London (London: County Council, 1908).

**54.** Godfrey, *Parish of Chelsea*, part II, p. 16.

**55.** Ibid., pp. 9–14.

**56.** Geddes, *Cities in Evolution*, p. 373.

**57.** See letter by Geddes to Reginald Blunt, Carlyle House, Chelsea, February 1895 (NLS MS 10508A, f. 93).

**58.** For Ashbee's work in Chelsea see Alan Crawford, *C. R. Ashbee: Architect, Designer, and Romantic Socialist* (New Haven: Yale University Press, 1985), pp. 237–259; for the fraternity houses see Saint, "Ashbee, Geddes, Lethaby," p. 214.

**59.** For Mackintosh's designs for Chelsea see *C. R. Mackintosh: The Chelsea Years, 1915–1923* (Glasgow: Hunterian Art Gallery, 1994).

**60.** Philip Boardman, *The Worlds of Patrick Geddes: Biologist, Town Planner, Re-educator, Peace-Warrior* (London: Routledge and Kegan Paul, 1978), p. 212.

**61.** Patrick Geddes, "The Scots College at Montpellier University," pamphlet reprinted from *Aberdeen University Review,* July 1927, p. 9.

**62.** Boardman, *Worlds of Patrick Geddes,* p. 235.

**63.** Letter, Patrick Geddes to Blackie Murdoch, June 1909 (NLS, MS 10512, f. 193).

**64.** Boardman, *Worlds of Patrick Geddes,* p. 141.

**65.** Patrick Geddes, *The Proposed University for Central India, at Indore. A Reprint from "Town Planning towards City Development." A Report to the Durbar of Indore by Patrick Geddes* (Indore: Holkar State Printing Press, 1918), p. 24.

**66.** Patrick Geddes, *Industrial Exhibitions and Modern Progress* (Edinburgh: Douglas, 1887), pp. 1–2.

**67.** Raymond Unwin, *Town Planning in Practise: An Introduction to the Art of Designing Cities and Suburbs* (London: Fisher Unwin, 1909), p. 141.

**68.** Boardman, *Worlds of Patrick Geddes,* p. 69.

**69.** Ernst Haeckel, *Generelle Morphologie,* quoted from Erhard Lange and Dietrich Alexander, eds., *Philosophenlexikon* (Berlin: Dietz, 1984), p. 331 (my translation).

**70.** Branford and Geddes, *Our Social Inheritance,* p. 306.

**71.** Geddes, *City Development. Report to the Carnegie Dunfermline Trust,* p. 123.

**72.** Geddes, *Industrial Exhibitions*, p. 23.

**73.** Patrick Geddes, "Civics: As Concrete and Applied Sociology. Part II," in *Sociological Papers 1905* (London: Macmillan, 1906), p. 94.

**74.** Friedrich Nietzsche, *Thoughts out of Season: Part II, The Use and Abuse of History*, trans. Adrian Collins, in *The Complete Works of Friedrich Nietzsche*, ed. Oscar Levy, 18 vols. (Edinburgh: T. N. Foulis, 1909), vol. 2, pp. 24–25.

## 6  The Metaphysical Imperative in Urban Design around 1900

**1.** See for example *Okkultismus und Avantgarde. Von Munch bis Mondrian 1900–1915*, exh. cat. (Frankfurt: Schirn Kunsthalle, 1995).

**2.** Richard Hamann and Jost Hermand, *Stilkunst um 1900* (Munich: Nymphenburger Verlagshandlung, 1975), pp. 10–11.

**3.** See especially chapter 4, "Idealismus statt Materialismus," in ibid., pp. 77–101.

**4.** Ibid., p. 93 (my translation).

**5.** Ferdinand Tönnies, *Gemeinschaft und Gesellschaft. Abhandlung des Communismus und des Sozialismus als empirische Culturformen* (Leipzig: Fues, 1887). The second edition had the title *Gemeinschaft und Gesellschaft. Grundbegriffe der reinen Soziologie.* (Berlin, 1912); the subtitle of this edition became the title of the first English translation: Ferdinand Tönnies, *Fundamental Concepts of Sociology (Gesellschaft und Gemeinschaft)*, trans. Charles P. Loomis (New York: American Book Company, 1940).

**6.** Ferdinand Tönnies, "The Concept of *Gemeinschaft*," in *Ferdinand Tönnies on Sociology: Pure, Applied and Empirical. Selected Writings*, ed. Werner J. Cahnmann and Rudolf Heberle (Chicago: University of Chicago Press, 1971), p. 65. The essay was originally written in 1925 and offers a brief but useful summary of Tönnies's concepts of community and society.

**7.** Ibid., p. 64.

**8.** Peter Saunders, *Social Theory and the Urban Question* (London: Hutchinson, 1981), p. 81.

**9.** For the history of communities in Great Britain see Walter Harry Green Armytage, *Heavens Below: Utopian Experiment in England* (London: Routledge and Kegan Paul, 1961); Dennis Hardy, *Alternative Communities in Nineteenth Century England* (London: Longman, 1979). For the history of communities in Germany see Ulrich Linse, ed., *Zurück, o Mensch, zur Mutter Erde. Landkommunen in Deutschland 1890–1933* (Munich: dtv, 1983). For the *Neue Gemeinschaft* see Iain Boyd Whyte, *Bruno Taut and the Architecture of Activism* (Cambridge: Cambridge University Press, 1982), pp. 10–11, 53; Corona Hepp, *Avant-garde. Moderne Kunst, Kulturkritik und Reformbewegung nach der Jahrhundertwende* (Munich: dtv, 1987), pp. 78–80.

**10.** Harald Szeemann, ed., *Monte Verità. Berg der Wahrheit. Lokale Anthropologie als Beitrag zur Wiederentdeckung einer neuzeitlichen sakralen Topographie* (Milan: Electa Editrice, 1980).

**11.** Wolfgang Herrmann, *In What Style Should We Build? The German Debate on Architectural Style* (Santa Monica: Getty Center for the History of Art and the Humanities, 1992).

**12.** Peter Behrens, *Feste des Lebens und der Kunst: Eine Betrachtung des Theaters als höchsten Kultur-Symbols* (1900), quoted in Hamann and Hermand, *Stilkunst*, pp. 213–214 (my translation).

**13.** William Morris, "The Prospects of Architecture in Civilization," in *On Art and Socialism: Essays and Lectures*, ed. Holbrook Jackson (Paulton: John Lehman, 1947), pp. 245–246.

**14.** Quoted in Hamann and Hermand, *Stilkunst*, p. 219 (my translation).

**15.** Quoted in Bernd Krimmel, "In the Matter of J. M. Olbrich," in Joseph Maria Olbrich, *Architecture: Complete Reprint of the Original Plates of 1901–1904* (London: Butterworth Architecture, 1988), p. 12.

**16.** Helen Rosenau, *The Ideal City in Its Architectural Evolution* (London: Routledge and Kegan Paul, 1959), pp. 4–5.

**17.** Antje von Graevenitz, "Hütten und Tempel. Zur Mission der Selbstbesinnung," in Szeemann, ed., *Monte Verità*, pp. 85–98.

**18.** Renate Ulmer, "Catalogue of Works," in Olbrich, *Architecture*, pp. 23–30.

**19.** William Richard Lethaby, "Architecture as Form in Civilization," in Lethaby, *Form in Civilization: Collected Papers on Art and Labour* (1922; London: Oxford University Press, 1957), p. 5.

**20.** William Richard Lethaby, *Architecture, Mysticism and Myth* (London: Percival, 1892); and see Godfrey Rubens, *William Richard Lethaby: His Life and Work, 1875–1931* (London: Architectural Press, 1986), p. 83.

**21.** Lethaby, *Architecture, Mysticism and Myth*, preface.

**22.** Ibid., p. 1.

**23.** Ibid., p. 3.

**24.** Ibid., p. 5.

**25.** Ibid., p. 7.

**26.** Ibid., p. 8.

**27.** Graevenitz, "Hütten und Tempel," p. 91 (my translation). See also Dolf Sternberger, *Panorama oder Ansichten vom 19. Jahrhundert*, 4th ed. (Frankfurt: Suhrkamp, 1974), pp. 132–135.

**28.** See Hans-Christian and Elke Harten, *Die Versöhnung mit der Natur. Gärten, Freiheitsbäume, republikanische Wälder, heilige Berge und Tugendparks in der Französischen Revolution* (Reinbek bei Hamburg: Rowohlt, 1989).

**29.** Cornelius Gurlitt, *Die deutsche Kunst des 19. Jahrhunderts* (Berlin, 1900), cited in Graevenitz, "Hütten und Tempel," p. 91.

**30.** K. P. C. de Bazel, "Bouwkunst," *Bouw- en Sierkunst* 1 (1898), p. 32, quoted in Wessel Reinink, *K. P. C. de Bazel—Architect* (Rotterdam: Uitgeverij 010, 1993), p. 41 (my translation).

**31.** Fritz Schumacher, *Studien. 20 Kohlezeichnungen von Fritz Schumacher* (Leipzig, 1900). See Hartmut Frank, ed., *Fritz Schumacher. Reformkultur und Moderne* (Stuttgart: Hatje, 1994).

**32.** See Graevenitz, "Hütten und Tempel," pp. 92–93; Janos Frecot, Johann Friedrich Geist, and Diethart Krebs, *Fidus 1868–1948* (Munich: Rogner & Bernhard, 1972).

**33.** See Iain Boyd Whyte, *Emil Hoppe, Marcel Kammerer, Otto Schönthal: Three Architects from the Master Class of Otto Wagner* (Berlin: Ernst & Sohn, 1989).

**34.** François J. M. Garas (1866–?) studied architecture at the Ecole des Beaux-Arts under Blondel. Garas was a member of the Société Nationale, at whose salons beginning in 1894 he exhibited schemes for country houses and "Temples pour les Religions futures." See Ulrich Thieme and Felix Becker, eds., *Allgemeines Lexikon der bildenden Künste von der Antike bis zur Gegenwart*, 37 vols. (Leipzig: Engelmann, E. A. Seemann, 1907–1950), vol. 13 (1920), p. 166.

**35.** Patrick Geddes, *Cities in Evolution: An Introduction to the Town Planning Movement and to the Study of Civics* (London: Williams & Norgate, 1915), p. 278.

**36.** Garas published a booklet with the title *Mes temples* (Paris: Michalon, 1907) which contains extracts of an intended larger publication with the same title. The table of contents of the larger volume, reprinted on page 2 of the booklet, includes three more temples dedicated to Industry, Music, and Theater. The larger book was obviously never published; the following account relies on the booklet.

**37.** Garas, *Mes temples*, p. 5.

**38.** Ibid., p. 17.

**39.** Ibid., pp. 17–21. The following summary is based on these pages.

**40.** Ibid., pp. 21–24.

**41.** See Wolfgang Pehnt, "Turm und Höhle," in *Moderne Architektur in Deutschland 1900–1950. Expressionismus und Neue Sachlichkeit*, exh. cat., ed. Vittorio Magnago Lampugnani and Romana Schneider (Stuttgart: Hatje, 1994), pp. 51–67.

**42.** Iain Boyd Whyte, "The Expressionist Sublime," in *Expressionist Utopias: Paradise, Metropolis, Architectural Fantasy*, exh. cat., ed. Timothy O. Benson (Seattle: University of Washington Press, 1993), p. 120.

**43.** Sternberger, *Panorama*, p. 35 (my translation).

**44.** Ernst Haeckel, *The Riddle of the Universe at the Close of the Nineteenth Century*, trans. Joseph McCabe (London: Watts & Co., 1900), p. 345.

**45.** This might imply a chronological order, in which temple projects were first located in the mountains (or in natural environments) and only later in cities. I choose this order for clarity of argument. In fact, the seclusion of temples on mountains and suggestions for similar buildings in cities happened more or less in parallel.

**46.** Already Richard Dadd's watercolor *The Rock and Castle of Seclusion* made a connection between a dominating building and a city, the latter significantly lacking any church or cathedral towers. But the specific circumstances under which this drawing was produced—Dadd was imprisoned after he had murdered his father—make the castle a symbol more of the painter's isolation from society than of any spiritual need. See Edward Lucie-Smith, *Symbolist Art* (London: Thames and Hudson, 1972), pp. 35–37.

**47.** Hermann Obrist, "Ein glückliches Leben. Eine Biographie des Künstlers, Forschers und Alleingängers: Hermann Obrist" (typescript, 1926–1927), quoted from Bernd Apke, "'Gehe hin und bilde dieses!' Die Bedeutung der Visionen Hermann Obrists für sein künstlerisches Werk," in *Okkultismus und Avantgarde*, p. 689 (my translation).

**48.** See *Hablik: Designer, Utopian Architect, Expressionist Artist, 1881–1934*, exh. cat. (London: Architectural Association, 1980).

**49.** Quoted from Anthony Tischhauser, introduction to ibid., p. 9.

**50.** See Regine Prange, "Das kristalline Sinnbild," in Lampugnani and Schneider, eds., *Moderne Architektur. Expressionismus und Neue Sachlichkeit*, pp. 69–97.

**51.** See Tischhauser, introduction to *Hablik*, p. 11.

**52.** For Townsend see Alastair Service, "Charles Harrison Townsend," in Service, ed., *Edwardian Architecture and Its Origin* (London: Architectural Press, 1975), pp. 162–182; A. Stuart Gray, *Edwardian Architecture: A Biographical Dictionary* (London: Duckworth, 1985), pp. 351–354.

**53.** See Anonymous, "New Institute, Bishopsgate," *The Builder* 67 (1894), 374–375, with two ills. after page 384; Service, "Charles Harrison Townsend," pp. 168–170.

**54.** Service, "Charles Harrison Townsend," p. 168.

**55.** See Alan Crawford, *C. R. Ashbee: Architect, Designer, and Romantic Socialist* (New Haven: Yale University Press, 1985), pp. 23–30. See also Helen E. Meller, ed., *The Ideal City* (Leicester: Leicester University Press, 1979), especially the introduction (pp. 9–39) and the reprint of Barnett's pamphlet "The Ideal City" from about 1893–1894 (pp. 55–66). For the history of the designs and the building see Service, "Charles Harrison Townsend," pp. 172–173, 175.

**56.** Dame Henrietta Barnett, *Canon Barnett: His Life, Work, and Friends* (1918), p. 225, quoted in Crawford, *C. R. Ashbee*, p. 25.

**57.** See also Horniman Museum, *An Account of the Horniman Free Museum and the Recreation Grounds, Forest Hill* (London: Horniman Museum, 1901).

**58.** Service, "Charles Harrison Townsend," p. 173.

**59.** See chapters 14–16 in Charles Robert Ashbee, *Where the Great City Stands: A Study in the New Civics* (London: Essex House Press, 1917), pp. 113–122.

**60.** Ibid., p. 113.

**61.** Ibid., p. 115.

**62.** Ibid., pp. 121, 120.

**63.** Ibid., p. 123.

**64.** Ibid., p. 120.

**65.** Charles Robert Ashbee, "What the City Might Do for the Craftsman," *Sociological Review* 9 (1916), p. 52.

**66.** William Richard Lethaby, "Of Beautiful Cities," in *Art and Life, and the Building and Decoration of Cities: A Series of Lectures by Members of the Arts and Crafts Exhibition Society, Delivered at the Fifth Exhibition of the Society in 1896* (London: Percival, 1897), p. 104.

**67.** Ibid., pp. 106–107.

**68.** See the collection *Art and Life*, cited in note 66.

**69.** Lethaby, "Of Beautiful Cities," pp. 103–104.

**70.** For the exhibition see Sybella Branford, "What the Crafts-man Can Do for the City," *Sociological Review* 9 (1916), pp. 49–52; W. T. Whitley, "Arts and Crafts at the Royal Academy," *The Studio* 69 (1916), pp. 66–77, 120–130, 189–196; anonymous, "The Arts and Crafts Exhibition," *The Builder* 111 (1916), pp. 245–246.

**71.** For Henry Wilson see Nicholas Taylor, "Byzantium in Brighton," in Service, ed., *Edwardian Architecture*, pp. 280–288; Gray, *Edwardian Architecture Dictionary*, p. 387.

**72.** Branford, "What the Craftsman Can Do for the City," p. 50. Branford's essay was published together with Ashbee's "What the City Might Do for the Craftsman," under the heading "The Arts and Crafts Exhibition: Its Civic and Educational Aspects."

**73.** Branford, "What the Craftsman Can Do for the City," p. 50. The Latin motto may be translated: "Civic service is a city's grace."

## 7  The City and Spirituality

**1.** Letter, Patrick Geddes to Frank C. Mears, 18 September 1922 (NLS, MS 10573, f. 134).

**2.** Thomas A. Markus, *Buildings and Power: Freedom and Control in the Origin of Modern Building Types* (London: Routledge, 1993), pp. 213–219.

**3.** Ibid., p. 214.

**4.** Dolf Sternberger, *Panorama oder Ansichten vom 19. Jahrhundert*, 4th ed. (Frankfurt: Suhrkamp, 1974), p. 17.

**5.** Robert Pemberton, *The Happy Colony* (London: Saunders and Otley, 1854); see Markus, *Buildings and Power*, p. 292. Also see the discussion of Pemberton's scheme in chapter 1 above.

**6.** Elisée Reclus, "A Great Globe," *Geographical Journal* 12 (1898), pp. 401–409.

**7.** Bernard Marrey, *Louis Bonnier, 1856–1946* (Liège: Mardaga, 1988), pp. 48–49, 183–195.

**8.** Reclus, "A Great Globe," p. 406.

**9.** Anonymous, "A Great Globe-Discussion," *Geographical Journal* 12 (1898), pp. 406–407.

**10.** Patrick Geddes, "A Great Geographer: Elisée Reclus," *Scottish Geographical Magazine* 21 (1905), pp. 549–550.

**11.** Patrick Geddes, "Note on Draft Plan for Institute of Geography," *Scottish Geographical Magazine* 18 (1902), pp. 142–144; John George Bartholomew, "A Plea for a National Institute of Geography," *Scottish Geographical Magazine* 18 (1902), pp. 144–148.

**12.** See Victor E. Thoren, *The Lord of Uraniborg: A Biography of Tycho Brahe* (Cambridge: Cambridge University Press, 1990).

**13.** Georg Braun and Frans Hogenberg, *Civitatis orbis terrarum* (Cologne, 1586ff), part IV, Latin edition, plate 27.

**14.** John Louis Emil Dreyer, *Tycho Brahe: A Picture of Scientific Life and Work in the Sixteenth Century* (Edinburgh: Adam and Charles Black, 1890).

**15.** Geddes, "Note on Draft Plan," p. 143.

**16.** Bartholomew, "Plea for a National Institute of Geography," p. 146.

**17.** Reclus, "A Great Globe," p. 403.

**18.** See Patrick Geddes, *City Development: A Study of Parks, Gardens and Culture-Institutes. A Report to the Carnegie Dunfermline Trust* (Edinburgh: Geddes and Company; Birmingham: Saint George Press, 1904), pp. 109–120.

**19.** Ibid., p. 120.

**20.** See Lyndsay Andrew Farrall, *The Origins and Growth of the English Eugenics Movement, 1865–1925* (Ann Arbor: University Microfilms, 1970), pp. 11–39.

**21.** Geoffrey Russell Searle, *Eugenics and Politics in Britain, 1900–1914* (Leyden: Noordhoff International Publishing, 1976), pp. 6–7.

**22.** See ibid., pp. 20–33.

**23.** John Edward Morgan, *The Danger of Deterioration of Race from the Too Rapid Increase of Great Cities* (paper read at the Social Science Congress, Sheffield, Tuesday, October 10, 1865) (London: Longman, Green and Co., 1866).

**24.** Max Nordau, *Degeneration* (London: William Heinemann, 1895), p. 35.

**25.** Francis Galton, *Inquiries into Human Faculty* (London: Macmillan, 1883), pp. 24–25, quoted in Farrall, *Origins and Growth of the English Eugenics Movement*, p. 55.

**26.** See Farrall, *Origins and Growth of the English Eugenics Movement*, pp. 27–53; Searle, *Eugenics and Politics*, pp. 9–33.

**27.** Searle, *Eugenics and Politics*, pp. 45–66; see also Nancy Stepan, *The Idea of Race in Science: Great Britain 1800–1960* (London: Macmillan, 1982), especially pp. 29–46.

**28.** Karl Pearson, *The Life, Letters and Labours of Francis Galton*, 4 vols. (Cambridge: Cambridge University Press, 1930), vol. 3, pp. 411–425.

**29.** Ibid., pp. 418, 420.

**30.** Ibid., p. 424.

**31.** Patrick Geddes, "A Synthetic Outline of the History of Biology," *Proceedings of the Royal Society of Edinburgh* 13 (1884–1886), pp. 904–911.

**32.** Geddes, "Theory of Growth, Reproduction, Sex, and Heredity," *Proceedings of the Royal Society of Edinburgh* 13 (1884–1886), pp. 927, 911.

**33.** Ibid., p. 912.

**34.** Ibid., p. 913.

**35.** Geddes, "Synthetic Outline of the History of Biology," p. 911.

**36.** Geddes, "Theory of Growth," p. 923.

**37.** In the essay "Theory of Growth," Geddes indicates the application of the anabolism/catabolism dichotomy to human beings. He later develops this application more fully together with J. Arthur Thomson in the book *The Evolution of Sex* (London: Scott, 1889).

**38.** Geddes, "Theory of Growth," pp. 929–930. Geddes drew only one side of the tree but stated that it had to be mirrored along the vertical axis to arrive at the full picture.

**39.** Ibid., p. 926.

**40.** Patrick Geddes and J. Arthur Thomson, *Evolution* (London: Williams & Norgate, n.d. [1911]), p. 182.

**41.** Stepan, *Idea of Race*, p. 119. Stepan gives no dates for Geddes's membership.

**42.** Geddes, "Synthetic Outline of the History of Biology," p. 910.

**43.** Ibid.

**44.** Letter, David Montague Eder to Patrick Geddes, 24 April 1908 (SUA, T-GED 9/831).

**45.** For Geddes's lecture notes see SUA, T-GED 8/3/7.

**46.** See Amelia Defries, *The Interpreter Geddes: The Man and His Gospel* (London: George Routledge & Sons, 1927), p. 109.

**47.** Geddes divides male human life, for example, into the following seven periods: youth (through age 15); adolescence (learning a profession, age 15–30); manhood (practicing a profession, 30–45); maturity proper (45–48); period of experience (48–60); period of wisdom (60–75 or 80); old age and decay (beyond 80). Geddes 1908 eugenics lecture (SUA, T-GED 8/3/7), card 4.

**48.** Ibid., card 5.

**49.** Ibid., card 8.

**50.** Patrick Geddes, "Mythology and Life: An Interpretation of Olympus; with Applications to Eugenics and Civics," *Sociological Review* 6 (1913), p. 56.

**51.** Ibid., p. 57.

**52.** Geddes, 1908 eugenics lecture (SUA, T-GED 8/3/7), card 13.

**53.** Patrick Geddes, "Woman?," unpublished typescript, n.d., pp. 8, 9–11 (SUA, T-GED 8/3/10).

**54.** Patrick Geddes, *Women, the Census, and the Possibilities of the Future* (Edinburgh: Outlook Tower, 1921), p. 9.

**55.** Ibid.

**56.** For Mumford's criticism of this project see Lewis Mumford, "The Geddesian Gambit," in *Lewis Mumford and Patrick Geddes: The Correspondence*, ed. Frank G. Novak, Jr. (London: Routledge, 1995), pp. 370–371.

**57.** Philip Boardman, *The Worlds of Patrick Geddes: Biologist, Town Planner, Re-educator, Peace-Warrior* (London: Routledge and Kegan Paul, 1978), p. 396.

**58.** For sketches of the crematorium see SUA, T-GED 8/3/1. For a philosophical discussion by Geddes of death see Patrick

Geddes and J. Arthur Thomson, *Life: Outlines of General Biology*, 2 vols. (London: Williams & Norgate, 1931), pp. 1375–1376.

**59.** Letter, Patrick Geddes to Adrian Berrington, 22 September 1909 (NLS, MS 10512, f. 225).

**60.** Patrick Geddes, *The Masque of Learning and Its Many Meanings: A Pageant of Education through the Ages* (Edinburgh: Patrick Geddes and Colleagues, 1912), p. 18.

**61.** Ibid.

**62.** Hesiod, *Theogony*, in Hesiod, *Theogony; Works and Days*, and Theogonis, *Elegies*, trans. Dorothea Wender (Harmondsworth: Penguin, 1973), pp. 23–25.

**63.** Ibid., pp. 23–24.

**64.** Geddes, *Masque of Learning*, p. 18.

**65.** Ibid., p. 19.

**66.** There exist also two pencil sketches by Geddes of the plan of this garden (SUA, T-GED 8/3/1; 22/1/823). There are slight differences between the plans and the perspective; the following description refers to all of these images.

**67.** One of Geddes's plans indicates different architectural features in addition to the above: a labyrinth, a city square with a statue, and cells for study (SUA, T-GED 8/3/1).

**68.** Patrick Geddes, *Town-Planning in Patiala State and City: A Report to the H. H. Maharaja of Patiala* (Lucknow: Perry's Printing Press, 1922), pp. 9–18.

**69.** See Constance Mary Villiers-Stuart, *Gardens of the Great Mughals* (London: Adam and Charles Black, 1913), pp. 199–228.

**70.** Geddes, *Town-Planning in Patiala*, pp. 9–18; Villiers-Stuart, *Gardens of the Great Mughals*, pp. 224–228.

**71.** Geddes, *Town-Planning in Patiala*, pp. 13, 16.

**72.** Ibid., pp. 16, 12.

**73.** Ibid., pp. 17–18.

**74.** J. Arthur Thomson and Patrick Geddes, "A Biological Approach," in James Edward Hand, ed., *Ideals of Science and Faith* (London: George Allen, 1904), p. 56.

**75.** Ibid., p. 55.

**76.** John Alexander Stewart, *The Myths of Plato* (London: Macmillan, 1905), p. 21.

**77.** Ibid., p. 7.

**78.** See Anjam Khursheed, *The Seven Candles of Unity: The Story of 'Abdu'l-Bahá in Edinburgh* (London: Bahá'í Publishing Trust, 1991), pp. 63–71, 85–99, 185–199.

**79.** Letter, Patrick Geddes to Frank C. Mears, 18 September 1922 (NLS MS 10573, f. 128).

**80.** Ibid., f. 134.

**81.** Francis Younghusband, quoted in "London Conference Opened," *Times* (London), 23 September 1924, p. 14. See also daily reports on the conference in the *Times*, 24–30 September; and William Loftus Hare, ed., *Religions of the Empire: A Conference on Some Living Religions within the Empire* (London: Duckworth, 1925).

**82.** See the collection of essays in *Sociological Review* 16 (1924), pp. 90–116, 187–215, 285–294, 300–316; and see Hare, ed., *Religions of the Empire*, pp. 401–508.

**83.** Victor Branford, "A Hall of Vision," in Patrick Abercrombie et al., *The Coal Crisis and the Future: A Study in Social Disorders and Their Treatment* (London: Le Play House Press and Williams & Norgate, 1926), p. v. The following description of the exhibition derives from this source.

**84.** Geddes, "A Great Geographer," p. 549.

**85.** Branford, "Hall of Vision," p. xvii.

**86.** Ibid.

**87.** Ibid., p. viii.


### 8   From the Temple of the City to the Cultural Acropolis

**1.** Victor Branford and Patrick Geddes, *The Coming Polity: A Study in Reconstruction* (London: Williams & Norgate, 1917), pp. 133–134.

**2.** John Ruskin, *The Stones of Venice*, in *The Works of John Ruskin*, ed. Edward Tyas Cook and Alexander Wedderburn, 39 vols. (London: Allen, 1904), vol. 10, pp. 180–269.

**3.** Johann Wolfgang von Goethe, "Von deutscher Baukunst. D. M. Ervini Steinbach," in *Von deutscher Art und Kunst. Einige fliegende Blätter* (Hamburg, 1773); repr., ed. Hans Dietrich Irmscher (Stuttgart: Philipp Reclam jun., 1988), pp. 93–104.

**4.** Patrick Geddes, *City Development: A Study of Parks, Gardens and Culture-Institutes. A Report to the Carnegie Dunfermline Trust* (Edinburgh: Geddes and Company; Birmingham: Saint George Press, 1904), p. 220.

**5.** Ibid., p. 202.

**6.** Ibid., p. 220. The idea of a cathedral, a temple building, as an encyclopedia Geddes might have derived from Lethaby, who described a temple as "a sort of model to scale, its form governed by the science of the time; it was a heaven, an observatory, and an almanack." William Richard Lethaby, *Architecture, Mysticism and Myth* (London: Percival, 1892), p. 5.

**7.** Geddes, *City Development. Report to the Carnegie Dunfermline Trust*, p. 202.

**8.** Hexagon sketches by Patrick Geddes in SUA, T-GED 14/1/37.

**9.** Amelia Defries, *The Interpreter Geddes: The Man and His Gospel* (London: George Routledge & Sons, 1927), p. 71.

**10.** Patrick Geddes, *Town Planning towards City Development: A Report to the Durbar of Indore*, 2 vols. (Indore: Holkar State Press, 1918), plan X.

**11.** Patrick Geddes and Frank C. Mears, *Cities and Town Planning Exhibition, Edinburgh, 13th March–1st April 1911, Explanatory Guide Book and Outline Catalogue* (Edinburgh: A. T. Hutchinson, 1911), p. 60.

**12.** Geddes, *City Development. Report to the Carnegie Dunfermline Trust*, pp. 190–192.

**13.** Geddes and Mears, *Cities and Town Planning Exhibition*, pp. 63–64.

**14.** Patrick Geddes, "Town-Planning Report—Jaffa and Tel-Aviv" (unpublished typescript, 1925; Tel Aviv-Yafo history museum).

**15.** Ibid., p. 23.

**16.** See Geddes, *City Development. Report to the Carnegie Dun-fermline Trust,* p. 208.

**17.** Defries, *The Interpreter Geddes,* p. 95.

**18.** Geddes, *City Development. Report to the Carnegie Dunfermline Trust,* p. 209.

**19.** Defries, *The Interpreter Geddes,* p. 55.

**20.** Friedrich Nietzsche, *The Joyful Wisdom,* trans. Thomas Common (Edinburgh: T. N. Foulis, 1910), p. 217.

**21.** Walter Crane, "Of the Decoration of Public Buildings," in *Art and Life, and the Building and Decoration of Cities: A Series of Lectures by Members of the Arts and Crafts Exhibition Society, Delivered at the Fifth Exhibition of the Society in 1896* (London: Percival, 1897), p. 149.

**22.** Geddes and Mears, *Cities and Town Planning Exhibition,* p. 26.

**23.** Geddes, "The Scots Renascence," *The Evergreen: A Northern Seasonal* 1 (Spring 1895), pp. 131–132.

**24.** Ibid., p. 132.

**25.** Christian Weller, "Reform der Lebenswelt. Die Entwicklung zentraler Gedanken Fritz Schumachers bis 1900," in Hartmut Frank, ed., *Fritz Schumacher. Reformkultur und Moderne* (Stuttgart: Hatje, 1994), pp. 52–53.

**26.** Letter, Patrick Geddes to the Directors of Town & Gown Association, 26 August 1909 (NLS, MS 10512, f. 205).

**27.** Anonymous, "Edinburgh University Hall: Re-opening of Ramsay Lodge," *Scottish Leader,* 14 April 1894.

**28.** See Patrick Geddes, *The Masque of Learning and Its Many Meanings: A Pageant of Education through the Ages, Devised and Interpreted by Patrick Geddes. Semi-Jubilee of University Hall, 1912* (Edinburgh: Patrick Geddes and Colleagues, 1912).

**29.** Defries, *The Interpreter Geddes,* pp. 46–47.

**30.** Anonymous, "The Masque of Learning at the Synod Hall: A Brilliant Spectacle," *The Scotsman,* 15 March 1912, p. 6.

**31.** Patrick Geddes, "Significance and Purpose of the Masques" (typescript, n.d.), pp. A–B (SUA, T-GED 12/1/395).

**32.** In the following I rely on Louise Bruit Zaidman and Pauline Schmitt Pantel, *Religion in the Ancient Greek City*, trans. Paul Cartledge (Cambridge: Cambridge University Press, 1992).

**33.** Ibid., p. 106.

**34.** Patrick Geddes, *The Proposed University for Central India, at Indore. A Reprint from "Town Planning towards City Development." A Report to the Durbar of Indore* (Indore: Holkar State Printing Press, 1918), p. 34. Geddes proposed combining the theater with a gymnasium and a wrestling pit.

**35.** Geddes, *City Development. Report to the Carnegie Dunfermline Trust*, pp. 181–189; Geddes, "Town-Planning Report—Jaffa and Tel-Aviv," pp. 33–34.

**36.** Alessandra Ponte, "The Thinking Machines from the Outlook Tower to the City of the World," *Lotus International*, no. 35 (1982), p. 51.

**37.** Geddes, *City Development. Report to the Carnegie Dunfermline Trust*, p. 202.

**38.** Ibid., p. 203.

**39.** Ibid., p. 202.

**40.** Patrick Geddes, "A Note of Graphic Methods," *Sociological Review* 15 (1923), pp. 230–231.

**41.** Victor Branford, *Interpretations and Forecasts: A Study of Survivals and Tendencies in Contemporary Society* (London: Duckworth, 1914), pp. 385–386. The bracketed addition is my inference.

**42.** Victor Branford, *Living Religions: A Plea for the Larger Modernism* (London: Le Play House Press and William & Norgate, 1924), p. 233.

**43.** Sybella Branford, "Citizenship and the Civic Association," *Sociological Review* 13 (1921), p. 233.

**44.** Quoted from John Alexander Stewart, *The Myths of Plato* (London: Macmillan, 1905), p. 193. Geddes used this translation and called attention to the words printed here in italics (see note 46 below).

**45.** Zaidman and Pantel, *Religion in the Ancient Greek City*, p. 178.

**46.** Manuscript notes by Geddes referring to John Alexander Stewart, *The Myths of Plato* (SUA, T-GED 11/1/91/2).

**47.** Patrick Geddes, *Cities in Evolution: An Introduction to the Town Planning Movement and to the Study of Civics* (London: Williams & Norgate, 1915), p. 254.

**48.** Figure 8.8 is taken from a series of glass slides used to illustrate lectures on Geddes's ideas of temples for the Greek gods and Muses.

**49.** Patrick Geddes, "Civics: As Concrete and Applied Sociology. Part II," in *Sociological Papers 1905* (London: Macmillan, 1906), p. 85.

**50.** Patrick Geddes, *The Returning Gods* (London: n.pub., 1914), p. 3.

**51.** Geddes, "Town-Planning Report—Jaffa and Tel-Aviv," pp. 56–57.

**52.** Defries, *The Interpreter Geddes*, p. 169.

**53.** See Volker M. Welter, "History, Biology and City Design: Patrick Geddes in Edinburgh," *Architectural Heritage* 6 (1996), pp. 60–82.

**54.** Geddes, *Proposed University for Central India*, pp. 19–20.

**55.** Arthur A. Goren, "The View from Scopus: Judah L. Magnes and the Early Years of the Hebrew University," *Judaism: A Quarterly Journal of Jewish Life and Thought* 45 (1996), pp. 203–223.

**56.** Geddes, "Town-Planning Report—Jaffa and Tel-Aviv," pp. 51–60.

**57.** Geddes, *City Development. Report to the Carnegie Dunfermline Trust*, p. 18.

**58.** Patrick Geddes, "A Proposed Co-ordination of the Social Sciences," *Sociological Review* 16 (1924), p. 55.

**59.** Ibid.

**60.** Patrick Geddes, "Civic Education and City Development," *Contemporary Review* 88 (1905), p. 422.

**61.** Patrick Geddes, "Civics: As Applied Sociology, Part I," in *Sociological Papers 1904* (London: Macmillan, 1905), p. 104.

**62.** Geddes, *Cities in Evolution*, p. 300. This is a paraphrase of the first verse of Psalm 127; see *Tanakh: A New Translation of the Holy Scriptures According to the Traditional Hebrew Text* (Philadelphia: Jewish Publication Society, 1985), p. 1264.

**63.** Printed map of Conjeevaram, India, annotated by Patrick Geddes (SUA, T-GED 22/1/1262).

**64.** Apart from the city crown projects mentioned in the text, Geddes proposes similar centers in other city design reports. For Balrampur he suggests an educational quarter with a public library, boys' and girls' schools, and sport facilities in the immediate vicinity of a small open-air stage (Patrick Geddes, *Town Planning in Balrampur: A Report to the Hon'ble the Maharaja Bahadur* [Lucknow: Murray's London Printing Press, 1917], pp. 12–13, 18, 44); in Baroda he plans a civic center with educational facilities including schools, library, and a theater (Patrick Geddes, *A Report on the Development and Expansion of the City of Baroda* [Baroda: Lakshmi Vilas Press, 1916], p. 30); in Indore he plans not only the university mentioned above but also an outlook tower and an open-air theater in combination with "an open air Gymnasium, and a couple of Wrestling Pits for youths and men" (Geddes, *Proposed University for Central India*, pp. 19, 34, 39); in Lahore he intends to create a green space with playgrounds crowned by a temple on a hill in the park, thus dominating the city (Patrick Geddes, *Town Planning in Lahore: A Report to the Municipal Council* [Lahore: Commercial Printing Works, 1917], p. 22); the preliminary report for Nagpur contains a brief section on a possible university in the city (Patrick Geddes, *Town Planning in Nagpur: A Report to the Municipal Council* [Nagpur: Municipal Press, 1917], p. 12); and in his report on Patiala state and city Geddes deals with new accommodations for students and professors at the Mohindra College, an open-air theater within a new "municipal flower garden," and the already-discussed palace garden reinterpreted as a garden for the Greek gods and Muses (Patrick Geddes, *Town-Planning in Patiala State and City: A Report to the H. H. Maharaja of Patiala* [Lucknow: Perry's Printing Press, 1922], pp. 17–18, 25–29, 62).

**65.** Patrick Geddes, "The Village World: Actual and Possible," *Sociological Review* 19 (1927), p. 115.

**66.** Geddes, *Cities in Evolution*, p. 211.

**67.** Bruno Taut, *Die Stadtkrone mit Beiträgen von Paul Scheerbart, Erich Baron, Adolf Behne* (Jena: Eugen Diederichs, 1919).

**68.** See most recently, for example, Regine Prange, *Das Kristalline als Kunstsymbol: Bruno Taut und Paul Klee* (Hildesheim: Georg Olms Verlag, 1991).

## Epilogue

**1.** For Gutkind see for example E. A. Gutkind, *Revolution of Environment* (London: Routledge, 1946), or *The Expanding Environment: The End of Cities, the Rise of Communities* (London: Freedom Press, 1953); for Glikson see Volker M. Welter, "Artur Glikson, Thinking Machines and the Planning of Israel," in Volker M. Welter and James Lawson, eds., *The City after Patrick Geddes* (Bern: Peter Lang, 2000), pp. 211–226.

**2.** Congrès Internationaux d'Architecture Moderne (CIAM), *Dix ans d'architecture contemporaine*, ed. Sigfried Giedion (Zurich: Editions Girsberger, 1951), p. 25.

**3.** Ibid., p. 6 (my emphasis).

**4.** For a debate of this shift that puts a strong emphasis on Lewis Mumford's influence, see Eric Mumford, "CIAM Urbanism after the Athens Charter," *Planning Perspectives* 7 (1992), pp. 391–417.

**5.** Congrès Internationaux d'Architecture Moderne 8 (CIAM 8), *The Heart of the City: Towards the Humanisation of Urban Life*, ed. Jaqueline Tyrwhitt, José Luis Sert, and E. N. Rogers (London: Lund Humphries, 1952), p. 168.

**6.**   Sigfried Giedion, "The Heart of the City: A Summing Up," in CIAM 8, *Heart of the City*, p. 160.

**7.**   "A Short Outline of the Core: Extracts from Statements Prepared during the 8th Congress of CIAM," in CIAM 8, *Heart of the City*, p. 168.

**8.**   Ibid., p. 166; italics in original.

**9.**   Sigfried Giedion, "Historical Background," in CIAM 8, *Heart of the City*, p. 25.

# Bibliography

## Primary and Archival Sources

Carnegie Dunfermline Trust, Dunfermline.

Edinburgh University Library, Special Collections.

National Library of Scotland (NLS), Manuscripts Division, Edinburgh.

Strathclyde University Archive (SUA), Glasgow.

Tel Aviv-Yafo History Museum, Tel Aviv-Yafo.

## Printed Sources by Patrick Geddes

*Aberdeen, Old and New: An Impression.* N.pl.: n.pub., n.d. [1896].

"An Analysis of the Principles of Economics." *Proceedings of the Royal Society of Edinburgh* 12 (1883–1884), 943–980.

"Beginnings of a Survey of Edinburgh." *Scottish Geographical Magazine* 35 (1919), 281–298.

(J. Arthur Thomson and Geddes.) "A Biological Approach." In James Edward Hand, ed., *Ideals of Science and Faith* (London: George Allen, 1904), pp. 49–80.

"Boundaries and Frontiers: Their Origin and Their Significance." *Westminster Review* 169 (1908), 257–260.

"The Charting of Life." *Sociological Review* 19 (1927), 40–63.

*Chelsea, Past and Possible: An Address to "The Utopians" of Chelsea.* N.pl.: n.pub., n.d. [1908].

(Geddes and Frank C. Mears.) *Cities and Town Planning Exhibition, Edinburgh, 13th March–1st April 1911, Explanatory Guide Book and Outline Catalogue.* Edinburgh: A. T. Hutchinson, 1911.

*Cities in Evolution.* Ed. the Outlook Tower Association and the Association for Planning and Regional Reconstruction,

London. London: Williams & Norgate, 1949. (Revised edition of the following.)

*Cities in Evolution: An Introduction to the Town Planning Movement and to the Study of Civics.* London: Williams & Norgate, 1915.

"The City Beautiful—In Theory and Practise." *Garden Cities & Town Planning Magazine* 3 (1913), 196–200.

"City Deterioration and the Need of City Survey." *Annals of the American Academy of Political and Social Science* 24 (1909), 54–67.

*City Development: A Study of Parks, Gardens and Culture-Institutes. A Report to the Carnegie Dunfermline Trust.* Edinburgh: Geddes and Company; Birmingham: Saint George Press, 1904.

"The City Survey: A First Step—I, II, III." *Garden City & Town Planning Magazine,* n.s. 1 (1911), 18–19, 31–32, 56–58.

*City Surveys for Town Planning.* Edinburgh and Chelsea: Geddes and Colleagues, 1911. (Reprint of a paper Geddes read at the Birkenhead Health Congress in 1910.)

"Civic Education and City Development." *Contemporary Review* 88 (1905), 413–426.

*Civics: The Conditions of Town Planning and City Design.* London: Hampton, 1910.

"Civics: As Applied Sociology. Part I." In *Sociological Papers 1904* (London: Macmillan, 1905), 103–118.

"Civics: As Concrete and Applied Sociology. Part II." In *Sociological Papers 1905* (London: Macmillan, 1906), pp. 57–111.

*The Civic Survey of Edinburgh.* Edinburgh: Outlook Tower; Chelsea: Crosby Hall, 1911. Reprint from Royal Institute of British Architects, ed., *Town Planning Conference, London, 10–15 October 1910: Transactions* (London: RIBA, 1910), pp. 537–574.

"The Classification of Statistics and Its Results." *Proceedings of the Royal Society of Edinburgh* 11 (1881), 295–322.

"The Coming of the Kingdom—On Earth: A Scientific Fellowship of Heart, Head, and Hand." In J. W. Stevenson, ed., *The Healing of the Nation: The Scottish Church and a Waiting People* (Edinburgh: T. & T. Clark, 1930), pp. 174–184.

(Victor Branford and Geddes.) *The Coming Polity: A Study in Reconstruction.* London: Williams & Norgate, 1917. New and enlarged edition, 1919.

*Co-operation versus Socialism.* Manchester: Co-operative Printing Society, 1888.

*Country and Town in Development, Deterioration, and Renewal.* N.pl.: n.pub., n.d. [c. 1909–1910].

*A Course of Three Lectures on Inland Towns & Cities: Their Main Origins.* Ed. Royal Geographical Society. N.pl. [London]: n.pub. [Royal Geographical Society], n.d.

"Edinburgh and Its Region, Geographic and Historical." *Scottish Geographical Magazine* 18 (1902), 303–312.

(Patrick Geddes, ed.) *The Evergreen: A Northern Seasonal* 1 (1895–1896/97).

*Every Man His Own Art Critic at the Manchester Exhibition, 1887.* Manchester: John Heywood, 1887.

*Every Man His Own Art Critic (Glasgow Exhibition, 1888).* Edinburgh: William Brown; Glasgow: John Menzies, 1888.

(Geddes and J. Arthur Thomson.) *Evolution.* London: Williams & Norgate, n.d. [1911].

(Geddes and J. Arthur Thomson.) *The Evolution of Sex.* London: Scott, 1889.

"A Great Geographer: Elisée Reclus." *Scottish Geographical Magazine* 21 (1905), 490–496, 548–555.

(Geddes and Gilbert Slater.) *Ideas at War.* London: Williams & Norgate, 1917.

*Industrial Exhibitions and Modern Progress.* Edinburgh: Douglas, 1887.

"The Influence of Geographical Conditions on Social Development." *Geographical Journal* 12 (1898), 580–587.

*Interpretation of the Pictures in the Common Room of Ramsay Lodge.*
Edinburgh: n.pub., 1928.

*John Ruskin: Economist.* Edinburgh: Brown, 1885. Reprinted as
"John Ruskin, as Economist." *International Monthly* 1
(1900), 280–308.

(J. Arthur Thomson and Geddes.) *Life: Outlines of General Biology.* 2 vols. London: Williams & Norgate, 1931.

"The Mapping of Life." *Sociological Review* 16 (1924), 193–203.

*The Masque of Learning and Its Many Meanings: A Pageant of Ed-
ucation through the Ages, Devised and Interpreted by Patrick
Geddes. Semi-Jubilee of University Hall, 1912.* Edinburgh:
Patrick Geddes and Colleagues, 1912.

"Morphology." In *Encyclopaedia Britannica*, 9th ed., 24 vols. (Edinburgh: A & C Black, 1875–1889), 16:837–846.

"Mythology and Life: An Interpretation of Olympus; with Applications to Eugenics and Civics." *Sociological Review* 6
(1913), 56–58.

(As "Rusticus.") "A Note on Boundaries and Frontiers." *Sociological Review* 11 (1919), 46–48.

"A Note on Graphic Methods." *Sociological Review* 15 (1923),
227–235.

"Note on Draft Plan for Institute of Geography." *Scottish Geographical Magazine* 18 (1902), 142–144.

"On the Conditions of Progress of the Capitalist and the Labourer." In *The Claims of Labour* (Edinburgh: Co-operative
Printing Co., 1886).

"Opening Address" (for a meeting "Discussion on Housing in
Scotland"). *Proceedings of the Royal Philosophical Society of
Glasgow* 44 (1913), 246–249.

(Victor Branford and Geddes.) *Our Social Inheritance.* London:
Williams & Norgate, 1919.

"A Proposed Co-ordination of the Social Sciences." *Sociological
Review* 16 (1924), 54–65.

*The Proposed University for Central India, at Indore. A Reprint from
"Town Planning towards City Development." A Report to the
Durbar of Indore.* Indore: Holkar State Printing Press, 1918.

"Religion on the Chart of Life." In William Loftus Hare, ed., *Religions of the Empire: A Conference on Some Living Religions within the Empire* (London: Duckworth, 1925), pp. 486–509.

*Report on Planning for the Lucknow Zoological Garden.* Lucknow: NK Press, n.d.

*A Report on the Development and Expansion of the City of Baroda.* Baroda: Lakshmi Vilas Press, 1916.

"A Re-statement of the Cell Theory, with Application to the Morphology, Classification, and Physiology of Protists, Plants, and Animals. Together with an Hypothesis of Cell-Structure, and an Hypothesis of Contractility." *Proceedings of the Royal Society of Edinburgh* 12 (1883–1884), 266–292.

*The Returning Gods.* London: n.pub., 1914.

Review of *The City* by Robert E. Park, Ernest W. Burgess, [and Roderick D. McKenzie]. *Sociological Review* 18 (1926), 167–168.

Review of *The Wealth and Welfare of the Punjab* by H. Clavert. *Sociological Review* 15 (1923), 65–68.

"Robert Smith, B.Sc., University College, Dundee." *Scottish Geographical Magazine* 16 (1900), 597–599.

(With Victor Branford.) "Rural and Urban Thought: A Contribution to the Theory of Progress and Decay." *Sociological Review* 21 (1929), 1–19.

"The Scots College at Montpellier University." Reprint (n.pl.: n.pub., n.d.) from *Aberdeen University Review,* July 1927.

"The Scots Renascence." *The Evergreen: A Northern Seasonal* 1 (Spring 1895), 131–139.

"Social Evolution: How Advance It?" *Sociological Review* 21 (1929), 334–341.

"A Suggested Plan for a Civic Museum (or Civic Exhibition) and Its Associated Studies." In *Sociological Papers 1906* (London: Macmillan, 1907), 197–236.

*Syllabus of a Course of Ten Lectures on Evolutionary Ethics, Based on Natural Science and Sociology.* London: Hampton, 1905.

*Syllabus of a Course of Ten Lectures on Evolution in Life, Mind, Morals and Society.* London: University of London, 1910.

*Syllabus of a Course of Ten Lectures on Great Cities: Their Place in Geography, and Their Relation to Human Development.* London: P. S. King and Son, 1905.

*Syllabus of a Series of Ten Lectures on the Study of London.* London: P. S. King and Son, 1909.

"A Synthetic Outline of the History of Biology." *Proceedings of the Royal Society of Edinburgh* 13 (1884–1886), 904–911.

"The Temple Cities." *Modern Review* 25 (1919), 213–222.

"The Temple Cities." In J. V. Ferreira and S. S. Jha, eds., *The Outlook Tower: Essays on Urbanization in Memory of Patrick Geddes* (Bombay: Popular Prakashan, 1976), pp. 461–475.

"Theory of Growth, Reproduction, Sex, and Heredity." *Proceedings of the Royal Society of Edinburgh* 13 (1884–1886), 911–931.

"Town Planning and City Design." *Sociological Review* 3 (1910), 56–60.

*Town Planning and City Design—in Sociology and in Citizenship.* London: Sociological Society, 1908.

*Town Planning in Balrampur: A Report to the Hon'ble the Maharaja Bahadur.* Lucknow: Murray's London Printing Press, 1917.

*Town Planning in Lahore: A Report to the Municipal Council.* Lahore: Commercial Printing Works, 1917.

*Town Planning in Nagpur: A Report to the Municipal Council.* Nagpur: Municipal Press, 1917.

*Town-Planning in Patiala State and City: A Report to the H. H. Maharaja of Patiala.* Lucknow: Perry's Printing Press, 1922.

*Town Planning towards City Development: A Report to the Durbar of Indore.* 2 vols. Indore: Holkar State Press, 1918.

*Two Steps in Civics: "Cities and Town Planning Exhibition" and the "International Congress of Cities," Ghent International Exhibition, 1913.* Liverpool: University Press, 1913. (Reprint from the *Town Planning Review,* July 1913, 1–16.)

"The Valley in the Town (the Fourth of the Talks from the Outlook Tower)." *Survey Graphic,* July 1925, 396–400, 415–416.

"The Valley Plan of Civilization (the Third of the Talks from the Outlook Tower)." *Survey Graphic*, June 1925, 288–290, 322–323, 325.

"The Valley Section." Ed. J. Tyrwhitt. *Architect's Yearbook* 12 (1968), 65–71.

"The Village World: Actual and Possible." *Sociological Review* 19 (1927), 108–119.

*Women, the Census, and the Possibilities of the Future.* Edinburgh: Outlook Tower, 1921.

"A World League of Cities." *Sociological Review* 18 (1926), 166.

*The World Without and the World Within.* Bournville: Saint George Press; London: George Allen, 1905.

## Printed Sources by Other Authors

Andersen, Hendrik Christian. *"World-Conscience": An International Society for the Creation of a World-Centre to House International Interest and to Unite Peoples and Nations for the Attainment of Peace and Progress upon Broader Humanitarian Lines.* Rome: World Conscience Society, 1913.

Andersen, Hendrik Christian, and Ernest M. Hébrard. *Creation of a World Centre of Communication.* Paris: n.pub., 1913.

Anonymous. "The Arts and Crafts Exhibition." *The Builder* 111 (1916), 245–246.

Anonymous. "Buddhism in the Empire." *The Times*, 25 September 1924, p. 9.

Anonymous. "Edinburgh University Hall: Re-opening of Ramsay Lodge." *Scottish Leader*, 14 April 1894.

Anonymous. "Forms of Islam in the Empire." *The Times*, 24 September, p. 11.

Anonymous. "Geography at the Summer Meetings." *Geographical Teacher*, no. 2 (June 1903), 77–78.

Anonymous. "A Great Globe-Discussion." *Geographical Journal* 12 (1898), 406–409.

Anonymous. "Hindu Reformations." *The Times*, 27 September 1924, p. 11.

Anonymous. "London Conference Opened." *The Times*, 23 September 1924, p. 14.

Anonymous. "'The Masque of Learning' at the Synod Hall: A Brilliant Spectacle." *The Scotsman*, 15 March 1912, p. 6.

Anonymous. "New Institute, Bishopsgate." *The Builder* 67 (1894), 347–375.

Anonymous. "Primitive Beliefs." *The Times*, 30 September 1924, p. 10.

Anonymous. "Proposed National Institute of Geography." *Scottish Geographical Magazine* 18 (1902), 217–220.

Anonymous. "Religions in the Empire: Zoroastrianism and Janism." *The Times*, 26 September 1924, p. 11.

Apke, Bernd. "'Gehe hin und bilde dieses!' Die Bedeutung der Visionen Hermann Obrists für sein künstlerisches Werk." In *Okkultismus und Avantgarde. Von Munch bis Mondrian 1900–1915*, exh. cat. (Frankfurt: Schirn Kunsthalle, 1995), pp. 687–701.

Armytage, Walter Harry Green. *Heavens Below: Utopian Experiment in England*. London: Routledge and Kegan Paul, 1961.

*Art and Life, and the Building and Decoration of Cities: A Series of Lectures by Members of the Arts and Crafts Exhibition Society, Delivered at the Fifth Exhibition of the Society in 1896*. London: Percival, 1897.

Ashbee, Charles Robert. "What the City Might Do for the Craftsman." *Sociological Review* 9 (1916), 52–54.

Ashbee, Charles Robert. *Where the Great City Stands: A Study in the New Civics*. London: Essex House Press, 1917.

Bannon, Michael J. "The Making of Irish Geography, III: Patrick Geddes and the Emergence of Modern Town Planning in Dublin." *Irish Geography* 2 (1978), 141–148.

Bartholomew, John George. "A Plea for a National Institute of Geography." *Scottish Geographical Magazine* 18 (1902), 144–148.

Bauman, Zygmunt. *Modernity and Ambivalence*. London: Polity Press, 1991; repr. 1993.

Benson, Timothy O., ed. *Expressionist Utopias: Paradise, Metropo-lis, Architectural Fantasy*. Exh. cat. Seattle: University of Washington Press, 1993.

Boardman, John, et al., eds. *The Oxford History of the Classical World*. Oxford: Oxford University Press, 1986.

Boardman, Philip. *The Worlds of Patrick Geddes: Biologist, Town Planner, Re-educator, Peace-Warrior*. London: Routledge and Kegan Paul, 1978.

Boyer, M. Christine. *The City of Collective Memory: Its Historical Imagery and Architectural Entertainments*. Cambridge: MIT Press, 1996.

Branford, Sybella. "Citizenship and the Civic Association." *Socio-logical Review* 13 (1921), 228–234.

Branford, Sybella. "What the Craftsman Can Do for the City." *Sociological Review* 9 (1916), 49–52.

Branford, Victor. "General Survey." In William Loftus Hare, ed., *Religions of the Empire: A Conference on Some Living Religions within the Empire* (London: Duckworth, 1925), pp. 511–514.

Branford, Victor. "A Hall of Vision." *Sociological Review* 17 (1925), 264–288.

Branford, Victor. "A Hall of Vision." In Patrick Abercrombie et al., *The Coal Crisis and the Future: A Study in Social Disorders and Their Treatment* (London: Le Play House Press and Williams & Norgate, 1926), pp. v–xxviii (appendix B).

Branford, Victor. *Interpretations and Forecasts: A Study of Survivals and Tendencies in Contemporary Society*. London: Duckworth, 1914.

Branford, Victor. *Living Religions: A Plea for the Larger Mod-ernism*. London: Le Play House Press and Williams & Nor-gate, 1924.

Branford, Victor. "A More Realistic Approach to the Social Syn-thesis." *Sociological Review* 22 (1930), 195–218.

Branford, Victor. *St. Columba: A Study of Social Inheritance and Spiritual Development*. Edinburgh: Geddes & Colleagues, 1912.

Branford, Victor. "Westminster: An Interpretative Survey. I. Method: The Non-national Unit. II. The Mediæval City: Its Survivals and Tendencies." *Sociological Review* 9 (1916), 253–284.

Braun, Georg, and Frans Hogenberg. *Civitatis orbis terrarum.* Cologne, 1586ff.

Brett, David. *C. R. Mackintosh: The Poetics of Workmanship.* London: Reaktion Books, 1992.

Bunyan, John. *The Pilgrim's Progress.* Ed. Roger Sharrock. Harmondsworth: Penguin, 1987. Originally published 1678.

Cherry, Gordon E. *The Evolution of British Town Planning: A History of Town Planning in the United Kingdom during the Twentieth Century and of the Royal Town Planning Institute, 1919–1974.* London: Leonard Hill, 1974.

Clarke, Paul Barry. *Citizenship.* London: Pluto, 1994.

Clunn, Harold P. *The Face of London: The Record of a Century's Changes and Development.* London: Marshall, 1933.

Cohen, Jean-Louis. *Le Corbusier and the Mystique of the USSR: Theories and Projects for Moscow, 1928–1936.* Princeton: Princeton University Press, 1987.

Congrès Internationaux d'Architecture Moderne (CIAM). *Dix ans d'architecture contemporaine.* Ed. Sigfried Giedion. Zurich: Editions Girsberger, 1951.

Congrès Internationaux d'Architecture Moderne 8 (CIAM 8). *The Heart of the City: Towards the Humanisation of Urban Life.* Ed. Jaqueline Tyrwhitt, José Luis Sert, and E. N. Rogers. London: Lund Humphries, 1952.

Conzen, Michael Robert Gunter. "The Use of Town Plans in the Study of Urban History." In Harold James Dyos, ed., *The Study of Urban History* (London: Arnold, 1968), pp. 113–130.

*C. R. Mackintosh: The Chelsea Years, 1915–1923.* Exh. cat. Glasgow: Hunterian Art Gallery, 1994.

Crane, Walter. "Of the Decoration of Public Buildings." In *Art and Life, and the Building and Decoration of Cities: A Series of Lectures by Members of the Arts and Crafts Exhibition Society,*

*Delivered at the Fifth Exhibition of the Society in 1896* (London: Percival, 1897), pp. 111–166.

Crawford, Alan. *C. R. Ashbee: Architect, Designer, and Romantic Socialist.* New Haven: Yale University Press, 1985.

Cross, Robert Craigie, and Anthony Douglas Woozley. *Plato's Republic: A Philosophical Commentary.* London: Macmillan, 1966.

Cumming, Elizabeth S. *The Arts and Crafts Movement in Edinburgh, 1880–1930.* Edinburgh: College of Art, 1985.

Cumming, Elizabeth. "A Gleam of Renaissance Hope: Edinburgh at the Turn of the Century." In Wendy Kaplan, ed., *Scotland Creates: 5000 Years of Art and Design.* London: Weidenfeld and Nicolson, 1990.

Cumming, Elizabeth. *Phoebe Anne Traquair.* Edinburgh: Scottish National Portrait Gallery, 1993.

Cumming, Elizabeth, and Wendy Kaplan. *The Arts and Crafts Movement.* London: Thames and Hudson, 1991.

Daiches, David. *The Scottish Enlightenment.* Edinburgh: Saltire, 1986.

Darwin, Charles Robert. *On the Origin of Species by Means of Natural Selection, or the Preservation of Favoured Races in the Struggle for Life.* London: John Murray, 1859.

Defries, Amelia. *The Interpreter Geddes: The Man and His Gospel.* London: George Routledge & Sons, 1927.

Dellheim, Charles. *The Face of the Past: The Preservation of the Medieval Inheritance in Victorian England.* Cambridge: Cambridge University Press, 1982.

Dethier, Jean, and Alain Guiheux, eds. *La ville, art et architecture en Europe, 1870–1993.* Exh. cat. Paris: Centre Pompidou, 1994.

Dickens, Charles. *Hard Times.* London: Bradbury, 1854; repr. London: Dent, 1964.

Dickinson, Robert E. *Regional Concept: The Anglo-American Leaders.* London: Routledge and Kegan Paul, 1976.

Dreyer, John Louis Emil. *Tycho Brahe: A Picture of Scientific Life and Work in the Sixteenth Century.* Edinburgh: Adam and Charles Black, 1890.

Eck, Caroline van. *Organicism in Nineteenth-Century Architecture: An Inquiry into Its Theoretical and Philosophical Background.* Amsterdam: Architectura & Natura Press, 1994.

Engels, Friedrich. "Die Lage der arbeitenden Klasse in England." In Karl Marx and Friedrich Engels, *Werke,* 39 vols. (Berlin [DDR]: Dietz, 1969), 2:225–506.

Farrall, Lyndsay Andrew. *The Origins and Growth of the English Eugenics Movement, 1865–1925.* Ann Arbor: University Microfilms, 1970.

Fehl, Gerhard, and Juan Rodríguez-Lores, eds. *Städtebau um die Jahrhundertwende. Materialien zur Entstehung einer Disziplin.* Cologne: Deutscher Gemeindeverlag, 1980.

Finley, Moses I. "The Ancient City: From Fustel de Coulanges to Max Weber and Beyond." In Finley, *Economy and Society in Ancient Greece,* ed. B. D. Shaw and R. P. Saller (London: Chatto & Windus, 1981), pp. 3–23.

Finley, Moses I. *The Ancient Economy.* London: Hogarth Press, 1985; repr. Harmondsworth: Penguin, 1992.

Fishman, Robert. *Urban Utopias in the Twentieth Century: Ebenezer Howard, Frank Lloyd Wright, and Le Corbusier.* New York: Basic Books, 1977.

Fowler, William Warde. *The City-State of the Greeks and Romans: A Survey Introductory to the Study of Ancient History.* London: Macmillan, 1893.

Frank, Hartmut, ed. *Fritz Schumacher. Reformkultur und Moderne.* Stuttgart: Hatje, 1994.

Frecot, Janos, Johann Friedrich Geist, and Diethart Krebs. *Fidus, 1868–1948.* Munich: Rogner & Bernhard, 1972.

Füredi, Frank. *Mythical Past, Elusive Future: History and Society in an Anxious Age.* London: Pluto Press, 1992.

Galton, Francis. "Eugenics as a Factor in Religion." In *Sociological Papers 1905* (London: Macmillan, 1906), pp. 52–53.

Galton, Francis. "Eugenics: Its Definition, Scope and Aims." In *Sociological Papers 1904* (London: Macmillan, 1905), pp. 43–50.

Galton, Francis. "Restrictions in Marriage" and "Studies in National Eugenics." In *Sociological Papers 1905* (London: Macmillan, 1906), pp. 1–13, 14–17.

Garas, François. *Mes temples.* Paris: Michalon, 1907.

Giedion, Sigfried. "The Heart of the City: A Summing Up." In Congrès Internationaux d'Architecture Moderne 8 (CIAM 8), *The Heart of the City: Towards the Humanisation of Urban Life*, ed. Jaqueline Tyrwhitt, José Luis Sert, and E. N. Rogers (London: Lund Humphries, 1952), pp. 159–163.

Giedion, Sigfried. "Historical Background to the Core." In Congrès Internationaux d'Architecture Moderne 8 (CIAM 8), *The Heart of the City: Towards the Humanisation of Urban Life*, ed. Jaqueline Tyrwhitt, José Luis Sert, and E. N. Rogers (London: Lund Humphries, 1952), pp. 17–15.

Godfrey, Walter Hindes. *The Parish of Chelsea* (part I). London: County Council, 1909.

Godfrey, Walter Hindes. *The Parish of Chelsea* (part II). London: County Council, 1913.

Goethe, Johann Wolfgang von. *Versuch die Metamorphose der Pflanzen zu erklären.* Gotha: C. W. Ettinger, 1790. Repr. in *Goethes naturwissenschaftliche Schriften. Zur Morphologie*, ed. Rudolf Steiner (Weimar: Böhlau, 1891), VI/1:23–94.

Goethe, Johann Wolfgang von. *Versuch über die Metamorphose der Pflanzen.* Stuttgart: Cottasche Buchhandlung, 1831. Repr. in *Goethes naturwissenschaftliche Schriften. Zur Morphologie*, ed. Rudolf Steiner (Weimar: Böhlau, 1891), VI/1:95–128.

Goethe, Johann Wolfgang von. "Von deutscher Baukunst. D. M. Ervini Steinbach." In *Von deutscher Art und Kunst. Einige fliegende Blätter* (Hamburg, 1773). Repr., ed. Hans Dietrich Irmscher (Stuttgart: Philipp Reclam jun., 1988), pp. 93–104.

Goethe, Johann Wolfgang von. "Vorarbeiten zur einer Physiologie der Pflanzen." In *Goethes naturwissenschaftliche Schriften. Zur Morphologie*, ed. Rudolf Steiner (Weimar: Böhlau, 1891), VI/1:296.

Gold, John R. *The Experience of Modernism: Modern Architects and the Future City, 1928–53*. London: E & FN Spon, 1997.

Goren, Arthur A. "The View from Scopus: Judah L. Magnes and the Early Years of the Hebrew University." *Judaism: A Quarterly Journal of Jewish Life and Thought* 45 (1996), 203–223.

Graevenitz, Antje von. "Hütten und Tempel: Zur Mission der Selbstbesinnung." In Harald Szeemann, ed., *Monte Verità. Berg der Wahrheit. Lokale Anthropologie als Beitrag zur Wiederentdeckung einer neuzeitlichen sakralen Topographie* (Milan: Electa Editrice, 1980), pp. 85–98.

Gray, A. Stuart. *Edwardian Architecture: A Biographical Dictionary*. London: Duckworth, 1985.

Gurney, Sybella. "Civic Reconstruction and the Garden City Movement." *Sociological Review* 3 (1910), 35–43.

*Hablik: Designer, Utopian Architect, Expressionist Artist, 1881–1934*. Exh. cat. London: Architectural Association, 1980.

Haeckel, Ernst. *The Riddle of the Universe at the Close of the Nineteenth Century*. Trans. Joseph McCabe. London: Watts & Co., 1900.

Hall, Peter. *Cities of Tomorrow: An Intellectual History of Urban Planning and Design in the Twentieth Century*. Oxford: Blackwell, 1992.

Hamann, Richard, and Jost Hermand. *Stilkunst um 1900*. Munich: Nymphenburger Verlagshandlung, 1975.

*Der Hang zum Gesamtkunstwerk*. Exh. cat. Zurich, Düsseldorf, and Vienna, 1983.

Hardy, Dennis. *Alternative Communities in Nineteenth Century England*. London: Longman, 1979.

Hare, William Loftus, ed. *Religions of the Empire: A Conference on Some Living Religions within the Empire*. London: Duckworth, 1925.

Harrison, Frederic. *The Meaning of History and Other Historical Pieces*. London: Trübner, 1862; London: Macmillan, 1894.

Harten, Hans-Christian and Elke. *Die Versöhnung mit der Natur. Gärten, Freiheitsbäume, republikanische Wälder, heilige Berge und Tugendparks in der Französischen Revolution.* Reinbek bei Hamburg: Rowohlt, 1989.

Hepp, Corona. *Avantgarde. Moderne Kunst, Kulturkritik und Reformbewegung nach der Jahrhundertwende.* Munich: dtv, 1987.

Herrmann, Wolfgang. *In What Style Should We Build? The German Debate on Architectural Style.* Santa Monica: Getty Center for the History of Art and the Humanities, 1992.

Hesoid. *Theogony.* In Hesoid, *Theogony; Works and Days,* and Theogonis, *Elegies,* trans. Dorothea Wender (Harmondsworth: Penguin, 1973), pp. 23–57.

Hobman, J. B., ed. *David Eder: Memoirs of a Modern Pioneer.* London, Victor Gollancz, 1945.

Hobsbawm, Eric J. *Nations and Nationalism since 1780: Programme, Myth, Reality.* Cambridge: University Press, 1990; repr. 1993.

Horkheimer, Max, and Theodor W. Adorno. *Dialektik der Aufklärung. Philosophische Fragmente.* Frankfurt: S. Fischer, 1969.

Horniman Museum. *An Account of the Horniman Free Museum and the Recreation Grounds, Forest Hill.* London: Horniman Museum, 1901.

Hörz, H., et al., eds. *Philosophie und Naturwissenschaften. Wörterbuch zu den philosophischen Fragen der Naturwissenschaften.* Berlin [DDR]: Dietz, 1983.

Howard, Ebenezer. *Garden Cities of To-morrow (Being the Second Edition of "To-morrow: A Peaceful Path to Real Reform).* London: Swan Sonnenschein, 1902; Builth Wells: Attic, 1985, repr. 1989.

Howard, Ebenezer. *To-morrow: A Peaceful Path to Real Reform.* London: Swan Sonnenschein, 1898.

Hug, Heinz. *Kropotkin zur Einführung.* Hamburg: Ed. SOAK im Junius Verlag, 1989.

Hughes, Thomas P., and Agatha C. Hughes, eds. *Lewis Mumford: Public Intellectual.* New York: Oxford University Press, 1990.

James, William. *Psychology: A Briefer Course.* London: Macmillan, 1892.

Johnston, Margo. "Ramsay Garden, Edinburgh." *Journal of the Architectural Heritage Society of Scotland* 16 (1989), 3–19.

Katznelson, Ira. "The Centrality of the City in Social Theory." In Irit Rogoff, ed., *The Divided Heritage: Themes and Problems in German Modernism* (Cambridge: Cambridge University Press, 1991), pp. 253–264.

Keith, William John. *Regions of Imagination: The Development of Rural British Fiction.* Toronto: University of Toronto Press, 1988.

Khursheed, Anjam. *The Seven Candles of Unity: The Story of 'Abdu'l-Bahá in Edinburgh.* London: Bahá'í Publishing Trust, 1991.

Kinkead-Weekes, Mark. *D. H. Lawrence: Triumph to Exile, 1912–1922.* Cambridge: Cambridge University Press, 1996.

Kitchen, Paddy. *A Most Unsettling Person: An Introduction to the Ideas and Life of Patrick Geddes.* London: Victor Gollancz, 1975.

Koeman, Cornelis. *Atlantes Neerlandici. Bibliography of Terrestrial, Maritime and Celestial Atlases and Pilot Books Published in the Netherlands up to 1880.* 5 vols. Amsterdam: Theatrum Orbis Terrarum, 1969–1971.

Krimmel, Bernd. "In the Matter of J. M. Olbrich." In Joseph Maria Olbrich, *Architecture: Complete Reprint of the Original Plates of 1901–1904* (London: Butterworth Architecture, 1988), pp. 11–16.

Kropotkin, Peter. *Fields, Factories and Workshops Tomorrow.* Ed. Colin Ward. London: Freedom Press, 1985. Originally published London: Hutchinson, 1899.

Kropotkin, Peter. *Mutual Aid: A Factor of Evolution.* London: William Heinemann, 1902; London: Freedom Press, 1987.

Kuehl, Warren F., ed. *Biographical Dictionary of Internationalists.* Westport, Conn.: Greenwood Press, 1983.

Lampugnani, Vittorio Magnago, and Romana Schneider, eds. *Moderne Architektur in Deutschland 1900–1950. Expressionismus und Neue Sachlichkeit.* Exh. cat. Stuttgart: Hatje, 1994.

Lange, Erhard, and Dietrich Alexander, eds. *Philosophenlexikon.* Berlin [DDR]: Dietz, 1984.

Lethaby, William Richard. "Architecture as Form in Civilization." In W. R. Lethaby, *Form in Civilization: Collected Papers on Art and Labour* (1922; London: Oxford University Press, 1957), pp. 1–13.

Lethaby, William Richard. *Architecture, Mysticism and Myth.* London: Percival, 1892.

Lethaby, William Richard. "Of Beautiful Cities." In *Art and Life, and the Building and Decoration of Cities: A Series of Lectures by Members of the Arts and Crafts Exhibition Society, Delivered at the Fifth Exhibition of the Society in 1896* (London: Percival, 1897), pp. 45–110.

Linse, Ulrich, ed. *Zurück, o Mensch, zur Mutter Erde. Landkommunen in Deutschland 1890–1933.* Munich: dtv, 1983.

Lucie-Smith, Edward. *Symbolist Art.* London: Thames and Hudson, 1972.

Lukács, Georg. *Die Zerstörung der Vernunft.* Berlin [DDR]: Aufbau, 1955; repr. 1984.

Mairet, Philip. *Autobiographical and Other Papers.* Ed. Charles Hubert Sisson. Manchester: Carcanet, 1981.

Mairet, Philip. *Pioneer of Sociology: The Life and Letters of Patrick Geddes.* London: Lund Humphries, 1957.

Markus, Thomas A. *Buildings and Power: Freedom and Control in the Origin of Modern Building Types.* London: Routledge, 1993.

Marrey, Bernard. *Louis Bonnier, 1856–1946.* Liège: Mardaga, 1988.

Marsh, Jan. *Back to the Land: The Pastoral Impulse in England from 1880 to 1914.* London: Quartet Books, 1982.

Martin, Elizabeth, ed. *A Concise Dictionary of Biology.* Oxford: University Press, 1990.

Marx, Karl, and Friedrich Engels. "Die deutsche Ideologie. Kritik der neuesten deutschen Philosophie in ihren Repräsentanten Feuerbach, B. Bauer, Stirner und des deutschen Sozialismus in seinen verschiedenen Propheten." In Karl Marx and Friedrich Engels, *Werke*, 39 vols. (Berlin [DDR]: Dietz, 1969), 3:9–532.

Massey, David. "Regional Planning 1909–1939: 'The Experimental Era.'" In Patricia L. Garside and Michael Hebbert, eds., *British Regionalism 1900–2000* (London: Mansell, 1989), pp. 57–76.

Matless, David. "Appropriate Geography: Patrick Abercrombie and the Energy of the World." *Journal of Design History* 6, no. 3 (1993), 167–178.

Matless, David. "Regional Surveys and Local Knowledges: The Geographical Imagination in Britain, 1918–1939." *Transactions of the Institute of British Geographers*, n.s. 17 (1992), 464–480.

McGrath, James, Samantha Searle, and Volker M. Welter, eds. *The Papers of Sir Patrick Geddes at Strathclyde University Archives*. 6 vols. Glasgow: Strathclyde University Archives, 1999.

McWilliam, Colin. *Scottish Townscape*. London: Collins, 1975.

Mears, Frank C. "Primitive Edinburgh." *Scottish Geographical Magazine* 35 (1919), 298–315.

Meller, Helen. "Cities and Evolution: Patrick Geddes as an International Prophet of Town Planning before 1914." In Anthony Sutcliffe, ed., *Rise of Modern Urban Planning, 1800–1914* (London: Mansell, 1980), pp. 199–223.

Meller, Helen. "Geddes and His Indian Reports." In *Patrick Geddes: A Symposium, 1 March 1982* (Dundee: Duncan of Jordanstone College of Art/University of Dundee, n.d. [1985]), pp. 1–25.

Meller, Helen, ed. *The Ideal City*. Leicester: Leicester University Press, 1979.

Meller, Helen. "Patrick Geddes." In Gordon Cherry, ed., *Pioneers in British Planning* (London: Architectural Press, 1981), pp. 46–71.

Meller, Helen. "Patrick Geddes: An Analysis of His Theory of Civics, 1880–1904." *Victorian Studies* 16 (1973), 291–315.

Meller, Helen. *Patrick Geddes: Social Evolutionist and City Planner.* London: Routledge, 1990.

Meller, Helen. "Planning Theory and Women's Role in the City." *Urban History Yearbook* 17 (1990), 85–98.

Meller, Helen. "Some Reflections on the Concept of Megalopolis and Its Use by Patrick Geddes and Lewis Mumford." In Theo Barker and Anthony Sutcliffe, eds., *Megalopolis: The Giant City in History* (New York: St. Martin's Press, 1993), pp. 116–129.

Millar, John. *The Origin of the Distinction of Ranks.* Edinburgh, 1806 (4th ed.); repr. Bristol: Thoemmes, 1990.

Morgan, John Edward. *The Danger of Deterioration of Race from the Too Rapid Increase of Great Cities.* Paper read at the Social Science Congress, Sheffield, Tuesday, October 10, 1865. London: Longman, Green and Co., 1866.

Morgan, Kenneth O., ed. *The Sphere Illustrated History of Britain, 1789–1983.* Oxford: Oxford University Press, 1984; repr. London: Sphere, 1991.

Morris, William. "Address at the Second Annual Meeting [of the SPAB], 28 June 1879." In *William Morris, Artist, Writer, Socialist,* ed. May Morris, 2 vols. (Oxford: Basil Blackwell, 1936), 1:119–124.

Morris, William. "Address at the Twelfth Annual Meeting [of the SPAB], 3 July 1889." In *William Morris, Artist, Writer, Socialist,* ed. May Morris, 2 vols. (Oxford: Basil Blackwell, 1936), 1:146–157.

Morris, William. "Paper Read at the Seventh Annual Meeting of the S.P.A.B., 1 July 1884." In *William Morris, Artist, Writer, Socialist,* ed. May Morris, 2 vols. (Oxford: Basil Blackwell, 1936), 1:124–145.

Morris, William. "The Prospects of Architecture in Civilization." In Morris, *On Art and Socialism: Essays and Lectures,* ed. Holbrook Jackson (Paulton: John Lehman, 1947), pp. 245–272.

Mumford, Eric. "CIAM Urbanism after the Athens Charter." *Planning Perspectives* 7 (1992), pp. 391–417.

Mumford, Lewis. *The City in History: Its Origin, Its Transformation, and Its Prospects.* London: Secker & Warburg, 1961.

Mumford, Lewis. *The Culture of Cities.* New York: Harcourt, Brace & World, 1938.

Mumford, Lewis. *Sketches from Life: The Autobiography of Lewis Mumford. The Early Years.* Boston: Bacon Press, 1982.

Mumford, Lewis. *The Story of Utopias.* 2d ed. New York: Viking, 1974.

Nettleship, Richard Lewis. *Lectures on the Republic of Plato.* Ed. G. R. Benson. London: Macmillan, 1898.

Neuer Berliner Kunstverein, ed. *Stadt und Utopie. Modelle idealer Gemeinschaften.* Berlin: Frölich & Kaufmann, 1982.

Nietzsche, Friedrich. *The Joyful Wisdom.* Trans. Thomas Common. In *The Complete Works of Friedrich Nietzsche*, ed. Oscar Levy, 18 vols. (Edinburgh: T. N. Foulis, 1910), vol. 10.

Nietzsche, Friedrich. *Thoughts out of Season. Part II. The Use and Abuse of History.* Trans. Adrian Collins. In *The Complete Works of Friedrich Nietzsche*, ed. Oscar Levy, 18 vols. (Edinburgh: T. N. Foulis, 1909), 2:1–100.

Nordau, Max. *Degeneration.* London: William Heinemann, 1895.

Norman, Philip. *Crosby Place.* London: County Council, 1908.

Novak, Frank G., Jr., ed. *Lewis Mumford and Patrick Geddes: The Correspondence.* London: Routledge, 1995.

*Okkultismus und Avantgarde. Von Munch bis Mondrian 1900–1915.* Exh. cat. Frankfurt: Schirn Kunsthalle, 1995.

Patrick Geddes Centre for Planning Studies. *Catalogue of the Cities Exhibition.* Edinburgh: University of Edinburgh, 1988.

Pearson, Karl. *The Life, Letters and Labours of Francis Galton.* 4 vols. Cambridge: Cambridge University Press, 1930.

Pehnt, Wolfgang. "Turm und Höhle." In Vittorio Magnago Lampugnani and Romana Schneider, eds., *Moderne Architektur in Deutschland 1900–1950. Expressionismus und*

*Neue Sachlichkeit,* exh. cat. (Stuttgart: Hatje, 1994), pp. 51–67.

Pemberton, Robert. *The Happy Colony.* London: Saunders and Otley, 1854.

Petruccioli, Attilio. "Patrick Geddes in Indore: Some Questions of Method." *Lotus International,* no. 34 (1982), 106–115.

Pevsner, Nikolaus. *The Buildings of England: London Except the Cities of London and Westminster.* Harmondsworth: Penguin, 1952.

Pevsner, Nikolaus. "Scrape and Anti-scrape." In Jane Fawcett, ed., *The Future of the Past: Attitudes to Conservation, 1174–1974.* London: Thames and Hudson, 1976.

Piccinato, Giorgio. *Städtebau in Deutschland 1871–1914: Genese einer wissenschaftlichen Disziplin.* Trans. Michael Peterek. Braunschweig: Vieweg, 1983.

Plato. *Meno.* In *Protogoras and Meno,* trans. W. K. C. Guthrie (Harmondsworth: Penguin, 1956), pp. 115–157.

Plato. *Phaedo.* In *The Last Days of Socrates,* trans. Hugh Tredennick, 2d ed., rev. Harold Tarrant (Harmondsworth: Penguin, 1993), pp. 109–185.

Plato. *The Republic.* Trans. Desmond Lee. 2d rev. ed. Harmondsworth: Penguin, 1987.

Ponte, Alessandra. "The Thinking Machines from the Outlook Tower to the City of the World." *Lotus International,* no. 35 (1982), 46–51.

Prange, Regine. *Das Kristalline als Kunstsymbol: Bruno Taut und Paul Klee.* Hildesheim: Georg Olms Verlag, 1991.

Prevost, M., et al., eds. *Dictionnaire de biographie française.* Paris: Librarie Letouzey et Aué, 1933–.

Reclus, Elie, and Elisée Reclus. *Renouveau d'une cité. (On the Social Work of Patrick Geddes at Edinburgh).* N.pl.: n.pub., 1896.

Reclus, Elisée. "The Evolution of Cities." *Contemporary Review* 67 (1895), 246–264.

Reclus, Elisée. "A Great Globe." *Geographical Journal* 12 (1898), 401–409.

Reilly, John Patrick. *The Early Social Thought of Patrick Geddes.* Ann Arbor: University Microfilms, 1975.

Reinink, Wessel. *K. P. C. de Bazel—Architect.* Rotterdam: Uitgeverij 010, 1993.

Robson, Brian Turnbull. "Geography and Social Science: The Role of Patrick Geddes." In David Ross Stoddart, ed., *Geography, Ideology and Social Concern.* Oxford: Blackwell, 1981.

Rosenau, Helen. *The Ideal City in Its Architectural Evolution.* London: Routledge and Kegan Paul, 1959.

Royal Institute of British Architects, ed. *Town Planning Conference, London, 10th to 15th October 1910; Exhibition of Drawings and Models at the Royal Academy from the 10th to the 22nd October.* Exh. cat. London: Clowes & Son, 1910.

Royal Institute of British Architects, ed. *Town Planning Conference, London, 10–15 October 1910: Transactions.* London: RIBA, 1910.

Rubens, Godfrey. *William Richard Lethaby: His Life and Work, 1875–1931.* London: Architectural Press, 1986.

Ruskin, John. *The Economist of Xenophon.* Trans. Alexander D. O. Wedderburn and W. Gershom Collingwood. In *The Complete Works of John Ruskin,* ed. Edward Tyas Cook and Alexander Wedderburn, 39 vols. (London: Allen, 1907), 31:1–98.

Ruskin, John. *Fors Clavigera: Letters to the Workmen and Labourers of Great Britain.* In *The Complete Works of John Ruskin,* ed. Edward Tyas Cook and Alexander Wedderburn, 39 vols. (London: Allen, 1907), vol. 27.

Ruskin, John. *Lectures on Architecture and Painting, Delivered at Edinburgh in November, 1853.* London: Smith, Elder and Co., 1854.

Ruskin, John. *The Stones of Venice.* In *The Complete Works of John Ruskin,* ed. Edward Tyas Cook and Alexander Wedderburn, 39 vols. (London: Allen, 1907), 10:180–269.

Saint, Andrew. "Ashbee, Geddes, Lethaby and the Rebuilding of Crosby Hall." *Architectural History* 34 (1991), 206–217.

Sandwich, Earl of. "The Saving of Crosby Hall." *Sociological Review* 24 (1932), 362–364.

Saunders, Peter. *Social Theory and the Urban Question.* London: Hutchinson, 1981.

Schorske, Carl E. "The Idea of the City in European Thought: Voltaire to Spengler." In Oscar Handlin and John Burchard, eds., *The Historian and the City* (Cambridge: MIT Press, 1963; repr. 1966), pp. 95–114.

Searle, Geoffrey Russell. *Eugenics and Politics in Britain, 1900–1914.* Leyden: Noordhoff International Publishing, 1976.

Sembach, Klaus-Jürgen. *1910—Halbzeit der Moderne.* Stuttgart: Hatje, 1992.

Service, Alastair. "Charles Harrison Townsend." In Service, ed., *Edwardian Architecture and Its Origin* (London: Architectural Press, 1975), pp. 162–182.

Sheppard, Francis Henry Wollaston. "Sources and Methods Used for the Survey of London." In Harold James Dyos, ed., *The Study of Urban History* (London: Arnold, 1967), pp. 131–145.

Smith, Peter John. "Planning as Environmental Improvement: Slum Clearance in Victorian Edinburgh." In Anthony Sutcliffe, ed., *The Rise of Modern Urban Planning, 1800–1914* (London: Mansell, 1980), pp. 99–133.

Smith, Peter John. "Slum Clearance as an Instrument of Sanitary Reform: The Flawed Vision of Edinburgh's First Slum Clearance Scheme." *Planning Perspectives* 9 (1994), 1–27.

Smith, Robert. "Botanical Survey of Scotland I: Edinburgh District." *Scottish Geographical Magazine* 16 (1900), 385–346, map after p. 440.

Smith, Robert. "Botanical Survey of Scotland II: North Perthshire District." *Scottish Geographical Magazine* 16 (1900), 441–467, map after p. 504.

Smith, William. *A Smaller Classical Dictionary of Biography, Mythology and Geography.* 14th ed. London: John Murray, 1872.

Smith, William G. "A Botanical Survey of Scotland." *Scottish Geographical Magazine* 18 (1902), 132–139.

Smout, Thomas Christopher. *A History of the Scottish People, 1560–1830*. London: Collins, 1969; repr. London: Fontana, 1985.

Sociological Society, Cities Committee. *Memorandum on the Need of City Survey Preparatory to Town-Planning*. London: Sociological Society, 1911.

Stepan, Nancy. *The Idea of Race in Science: Great Britain, 1800–1960*. London: Macmillan, 1982.

Stephens, Riccardo. *The Cruciform Mark: The Strange Story of Richard Tregenna, Bachelor of Medicine (Univ. Edin.)*. London: Chatto & Windus, 1896.

Sternberger, Dolf. *Panorama oder Ansichten vom 19. Jahrhundert*. 4th ed. Frankfurt: Suhrkamp, 1974.

Stewart, John Alexander. *The Myths of Plato*. London: Macmillan, 1905.

Stout, George Frederic. *A Manual of Psychology*. 2 vols. London: University Tutorial Press, 1898–1899.

Sutcliffe, Anthony. *The Rise of Modern Urban Planning, 1800–1914*. London: Mansell, 1980.

Szeemann, Harald, ed. *Monte Verità. Berg der Wahrheit. Lokale Anthropologie als Beitrag zur Wiederentdeckung einer neuzeitlichen sakralen Topographie*. Milan: Electa Editrice, 1980.

*Tanakh: A New Translation of the Holy Scriptures According to the Traditional Hebrew Text*. Philadelphia: Jewish Publication Society, 1985.

Taut, Bruno. *Die Auflösung der Städte*. Hagen, 1920.

Taut, Bruno. *Die Stadtkrone mit Beiträgen von Paul Scheerbart, Erich Baron, Adolf Behne*. Jena: Eugen Diederichs, 1919.

Taylor, Nicholas. "Byzantium in Brighton." In Alastair Service, ed., *Edwardian Architecture and Its Origin* (London: Architectural Press, 1975), pp. 280–288.

Thieme, Ulrich, and Felix Becker. *Allgemeines Lexikon der bildenden Künstler von der Antike bis zur Gegenwart*. 37 vols. Leipzig: Engelmann, E. A. Seemann, 1907–1950.

Thompson, Edward Palmer. *William Morris: Romantic to Revolutionary.* London: Merlin Press, 1955; repr. 1977.

Thoren, Victor E. *The Lord of Uraniborg: A Biography of Tycho Brahe.* Cambridge: Cambridge University Press, 1990.

Tönnies, Ferdinand. "The Concept of *Gemeinschaft.*" In *Ferdinand Tönnies on Sociology: Pure, Applied and Empirical. Selected Writings,* ed. Werner J. Cahnmann and Rudolf Heberle (Chicago: University of Chicago Press, 1971), pp. 62–72.

Tönnies, Ferdinand. *Fundamental Concepts of Sociology (Gesellschaft und Gemeinschaft).* Trans. Charles P. Loomis. New York: American Book Company, 1940.

Turner, Frank M. *The Greek Heritage in Victorian Britain.* New Haven: Yale University Press, 1981.

Tyrwhitt, Jaqueline. "Cores with Urban Constellations." In Congrès Internationaux d'Architecture Moderne 8 (CIAM 8), *The Heart of the City: Towards the Humanisation of Urban Life,* ed. Jaqueline Tyrwhitt, José Luis Sert, and E. N. Rogers (London: Lund Humphries, 1952), pp. 103–105.

Tyrwhitt, Jaqueline, ed. *Patrick Geddes in India.* London: Humphries, 1947.

Ulmer, Renate. "Catalogue of Works." In Joseph Maria Olbrich, *Architecture: Complete Reprint of the Original Plates of 1901–1904* (London: Butterworth Architecture, 1988), pp. 23–30.

Unwin, Raymond. *Town Planning in Practise: An Introduction to the Art of Designing Cities and Suburbs.* London: Fisher Unwin, 1909.

Various authors. "Living Religions and Their Life-Emphasis." *Sociological Review* 17 (1925), 255–293.

Various authors. [Papers preparatory for the Conference on Some Living Religions within the Empire.] *Sociological Review* 16 (1924), 90–116, 187–215, 285–294, 300–316.

Villiers-Stuart, Constance Mary. *Gardens of the Great Mughals.* London: Adam and Charles Black, 1913.

Voigt, Wolfgang. "Die Gartenstadt als eugenisches Utopia." In Franziska Bollerey et al., eds., *Im Grünen wohnen—im Blauen planen* (Hamburg: Christians, 1990), pp. 301–314.

Wannop, Urlan, and Gordon E. Cherry. "The Development of Regional Planning in the United Kingdom." *Planning Perspectives* 9 (1994), 29–60.

Weber, Max. *The City by Max Weber*, trans. and ed. Don Martindale and Gertrud Neuwirth. New York: Free Press, 1958.

Weber, Max. "Die Stadt." *Archiv für Sozialwissenschaft und Sozialpolitik* 47 (1921). Repr. in Weber, *Wirtschaft und Gesellschaft. Grundriß der verstehenden Soziologie*, ed. Johannes Winckelmann (Cologne and Berlin: Kiepenheuer & Witsch, 1964), pp. 923–1033.

Weismann, August. *Essays upon Heredity.* 2 vols. Oxford: Clarendon, 1891.

Weller, Christian. "Reform der Lebenswelt. Die Entwicklung zentraler Gedanken Fritz Schumachers bis 1900." In Hartmut Frank, ed., *Fritz Schumacher. Reformkultur und Moderne* (Stuttgart: Hatje, 1994), pp. 41–65.

Welter, Volker M. "Arcades for Lucknow: Patrick Geddes, Charles Rennie Mackintosh and the Reconstruction of the City." *Architectural History* 42 (1999), 60–82.

Welter, Volker M. *Collecting Cities: Images from Patrick Geddes' Cities and Town Planning Exhibition.* Glasgow: Collins Gallery, 1999.

Welter, Volker M. "The Geddes Vision of the Region as City: Palestine as a Polis." In Jeannine Fiedler, ed., *Social Utopias of the Twenties: Bauhaus, Kibbutz and the Dream of the New Man* (Wuppertal: Müller + Busmann, 1995), pp. 72–79.

Welter, Volker M. "History, Biology and City Design: Patrick Geddes in Edinburgh." *Architectural Heritage* 6 (1996), 60–82.

Welter, Volker M. "Slum, Semi-slum, Super-slum: Some Reflections by Patrick Geddes on Edinburgh's New Town." *Architectural Heritage* 8 (1999), 66–73.

Welter, Volker M. "Die Stadt als Freilichtmuseum. Patrick Geddes in Edinburgh." *Die Alte Stadt* 25 (1998), 347–358.

Welter, Volker M. "Stages of an Exhibition: The Cities and Town Planning Exhibition of Patrick Geddes." *Planning History* 20 (1998), 25–35.

Welter, Volker M., and James Lawson, eds. *The City after Patrick Geddes.* Bern: Peter Lang, 2000.

West, Shearer. *Fin de Siècle.* London: Bloomsbury, 1993.

White, Ebe Minerva. *The Foundations of Civics.* London: Syndicate Publishing, 1927.

White, Hayden V. "The Burden of History." In *History and Theory: Studies in the Philosophy of History* (Middletown, Connecticut: Wesleyan University Press, 1966), pp. 111–134.

Whitley, W. T. "Arts and Crafts at the Royal Academy." *The Studio* 69 (1916), 66–77, 120–130, 189–196.

Whyte, Iain Boyd. *Bruno Taut and the Architecture of Activism.* Cambridge: Cambridge University Press, 1982.

Whyte, Iain Boyd. *Emil Hoppe, Marcel Kammerer, Otto Schönthal: Three Architects from the Master Class of Otto Wagner.* Berlin: Ernst & Sohn, 1989.

Whyte, Iain Boyd. "Expressionismus und Architektur in den Niederlanden." In *Wendigen 1918–1931. Amsterdamer Expressionismus. Ein Architekturmagazin der 20er Jahre. Vom Städtebau zur Schriftgestaltung,* exh. cat. (Darmstadt: Institut Mathildenhöhe, 1992), pp. 37–56.

Whyte, Iain Boyd. "The Expressionist Sublime." In Timothy O. Benson, ed., *Expressionist Utopias: Paradise, Metropolis, Architectural Fantasy,* exh. cat. (Seattle: University of Washington Press, 1993), pp. 118–137.

Whyte, Iain Boyd. "Stadt und Land: Patrick Geddes in Edinburgh." In Dieter Schädel, ed., *Architektur als Kunst,* Schriftenreihe des Vereins Fritz-Schumacher-Kolloquium e.V. (Hamburg: Sautter & Lackmann, 1995), pp. 20–23.

Williams, Raymond. *The Country and the City.* London: Chatto & Windus, 1973; repr. London: Hogarth Press, 1993.

Williams, Rosalind. "Lewis Mumford as a Historian of Technology in Technics and Civilization." In Thomas P. Hughes and Agatha C. Hughes, eds., *Lewis Mumford: Public Intellectual* (New York: Oxford University Press, 1990), pp. 43–65.

Wright, Terence R. *The Religion of Humanity: The Impact of Comtean Positivism on Victorian Britain.* Cambridge: Cambridge University Press, 1986.

Youngson, Alexander John. *The Making of Classical Edinburgh.* Edinburgh: Edinburgh University Press, 1966; repr. 1988.

Zaidman, Louise Bruit, and Pauline Schmitt Pantel. *Religion in the Ancient Greek City.* Trans. Paul Cartledge. Cambridge: Cambridge University Press, 1992.

Zueblin, Charles. "The World's First Sociological Laboratory." *American Journal of Sociology* 4 (1899), 577–592.

## Theses

Cuthbert, Michael. "The Concept of the Outlook Tower in the Work of Patrick Geddes." Master's thesis, University of St. Andrews, Department of Scottish History, 1987.

Green, Peter. "Patrick Geddes." Doctoral thesis, University of Strathclyde, 1970.

Hyman, Benjamin. "British Planners in Palestine, 1918–1936." Doctoral thesis, London Schools of Economics and Political Science, University of London, 1994.

Purves, Graeme. "The Life and Work of Sir Frank Mears: Planning with a Cultural Perspective." Doctoral thesis, Heriot-Watt University, 1987.

# Illustration Credits

**Sources of Illustrations**

Every effort has been made to trace copyright holders. The author and the publisher would be interested to hear from anyone not acknowledged, and will add credits as needed in any subsequent editions.

**2.1:** from Amelia Defries, *The Interpreter Geddes: The Man and His Gospel* (London: George Routledge & Sons, 1927).

**2.3:** from Patrick Geddes, *Cities in Evolution: An Introduction to the Town Planning Movement and to the Study of Civics*, repr., ed. the Outlook Tower Association and the Association for Planning and Regional Reconstruction, London (London: Williams & Norgate, 1949).

**3.4:** from Patrick Geddes, *The Civic Survey of Edinburgh* (Edinburgh: Outlook Tower; Chelsea: Crosby Hall, 1911).

**3.5:** from Patrick Geddes, *Cities in Evolution: An Introduction to the Town Planning Movement and to the Study of Civics* (London: Williams & Norgate, 1915).

**4.1:** from *The Evergreen: A Northern Seasonal* 1 (1895).

**4.3:** from Victor Branford and Patrick Geddes, *The Coming Polity: A Study in Reconstruction* (London: Williams & Norgate, 1917).

**5.1:** from Sociological Society, Cities Committee, *Memorandum on the Need of City Survey Preparatory to Town-Planning* (London: Sociological Society, 1911).

**5.2:** from Victor Branford and Patrick Geddes, *Our Social Inheritance* (London: Williams & Norgate, 1919).

**5.3:** from Patrick Geddes, *Town Planning in Balrampur: A Report to the Hon'ble the Maharaja Bahadur* (Lucknow: Murray's London Printing Press, 1917).

**6.1:** from Joseph Maria Olbrich, *Architektur* (Berlin: Wasmuth, 1904).

**6.6:** from *Wagnerschule 1901* (Vienna: no publisher, 1901).

**6.7:** from *Wagnerschule 1902* (Leipzig: Baumgartner's Buchhandlung, [1903]).

**6.12:** from *Academy Architecture* 9 (1896).

**6.13:** from *The Builder* 82 (1902).

**6.14:** from Charles Robert Ashbee, *Where the Great City Stands: A Study in the New Civics* (London: Essex House Press, 1917).

**6.16, 6.17:** from *The Studio* 69 (1916).

**7.1:** from *The Illustrated London News* 18 (1851).

**7.2:** from Robert Pemberton, *The Happy Colony* (London: Saunders and Otley, 1854).

**7.6:** from *Scottish Geographical Magazine* 18 (1902).

**7.8:** from Patrick Geddes, *City Development: A Study of Parks, Gardens and Culture-Institutes. A Report to the Carnegie Dunfermline Trust* (Edinburgh: Geddes and Company; Birmingham: Saint George Press, 1904).

**7.9:** from *Proceedings of the Royal Society of Edinburgh* 13 (1884–1886).

**7.10:** from Patrick Geddes, *Women, the Census, and the Possibilities of the Future* (Edinburgh: Outlook Tower, 1921).

**7.11, 7.16, 7.17, 8.1:** from Patrick Abercrombie et al., *The Coal Crisis and the Future: A Study in Social Disorders and Their Treatment* (London: Le Play House Press and Williams & Norgate, 1926).

**8.2:** from Patrick Geddes, *Town Planning towards City Development: A Report to the Durbar of Indore* (Indore: Holkar State Press, 1918).

**8.14:** from *Sociological Review* 16 (1924).

**8.18, 8.19:** from Bruno Taut, *Die Stadtkrone* (Jena: Diederichs, 1919).

All other figures are from archival and private collections as listed in the photographic credits.


## Photographic Credits

Archives nationales/Institut français d'architecture, Archives d'architecture du XXe siècle (AN/IFA), Paris: **7.3.**

Bildarchiv Foto Marburg, Marburg, and Art Resource, New York: **6.2, 6.4, 6.5.**

© Copyright The British Museum, London: **6.9.**

Central Saint Martins Museum and Study Collection ©, London: **6.15.**

Musée des Beaux-Arts de Lyon, Lyons, and Studio Basset, Caluire: **8.16, 8.17.**

Trustees of the National Library of Scotland, Edinburgh: **5.2, 5.3, 6.12, 6.13, 6.14, 6.16, 6.17, 7.2, 7.11, 7.12, 7.16, 7.17, 8.1, 8.14.**

Norval Photographers, Dunfermline: **8.4.**

Royal Commission on the Ancient and Historic Monuments of Scotland, Crown Copyright: **7.14, 7.15, 8.5, 8.6, 8.7.**

Special Collections, Edinburgh University Library: **3.3, 3.4, 6.8, 7.1, 7.9.**

Staatliche Museen zu Berlin, Kunstbibliothek, Berlin: **6.1.**

Staats- und Universitätsbibliothek Hamburg, Hamburg: **6.3.**

Strathclyde University Archives: **1.1, 2.2, 2.4, 3.1, 4.3, 5.4, 5.5, 5.6, 5.7, 5.8, 7.4, 7.5, 7.7, 8.3, 8.8, 8.9, 8.10, 8.11, 8.12, 8.13, 8.15.**

Volker M. Welter: **2.1, 2.3, 3.2, 3.5, 4.1, 4.2, 5.1, 7.6, 7.8, 7.10, 7.13, 8.2, 8.18, 8.19.**

Wenzel Hablik Museum, Itzehoe (photographs: Kai Falck): **6.10, 6.11.**

Iain Boyd Whyte: **6.6, 6.7.**

# Index

Page numbers in boldface refer to illustrations or tables

Buckingham, James Silk, 142
Bunyan, John, 48
Burgess, Ernest W., 65

## C

Carlyle, Thomas, 12, 122
Catabolic metabolism. *See* Metabolism
Cerdà, Ildefonso, 8-9, 145
Chaikin, Benjamin, **230, 231, 232**
Cherry, Gordon E., 71
CIAM. *See* Congrès Internationaux d'Architecture Moderne
Cities and Town Planning Exhibition, 70,
76, 99-102, 109, 124-125, 127,
**128-129**, 131-133, 224
in Belfast (1911), 100
in Chelsea, London (1911), 100, 125,
**126**, 217
in Dublin (1911), 100
in Edinburgh (1911), 100, **127**, 218
in Ghent (1913), 101, **102**
City Beautiful movement, 145
City crown (*Stadtkrone*), **237, 238**, 244-
248, **246, 247**. *See also* Cultural
acropolis; Metaphysical city center
City design (city development), 50-52, 77,
91, 93, 100, 115-116, 118, 125,
132-134, 199, 212, 226, 229, 237,
240, 243-244, 250
City-group. *See* Conurbation
City of Destruction, 48, **48**
City proper (true or great city), 36-37, 47-
48, 51, 77, 90-91, 211, 217, 233,
241, 243-244
City symbols of Geddes
cathedral, 92, 216, 222, 227, 235,
244
"Chapel of the City," Edinburgh, 217-
218
city cross, 217

hexagon and octagon, 216-220, **218,
219**, 229, 243
Civics, Geddes's concept of, 49-50, 78, 210
Civic survey. *See* Survey, civic, historical,
and regional
Classical Greek cities and culture, as
model, 29-30, 68, 85, 97, 139, 172,
248. *See also* Athens; Greek gods;
Muses, Greek; Plato; *Polis*
for Geddes, 16, 51, 67-68, 77, 99-100,
192-193, 196-199, 207, 224, 226,
231-235, **236**, 248
Classical Roman cities and culture, as
model, 85, 244-245. *See also* Rome
Classification schemes, 13-16
Cloister, 36-37, 42, 44, 47-48, 51-52, 77,
90, 92, 196-197, 207, 210, 216,
229, 233, 235, 244
Comte, August, 90. *See also* Temporal and
spiritual powers
Conference on Some Living Religions
within the Empire (London, 1924),
172, 206-207. *See also* Geddes,
Patrick: Hall of Vision
Congrès Internationaux d'Architecture
Moderne (CIAM), 253-254
Conjeevaram (Kanchipuram). *See* India,
Geddes in
Conservative surgery, 109, 116, 118-120,
250
Conurbation, 74-75, 80, 243, 251. *See also*
Region-city
Crane, Walter, 163, 221
Cultural acropolis, 234-235, 238, 240,
243-244, 247-248, 250, 254,
310N64. *See also* City crown;
Metaphysical city center

## D

Dadd, Richard, 157, **158**, 298N46

Daguerre, Louis Jacques Mandé, 176

Darwin, Charles, theory of evolution, 9, 63, 96, 132, 187, 207

De Bazel, K. P. C., 147

Defries, Amelia, 33, 223

Dreyer, John Louis Emil, 182

Dundee (Scotland)
    botanic garden, University College, 200
    University College, 235

Dunfermline (Scotland)
    Nature Palace, Pittencrieff Park, 185, **186**, 187, 200, 204, 226
    Pittencrieff Park, planning of, 133, 185, 217, 220, 226-227, **228**, 238, 243

**E**

Eck, Caroline van, 94

Economics, Geddes's ideas on, 15-16

Eder, David Montague, 22, 192, 227, 271N44. *See also* Palestine, Geddes in: Hebrew University

Edinburgh, XIX, 7-8, 66-67, **67**, 70-72, 75-76
    "Chapel of the City," 217-218
    Geddes and, 18, 66, 70-71, 76, 78, 116, 125, 127, 185, 222, 235
    National Institute of Geography, 179-181, **182**, **183**, 184-185, 201, 203-204, 216, 230, 235 (*see also* Brahe, Tycho; Galeron, Paul Louis Albert)
    Outlook Tower, XIX, 78, **79**, 89-99, 125, 180, 205, 220, 224, 230, 235 (*see also* Outlook towers)
    Ramsay Garden, 223-224, 231, 235
    region of, 66, 70-73, 78

Engels, Friedrich, 12, 84-85

Environment, function, and organism. *See* Place, work, and folk

Eugenics, 188-190, 193, 229

**F**

Fabian Society, 192-193, 229

Fellowship of the New Life, 20

Fidus (Hugo Höppner), 148, 153

Finlay, Moses I., 83

Flahault, Charles, 61-63, 65

Förster, Ludwig, 8

Four social types, 44, 90-92, 94, 96-97, **98**, 100, 103-105, **104**, 111-112, 114, 196, 200, 215, 222, 235. *See also* Intellectuals and emotionals; Temporal and spiritual powers

Fowler, William Warde, 68, 72

Foyer, waterfalls of (Inverness district, Scotland), 19

Friedrich, Caspar David, 157

Furnes, Belgium, **236**

**G**

Galeron, Paul Louis Albert
    celestial globe, 180-181, **181**, 185, 205
    National Institute of Geography, Edinburgh, 180, **182**, **183**

Galton, Francis, 188-189

Garas, François, 153, 205, 297NN34,36
    Temple à la Pensée, 153-154, **155**, 156

Garden city, 56-58, 75, 101, 125, 142, 231, 243

Garnier, Tony
    Cité Industrielle, 244-245, **246**
    Tusculum, reconstruction of, 244-245, **245**

Geddes, Patrick
    Bahá'í Temple, Allahabad, design for, 204-206, **205**, **206**, 216, 219
    Balrampur, town planning in, 117-118, 310N64
    Baroda, town planning in, 118, 310N64

Geddes, Patrick (cont.)

*The World Without and the World Within,* 40-41, 43

Genealogical tree, 190-191, **190**, 197

*Genius loci,* 144, 166, 254

Geddes on, 21, 39, 46-47, 52, 94, 114-116, 118, 121-122, 124, 134, 216, 221, 240-241

Geoffroy Saint-Hilaire, Etienne, 96

Giedion, Sigfried, 254

Glasgow, 70, 74-75

Glikson, Artur, 253

Godfrey, Walter Hindes, 111, 122

Goethe, Johann Wolfgang von, 95-96, 216. *See also* Morphology and metamorphosis

Goetheanum. *See* Steiner, Rudolf

Graevenitz, Antje von, 146

Great city. *See* City proper

Greek gods, 192-193, **194, 195**, 197-198, 201, 207, 226, 231, 233. *See also* Classical Greek cities and culture, as model; Geddes, Patrick: temple of Greek gods; Muses, Greek

Greiffenhagen, Maurice

*The Arts (Serving the City),* 170, **170**

Gropius, Walter, xx

Guarini, Guarino, 160

Gurlitt, Cornelius, 147

Gutkind, Erwin Anton, 253

**H**

Habermas, Jürgen, xvii

Hablik, Wenzel, 159-160, **160, 161**, 162

Haeckel, Ernst, 132, 157, 159, 221. *See also* Morphology and metamorphosis; Recollection or recapitulation

biogenetic fundamental law, xviii, 132-133, 191

Hagia Sophia, Istanbul, as model for temples, 170-171, 210

Hallward, Reginald, 171

Hamann, Richard, 137-138

Harrison, Frederic

*The Meaning of History,* 86-88, 94-95

Haussmann, Georges-Eugène, 8

Hébrard, Ernest M., 76

Hebrew University, Jerusalem. *See* Palestine, Geddes in

Hermand, Jost, 137-138

Hesiod, 198

Hilberseimer, Ludwig, 252-253

Historical survey. *See* Survey, civic, historical, and regional

Hoffbauer, Thédore Joseph, 8

Hogenberg, Frans, 182, 184

Höppner, Hugo. *See* Fidus

Horkheimer, Max, 252

Horne, Herbert P., 221

Howard, Ebenezer, 56-59, 74, 142, 251. *See also* Garden city

Huxley, Thomas Henry, 9-11

**I**

India, Geddes in, 22-24, 116-119

Bahá'í temple, Allahabad, design for, 204-206, **205, 206**, 216, 219

Balrampur, town planning in, 117-118, 310N64

Baroda, town planning in, 118, 310N64

Conjeevaram (Kanchipuram), town planning in, 241, **242**, 243

Indore, town planning in, 130, 217, **219**, 226, 235, 237, **237, 238**, 310N64

Lahore, town planning in, 118, 310N64

Lucknow, town planning in, 118

Nagpur, town planning in, 310N64

Patiala state and city, town planning in, 310N64 (*see also* India, Geddes in: Pinjaur)

Pinjaur, town planning in, 200, **201** (*see also* Geddes, Patrick: garden for the (nine) Greek Muses; India, Geddes in: Patiala state and city)

Indian cities and culture, as model, 85-86, 97, 248

for Geddes, 97, 100, 118, 200, 226, 241, 243

Indore. *See* India, Geddes in

Inlook tower. *See* Thinking cell or inlook tower

Intellectuals and emotionals, 44, 47, 90-92, 97, **104**, 114-115, 196, 200, 207, 222, 233. *See also* Four social types; Temporal and spiritual powers

International Exhibition of Industry, Science and Art (Edinburgh, 1886), 131

**J**

James, William, 40-41, 275N37

Jeanneret-Gris, Charles-Edouard. *See* Le Corbusier

Jerusalem. *See* Palestine, Geddes in

Johnson-Marshall, Percy, XXI

**K**

Kanchipuram. *See* India, Geddes in: Conjeevaram

Klenze, Leopold von, 147

Kropotkin, Peter, 44, 57-58, 63, 74

**L**

Lahore. *See* India, Geddes in

Lanchester, Henry V., 113

Lawrence, D. H., 22

Le Corbusier (Charles-Edouard Jeanneret-Gris), 283N71

Le Play, Frédéric, 11

Lethaby, William Richard, 147, 159, 179, 200

*Architecture, Mysticism and Myth*, 145-146, 306N6

sacred way for London, 168-169, **169**, 171

London, 51, 55, 58, 69, 101, 108, 112-115, 168-169, 176. *See also* Cities and Town Planning Exhibition: in Chelsea; Lethaby, William Richard: sacred way for London; Royal Anthropological Institute; Royal Economic Institute; Royal Geographical Society; Royal Society of Arts; Townsend, Charles Harrison

Chelsea, Geddes on, 47, 99, 115, 120-122, 124

Crosby Hall, Chelsea, 120-122, **121**, **123**, 124-125, **126**

More Hall, Chelsea, 121-122, 124

Richmond (garden city), 231

survey of, 110-111, 122

Toynbee Hall, 162-163, 165 (*see also* Barnett, Samuel Augustus)

Westminster, historical survey of, by Geddes, 112-113, **113**, 114-115, 133, 207, **209** (*see also* Survey, civic, historical, and regional)

Lucknow. *See* India, Geddes in

Lukács, György (Georg), 94

**M**

Mackintosh, Charles Rennie, 124

Mairet, Philip, 210, **211**

MARS group. *See* Modern Architectural
 Research Group
Marx, Karl, 12, 84-85
Mawson, Thomas H., 251
McKenzie, Roderick, 65
Mears, Frank, 23, 71, **130**, 131, 197, 205,
 **205, 206,** 219, 227, 229, **230, 231,**
 **232,** 237, **237, 238,** 272N48
Medieval cities and culture, as model, 28,
 57, 63, 85, 97, 139, 248
 for Geddes, 52, 77, 90, 92, 100, 196,
 215, 224, 226, 235, **236,** 248
Melnikoff, Avraham, **239**
Metabolism, 45, 189-191, 193, 196, 201,
 203
Metamorphosis. *See* Morphology and
 metamorphosis
Metaphysical city center, 142-145, 175,
 230-231, **236,** 241. *See also* City
 crown; Cultural acropolis
Millar, John, 64
Modern Architectural Research Group
 (MARS), 253-254
Montesquieu, Charles-Louis de Sécondat,
 Baron de, 83
Monte Verità (Ascona, Switzerland), 22,
 140-141
Montpellier (France), 61, 197
 Geddes in, 18, 197
More, Sir Thomas, 120-122
Morgan, John Edward, 188
Morphology and metamorphosis, 95-96,
 99, 103, 189. *See also* Goethe, Jo-
 hann Wolfgang von; Haeckel,
 Ernst
Morris, William, 12, 29, 100, 108, 114,
 120, 140
Mumford, Lewis, XVIII-XIX, XXI, 21, 77, 112,
 253, 289N71
Mundaneum, 76, 283N71
Muses, Greek, 197-198, 201, 203-204,
 231. *See also* Classical Greek cities

and culture, as model; Geddes,
 Patrick: garden for the (nine)
 Greek Muses; Greek gods
Museum, Geddes's ideas on, 93, 120, 127,
 130-131, 133, 198, 204, 234-235,
 237, 250
Muthesius, Hermann, 140

**N**

Nagpur. *See* India, Geddes in
Nash, John, 115
Natural occupations, 60, **60,** 61-65, **65,** 77,
 80, 103-104, **104,** 105, 196, 229.
 *See also* Valley region and valley
 section
Necessaries and super-necessaries, 15-16
Neotechnic age. *See* Paleotechnic and
 neotechnic ages
Neue Gemeinschaft, Berlin, 140
New Lanark (Scotland), 142
Nietzsche, Friedrich, 134, 137, 148, 156,
 159
 "Architecture for Thinkers," 221
Nordau, Max, 188
Notation of Life, XVIII-XIX, XXI, 31-32, **32,**
 33, 38-42, 44, **45,** 46, 48, 50, 67,
 77, 90-91, 111, 118, 197, 199-200,
 220, 229, 239-240. *See also* Act-
 Deed formula; Town-City formula
Nuremberg (Germany), 100

**O**

Obrist, Hermann, 159
Olbrich, Joseph Maria, 141, 171
 Mathildenhöhe with Ernst Ludwig
 House, Darmstadt, 142, **143, 144,**
 145, 223
 Secession building, Vienna, 141-142,
 147-148, **152**
Orage, Alfred Richard, 22

Royal Economic Institute, London, 238-239, **240**

Royal Geographical Society, London, 238-239, **240**

Royal Institute of British Architects, First International Conference on Town Planning (London, 1910), xx, 99, 125 (*see also* Cities and Town Planning Exhibition)

Royal Society of Arts, London, 33

Ruskin, John, 7-8, 12, 16, 29, 70, 100, 108, 216

**S**

Schelling, Friedrich Wilhelm Joseph von, 111

Schinkel, Karl Friedrich, 147, 157

Schönthal, Otto, 153, **153**

School for Oriental Studies, London, 206. *See also* Conference on Some Living Religions within the Empire

Schorske, Carl E., 84

Schumacher, Fritz, 197, 222
    crematorium, Dresden-Tolkewitz, 148, **152**
    Monument for Nietzsche, 148, **149**
    Temple of the Holy Grail, 148

Scott, Walter, 108

Sitte, Camillo, 100, 251

Smith, Adam, 83

Smith, Robert, 66

Social inheritance, 92-93, 112, 191. *See also* Geddes, Patrick: *Our Social Inheritance*

Society of Antiquaries of London, 107

Society of Antiquaries of Scotland, 107

Sociological Society, London, 21, 33, 206

Soria y Mata, Arturo, 9

Soul or spirit of the city. *See Genius loci*

Spencer, Herbert, 189

Steiner, Rudolf, 205

Stewart, John Alexander, 204. *See also* Plato

Stout, George F., 40-43, 112, 275N37

Super-necessaries. *See* Necessaries and super-necessaries

Survey, civic, historical, and regional, 69, 78, 104, 109, **110**, 111, 125, 131-132, 134

Survey of London. *See* London

**T**

Taut, Bruno, **246**, **247**, 248, 253-254. *See also* City crown

Tel Aviv. *See* Palestine, Geddes in

Temporal and spiritual powers, 90, 241. *See also* Comte, Auguste; Four social types; Intellectuals and emotionals

Thinking cell or inlook tower, xx, 24, 220-221, 224. *See also* Nietzsche, Friedrich: "Architecture for Thinkers"

Thinking machines, xix, 13, 31, 239

Thomson, John Arthur, 11, 132. *See also* Geddes, Patrick: *Life: Outlines of General Biology*

Thought diagrams. *See* Thinking machines

Tönnies, Ferdinand, 138-139

Town-City formula, 32-40, **33**, **36**, **41**, 42, 48, 50-51, 74, 90, 210, 216, 240. *See also* Act-Deed formula; Notation of Life

Town-country conflict, 55-56, 60, 64, 72, 74

Townsend, Charles Harrison, 165
    Bishopsgate Institute, London, 162-163
    Whitechapel Art Gallery, London, 162-164, **163**